MW00784803

ARMORED CHAMPION

ARMORED CHAMPION

THE TOP TANKS OF WORLD WAR II

Steven Zaloga

STACKPOLE
BOOKS

Published by
STACKPOLE BOOKS
5067 Ritter Road
Mechanicsburg, PA 17055
www.stackpolebooks.com

Printed in the United States of America

10 9 8 7 6 5 4 3 2 1

Unless otherwise noted, the photos in this book come from official U.S. government sources including the National Archives and Records Administration II in College Park, Maryland; the U.S. Army Military History Institute at Carlisle Barracks, Pennsylvania; and the Patton Museum, formerly at Fort Knox, Kentucky; as well as the author's personal collection.

Library of Congress Cataloging-in-Publication Data

Zaloga, Steve, 1952–
Armored champion : top tanks of World War II / Steven Zaloga.
pages cm
Includes bibliographical references and index.
ISBN 978-0-8117-1437-2 (alk. paper)
1. World War, 1939–1945—Tank warfare. 2. Tanks (Military science)—History—20th century. 3. Armored vehicles, Military—History—20th century. I. Title. II. Title: Top tanks of World War II.
D793.Z339 2015
940.54'2—dc23

2014044753

Contents

CHAPTER 1

What Makes a Great Tank?

WHAT WAS THE BEST TANK OF WORLD WAR II? This book argues that there was no single "best tank of World War II." While the Tiger may have been the best tank in the summer of 1943, it was merely an engineer's dream in 1941. Instead, this book takes snapshots in time to examine the best tanks at critical points during World War II. The approach that I have taken is not merely to provide opinions. Instead, I have supplied extensive documentation from archives, government studies, and a wide selection of published sources. Much of this has never been published in English before. Even if readers do not agree with my judgments, I hope that this book will provide them with ample data to draw their own conclusions.

What makes a tank great? The most obvious is the holy trinity of tank design: armor, firepower, and mobility. Nevertheless, evaluating these features depends on the date. A tank protected with 45mm armor was invulnerable in 1941, but it was doomed to quick defeat by 1945. A tank armed with a 76mm gun was a world-beater in 1941, but by 1945 was a pop-gun in a tank-versus-tank duel.

Besides the holy trinity, other factors are equally vital: crew training, tactics, affordability, and dependability. The T-34 tank was clearly the best tank on the 1941 battlefield in purely technical terms. But it was a dismal failure on the battlefield due to poor crew training, poor unit organization, and wretched employment. The Panther tank was a fearsome adversary in the summer of 1944, but by the winter of 1944–45 it had lost its edge because of inexperienced crews and crippling technical deterioration.

If we were only measuring the technical aspects of tank designs, it would be very easy to come up with a nice and simple technical comparison chart and pick the winner by straightforward numerical evaluation. But war, like all human endeavors, is complicated by a variety of factors that are not easily subject to numerical evaluation. Purely mathematical evaluations contain a false disguise of objectivity. A table of clean little numbers seems utterly scientific and fair, but inevitably contains bias and distortion.

Any comparative table is based on value judgments that arbitrarily skew the assessment in one direction or another. From our current perspective, we think of tanks in the modern framework of "main battle tanks." Contemporary armies employ a single, versatile type of tank that can serve in all tactical roles, whether it is tank-versus-tank fighting, fast exploitation, or close combat infantry fire support. But in 1939, most armies saw the need for multiple types of tanks, each tailored for specific tactical requirements. Most armies had a trio of types: a light tank or tankette for reconnaissance, an infantry tank to support rifle troops in close combat, and a cavalry tank for the fast exploitation mission. The qualities that make a great infantry tank, such as thick armor and good high-explosive firepower, are not as relevant in the cavalry tank role where speed and antitank firepower are more valuable. So it becomes very difficult to create a comparative table to determine the "best tank" since the criteria being used are likely to favor one tactical role with the risk of deprecating the combat values of another tank type. This is especially true in the 1939–42 period when most armies had hybrid tank fleets. By 1945, armies were moving in the direction of main battle tanks with the bulk of their fleets based on a single type, but there were still separate categories for light and heavy tanks roughly corresponding to the old scout and infantry tanks.

Cost is also a significant factor in war. Some armies would prefer to have a large but inexpensive tank fleet; others prefer to have a smaller number of better-quality tanks. In a tank-versus-tank fight, the better expensive tank may dominate, but from the broader perspective, a larger number of mediocre tanks may provide the critical edge on the battlefield.

With these factors in mind, three assessments of tank effectiveness can be made. In this book, I am calling them "Tanker's Choice," "Battlefield Dynamics," and "Commander's Choice." As I will explain in a moment, "Battlefield Dynamics" is a very important criteria, but almost impossible to quantify. So, I will offer a "Tanker's Choice" and "Commander's Choice" for Top Tank of a given era. I do not pretend that my choices are the only plausible ones. Judgments such as these are subjective, and in some cases I have deliberately selected a more provocative choice. Readers can make their own judgments, and it is my hope that this book will provide the data and historical context to improve the choices.

TANKER'S CHOICE

Tanker's Choice is the most basic assessment, focusing on the holy trinity of protection, firepower, and mobility. A tank crew would obviously choose a tank with the best features in these three categories. Tank crews really don't care if the tank is horribly expensive; they aren't paying for it. They simply want the best tank. Tanker's Choice is often threat-driven. This evaluation is closely tied to the capabilities of the main threat against its survivability.

Several armies conducted operational research during World War II and in the years after to try to quantify technical effectiveness. After World War II, the British Army Operational Research Group (AORG) attempted to calculate the technical effectiveness of tanks in tank-versus-tank engagements using both theoretical parameters and data collected from the 1944–45 campaigns. Effectiveness was defined as "the reciprocal of the number of tanks required per enemy tank to achieve parity in battle." One of these studies tried to compare the PzKpfw IV Ausf. H against several common British tanks. In the evaluation, the PzKpfw IV was given a rating of "1" and the British tanks were rated against this baseline.[1] The results are shown in more detail in Chapter 8.

Soviet tank experts also made a similar evaluation in the 1970s as a means to employ computer simulation to model the modern battlefield. The main Soviet tank research center, VNII Transmash (Scientific Research Institute of the Transportation Industry), created a computer model of a factor they called "combat potential." As in the British case, one tank was established as the baseline vehicle and assigned the value of "1." The other tanks were then evaluated against the baseline tank based on armor, firepower, and mobility, and given a value based on this assessment. Some of their evaluations were extended back to take a look at the World War II battlefield. Unlike the British assessment, the calculations behind the Soviet method have not been published. Some examples will be found in subsequent chapters.

This book will not use such a strict numerical assessment, but will provide the data to make an informed judgment about the Tanker's Choice for a given period.

BATTLEFIELD DYNAMICS

Battlefield Dynamics are one of the most critical aspects of the success or failure of a tank in battle. The two most important criteria are crew quality and battlefield circumstances. History has shown time and time again that a mediocre tank in the hands of a good crew will usually triumph against a better tank with a poor crew. Some obvious examples are the performance of German tanks in 1941 against the Red Army. The Red Army had superior tanks, such as the T-34 and KV, and massively outnumbered the Wehrmacht.[2] Yet the Red Army suffered massive defeats in tank combat. Another example, outside of the time period for this book, has been the performance of Israeli tank crews against Arab tank crews.

It is very difficult to place a quantitative value on crew quality. I recently wrote a book on tank fighting in Normandy pitting the M4 Sherman tanks of the 2nd Armored Division against the PzKpfw IV tanks of the *Panzer-Lehr Division* during Operation Cobra in July 1944.[3] The crews of the 2nd Armored Division had excellent, prolonged training and had seen a moderate amount of combat, including North Africa in November 1942 and Sicily in 1943. The *Panzer-Lehr Division* had only been formed at the end of 1943. Its officer cadre came from Wehrmacht tank training schools and were mostly combat-hardened veterans who had fought in Poland, France, and Russia. Its rank-and-file crewmen were mostly new recruits but they had already seen more than a month of fighting in Normandy against the British before their encounters with U.S. tanks at the end of July 1944. Both sides had training and experience advantages in different areas. It is no simple matter to quantify the capabilities of such opponents.

Battlefield circumstances are extremely important in the outcome of any tank-versus-tank fighting. The popular view of tank warfare is an armored joust. Two armored opponents are positioned opposite one another on the field of battle, with the more valiant or better-armed opponent the eventual victor. This has been cemented in the public mind by the scene in the movie *Patton* where George C. Scott muses that the battle could be decided at a lesser cost in blood if he and Rommel faced each other, man to man, in a tank. This is, of course, romantic nonsense.

Tank-versus-tank fighting was more often than not an opportunistic clash fought from ambush with one tank knocking out the other before the opposing tank even identified the presence of the enemy. The great "tank aces" of World War II were mostly bushwhackers, usually having a decided advantage in firepower or armor, and often having both. The hero of all Nazi fanboys is the Waffen-SS Tiger ace Michael Wittmann. Yet Wittmann fought from a Tiger heavy tank in 1943–44 when the Tiger could kill its opponents long before they were close enough to inflict damage on his tank. Most of the "tank aces" of World War II were simply the crews lucky enough to have an invulnerable tank with a powerful gun. How many "tank aces" operated the ordinary tanks—the PzKpfw III, PzKpfw IV, or Sherman?[4]

Aside from the clash between grossly unequal tank types, most tank skirmishes were won depending on battlefield advantages, not technical advantages. Let's create an example. A stationary, well-camouflaged tank is sitting in ambush; its opponent is a tank moving forward along a road with no knowledge that the enemy tank is waiting for it. Clearly the tank in ambush position has a much greater chance of success than the other tank crew that is oblivious to the position of the other tank. In the 1950s, the Operation Research Organization (ORO) of Johns Hopkins University conducted a number of studies on tank warfare, especially in the Korean War, to determine what factors lead to success in tank-versus-tank fighting.[5] This strongly indicated the side that spotted the enemy force and engaged first had up to a six-fold advantage. The simplest condensation of the rule of tank fighting is "See first, engage first, hit first." Tanks in a stationary defensive position had an obvious advantage against tanks moving to contact, since the stationary tanks were more likely to spot the approaching enemy first and engage first. The ORO research from tank battles in the Korean War suggested that tanks in well-prepared defensive positions enjoy a 3 to 1 advantage against attacking tanks. The other important element of the equation here is crew quality. It is not enough to see first and engage first. It is also necessary to hit first, meaning a crew that is well trained enough to have a high probability of getting a hit on the first shot. This is not as easy as it seems.

Even though these Battlefield Dynamics are absolutely critical to tank combat, they are almost impossible to quantify. Situational factors of the battlefield are unique to every single engagement; crew quality is difficult to measure. As a result, these factors will be mentioned in the ensuing chapters, but in most cases they will not be used to pick the Top Tanks.

COMMANDER'S CHOICE

Tank crews obviously want the best possible tank in terms of technical virtues since their survival depends upon it. But this is not necessarily the criteria of senior commanders. A tank such as the Tiger in 1943 would be the obvious Tanker's Choice. But the Tiger was a horribly expensive tank. The German army could have bought ten StuG III assault guns or three Tiger tanks. It can certainly be argued that ten assault guns give more combat power than three tanks. So cost is an important factor in assessing the combat power available to an army.

The other issue is reliability. Many of the heavy tanks of World War II, such as the Tiger, had poor reliability. They were at the "bleeding edge of technology" and existing power-train technology was at its outer limits when dealing with tanks of this weight. As will be described in more detail below, the ordinary vehicles such as the StuG III and PzKpfw IV had much better reliability than the Tiger and Panther. Factoring in reliability, the Wehrmacht could have had seven operational StuG III or one operational Tiger tank. From a general's perspective, seven assault guns offer far more combat power than one heavy tank, no matter how powerful. The Commander's Choice is therefore capabilities-driven. How much combat power can a given tank type contribute to the battle? These factors will be used in assessing the Commander's Choice for Top Tank.

A TANK PRIMER

Many readers of this book will already be familiar with World War II tank technology, but some will not be. This section will provide a thumbnail sketch of some of the basic criteria used in judging the Top Tanks.

Armor Protection

The survivability of the tank on the battlefield depends largely on its armor. Since World War I, armor has usually been provided either in the form of rolled armor plate or cast armor, with plate armor the most common. Until the 1930s, most armor plate was assembled using rivets. This traditional fabrication method has some problems, notably the possibility that if the rivet is hit by a projectile, the impact could shear off the inner head, sending it careening inside the tank. The solution to this problem was to seal-weld the rivet heads, a process sometimes used in the early 1940s. However, by 1945 welded armor was the preferred solution.

The protective value of armor depends largely on its thickness. World War I tanks typically had armor from about 1/4 inch thick (6mm) to 1 inch thick (25mm), more often on the lower end of this scale. The initial intention was to provide protection against rifle and machine-gun bullets. It usually took about 15mm of armor to protect against light machine guns in the .30-cal (7.62mm) range, or about 25mm to protect against heavy machine guns in the .50-cal (12.7mm) range.

Armor protection did not increase very dramatically after World War I, and most tank designs of the period focused on the traditional threat posed by machine guns and field guns. A typical tank of the mid-1930s, the Soviet T-26 light infantry tank, had 15mm on the front surfaces, except for the turret front which had 20mm. With the advent of the dedicated antitank gun during this period, epitomized by the German Rheinmetall 37mm gun, tanks began to face a new threat. This gun could penetrate contemporary tank armor at nearly any practical combat range. As a result, some armies began to increase the thickness of their tank armor to provide it with "shell-proof" capabilities. A good example of this

The 40mm cast armor of the Hotchkiss H39 was very effective in protecting the tank against German weapons up to the 37mm gun. This H39 from the 3rd Light Mechanized Division was knocked out during the tank melee at Hannut on 13 May 1940 by two 37mm hits at close range from PzKpfw III tanks. There are numerous gouges in the armor from hits by 7.92mm and 20mm fire from the PzKpfw I and PzKpfw II tanks that did not penetrate.

was the French Renault R35 infantry tank that entered production in 1936 after the advent of the German 37mm gun. This tank used cast armor that was 40mm thick to defeat the threat of the 37mm antitank gun. World War II saw a continued race between guns and armor, with tank armor steadily increasing to resist more and more powerful guns.

It has never proved practical to use thick armor on all surfaces of the tank—otherwise the tank would simply become too heavy. Armor thickness generally varies due to the probability of a surface being hit, so the front of the turret and glacis plate on the front of the hull usually have the thickest armor, the hull and turret sides less armor, and the tank roof

The formidable frontal armor of the Panther led the Allies to conduct a series of tests using various types of ammunition against captured tanks at Isigny, France, in July and August 1944. This photo from the report shows the results against one of the targets, with penetrations from the new 17-pounder APDS (armor-piercing, discarding sabot) projectiles, a plate failure around the machine-gun position, and numerous gouges from rounds that failed to penetrate.

The U.S. Ninth Army conducted their own trials against a Panther on 10 January 1945, using an M4A3 (105mm) assault gun firing HEAT (high-explosive antitank) and an M4A3 firing 75mm armor-piercing and high-explosive. While it may not be apparent in this view, several of the HEAT rounds made clean penetrations of the glacis plate and would have killed the crew.

and belly the least armor. Armor can be compared to a shield of an ancient warrior: the shield is used to protect the areas most likely to be struck in combat.

Tank designers tried to determine which surfaces were the most likely to be hit and to allot the armor accordingly. Historical data provides some idea of the probability of hits on the tank. This data stems from investigations of 107 M4 Sherman tanks of the U.S. Army in 1944–45.[6]

The Red Army carried out a far more exhaustive study of where tanks were hit in combat, examining 7,639 T-34 tanks from the time of the Stalingrad battles in 1942 to the end of the war in 1945. The data is summarized on page 8.

A destroyed M4A3 medium tank in Luxembourg in September 1944. Judging from the missing center bogie, this tank probably ran over a mine that set off the wet stowage ammunition racks in the hull floor. The off-kilter turret is a sure sign of a catastrophic ammunition fire.

While the Sherman has developed a reputation for its vulnerability to fire, German tanks were not exempt. This PzKpfw IV Ausf. H suffered a catastrophic ammunition fire during the fighting with the Canadians on the road between Caen and Vaucelles in Normandy in the summer of 1944.

A GI looks down in amazement at the gouges from no fewer than seven rounds that ricocheted off the glacis armor of this King Tiger near Moinet, Belgium, in January 1945. The tank was eventually penetrated on the left side, striking ammunition which set off a catastrophic fire that blew off the turret.

HITS ON U.S. ARMY M4 MEDIUM TANKS IN WWII	
Turret front	9%
Hull front	21%
Turret side	18%
Hull side	32%
Suspension	19%
Hull rear	1%

Although thickness is the primary determinant in the protective quality of armor, it is not the only one. By angling the armor relative to the enemy weapon, the effective thickness of the armor can be increased. So for example, in the case of a tank with 20mm armor, the vertical plate has an effective thickness of 20mm. When angled 30 degrees, the effective thickness increases to 22mm, and when angled to 45 degrees its effective thickness is 28mm. Armor at extremely inclined angles can also increase the chances that the enemy projectile will deflect off the surface. So the comparative charts in the following chapter will list the actual thickness of the tank armor as well as its effective thickness to give a more complete picture of its protective value.

The protective qualities of tank armor can also be affected by production techniques. German tanks in the early war years, notably the PzKpfw III and

HITS ON T-34 TANKS, 1942–45 (%)	Front	Side	Rear	Total
Turret	14.5	17.2	2.8	34.6
Hull	15.6	46.8	3	65.4
Tank	30	64	6	(100)

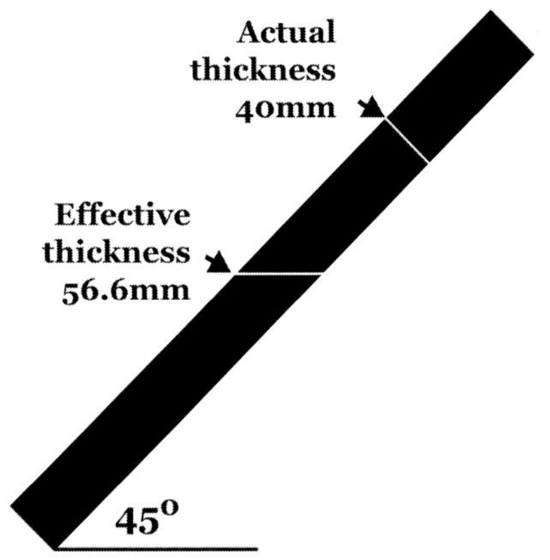

The angle of an armor plate to attack improves its protective values since its effective thickness relative to the ballistic path increases.

PzKpfw IV, used face-hardened armor that offered better protective qualities than homogeneous armor when hit by standard armor-piercing projectiles. However, the introduction of improved antitank projectiles such as APC (armor-piercing, capped) undermined the advantages. Not all steel armor plate has the same protective quality due to variations in hardness and the use of different alloys.[7] Different countries preferred different armor qualities. For example, the Soviet Union favored very hard armor, but the U.S. Army favored medium hardness armor that was more ductile.[8]

Nor was armor quality constant through the war. Evidence would suggest that German tank quality began to decrease by the autumn of 1944 due to

Early tank and antitank guns used solid armor-piercing shot that was often not very destructive. Here a crewman of this PzKpfw IV Ausf. D from *Panzer-Regiment.1* in Belgium inspects the penetration by a single 25mm antitank gun hit on the lower bow plate; the hit disabled the tank's transmission.

shortages of critical alloys. There was a severe decline in the quality of cast armor for T-34 turrets in 1942 when Soviet tank plants were hastily shipped east, but it later improved in 1944–45. This book does not have the length to discuss armor manufacturing technology in great depth, but readers should be aware of the complexities of armor protection.

Tank Vulnerability

What killed the most tanks on the World War II battlefield? The simple answer is that enemy guns were the primary killer. However, the percentage varied by time and theater, and the data seldom distinguished between enemy tanks versus antitank guns. Here are a few samples of historical data to give a sense of the source of casualties.

BRITISH TANK LOSS TO ENEMY WEAPONS IN NORTH AFRICA, 1941–43[9]

(%)	1941	1942	1943
Gunfire	86.4	78.7	76.9
Mines	7.3	16.7	23.1
Misc. weapons	6.1	4.4	0

ALLIED TANK LOSSES IN EUROPEAN THEATER OF OPERATIONS, 1944–45

(%)	Gunfire	Mines	RPG*	Misc.	Non-combat
U.S. 1944	47.6	16.4	11.7	4.5	19.7
British 1944	49.7	17.3	12.7	4.2	16.2
Canadian 1944	64.8	12.6	4.8	5.5	22.4
U.S. 1945	50.9	18.2	11.4	5.4	14.1
British 1945	53.6	22.0	21.4	3.0	19.2
Canadian 1945	32.9	12.3	10.6	6.9	37.2

*Rocket-propelled grenade, e.g. *Panzerfaust* or *Panzerschreck*

GERMAN KILL CLAIMS AGAINST SOVIET TANKS AND AFVS, JANUARY–APRIL 1944[10]

	January	%	February	%	March	%	April	%	Total	%
Panzer	1,401	38.1	853	44.7	122	11.8	820	53.1	3,196	39.2
Antitank guns	1,050	28.6	341	17.9	327	31.7	251	16.2	1,969	24.1
StuG and *Pz.Jäger*	757	20.6	472	24.7	297	28.8	236	15.3	1,762	21.6
Artillery, mines, other	348	9.4	148	7.7	142	13.7	63	4.0	701	8.6
Other AT weapons	114	3.1	91	4.7	143	13.8	172	11.1	520	6.4
Total	***3,670***		***1,905***		***1,031***		***1,542***		***8,148***	

SOVIET AFV LOSSES, 1944–45[11]

	Losses	Gunfire	Mines	Aviation	Other
4th Guards Tank Army, Orlov Operation, 1943	360	312	41	7	
4th Guards Tank Army, June–Sept. 1944	239	230	3	6	
1st Guards Tank Army, Lvov Operation, 1944	324	310		14	
1st Guards Tank Army, Carpathian Operation, 1944	286	256	4	14	12
3rd Guards Tank Army, Lvov-Carpathian Operation, 1944	381	322	10	49	
Leningrad Front, 1944	151	112	39		
2nd Byelorussian Front, Feb.1945	674	645	3		26
4th Ukrainian Front, May 1945	525	503	17	5	
	2,940	2,690 (91%)	117 (4%)	95 (3%)	38 (1%)

SOVIET COMBAT LOSSES, 1944–45: COMBAT VS. TECHNICAL CAUSES

	Total Losses	Combat Losses	%	Technical Losses	%	Other	%
All AFV	25,694	22,039	85.5	2,405	9.3	1,317	5.5
T-34 tanks	4,821	4,131	85.5	450	12.5	240	2

T-34 TANKS PENETRATED IF HIT, 1941–45

	Penetrated (%)	Not Penetrated (%)
To Sept. 1942	46	54
Stalingrad Operation, Nov. 1942–Jan. 1943	55	45
Central Front, Kursk-Orlov Operation, 1943	88	12
1st Byelorussian Front, July–Sept. 1944	92	8
1st Byelorussian Front, Jan.–Mar. 1945	98.7	1.3
1st Ukrainian Front, Jan.–Mar. 1945	99	1
4th Ukrainian Front, Jan.–Mar. 1945	97	3
1st Byelorussian Front, Berlin Operation	87	13

The effectiveness of tank armor also varied through time due to improvements in tank and antitank guns. A Soviet study examined the combat losses of the T-34 tank in 1941–45 and the statistics show the shift toward heavier firepower on the Russian Front.

This was also reflected in the growing vulnerability of tanks from 1941 to 1945. A Soviet study examined the probability of a T-34 tank being penetrated if hit throughout the war, based on various reports. As can be seen, through 1942 the T-34 had about an even chance of being penetrated if hit up to

COMBAT LOSSES OF THE T-34 TANK BY GERMAN WEAPONS, 1941–45 (%)[12]

	20mm	37mm	50mm	75mm	88mm	105mm	128mm	RPG	Unknown
To Sept. 1942	4.7	10.0	61.8	10.1	3.4	2.9			7.1
Stalingrad Operation, Nov. 1942–Jan. 1943			52.1	12.1	7.8				28.0
Central Front, Kursk-Orlov, 1943		10.5	23.0	40.5	26.0				
1st Byelorussian Front, July–Sept. 1944				39.0	38.0			9.0	14.0
1st Byelorussian Front, Jan.–Mar. 1945				29.0	64.0		1.0	5.5	0.5
1st Ukrainian Front, Mar. 1945			0.5	19.0	71.0	0.6		8.9	
4th Ukrainian Front, May 1945				25.3	51.5	0.9		9.0	13.3
1st Byelorussian Front, Oder-Berlin, 1945			1.4	69.2	16.7			10.5	2.2
2nd Guards Tank Army, Berlin Operation, 1945		5.4		36.0	29.0	6.6		22.8	

This is an example of the penetration of a German *Panzerschreck* or *Panzerfaust*–shaped charge warhead detonating against the left hull side of a French Army M4A2 in November 1944. Shaped-charge warheads usually leave a distinct pattern of spall away from the point of penetration, as can be seen here.

An ordnance lieutenant from the 6th Armored Division looks at the damage to an M4A3 Sherman tank in November 1944. A German 75mm gun hit the turret at least five times from the rear left quadrant. Two rounds penetrated while three ricocheted off.

Thin armor hit with high-explosive projectiles tends to suffer catastrophic failure. This Jagdpanzer 38 (Hetzer) was hit on the side by a couple of 76mm rounds from a Soviet SU-76M in the January 1945 fighting; they completely collapsed the left side armor. This vehicle was fished out of the Czarna Nida River in Poland in the 1990s when a summer drought lowered the water level.

the time of the Stalingrad battles. By the final 1945 battles, the T-34 almost always was penetrated if hit.

Firepower

Tanks of World War I were usually armed with machine guns and small cannon since their main mission was to fight enemy infantry and machine-gun nests. Tank-versus-tank fighting was a rarity. The French army conducted over 4,350 tank missions in 1917–18, yet never encountered a single German tank; the British army only had one encounter with a German tank.

Not surprisingly, tanks in the interwar period tended to carry much the same sort of weaponry. Light tanks often used one or more machine guns as their basic armament; short, low-velocity 37–47mm guns were common on medium tanks. The Red Army was the first to widely use a dual-purpose tank gun, a 45mm gun derived from the German Rheinmetall 37mm antitank gun. In contrast to its 37mm ancestor, the 45mm gun was designed to fire both an antitank projectile and a high-explosive projectile. This gun became the predominant Red Army tank armament, equipping both infantry tanks such as the T-26 and cavalry tanks such as the BT. The versatility of this weapon became evident in 1937 during the Spanish Civil War, which saw the first widespread tank-versus-tank encounters. The T-26 dominated these skirmishes against machine-gun-armed opponents such as the German PzKpfw I and Italian L-3 tankette. By this stage, European armies began to realize that reliance on machine-gun armament was shortsighted, and most tanks designed after this point, except for reconnaissance light tanks, carried some form of gun armament. This did not mean the end of machine-gun armament on tanks. Machine guns remained an important secondary weapon for use against infantry. Rather, they were no longer the principal weapon of most new tank designs, but instead supplemented guns.

One of the most common misconceptions about tank guns is that their antiarmor performance is largely dependent on their caliber. The presumption is that a 76mm gun is more powerful than a 75mm gun. This is entirely false. Armor penetration is largely a factor of the velocity of the projectile. A rough measure of the energy of a tank projectile is mass x velocity (squared). In other words, increases in projectile velocity are far more important than increases in weight of the projectile. Projectile velocity can be accelerated in several ways. The most important source of velocity is the amount and type of propellant. So for example, in the case of German 75mm tank guns, the early war short 75mm gun used a round with only 12 ounces of propellant, which increased to 5.35 pounds in the mid-war "long" 75mm KwK 40 on the PzKpfw IV Ausf. G, and finally to 8.1 pounds in the Panther's very long 75mm KwK 42. As can be seen from the chart below, this resulted in substantially higher

Tank ammunition, even if the same caliber, is not interchangeable. These three 37mm armor-piercing rounds from the author's collection are (from left to right) American, German, and Czechoslovak.

COMPARATIVE PERFORMANCE OF GERMAN 75MM APCBC PROJECTILE

75mm Gun	Length	Propellant weight kg (lb)	Initial muzzle velocity (m/s)	Penetration (mm)*
KwK	L/24	.34 (.75)	1,263	62
KwK 40	L/48	2.4 (5.35)	2,460	141
KwK 42	L/70	3.7 (8.1)	3,070	190

*Against vertical RHA plate, point-blank; RHA= rolled homogeneous armor

COMPARATIVE PERFORMANCE OF U.S. 75MM GUNS FIRING M61 APCBC ROUND

Gun Type	Length	Muzzle Velocity	Penetration*
M2	L/31	1,926 ft/s	2.6 inches
M3	L/40	2,024 ft/s	2.9 inches

*RHA plate at 20 degrees at 500 yards

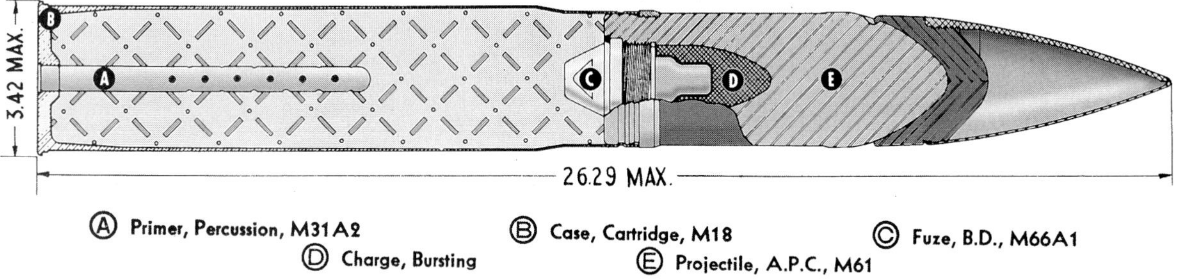

The APCBC (armor-piercing capped, ballistic cap) ammunition was one of the most common types in use in the later years of the war. The basic steel core (E) has a blunt soft metal cap welded to the front, followed by a thin steel windshield for better ballistic performance.

muzzle velocity and armor penetration even though the projectile was essentially unchanged.

The other important factor in armor penetration of tank guns is barrel length. A tank gun firing the same type of projectile with the same propellant load will get more muzzle velocity with a longer barrel than a shorter barrel since the longer barrel provides more time for the detonation of the propellant to impart its energy to the projectile. Good examples of this are the American 75mm tank guns. On a technical note, gun barrel length is usually expressed as "caliber" (L/), which is the length of the gun tube divided by the bore diameter. So the M3 gun had a length of 3,010mm divided by its 75mm bore diameter, which equals L/40.

Another factor affecting armor penetration is the design of the projectile. Armor-piercing (AP) projectiles early in the war were simple steel bullets, often with an aerodynamically sleek design for better flight characteristics. As the speed of these projectiles increased, there was a tendency for the steel to shatter on impact with sloped armor, especially face-hardened armor. One solution was to cement a soft metal cap, typically iron, to the nose of the projectile. The cap cushioned the forces on the projectile on impact, helping to make it more resistant to shattering. In its simplest form, these were called APC (armor-piercing capped). These gave way to a more sophisticated version that added a thin metal "windshield" in front of the cap for better aerodynamic performance. These were called APCBC (armor-piercing capped, ballistic cap) and became the common antiarmor projectile in the later war years.

To squeeze more performance out of antitank projectiles, a variety of more novel projectiles were developed. One innovation was to encase a very dense and hard sub-caliber penetrator within a larger, light metal projectile. During World War II, the penetrator was usually a very hard and heavy material such as tungsten carbide, which is denser and harder than steel (13 vs. 7.8 grams per cubic centimeter). It was usually encased in a light, soft metal such as duraluminum. The main advantage of this type of projectile was that its lighter weight gave it greater speed. In addition, on impact the soft outer shell peeled away, and the projectile's energy was concentrated on a smaller impact point of the hard metal penetrator. This type of projectile was called APCR (armor-piercing composite rigid) by the British, but was known as HVAP (high-velocity armor-piercing) by the U.S. Army; HVAP is used in this book. By way of comparison, the HVAP round for the 88mm gun on the King Tiger tank had a penetration of about 260mm at 500 meters compared to about 210mm for the more conventional APCBC round. The German army began to use this type of ammunition in 1941 to improve the performance of the 50mm tank gun on the PzKpfw III in 1941 against the threat of the T-34 tank. The Red Army began using it in 1942–43 and the U.S. Army in the late summer of 1944.

There were two main disadvantages to this type of ammunition. First, the HVAP round had the same frontal area as an APCBC round while only about 70 percent of the weight. As a result, its ballistic performance fell off faster at longer ranges, or in technical jargon, it had a lower ballistic coefficient. The second problem with HVAP was that the penetrator was made of tungsten carbide, a precious commodity in World War II and one badly needed by defense industries for machine tools. As a result, HVAP production was severely constrained by most armies. In the case of the U.S. Army, the goal in late 1944 was to equip each tank with one round of HVAP. The Red Army, due to more ample supplies of tungsten, was able to equip its tanks in 1944–45 with more of these rounds, often five to six per tank. The German army made extensive use of HVAP in 1941–43, but due to dwindling supplies it became scarce in 1944–45.

Another approach to launch a high-velocity, sub-caliber penetrator was the APDS (armor-piercing, discarding sabot), also called SVDS (super-velocity discarding sabot). Instead of encasing the penetrator in soft metal, it was placed in a light metal sabot, usually made of aluminum. When the projectile left the gun barrel, the separate "petals" of the sabot peeled off, leaving the penetrator to fly to its target at very high speed. In the case of the British 17-pounder, the APDS round offered about a 1,000 ft/s increase in speed over the conventional APC round, a sizzling 3,950 ft/s initial muzzle velocity. The main problem with the APDS rounds in 1944–45 were the mechanics of the sabot separation.[13] Unless all the petals fell away neatly and simultaneously, the penetrator suffered slight deviations in its ballistic trajectory, which translated into dispersion and decreased accuracy at longer ranges.

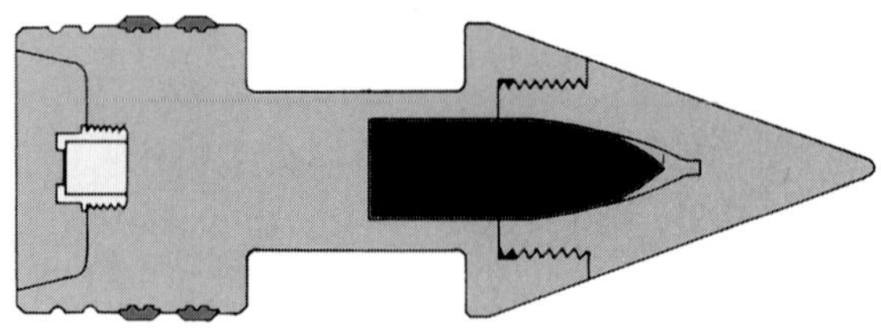

BR-365P 85mm HVAP

The shape of HVAP projectiles varied from army to army. Soviet HVAP projectiles such as this 85mm BR-365P were called "arrow-head" due to their shape. The tungsten-carbide core was surrounded by an aluminum ballistic body.

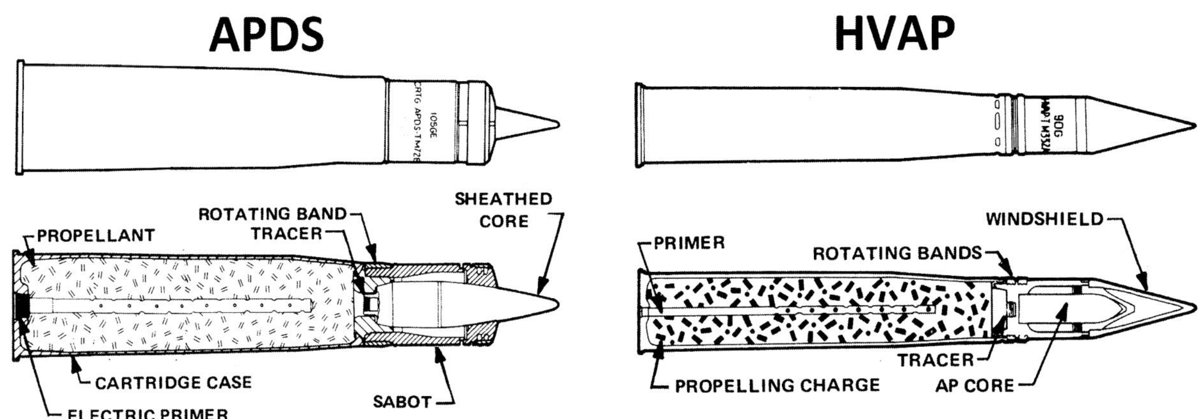

The two principal types of hyper-velocity armor-piercing ammunition in World War II were APDS (armor-piercing, discarding sabot) and HVAP (high-velocity armor-piercing). When the APDS projectile leaves the gun, the sabot and other parts separate from the core, and only the armor-piercing core impacts the target. When the HVAP projectile leaves the gun, the lightweight structure around the tungsten-carbide core remains with the core until impact.

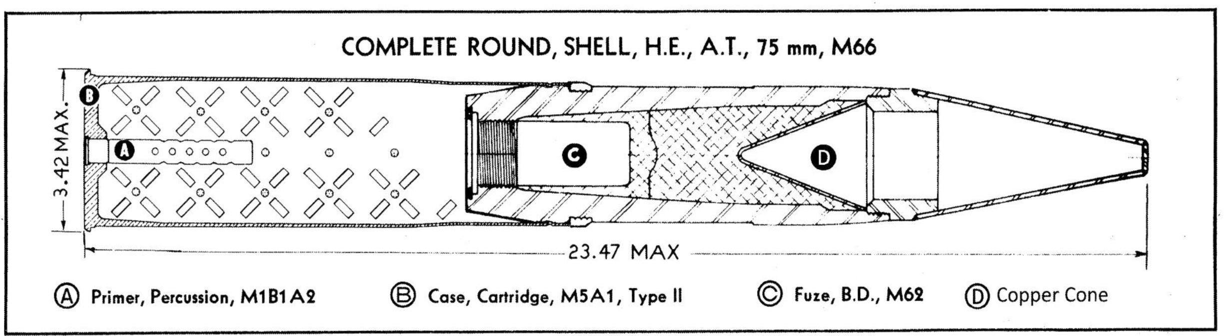

HEAT (high-explosive antitank) was not widely used for tank guns in World War II since the impact fuzes did not work quickly enough for the shaped charge to detonate properly. In a shaped-charge warhead, the explosive behind the copper cone detonates and explosively compresses the copper liner into a hypersonic stream of metallic particles that penetrate the armor.

These problems were gradually worked out after the war. Generally speaking, HVAP offered better accuracy, but APDS offered better penetration in the 1944–45 time frame.

The projectile with the best armor penetration during World War II was the HEAT (high-explosive antitank). However, this seldom proved practical for tank-versus-tank fighting in 1939–45. The HEAT projectile used a shaped-charge warhead consisting of a hollow copper cone backed by a layer of explosive. On impact, the detonation of the explosive collapsed the copper into a hypersonic jet of metal particles that could bore through a substantial amount of steel armor. This type of warhead was first used on antitank rockets such as the U.S. Army 2.36 Bazooka antitank launcher. Other armies adapted it to various types of guns, mainly low-velocity guns and howitzers. It was not used by high-velocity tank guns in World War II for two reasons. Rifled tank guns spun the projectile and decreased the penetration of its jet by 30–50 percent. There were also problems detonating the high-explosive warhead quickly enough after impact. When impacting at high velocity, the copper cone at the front of the projectile was crushed or deformed before the base-detonating impact fuze could trigger the explosives. This was not as great an issue with handheld rocket weapons or howitzer rounds that were so slow that the fuze could work in time. This problem was not solved until after World War II with the invention of piezo-electric fuzes that could detonate the high-explosive warhead in microseconds before the copper cone was damaged. These became the predominant form and antitank ammunition in NATO through most of the 1950s and 1960s.

How much ammunition was needed on board a tank? Contrary to popular computer games, it took a lot of ammunition to hit another tank in typical World War II combat. For example, the Tiger tanks of *Panzer-Abteilung 502* during 24–30 June 1944 claimed the destruction of 27 Soviet tanks and AFVs, expending 1,079 88mm armor-piercing rounds. This equals 40 rounds for each Soviet vehicle destroyed. In the next engagements during 4–27 July, 85 Soviet tanks and AFVs were destroyed, for an expenditure of 555 rounds or about 6.5 rounds per target destroyed. The difference between the two engagements were battlefield circumstances. The first set of engagements took place at very long ranges, often 2 kilometers; the second set were meeting engagements at closer ranges.

These high rates of ammunition expenditure per kill claim were not unusual. From 1 December 1943 to 31 May 1944, 23 StuG III brigades on the Russian Front fired a total 51,595 armor-piercing rounds against Soviet tanks and other armored targets. This resulted in claims for 1,899 Soviet AFVs destroyed as well as 132 disabled.[14] This indicates that it took more than 25 rounds of ammunition for every Soviet tank destroyed or disabled. German 88mm Flak guns used in an antitank role in the Western Desert in 1942 might seem the ideal tank-killing weapon since they were on stable, stationary mounts with an excellent telescopic sight, firing in open desert, using a very powerful, high-velocity projectile. Yet unit records over the course of several days showed that on average, it took 11 rounds for every tank claimed.[15]

Another factor worth considering here is the issue of kill claims. When an airplane is shot down in combat, it is almost invariably a total loss. This is not the case in tank combat. In many cases, tanks are temporarily put out of action by a less-than-fatal hit. For example, a track is hit by an antitank gun, stopping the tank. Or an antitank projectile penetrates the tank, killing or injuring several crewmen but leaving the rest of the tank unharmed. In these cases, the tank can be recovered and put back into action. Tanks are usually not written off as total losses unless they suffer a catastrophic fire intense enough to damage the armor. Most often this resulted from an ammunition fire. As in the case of aircraft kill claims, tank kill claims by the various armies tended to be exaggerated. Sometimes this was done due to the usual chaos and confusion of battle. Several tanks simultaneously would engage an enemy tank, and when it was finally hit all would claim it as their victim. Sometimes, exaggerated kill claims also served propaganda purposes.[16]

Although most attention is paid to the antitank performance of tank guns, high-explosive throwing power remained a more critical ingredient for most tank combat. Tank buffs tend to focus on tank-versus-tank fighting. Large-scale tank-versus-tank battles such as the Battle of Kursk in the summer of 1943 are viewed as the norm rather than as the exception. This tendency has been further reinforced by video games such as the popular "World of Tanks" that focus entirely on tank-versus-tank fighting. Many military buffs grow up reading about fighter plane combat and see tank fighting as an analog to air combat. They were not.

Yet in terms of day-to-day tank combat, the vast majority of engagements were between tanks and infantry and their supporting arms such as antitank guns. For example, in the European Theater of Operations (ETO), 71 percent of 75mm tank gun expenditure and 73 percent of 76mm gun expenditure by the U.S. Army was high-explosive; the remainder was smoke and armor-piercing. Less than 20 percent of the targets were other tanks or armored vehicles. In the case of the German army, the 23 StuG III assault gun brigades on the Russian Front fired a total of 315,280 rounds, of which 263,685 (83.7 percent) were fired against unarmored targets such as infantry, buildings, and vehicles, while 51,595 (16.3 percent) were fired against tanks and other armored targets from 1 December 1943 to 31 May 1944.

TARGETS OF U.S. ARMY TANKS, 1942–45[17]

Target	Average, All Theaters	Highest % by Theater
Fortifications	21.2	36.4 (SW Pacific)
Buildings	17.3	28.0 (Italy)
Troops	15.5	23.9 (Pacific)
Tanks	14.2	24.4 (North Africa)
Antitank guns and artillery	12.8	18.8 (Italy)
Other	10.8	15.6 (North Africa)
Trucks	8.2	12.6 (ETO)

A U.S. study of targets engaged by tanks found that enemy tanks represented only about 15 percent of the targets engaged by U.S. tanks during the war. The target set varied by theater, with tank-versus-tank fighting more common in North Africa and least common in the Pacific; correspondingly, non-tank targets were more common in the Pacific.

Most armies in World War II eventually discovered that the ideal tank gun was a dual-purpose weapon able to fire both a lethal antitank projectile and a high-explosive round with a large content of high-explosive. In reality, the balance between both characteristics was elusive. This was especially the case in the early war years of 1939–42 when common tank guns such as the German 37mm gun and the British 2-pounder had good antitank performance but poor high-explosive throwing power due to the small size of the projectile. For example, the German 37mm high-explosive round had only 25 grams (1 ounce) of high explosive. This problem became less acute in the mid-war years with the advent of larger caliber tank guns in the 75mm range, which had projectiles large enough to accommodate high-explosive charges of 1.5 pounds or more.

Combat Ranges

The effectiveness of World War II tank guns was highly dependent on the engagement range. Performance quickly fell off at long ranges as the projectile lost speed and accuracy decreased due to ballistic drop. Tank gun sights did not offer accurate range determination; this is dealt with in more detail below in the Command and Control section. Studies after the war found that typical combat ranges varied through time. In the blitzkrieg era, ranges were limited by the guns such as the typical 37mm tank and antitank guns. Later in the war, combat ranges were often limited by terrain factors. Open desert terrain or the Ukrainian steppes permitted longer ranges than mountainous terrain such as in Italy or built-up terrain such as northwest Europe. One U.S. study summarized typical engagement ranges as follows:

AVERAGE TANK ENGAGEMENT RANGES[18]

North Africa, 1941–43	900 yards
Sicily–Italy, 1943–45	350 yards
ETO, 1944–45	800 yards

The French tank commander in the Char B1 bis or Somua S35 had a 4-power L.762 monocular telescopic sight to aim the 47mm SA35 gun. This is a simulated view through that sight at a range of 200 meters. The "stairs" on the left were for the MAC 31 machine gun (M= *mitrailleuse*) while the "stairs" on the right side had two separate gradations: the one on the left marked BR (R = rupture, armor-piercing) and the one on the right marked Ex (*explosif*, high-explosive). The commander rotated the reticle dial on the telescope to match the cross hair with the appropriate range gradation, moving the cross hair to provide the necessary super elevation, and then elevated the gun to align the realigned cross hair with the point where he wished to aim.

The German gunner on the PzKpfw IV Ausf. D tank had a 2.5-power Leitz TZF5b (*Turmzielfernrohr*) monocular telescopic gun sight to aim the 75mm KwK 37 gun. This simulated sight shows the appearance of a French Char B1 bis 200 meters away. The difference is noticeable when compared to the higher magnification of the French 47mm gun sight shown here.

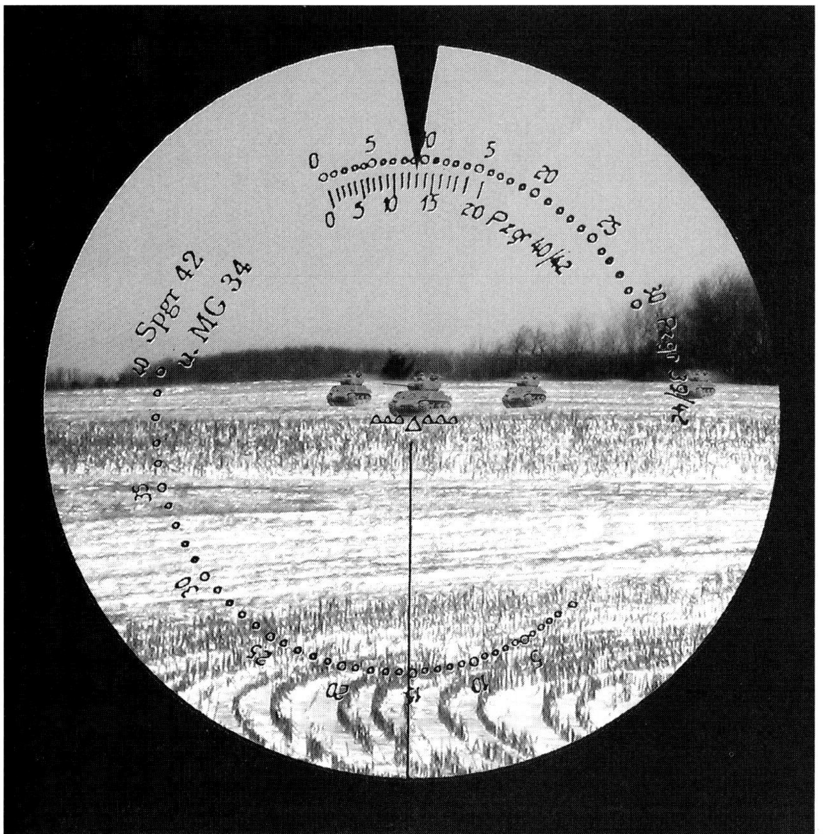

The German gunner in a Panther Ausf. G tank aimed the 75mm KwK 42 gun through a TFZ 12a monocular telescope. The telescope operated at two magnifications, 2.5 and 5 power, with the lower magnification used for general observation, at which point the gunner switched to the higher magnification for precision aiming. The view shown here depicts what a gunner would see at the typical engagement range of 900 meters at 5 power. The sight's engraved reticle provided a limited stadiametric ranging capability, which allowed a well-trained gunner to estimate the range based on the size of the target compared to the large triangle. The small gradations around the periphery of the reticle were to help adjust the weapon depending on the weapon and type of ammunition being used. The gunner would dial in either the machine-gun or main gun gradations, seen here set at 900 meters for the *Pz.Gr.39/42* armor-piercing projectile.

The gunner in an M4A3 (76mm) Sherman would aim the 76mm M1A2 gun with a 5-power M71D monocular telescopic sight. The reticle had range gradations for the standard M62 armor-piercing projectile; the performance of the M62 HE projectile was essentially similar at ranges under 1,000 yards. The reticle pattern was graduated in yards, so the commander estimated the range to target, including this in his firing commands, and the gunner adjusted the sight on the target accordingly.

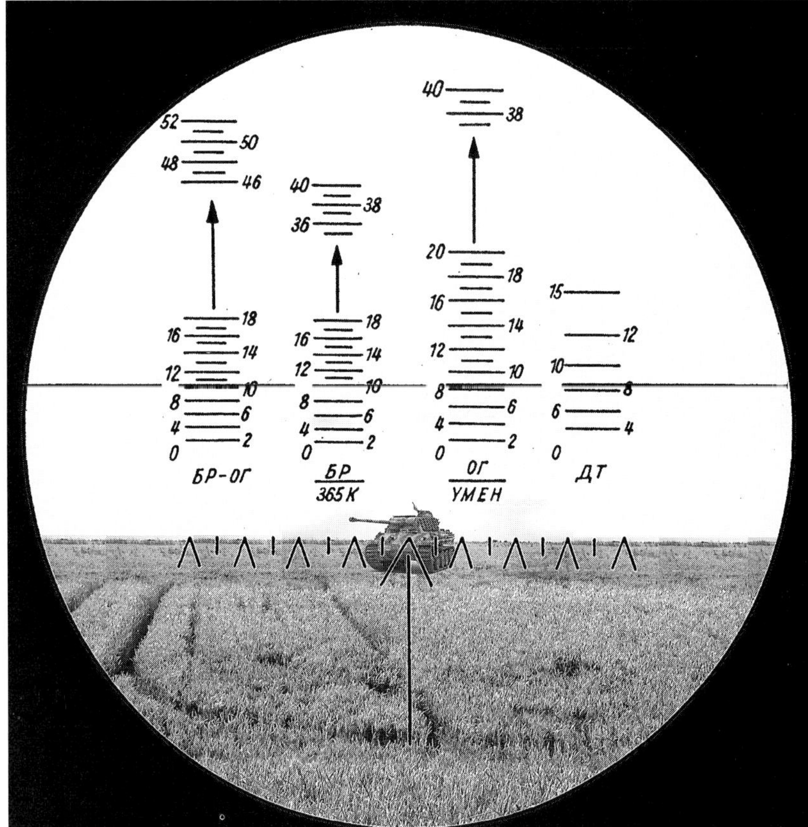

The Soviet gunner in a T-34-85 used a 4-power TSh-16 sight for aiming the ZIS-S-53 gun. The illustration here simulates the engagement of a Panther tank at 1,000 meters. The stadiametric rangefinder etched into the reticle has four vertical "stairs" for providing ballistic corrections for the four main types of the ammunition (from left to right): armor-piercing, armor-piercing hyper-velocity, high-explosive, and DT machine-gun. The lower lines consisting of upside-down Vs and dashes provide a simple stadiametric scale, with the width of the center V roughly equivalent to the length of a tank when viewed at 1,000 meters.

Mobility

The distinction between infantry and cavalry tanks early in the war led to strong variations in tank mobility. Infantry tanks tended to place the accent on armor protection over speed, while cavalry tanks tended to place the emphasis on speed. By mid-war, these distinctions had begun to erode and most tanks were expected to have a road speed in the range of 25–30 miles per hour and a cross-country speed around 15 miles per hour.

Tank mobility begins with engine power. Gasoline engines were the predominant type during the war, though some major tank forces such as the Red Army had shifted in favor of diesel for their medium and heavy tanks. One of the more popular canards was that gasoline engines made tanks more prone to fires. There is very little statistical evidence to support this, and more wartime research indicated that ammunition fires were the primary cause of catastrophic tank fires.

The prevalence of gasoline engines in tanks was in part due to the origins of the engines. Most countries adopted existing engines for tanks rather than developing dedicated tank engines. The U.S. Army in the early war years favored aircraft radial engines, though later adopted a variety of other types when the aircraft industry received priority for engine production. A popular tank engine in the 1930s was the World War I Liberty in-line aircraft engine, which formed the basis for the Soviet BT tanks of the 1930s and many early British tanks. The French army used a variety of engine sources, although bus and truck engines were widely adopted on the common infantry tanks. Some armies developed engines specifically for tanks and these were often diesels. The Japanese were the first to widely use diesel engines on tanks; the Soviets followed with the development of the V-2 diesel engine for the T-34 and KV in 1939–40.

A critical but often overlooked element in tank mobility was the transmission and power-train.

Tank transmissions were frequently derived from tractor or automotive transmissions, but the peculiarities of tank propulsion often required substantial redesign of components such as the final drives. Power-trains were a frequent source of reliability problems, and some World War II tank designs were seriously undermined by inadequate power-trains.

Tank suspensions in World War II started with a range of leaf spring–based types which offered a good balance between light weight and adequate cross-country performance. At the extreme was the Christie spring suspension, intended for high-speed tanks, which offered considerable wheel travel in terrain but at the expense of stealing considerable internal hull volume. The U.S. Army favored volute springs over leaf springs, and this system proved robust enough for tanks into the 30-ton class. Torsion bar suspensions began to appear in the late 1930s, first widely used on the PzKpfw III Ausf. F. This was gradually adopted by most tank manufacturers by the end of the war since it offered good road-wheel travel while not taking up much internal hull volume.

Track design has a considerable impact on mobility, both in terms of rolling resistance and ground pressure. Most armies relied on simple, narrow-pitch cast metal track with simple pins. (Pitch is the measure of the length between two links of track.) The U.S. Army preferred a family of track including rubber-padded track blocks as one option for better road performance, albeit at a higher unit cost. Track width was a critical ingredient in establishing the ground pressure of a tank. Almost any form of track is useful on roads or in dry terrain conditions, but soft ground in the form of mud or snow requires the better flotation made possible with wider tracks. Track widths on western European and American tanks tended to be narrow through 1941 when the German army encountered the mud and snow of the Russian Front. The short-term expedient was to introduce wider winter track or added track extensions. German tank designs after 1941 took the lead offered by the Soviet T-34 tank and moved toward wider tracks. The U.S. Army stuck with relatively narrow track through 1944 due to its reduced rolling resistance, but the mud and snow of the European Theater in the autumn of 1944 led to a hasty adoption of extended end connectors, and eventually new suspensions with wider tracks in early 1945.

The Christie spring suspension as used on tanks such as the T-34 and Cromwell provided a smoother ride and offered greater wheel travel. On the downside, the spring towers consumed considerable internal hull volume and could be difficult to service.

Narrow tracks are good for low rolling resistance on roads and dry ground but they suffer in mud and snow. One solution was to use extended end connectors in the wet autumn and winter months, the approach preferred by the U.S. Army in 1944–45. Germany called their type of extended track *Ostketten* ("eastern track") since they were intended for use on the Russian Front.

Command and Control

Most armies had tactical doctrines that expected tanks to operate in formations no smaller than a platoon in size, roughly four to five tanks. Unlike infantry that can rely on voice communications for small formations, tanks require some other means to coordinate their battlefield actions. In World War I, this usually involved some form of visual signaling, sometimes a semaphore or arm signals but most often some form of flags. Flags remained a standard form of tank communication in the early years of World War II, but this method was never satisfactory. Flags were difficult to see if the tanks were more than a short distance away, and the visibility of flag commands was further undermined by smoke on the battlefield and the difficulty of seeing small detail through typical tank vision devices. Finally, flag signaling often involved the tank commander exposing himself outside the tank to conduct the signaling, a risky operation on the battlefield.

Radio was a possible technical solution, but radios were on the "bleeding edge of technology" in the early war years. Early tactical AM radios relied on tube technology and were fragile. The first tank radios relied on Morse code, which required a skilled operator. Voice radio became available in the late 1930s, but the sets required a dedicated operator. Due to cost and other factors, the best approach

One of the more common methods for communication within the tank was an intercom system, with each crewman receiving a throat mike as in the case of the U.S. system seen here. The crewman pressed a button on the small switchbox to activate the mike.

Throat mikes were not entirely popular, and some later systems such as this American example in 1944 used a handheld mike that offered better sound properties.

in the 1939–41 period was to issue a full transmitter-receiver to the platoon commander and simple receivers to the other tanks. Very few armies made radios standard in the early war years. Germany was one of the pioneers in this regard because senior commanders appreciated the need for real-time communication in high-speed warfare.[19] Britain was another of the pioneers, especially for use in cruiser tanks and reconnaissance tanks.[20] France intended to deploy radios in all cavalry tanks and in the battle tanks such as the Char B1 bis, but largely refrained from using it in infantry tanks due to cost and training issues.[21] The Red Army intended to make widespread use of radios, but cost and poor radio technology limited it; for example, in the case of the Soviet T-26 tank, the most widely produced tank of the 1930s, about half the tanks were fitted with radios. After the start of the war in 1941, the Soviet use of radios decreased in 1942–43 due to shortages, rising again in 1944–45 as production capacity improved.

Radio technology improved dramatically during the war. One important innovation was the adoption of preset channels which made it easier for crews with limited training to use. The early German tank radios had two preset channels. The U.S. Army made a major leap forward in 1941 by switching to FM (frequency modulation) radios. These had a significant advantage over AM (amplitude modulation) radios since they could be filtered to reduce signal noise. AM radios were very vulnerable to signal noise induced by the tank itself, including the tank's electrical ignition system and metal-on-metal contact of the tracks and running gear.

Besides their use for communication between tanks, radios also proved useful in communicating with the infantry units that the tanks were supporting. In most armies, the pattern was for the platoon or company commander to communicate with the headquarters of the infantry unit being supported, usually no lower than company or battalion level. This was a cumbersome and time-consuming procedure, since the tanks were often assigned to support smaller infantry formations at company level. So for example, if an infantry platoon spotted an enemy antitank gun that threatened the accompanying tanks, the platoon had to inform the company headquarters, which used its radio to inform the tank platoon commander. The delays imposed by this poor network could be fatal in combat.

The slow evolution of tank-infantry radio communications was due to the fact that radio distribution in small infantry units was quite limited until late in the war. For example, the German infantry battalions were not regularly issued radios until 1943, with the potential to deploy some of these in the infantry companies. The U.S. and British armies were the most lavish in equipping small units with radio; the U.S. Army began issuing small radios at platoon level starting in 1941. However, it was not until the fighting in France in 1944 that the issue of tank-infantry communication at the platoon or company level arose. The U.S. Army pioneered this tactic by equipping some tanks in each company with a SCR-300 radio and, starting in September 1944, with a dedicated tank-infantry radio, the VRC-3. These radios could communicate between the tank formation and the associated infantry company's SCR-300 radio. For communication with smaller infantry formations, many U.S. tanks were fitted with field telephones in boxes at the rear to permit neighboring infantry to talk to the tank crews and pass on vital instructions.[22] The German army began steps to link its panzer regiments to its associated panzergrenadier regiments in early 1944 at company level, a process complicated by shortages of equipment.[23] However, tank-infantry radio communication was at a very immature stage of development at the end of World War II.

The advent of tank radios was usually accompanied by improvements in internal crew communications. Tanks in the early war period as often as not depended on simply voice communication or voice tubes between the commander and crew. In some tanks, the tank commander communicated to the driver by foot signals against his right or left shoulder to indicate the direction he wanted him to drive. Once radio use became more common, crew intercommunication systems began to appear, with each crewman receiving headphones.[24] This significantly improved crew coordination under noisy and chaotic battlefield conditions.

One of the most critical ingredients in tank command and control was crew size. Many early tanks,

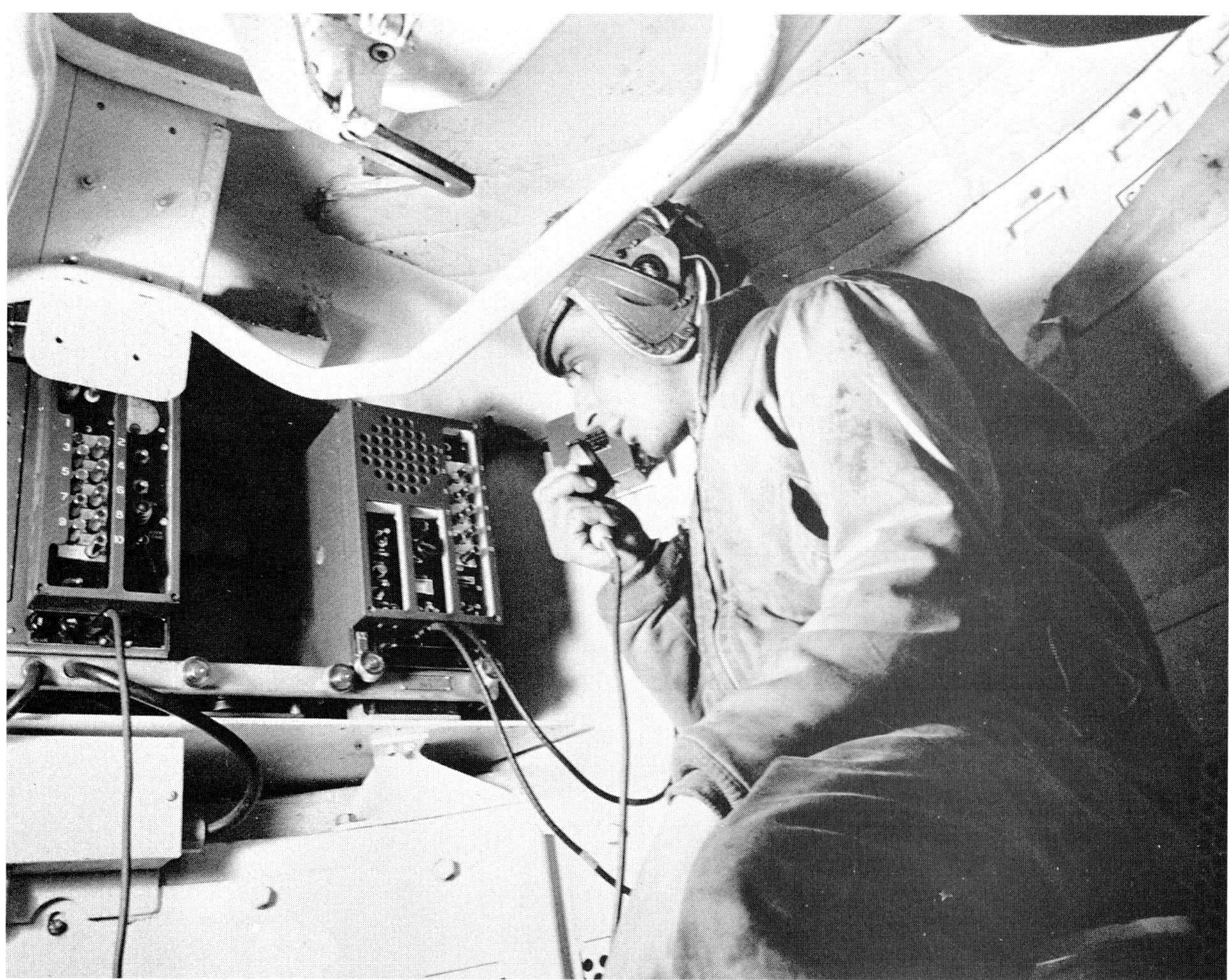

By 1944, the trend was to equip all tanks with at least a radio receiver, and preferably both a transmitter and receiver. The American and British practice was to mount the radio in a bustle in the turret for easier access by the tank commander. As shown in this M4 Sherman, the U.S. practice was to cross-train the loader to assist the commander with the radio.

starting with the Renault FT in 1917, had a two-man crew consisting of a driver and a commander/gunner. This was adequate for slow-moving tanks in the infantry support role. Once tactics became more complex and tank mobility improved, larger crews were needed. Crew size gradually increased to three, consisting of a driver and two men in the turret. This was better but not ideal, since the commander had to double up either as loader or gunner. The most important innovation came in the early 1930s as a result of German tactical trials when it was discovered that two-man turrets were not efficient on the battlefield. As a result, when the next generation tanks were designed in the mid-1930s, the new Krupp turrets had three men: the commander, gunner, and loader. This design had two critical advantages: It freed the commander of any responsibilities as loader or gunner and allowed him to concentrate his attention to coordinating his own tank crew as well as the actions of his tank within the tank platoon. This was absolutely vital in the maturation of modern tank small-unit tactics.

The importance of three-man turret crews became very evident in the blitzkrieg era of 1939–41 when the Germans found that their French and Russian tank opponents behaved in a sluggish and uncoordinated fashion due the poor ergonomic factors of their one- or two-man turrets. The other

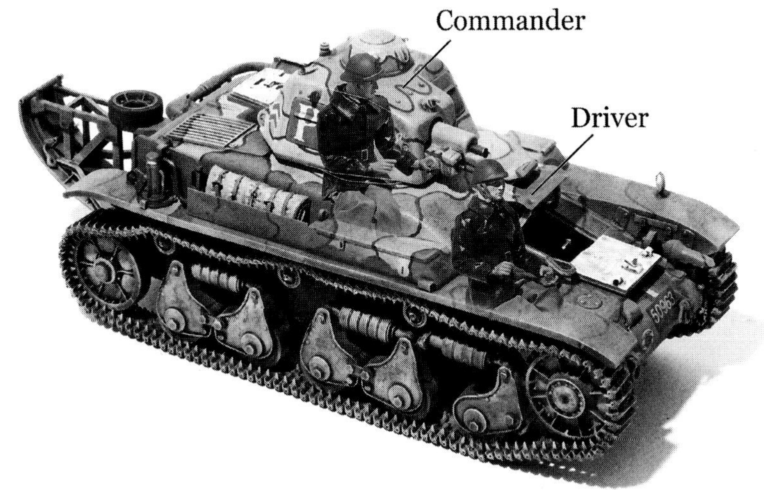

The Renault R35 was typical of many tanks of the 1930s with a simple two-man crew. This burdened the commander with additional chores including the loading and aiming of the main gun and co-axial machine gun.

The PzKpfw II added an additional crewman to deal with the radio. Early radios required careful tuning and telegraphic skills.

innovation of the Krupp turrets on the PzKpfw III and PzKpfw IV was the provision of a special commander's cupola that provided all-around vision. This gave the commander far better situational awareness than typical tank turrets of the period which offered very limited views through periscopes or episcopes. The independent commander feature became the hallmark of most successful tank designs in the mid-war years of 1942–43.

The other important element of tank command and control was the tank's vision systems. This fell into two main categories: general purpose vision devices and tank gun aiming devices. Early tank vision systems were often limited to simple view slits, which were vulnerable even to small-arms fire. By the 1920s, these were gradually replaced with episcopes consisting of armored glass mirrors, with the operator indirectly viewing outside the

The Krupp turrets on the PzKpfw III and PzKpfw IV pioneered the classic three-man turret configuration. This freed the commander to concentrate on leading the tank in combat, a vital tactical innovation in tank warfare.

The Czech LT-38, better known in German service as the PzKpfw 38(t), was typical of tanks of the late 1930s and early 1940s with a four-man crew. The commander still had to double as gunner, but a loader was added to simplify his tasks. In the hull, the bow gunner also served to operate the radio.

tank through the episcope lenses. This made the crew less vulnerable to injury from small-arms fire against the view slit, and in the event that the upper episcope glass was damaged, it could be replaced by spares. Episcopes gradually fell out of favor since they still required a slit in the armor, which was vulnerable if hit by an antitank round. Instead, periscopic sights became favored since they exited through the roof armor, which was far less vulnerable to enemy fire. These were first introduced on the Polish 7TP light tank and later copied on British, Soviet, and American tanks. Periscopes also could be rotated, giving the crew better situational awareness.

As mentioned above, by 1944–45 most of the major armies adopted special commander cupolas to provide him with all-around exterior vision. The Germans had been doing this since the PzKpfw III

Crew performance in the chaos of combat was frequently impeded by cluttered fighting compartments. This photo is of the interior of an M2A4 light tank and shows the typical amount of obstruction in the fighting compartments of many tanks of the late 1930s and early 1940s. These tanks usually had a simple folding seat for the turret crew, attached to the turret ring.

A step forward in the fightability of turrets was a simple turret basket. This example is found in an M22 Locust light tank and is fairly typical of tank designs in the 1942–43 period.

medium tank, but later designs such as the U.S. Army's 1944 all-vision cupola offered a simpler design that did not require each periscope or view device to be opened separately every time it was used. In reality, tank vision devices during World War II were never entirely satisfactory, and many armies encouraged tank commanders to operate with their head outside the hatch to maintain better situational awareness.

Tank gun fire controls usually relied on telescopic sights for aiming the weapon. There were some alternatives to this; the U.S. Army used a periscopic sight on the early M4 Sherman tanks to avoid the need for a hole in the turret front for the telescope. However, the linkage between the periscopic gun sight and the gun was prone to being jarred and it was more difficult to boresight the weapon. The British, who were operating the M4

One way to avoid the turmoil in the turret was to provide the crew with a turret basket. This is an example on an early M4 of the 5th Armored Division during training in December 1942. Sherman baskets grew progressively less extensive in 1943–44 to provide faster access to ammunition.

Sherman by 1942, encouraged the U.S. Army to switch back to telescopic sights, which became standard again in late 1942 with the M55 telescope in the M34A1 gun mount.

Tank gun mounts also had an important role in gun accuracy. In the late 1930s, some armies still used gun mounts that were free in elevation and elevated using a simple shoulder pad on the gun mount. This was adequate for very short-range engagements; however, for longer range engagements, a geared elevation system was essential so that corrections could be made after the first shot. In the U.S. Army, the transition occurred between the M3 and M3A1 light tanks. The British army still used a free-elevation system in the Matilda infantry tank and early Crusader Cruiser tanks of the 1940–41 period. The geared elevation feature became standard in most armies by 1942.

Gun accuracy at longer ranges was largely dependent on accurate range determination to the target so that the gunner could super-elevate the gun to compensate for the ballistic drop of the projectile. In the German army, the preference was to use reticles in the gun telescope which a well-trained gunner could use to estimate range to target. In the U.S. Army, tank commanders were issued binoculars with reticles and it was the role of the commander to call out range instructions to the

One reason for the amount of clutter inside tanks was the sheer amount of gear that had to be stowed. This is an example of the equipment stowed outside and inside the M3 light tank.

gunner. These types of systems were not especially accurate in long-range engagements, but until the advent of long 75–90mm guns in 1944–45, it was not a major concern. During the final years of the war, armies began to experiment with coincidence rangefinders for tanks, similar to the type widely used by antiaircraft and battleship guns. These did not reach service in World War II, but became commonplace in the 1950s. Soviet studies concluded that the World War II reticle-based rangefinders had an error rate of 15 percent compared to about 2.6 percent for coincidence rangefinders.

Another fire-control innovation that emerged in 1944–45 was night-fighting equipment. Britain developed the Canal Defense Light concept using a powerful searchlight mounted on Matilda or Grant tanks. Although this was built in significant numbers for both the U.S. and British armies, the high level of secrecy attached to the project doomed any attempts to use the system as intended in the summer and autumn of 1944. It was eventually abandoned without any extensive use. Germany, Britain, and the United States worked on infrared night vision systems. The British and American systems were primarily oriented toward night driving rather than combat. The German Uhu system involved IR searchlights on a supporting half-track vehicle and metascopes on the tanks. A small number of Uhu sets were issued in 1945, but the system was technologically immature to the point of being useless.

There are rumors that the Uhu sets were used in combat in 1945, though evidence is not especially clear.

Aside from tank gun optics, one of the innovations in tank fire controls in World War II were early attempts at gun stabilization. The only army to pursue this on a large scale was the U.S. Army, which used a one-axis stabilization system on the M4 Sherman tank. The aim of this system was to permit firing while on the move at slow speeds or to keep the gun on target before halting and making final fine adjustments. This device was controversial due to the maintenance and training burden it imposed. Some of the better-trained gunners favored the system, but heavy attrition of trained gunners after the summer of 1944 led to an influx of less well-trained gunners who did not find the system as valuable.

The Crew

The quality of the tank crew greatly affects the performance of the tank. Probably the clearest example of this was the ineffectiveness of the T-34 tank in the battles of the summer of 1941 at the start of the Russo-German war. The T-34 tank was clearly superior to its German opponents from nearly every technical standpoint, but its battlefield performance was unexceptional. Unit after-action reports were full of complaints about the poor preparation and training of the tank units prior to the start of the campaign due to the lack of familiarity with this new tank type and a general deficit of training.[25]

The U.S. Army experience provides another perspective on this issue. U.S. tank units deployed to France in 1944 had in many cases been training for two years or more prior to the combat debut, and so had excellent preparation in tank operation. Yet these tank battalions frequently suffered half of all wartime tank casualties in their first month of combat.[26] No matter how good the technical training, combat experience was a critical ingredient in successful tank employment.

The Soviet army conducted studies of the effect of tank crew quality during an engagement between equivalent tanks. The criteria was based on the probability of locating and identifying the opposing tank, being the first to fire, and actually hitting the enemy tank. In the case of a well-trained crew facing an equally well-trained opponent, the friendly tank had only a 38 percent chance of knocking out the enemy tank. On the other hand, in the case of a well-trained crew facing a poorly trained enemy, the probability increased to almost 63 percent. Correspondingly, two poorly trained crews facing one another had a very low probability of knocking out the enemy tank.

Durability/Reliability

One of the most important but overlooked aspects of tank effectiveness was their durability. Tanks had emerged from the First World War as an important but fragile innovation. The early tanks were a reincarnation of medieval siege engines, powerful weapons capable of cracking open a fortified trench line but mechanically very delicate. A big question in the interwar years was whether tanks were durable enough to sustain offensive missions. The principal cause of casualties in the early tanks was

PROBABILITY OF DESTROYING ENEMY TANK BASED ON CREW QUALITY[27]

Qualifications of the Friendly Tank Crew	Qualifications of the Enemy Tank Crew		
	High (%)	Medium (%)	Low (%)
High	38.4	51.2	62.7
Medium	13	18.8	24
Low	1.1	2.4	3.6

Tank reliability can be enhanced by careful design. The Sherman had a modular transmission that could easily be unbolted and replaced. In contrast, German tanks such as the Panther and Tiger had the transmission encased in armor, making repairs difficult.

simple mechanical breakdown. For example, the German A7V tank of World War I could seldom operate for more than a day without requiring depot-level rebuilding. French and British tank reliability was somewhat better, but few tanks would still be functioning after operations involving more than 10–20 miles of travel.

During the 1930s, tank reliability began to improve. The most common tank of the 1930s was the Vickers 6-Ton tank, most notably its license-built Soviet derivative, the T-26. The T-26 light tank required medium overhaul at district workshops after 150 engine hours and factory rebuilding or replacement after 600 hours. Tracks and track pins began to wear out after 500 miles of travel; side clutches became worn out and the power-train was gradually knocked out of alignment from hard cross-country travel.

When the T-26 saw its combat debut in the Spanish Civil War in October 1936, the first group of about 50 tanks were all largely worn out after 2 months of operations. During the Teruel campaign in December 1937–February 1938, the 104 T-26 tanks that participated were repaired 586 times over 65 days of fighting, or roughly once every 11 days. Most of these were ordinary field repairs involving tracks and minor engine repairs. However, there were 63 medium and capital repairs requiring 58 engine replacements, 6 transmissions, 15 main clutches, and 22 side clutches. In other words, every other tank had its engine replaced after only about 2 months of combat use.

To help minimize wear on the tanks, the Spanish army turned to the use of transport trucks to move the tanks between battles, a tactic first developed by the French army in World War I to extend

Another key factor in tank durability was the provision of spare parts. The M4 Sherman series had excellent reliability in U.S. Army service in no small measure due to an ample supply of spare parts and a robust infrastructure for maintenance, including wrecker trucks and armored recovery vehicles. This is an M4 of the 2nd Armored Division being repaired in Normandy in the summer of 1944.

the effective combat life of their tanks.[28] During the Soviet invasion of Poland in September 1939, the Red Army deployed 1,675 T-26 tanks on what was essentially an uncontested road march into eastern Poland. Of these, 302 tanks, or roughly one-fifth of the force, broke down for mechanical reasons; in contrast there were only 15 combat casualties.[29] Throughout the 1930s and the early years of World War II, tanks crews were obliged to keep detailed logbooks charting their engine and track usage.

The Soviet examples given here were not especially unusual. During the Battle of France in 1940, the British Army estimated that about 75 percent of its tank casualties were due to mechanical breakdowns. In the case of the French Char B1 bis, the evidence suggests that about half of the tank casualties were the result of mechanical breakdowns, particularly its delicate transmission.[30]

Tank durability remained a nagging problem throughout the war, even though on average the mechanical life expectancy of most tank types

AVERAGE TANK LIFE EXPECTANCY, 1942–43	
Matilda	1,000 miles
Crusader	1,000–1,200 miles
M3 Grant, M4 Sherman	1,500 miles
Valentine	2,000–2,500 miles
M3 Stuart	3,500 miles

The T-34 had an unusual layout with the transmission at the rear of the tank. This provided easier access for repair and more direct connection to the engine but required lengthy connecting rods to the clutch, which made operations more strenuous for the driver.

increased. The South African army, which operated a variety of British and American tank types, estimated their average life expectancy.[31] The figures on page 35 underestimate U.S. tank durability; later studies give the Sherman at least a 2,000-mile life expectancy.

Aside from inherent manufacturing features, dependability was also strongly affected by availability of spare parts. The British army suffered from low rates of tank availability in the early desert campaign in 1941–42 due to spare parts shortages, and as a result made a determined effort to increase spare parts production through the mid years of the war. Spare part production for tanks in Britain as a percentage of tank production contracts went from 4 percent in 1939 to 12 percent by 1940, 22 percent by 1942, 37 percent by 1943, and 45 percent by 1944.[32]

As in the British army's case, the German army continued to increase its spares production in the early war years, based on the growing recognition that this was essential to keep the tanks rolling. For example, in October 1940 spares deliveries for tanks were only 352 metric tons, but this steadily increased to 1,190 metric tons by March 1942.[33] The German objective was about 30 percent of the contract devoted to spares and repair parts in 1941.[34]

The German army generally enjoyed better tank reliability than many of its opponents in the early years of the war, but still faced constant problems with the mechanical attrition of its tank force. During the month-long Battle of France in June–July 1940, the *3.* and *4.Panzer-Divisions* deployed 674 tanks at the start of the campaign and at the conclusion had about half (55 percent) still operational, about a quarter destroyed in combat (24 percent), and about a fifth (22 percent) broken down or battle damaged and inoperable.[35] During the campaign in Russia in the late summer of 1941, long road marches led to an especially high level of mechanical problems. Many panzer divisions could barely keep half of their tanks operational at any given time. The mechanical state of the panzer force was even worse in the winter of 1941–42 due to the advent of harsh winter conditions.[36] This issue is covered in more detail in subsequent chapters.

Cost

Josef Stalin is reported to have quipped, "Quantity has a quality all its own." One of the dilemmas facing all armies is whether to field a tank force with large quantities of inexpensive and mediocre tanks, or a small number of more effective but expensive tanks. Usually, armies try to come up with some sort of balance. While the German army might have desired to field panzer divisions completely equipped with the superb Tiger I tank in 1943, in reality, there were not the resources to do so since the Tiger cost almost three times as much as the standard medium tanks. Germany also continued to build armored vehicles on the light PzKpfw 38(t) chassis until the end of the war since the Czech factories where they were built could not manufacture larger and heavier tanks due to a lack of suitable machine tools. Likewise, the Red Army continued to manufacture the dreadful little T-60 and T-70 tanks through 1942 and 1943 since the automotive plants manufacturing them were not well enough equipped with the proper machine tools and armor plate facilities to build the larger T-34 tank.

The charts presented here show some typical price data for tanks during World War II. It is very difficult to compare prices between two countries since the accounting methods were so different and the exchange rates likely to be artificial. For example, many German weapons prices reflected the payment to the manufacturer for the "tin box" even though some major components such as the gun and power-train were provided to the assembly plant as government-furnished equipment (GFE). So for example in the case of the Panther tank, the basic price was listed as 117,100 RM (Reichsmark), but the gun cost an additional 12,000 RM.[37]

The price of tanks also varied from factory to factory due to the availability of machine tools and other equipment. For example, for one of the Panther production batches, the additional state investment in machine tools and facilities at some plants such as Daimler-Benz in Berlin and MNH in Hannover was about 25,000 RM per tank, about 82,000 RM per tank at the new Nibelungen Werk in St. Valentin, and some 190,000 RM at Demag in Falkensee.[38] In addition, there was wide variation in prices at the various plants due to different rates of taxation depending on whether the plant was private or state-owned.[39] Other problems with assessing German prices were the politicization of the process resulting from the 1943 "Adolf Hitler Panzer Program" and the temptation of Albert Speer's armaments ministry to claim enormous cost efficiencies on new tank types such as the Panther and to hide or disguise capital investments needed for production. It's worth noting that the price for a Tiger I tank for the German army was about 300,000 RM, but the

SOVIET TANK PRICES, 1940–42 (RUBLES)[40]

Plant	Type	1940	1941	1942
Zavod No. 174	T-26	56,000	-	-
Zavod No. 174	T-50	-	165,200	92,050
Zavod No. 183	T-34	429,256	249,272	166,310
Zavod No. 112	T-34	-	-	209,700
UZTM	T-34	-	-	273,800
UZTM	KV-1	720,000	410,000	300,000

example sold to Japan was priced at 645,000 RM, an amount more likely to reflect the actual cost including industrial infrastructure investment.

The chart below on U.S. Army tank prices covers the basic vehicle, the vehicle plus the GFE including tank guns and sights, and finally the cost for Lend-Lease export which presumably adds spares, technical documents, and shipping costs.

A further complication is that costs were not constant. The price of a given tank, for example the T-34, varied depending on the contract batch, the plant, and the specific production series. As the chart below demonstrates, the amount of work needed to manufacture a T-34 tank declined through the war due to efficiencies and automation, but varied considerably from plant to plant.

SOVIET TANK PRICES, 1944–45 (RUBLES)[41]	
T-70 light tank (line)*	60,770
T-70 light tank (radio)	63,270
T-34 medium tank (line)*	162,000
T-34 medium tank (radio)	171,230
T-34-85 medium tank	181,000

*The Red Army called tanks without radios line tanks (*lineyniy tank*).

MAN-HOURS PER T-34 TANK, 1942–43[42]

Plant	1 Jan. 1942	1 Jan. 1943	1 Jan. 1944	1 Jan. 1945	1 July 1945
No. 183	5,300	5,100	3,617	3,251	3,209
No. 112	9,000	7,500	5,497	4,439	3,388
No. 174	8,092	7,205	4,574	3,209	3,094

BRITISH TANK COSTS (£)[43]

Tank	Cost	Tank	Cost
Tetrarch	6,650	Matilda	15,000
Cruiser Tank Mark I (A9)	10,000	Cromwell III	14,800
Cruiser Tank Mark II (A10)	11,500	Cromwell IV	17,600
Cruiser Tank Mark III (A13)	10,000	Comet	10,500
Crusader I and II	9,600	Churchill I	15,000
Crusader III	7,400–7,600	Churchill IV (75mm)	12,966–13,000
Covenanter	7,700	Churchill IV (95mm)	23,100
Valentine I	9,600	Centurion I	29,500
Valentine III	10,000		
Valentine IX	10,200		
Valentine IV	10,800		

U.S. TANK COSTS ($)[44]			
Type	**Base Price**	**With GFE**	**Lend-Lease**
M3A1 (gas) light tank	32,195	32,915	42,236
M5A1 light tank	25,949	27,057	37,661
M24 light tank	36,439	39,653	N/A
M3 medium tank	53,250	55,244	64,814
M4, M4A1 (75mm) medium tank	44,699	47,725	60,534
M4A1 (76mm) medium tank	47,569	51,509	69,288
M4 (105mm) assault gun	41,961	45,766	64,873
M4A2 (75mm) medium tank	42,788	45,814	60,214
M4A2 (76mm) medium tank	41,923	45,863	66,987
M4A3 (75mm) medium tank	41,530	44,556	60,214
M6A1 heavy tank	167,792	171,615	N/A
M26 heavy tank	76,266	81,324	83,273

GERMAN TANK PRICES (REICHSMARK)[45]	
PzKpfw I Ausf. B*	38,000 RM*
PzKpfw II Ausf. A	52,640 RM
PzKpfw II D/E	52,728 RM*
PzKpfw II Ausf. F	49,228 RM*/ 52,728 RM
PzKpfw III Ausf. M	96,163 RM*/103,163 RM
StuG III Ausf. G	82,500 RM
PzKpfw IV	103,462 RM
PzKpfw IV Ausf. F2	115,962 RM
PzKpfw IV Ausf. G	125,000 RM
PzKpfw V Panther	117,100 RM*/176,100 RM
PzKpfw VI Tiger	250,800 RM*/299,800 RM
PzKpfw VI Tiger II	321,500 RM

*Price without gun, radio, or other components

CHAPTER 2

The Approach to War: 1919–36

TO BETTER APPRECIATE THE TANKS AVAILABLE at the start of World War II, it is important to understand tank development after World War I. This chapter examines the quintessential tanks of the pre-war period up to the first stirring of global war in 1936. This date has been chosen because 1936 marks the start of the great European arms race that preceded World War II. The tanks that entered service after 1936 will be covered in the next chapter on the blitzkrieg era.

The mid-1930s were something of a "pre-game warmup" for the global war that followed. The Spanish Civil War started in 1936 and was the first conflict since World War I where tanks were used in significant numbers. In Asia, both China and Japan were girding for war, which finally started in earnest in 1937 with the Marco Polo bridge incident.

The most significant tanks of this period entered production in the early 1930s. There was very little tank production from the end of World War I until 1930 due to the financial and military exhaustion of the great powers and the large inventory of tanks left over from the war. Tank production had resumed in fits and starts in the late 1920s; some of these efforts were delayed programs to manufacture World War I tanks. The Renault FT proved to be one of the most influential tanks of the war and led to some copies or derivatives, such as the American 6-Ton tank, Italian Fiat 3000, and Soviet Russki-Reno and MS-1. France attempted to continue the evolution of the design with the Renault NC, but fewer than 30 were built and most were exported. Aside from experimental tanks, one of the few remaining French types to reach production was the super-heavy Char 2C, a tank designed for the 1919 Allied offensive but completed only in 1920 because of problems with

The predominant tank of the 1920s was the Renault FT, the most modern and widely produced tank of World War I. Aside from its use by France, it was also the seed for many other tank forces, including those of the United States and Soviet Union. In the 1930s, the French army rebuilt many of its older tanks to extend their lives, including the addition of the more modern Reibel 7.5mm machine gun, as seen on the tank to the right. The tank on the left is a standard gun-armed version with the 37mm SA18 gun.

Copies of the Renault FT were built in several countries; in Italy it became the Fiat 3000. This particular tank was still in service in July 1943 during the fighting on Sicily.

Many Renault FTs and their copies remained in service through the start of World War II. This is a 6-Ton tank, the American copy of the Renault FT. This example was in training use at Fort Belvoir in November 1940 when the mishap occurred. Many of these old tanks were shipped to Canada to expedite tank crew training.

the engine. The British rhomboid Landships and the German A7V had far less appeal, and these configurations largely disappeared after the war. The British army saw the rhomboid Landships as a dead end and moved to turreted tanks in 1923 with the Vickers Medium Mark I. A total of 168 Medium Mark I and Mark II were manufactured in 1922–27, and small numbers were later exported.

THE TANKETTE FAD

The single most influential source of new tanks in the late 1920s and early 1930s was the British armaments firm Vickers Armstrong. These tanks were commercial designs, intended for export, and not specifically designed for the British army. Many of the early designs were the products of two exceptional engineers, Sir John Carden and Vivian Loyd.[1] Their designs led to the great tankette fad of the early 1930s.

The idea of a small, one-man tank had emerged after World War I as a scout tank for the larger tanks. The aim was to build an elementary vehicle around a simple 20-horsepower automobile engine. The first was assembled by Col. G. Martel in 1925. This design inspired the prolific British military writer Capt. Basil Henry Liddell Hart to promote these small vehicles as a "mechanized infantryman." The homebuilt Martel design was taken up by the

Many of the smaller and impoverished European armies saw tankettes as a more cost-effective solution to full-size, turreted tanks. Poland acquired over 600 TK and TKS tankettes based on the Carden-Loyd tankette. These are seen here in September 1939 during the defense of Warsaw.

automotive firm of Morris, and an improved two-man version was built. Carden and Loyd had set up an automotive business in London after the war, and they eventually became involved in this project. The British army ordered eight each of the Morris-Martel and Carden-Loyd tankettes in 1926 for the Experimental Mechanised Force. The initial designs were technically immature, and the Carden-Loyd version underwent several evolutionary stages before finally emerging as the Mark VI in 1927. One of the main problems with the early designs was a wretchedly short track life. The narrow-pitch cast-iron track of the Mark VI finally reached a durability of 600 miles, which was considered quite good for its day. The British army eventually ordered 250 Mark VIs in 1929–30, though by this stage they had given up on them as tankettes and referred to them as Machine Gun Carriers. From the British perspective, the Mark VI can be seen as an early forerunner of World War II's ubiquitous infantry carriers.

Other armies continued to view the tankette as a viable armored fighting vehicle and not simply as a means to mechanize the infantry. In 1929–30, Vickers sold test batches of the Mark VI to several countries. Poland, Czechoslovakia, and the Soviet Union decided to manufacture their own versions under license. Poland built tankettes in two series: the TK-3 in 1931–33 with 300 manufactured, and the improved TKS in 1934–36 with a further 300 built. These were the most numerous Polish armored vehicle in the 1939 campaign.[2]

The Red Army saw the Carden-Loyd as a means to quickly mechanize its backward tank force, and some 3,297 T-27 tankettes were delivered in

1931–34, making it the most numerous armored vehicle of the early 1930s. The Czechoslovak army eventually ordered 74 Tancik vz. 33 in 1930–34.[3] Italy purchased 4 Carden-Loyd Mark VI in 1929 and built 29 under license as the Carro veloce CV 29. The Italian army was not entirely happy with the design, and Fiat-Ansaldo was commissioned to develop an improved type which emerged in 1933 as the CV 3/33. This underwent considerable evolutionary change during its manufacture such as the CV 3/35 and the CV 3/38. The series was later renamed the L.3 (L= *leggero*, light). In total about 1,320 were built for the Italian army and about 400 for export.[4] France also acquired test batches of the Mark VI Machine Gun Carrier but, like the British army, concluded it was better suited to infantry mechanization than for use as a tank. An unarmed French analog was manufactured in 1931–40 as the Renault UE with about 5,300 built. These were used primarily for towing antitank guns and as supply vehicles.

The tankettes had an uninspiring combat record. Their light armor was proof against rifle fire, but by the mid-1930s several armies were developing ammunition for standard 7.62–7.92mm machine guns that could penetrate their thin armor. In terms of mobility, the tankettes were adequate on roads and dry ground but vulnerable to ditching in mud or snow. They were so small they could be stopped by trenches and natural obstructions such as irrigation ditches. Their firepower, usually a single machine gun, was useful for infantry support, but its traverse was extremely limited.

The Italian L.3 first saw combat use in Ethiopia in 1935. During the battle of the Dembeguina Pass on 15 December 1935, a detachment of nine CV 3/33 tankettes was wiped out when they became trapped and attacked from the rear. A relief column with a further ten tankettes was also wiped out after the Ethiopian troops realized they could be immobilized by placing large boulders on the roads.[5] Italian

The Italian army's principal tank of the 1930s was the L.3 tankette series. It was also widely exported, and the Hungarian army acquired sixty-five of the L.3/35 with an enlarged cupola and a different machine-gun armament.

The combat use of the L.3/35 by Italian units in the Spanish Civil War in 1936–37 revealed the shortcomings of these small vehicles, especially when confronted by more modern tanks such as the Soviet T-26.

tankettes took part in the first tank-versus-tank battle since World War I on 29 October 1936 south of Madrid during the Spanish Civil War. Three Italian tankettes, including one armed with a flamethrower, were attached to a Nationalist infantry unit and attempted to resist a Republican attack near the town of Seseña. The Republican forces were supported by a newly arrived contingent of fifteen T-26 light tanks. The small tankettes were hopelessly outgunned since their 8mm machine guns could not penetrate the armor of the T-26 tanks. Embarrassing proof of their inferiority came when one of the tankettes was knocked out by a T-26 simply pushing it off the road into a ditch.[6] Later confrontations between Italian tankettes and T-26 tanks during the Spanish Civil War did not go any better, and the Italian units soon learned to avoid direct confrontations with Republican tank units.

The L.3 remained in Italian service during the early battles of World War II, including the 1940 campaign against France, the Balkan campaigns against Yugoslavia and Greece, the battles with the British in the North African desert in 1940–41, and even the campaign in Russia in 1941. By this time, they were hopelessly obsolete but remained in service since the impoverished Italian army had so few modern tanks.

The Poles made extensive use of the TK and TKS tankettes in the 1939 campaign where they were used for both infantry and cavalry support. They had their occasional successes when used against German infantry. A small number of tankettes upgraded with 20mm guns even managed to knock out a few German light tanks. However, they were completely useless when the German 37mm antitank guns were present on the battlefield and hopelessly outmatched in most tank-versus-tank encounters.

The Red Army still had 2,279 T-27 tankettes in service at the time of the German invasion on 22

June 1941, plus a further 182 that had been converted into unarmed tractors. They were mainly relegated to a training role by this stage, though a few were thrown into combat in desperate circumstances.

Overall, the tankette concept proved to be shortsighted. They were mostly adopted as expedient tanks by impoverished armies such as those of Italy and Poland that could not afford larger and more expensive tanks.

LIGHT TANKS OF THE 1930S

As in the case of tankettes, Vickers proved to be the most influential source for light reconnaissance tanks in the early 1930s. These differed from the tankettes in one crucial respect: They were large enough that their machine-gun armament could be mounted in a turret. They gradually grew larger than the tankettes, with suspensions that were more suitable for cross-country travel. Several different Carden-Loyd and Vickers-Armstrong designs were on offer, including amphibious types. The first Mark I light tank was built for the British army in 1928, and 115 Mark I–Mark V tanks were purchased by the British army through 1935, plus a further 60 for the Indian army. Eventually, 11 countries bought Vickers light tanks, and in many of the smaller armies—such as those of Belgium, Latvia, Lithuania, Switzerland, and the Dutch East Indies—they were the backbone of their tank force

Landsverk in Sweden attempted to get into the tank export business in the 1930s with their attractive L-60 light tank. License production rights were obtained by Hungary, which manufactured it as the Toldi during the first years of World War II.

The Vickers 6-Ton tank was one of the most successful light export tanks of the mid-1930s. Poland acquired both the gun type with short 47mm gun and the twin-turret type with machine guns. The Polish vehicles were later modified with a cowl over the radiator cover for better protection. These served in 1939 in the 10th Mechanized Brigade.

Vickers also enjoyed sales with the Vickers-Carden-Loyd Model 1931 amphibious tank and sold twenty-nine to China in the 1930s. They served with the 1st Armored Battalion in Shanghai and saw combat with the Japanese.

up to the start of World War II. In numerical terms, the sale of 8 amphibious tanks to the Soviet Union in 1930 had the largest outcome. These tanks served as the basis for the later Soviet T-37 amphibious tank, with some 2,549 manufactured in 1933–36. Its further evolution, the T-38 amphibious tank, added another 1,382 tanks in 1936–39 for a grand total of 3,931. To put this in some perspective, this production was more than all British or German tank production in 1930–39.

Aside from direct derivatives of the Vickers light tanks, some nations manufactured tanks that were clearly inspired by these designs. The French cavalry's AMR 33 and AMR 35 have a clear link to the British designs. The culmination of the Vickers light tank series was the Mark VI, including the later Mark VIB. These entered production in 1936 and the British army ordered about 1,320 of the different variants, making it the most important British tank of the prewar period in terms of numbers built.

Germany's PzKpfw I is often derided as nothing but a training tank, but by the standards of the early 1930s it was a robust and well-engineered design. It was armed with twin 7.92mm machine guns.

This type saw its combat debut in France in 1940 and in the desert war against Italy in North Africa. It remained in service in North Africa well into 1942, though its role was increasingly limited to a cavalry scouting function due to its modest armament.

Germany had been restricted by the Versailles Treaty after World War I from building or deploying tanks. The rise of Hitler's Nazi Party and their accession to power in 1933 led to a growing remilitarization. Although Germany had deployed only a handful of A7V tanks in 1917–18, the revived German army showed a great deal more interest in tanks than had the Kaiser's army. Germany had been clandestinely developing tanks in collusion with Soviet Russia in the late 1920s, most notably the Grosstraktor medium tank. This was recognized to be a technical dead-end, but development of new medium tanks was expected to take several years before they would be ready for production. In the meantime, the German army wanted significant numbers of new tanks to equip their new panzer units and to begin large-scale tactical experiments. Lacking an established tank industry, the army leaders realized that an inexpensive light tank would be the best short-term solution. This led to production of the PzKpfw I, starting in 1934. This tank was roughly comparable to the Vickers light tanks with similar firepower, armor, and mobility. Although the PzKpfw I was later derided as a mere training tank, the design was quite modern and efficient by early 1930s standards. One of its most important if unheralded attributes was good durability, about 1,800 kilometers between major overhauls compared to about 800 kilometers for contemporaries such as the Soviet T-26 tank.

The PzKpfw II was an attempt to design an inexpensive tank with better antitank capability in the form of its 20mm cannon. It was the backbone of the German panzer divisions into 1941 until enough PzKpfw III and PzKpfw IV were available. Here, a crew from *Panzer-Abteilung 40* performs routine maintenance on the 20mm gun barrel of their tank on the Finnish Front in June 1941.

For most of the 1930s, the U.S. Army's infantry branch preferred twin-turreted light tanks such as this M2A2 of the 66th Infantry Regiment (Tank) at Fort Benning. Beyond it is an experimental tank support gun, an M2A1 light tank hull fitted with a 1.85-inch gun in an open turret.

In contrast to the Infantry, the U.S. Cavalry branch preferred single-turret tanks such as this M1A1 Combat Car of C Troop, 1st Cavalry (Mechanized). The turret armament consisted of a .30-cal and .50-cal machine gun, with the .50-cal heavy machine gun considered its primary antitank weapon.

Vickers developed a family of light tanks for the cavalry role. The Mark VIB was the predominant type in the British army at the start of the war, armed with a .50-cal and .30-cal machine gun.

The Renault Char D1 was yet another elaboration of the basic Renault FT layout, but in a significantly larger and better armored configuration. It saw combat in France in 1940 and in Tunisia in 1943.

By 1935, the German army realized that tanks needed some form of weapon to defend themselves against enemy tanks. Because of the delay in manufacturing their new medium tanks, the PzKpfw III and PzKpfw IV, they adopted an interim light tank, the PzKpfw II, which had a 20mm gun with modest antiarmor capability against other light tanks.

GUN TANKS

The tankettes and light tanks described above were mostly armed with light machine guns, though there were occasional experiments to mount heavy machine guns or automatic cannon in the 20mm range. As in the other categories, Vickers-Armstrong was the pacesetter with its Medium E tank, better known as the 6-Ton tank. Originally, this was offered in two versions: the Type A "trench sweeper" fitted with two turrets armed with machine guns, and the Type B armed with a short 47mm gun advertised as a dual-role weapon suitable for use against enemy infantry or tanks. The suspension was a patented double-bogie system with springs that offered a much superior ride to the simple rigid frame suspensions widely used on medium tanks up to that point. Propulsion was a four-cylinder horizontal Armstrong Siddeley in the rear and the transmission and drive sprocket in front. Its armor was fairly standard for the period and only intended to protect against machine-gun fire.

Sales of the Vickers 6-Ton tank caught on immediately. Poland was one of the first customers, buying 38 tanks, including 22 Type A with machine-gun turrets and 16 Type B with the 47mm gun. Poland also bought license production rights and manufactured the type in modified form as the 7TP with an Austrian Saurer diesel engine. In its later 1937 configuration, it was armed with an excellent Bofors 37mm gun. This type was the best Polish tank in 1939, with about 135 in service.

A far more consequential sale was made to the Soviet Union in 1930 for fifteen Type A tanks along with license production rights. The Red Army was shopping around for a new tank to support its rifle divisions, and the Vickers design was considerably more modern than any indigenous designs. After

The Soviet Union purchased license production rights for the Vickers 6-Ton tank. The initial version of the T-26 light infantry tank used the twin-turret configuration with a 7.62mm DT machine gun in each turret.

In 1933, the T-26 was modernized with the development of a new turret armed with the dual-purpose 45mm gun. About half of the production run was fitted with radios that used this archaic clothesline aerial to insulate them from the metal hull.

trials of the Vickers, the Red Army started production of its own examples in 1931 as the T-26 light tank. The original version of the T-26 followed the Type A layout with twin turrets but substituted the Soviet DT machine gun for the Vickers. There was some interest in a more powerful armament, and a portion of the tanks began to receive a Soviet copy of the French 37mm SA 18 gun, the same weapon from the Renault FT. These gun-armed tanks had the cannon in one turret and a machine gun in the other. Plans were underway to arm them with an improved 37mm gun with a longer barrel, but this was short-lived.

In the meantime, the Soviet infantry had been examining a variety of antitank guns and accompanying guns. A license was purchased from Rheinmetall to manufacture their new 37mm antitank gun starting in 1930. Once production had begun, the artillery plant proposed increasing the bore of the gun to 45mm to permit the use of a more effective high-explosive round. The original 37mm gun fired a round with only 25 grams of high explosive while the new 45mm high-explosive fragmentation round had 118 grams of TNT. This was attractive to the infantry since it made the gun a dual-role cannon, so it was adopted for service in the spring of 1932. With the infantry accepting this weapon as its principal antitank gun, it made sense to examine it for tank use as well, but the gun was too large to be accommodated in the small turrets of the baseline

The T-26 was exported to Republican forces during the Spanish Civil War in 1936–37. It was by far the best tank in use in this conflict and made it clear that the days of machine-gun-armed tanks were numbered.

T-26. At the same time, the Soviets realized that a larger turret could accommodate both the 45mm gun and a DT machine gun. The new T-26 tank with 45mm gun entered completed tests in 1933 and was accepted for service, sometimes called the T-26 Model 1933. For its day, this was the most powerful tank in its class with an excellent dual-purpose gun and a machine gun. It remained in production in improved forms through 1941 with over 10,300 infantry tanks manufactured and a total of over 12,000 of all variants, including flamethrower tanks and self-propelled gun versions. This made it by far the most numerous tank of the 1930s, with production exceeding the total of combined British, French, and German tank production in 1930–39.

Besides license-built copies of the Vickers 6-Ton tank such as the Soviet T-26 and Polish 7TP, the Vickers design inspired several other important light tank designs. The U.S. Army purchased a Vickers 6-Ton tank, but like the British army they were concerned about the durability of the suspension. Instead of the Vickers suspension, the U.S. Army began to move toward the use of a vertical-volute spring suspension that entered serial production of the first M1 light tanks and M1 combat cars. This would eventually become one of the most distinctive features of U.S. tanks of World War II, including the M3 and M5A1 Stuart light tanks, M3 Lee medium tank, and early M4 Sherman tanks.

Czechoslovakia considered adopting the Vickers 6-Ton tank but eventually decided to build its own tanks, the LT vz. 34 and LT vz. 35, both of which were influenced by the British design. Likewise, the Italian medium tanks of the late 1930s, notably the M11/39 and M13/40, also show a strong Vickers influence in their general layout.

SPEED DEMON

One of the more unusual tanks of the interwar years was the Christie wheel-and-track tank. J. Walter Christie was an American automotive engineer best known before World War I for his fire engines. During World War I, he began to design tracked vehicles for the army, mostly self-propelled field artillery vehicles. In the 1920s, he conceived of a convertible fast tank that could be propelled by either tracks or wheels. The tracks could be used when traveling cross-country but removed when traveling on roads, allowing the tank to travel at much higher speeds. This was accomplished by a novel suspension that allowed the lead road wheel to be steered and that connected one of the rear road wheels to the power-train via a chain drive to propel the tank on roads.

Christie had a flamboyant and eccentric personality that rubbed the U.S. Army bureaucracy the wrong way. He was a skilled showman and promoter, and eventually convinced several Congressmen of the brilliance of his new tank design. The U.S. Army was pressured into purchasing a single Christie tank in 1929 for $62,000. This was an enormous sum of money at the time for a tank, and the Army was not pleased when it was learned that Christie was offering the same tank to foreign buyers for considerably less. Furthermore, it was not a real tank, lacking a turret and armament.

Promoters and critics of Christie's designs waged a boisterous campaign in the press, and after Congressional hearings the Army was pressured into buying seven more tanks. These were all delivered by 1932 and armed with a simple circular turret with a 37mm gun and co-axial .30-cal machine gun. Three of the tanks were issued to the Infantry at Fort Benning as the Convertible Medium Tank T3 while the other four were issued to the Cavalry

The Christie T3 medium tank was never popular in U.S. Army service due to its technical problems. Two of the seven purchased are seen here serving with the 67th Infantry (Tanks) during summer wargames.

at Fort Knox as the Combat Car T1. No further purchases were made due to the continuing disputes between Christie and the Army and Army decisions to impose limits on the weight of tanks.

The Christie tanks were never popular in the Army. Many bugs in the design had not been worked out, and spare parts remained a problem throughout their career because of the difficult relationship with Christie's company. The Cavalry, which might have been expected to be the main advocate for such a design, had very mixed feelings about it. Although more advanced than any other tank in service, the Christie tank soon developed the reputation of a hanger queen due to frequent maintenance problems. During 1932, there was only one day in which all four of the Cavalry's T1 Combat Cars were in running condition. The mechanized detachment commander derided the design as only a "mobile cradle for an engine." The Liberty engine and transmission were a frequent problem and led to a number of unsuccessful attempts to develop substitutes. The Cavalry found that the convertible feature was of dubious use due to the long time it took to switch the tank from tracks to wheels and back again. The spring suspension took up so much space in the hull that the fighting compartment was deemed inadequate for a combat vehicle. The Cavalry was also unhappy with the 37mm gun armament, and three of the combat cars had the weapon and mounting removed and a simple mount for a

The BT-7 was a complete rework of the BT-5 with a new hull. The later series also introduced an improved turret with angled sides as seen here.

SOVIET TANK PRODUCTION, 1932–40[7]

Type	1932	1933	1934	1935	1936	1937	1938	1939	1940
BT tanks	396	1,005	1,105	500	1,063	788	1,221	1,402	779
T-26 types	1,032	1,405	1,420	1,236	1,215	550	1,054	1,399	1,601
T-28 types	0	41	50	32	101	46	100	140	13
T-35 types	0	1	10	7	15	10	11	6	0
T-37/T-38/ T-40	0	138	951	1,104	1,410	216	0	158	41
T-34	0	0	0	0	0	0	0	0	117
KV	0	0	0	0	0	0	0	0	243
T-27 tankette	1,610	919	14	0	0	0	0	0	0
Totals	***3,038***	***3,509***	***3,550***	***2,906***	***3,804***	***1,610***	***2,386***	***3,105***	***2,794***

.50-cal heavy machine gun substituted. The Christie tanks faded from view in the late 1930s as newer light tanks and combat cars entered service.

Even though the Christie tank made little impression in the United States, it spurred far more excitement in Europe. In 1929–30, it started a bidding war between Poland and the Soviet Union, both of whom thought it would form an excellent basis for their new tank force. The Soviet Union eventually signed a contract with Christie that included license production rights. After initial tests, the Red Army decided to deal with some of the technical shortcomings and put it into service as the central element in the mechanization of their cavalry. It was locally called the BT tank, an acronym for "fast tank" in Russian. The first batch of BT-2 tanks were equipped with simple cylindrical turrets armed with machine guns. When the T-26 tank received its 45mm turret, the Red Army decided to standardize this design for both the infantry and cavalry tanks, and this version became the BT-5. The BT was powered by the M-17 engine, a Russian copy of the World War I American Liberty aircraft engine. Compared to most tanks of the day that were barely capable of 20 miles per hour, the BT-5 had a sizzling speed of 45 miles per hour on wheels and 30 miles per hour on tracks. It was the second most widely produced tank of the 1930s after its stablemate the T-26, with some 6,565 manufactured.

The BT-5 saw its combat debut in 1937 during the Spanish Civil War and also saw combat in the little-known border wars between Japan and the Soviet Union along the Mongolian frontiers in 1938–39. The BT tank was extensively used at the beginning of the war with Germany in June 1941. In spite of its importance in interwar tank design, its greatest claim to fame came later from its evolutionary offspring, the legendary T-34, which shared its Christie suspension. (The T-34 will figure prominently in later chapters.) Yet the BT tank was outstanding its own right. It was the fastest tank of its generation, even on tracks, and was well armed and well armored for its day. Compared to the T-26, it had better armor, the same basic armament, and better cross-country performance.

MULTI-TURRET TANKS

During the 1920s and 1930s, there was a fad for multi-turreted tanks, especially multiple turrets on various heavy tank designs. The first of these was the monstrous Char 2C breakthrough tank. There were plans to build about 300 of these for the Allied offensive of 1919. That never happened, and in the end only 10 Char 2C were built. It was the largest, best armed, and best armored tank of the World War I era, with a 75mm gun in the main turret and a separate machine-gun turret in the rear. Vickers Armstrong can lay claim to reviving the multi-turret idea both with their Vickers 6-Ton tank and with their impressive Independent heavy tank of 1926. This had a 3-pounder main gun in the main turret and four small machine-gun turrets around the main turret. This type never entered serial production for the British army. Nevertheless, it served as inspiration for a number of multi-turret tanks in the Soviet Union, Germany, and Japan.

The Vickers influence can be most clearly seen in the Soviet T-35 heavy tank. This followed the general layout of the Independent, though it was significantly larger. It had a short 76mm gun in the main turret and four subsidiary turrets, two with 45mm guns and two with machine guns. Only sixty-one were built in 1933–39, and the Red Army soon learned that the multi-turret concept had gone too far. The separate turrets were impossible for the commander to control given the primitive communications on the tanks. Nevertheless, these land

The French FCM Char 2C was the ultimate World War I tank, combining the rhomboid shape of British Landships with the innovative turret of the Renault FT. Due to its enormous size, a small machine-gun turret was added on the rear to defend the tank from infantry. The six remaining tanks were in transit to the front in 1940 when the train was blocked; the tanks were demolished by their crews before ever seeing combat.

The Vickers Independent, although never put into quantity production, served as an inspiration around the world for multi-turreted tanks.

The ultimate example of the interwar multi-turreted tanks was the Soviet T-35. This had a main turret with a 76mm gun and four subsidiary turrets, two with 45mm guns and two with machine guns. By the time they saw combat in 1941, they were worn out and most were lost from mechanical breakdowns.

The Soviet T-28 was one of the most powerful tanks of the interwar years, armed with a short 76mm gun and two subsidiary machine-gun turrets. It was also unusual among Soviet tanks of the mid-1930s for being an entirely indigenous design, not based on license manufacture. This particular tank of the 5th Tank Division, 3rd Mechanized Corps, was knocked out near Alytus, Lithuania, during the 1941 Operation Barbarossa campaign.

An alternative to multiple turrets was to mount additional machine guns in barbettes around the fighting compartment. After a prolonged gestation due to a lack of funds, the U.S. Army's M2 medium tank entered production in 1939, by which time it was woefully obsolete.

battleships were a popular fixture of the parades in Red Square in Moscow. Most of these tanks were abandoned without seeing combat in 1941 due to their mechanical frailties.

A slightly more practical design was the T-28 medium tank. This resembled a shrunken version of the T-35 since it used the same main turret with 76mm gun. However, instead of four sub-turrets, it had only two, both in the front and both armed with machine guns. A total of 503 were manufactured in 1933–40 and they saw extensive combat use in the Russo-Finnish War of 1941 and again in the Barbarossa campaign of 1941. Although not a particularly important tank in the Red Army due to its modest numbers, it was still the most numerous medium tank design of the 1930s.

Germany's experimental Grosstraktor of 1929 was configured like the Char 2C with a main turret in front and a small machine-gun turret in the rear for self-defense. It mainly convinced the German army that multi-turreted tanks were a bad idea. Japan's Type 95 heavy tank of 1934 bears a passing resemblance to the Independent, but instead of having multiple machine-gun turrets it had only a single sub-turret with 37mm gun in addition to its main turret. The Japanese continued to experiment with multi-turreted tanks right until 1940, but none reached service use.

The French worked on several medium tanks during the late 1920s and early 1930s. The most important was the Char B battle tank, which started development immediately after World War I. However, its development was so protracted that it did not enter production to any significant extent until 1936, so it will be considered in the next chapter. The only French medium tank to enter production prior to 1936 was the Char D1 infantry tank. This was originally conceived as a follow-on to the Renault FT, but larger, with better armor and a more powerful gun. It still retained the archaic shape of its ancestor. It was accepted for service in 1929; production began in 1931 and 160 tanks were finished by 1935. Compared to later medium tanks, it was slow with a top speed of only 11 miles per hour, but it was well armored with 30mm frontal armor comparable to the German PzKpfw IV of 1940, and had a good dual-purpose 47mm gun. As the only modern tank in the French inventory until 1936, the D1 tanks saw too much use in wargames and training, and in the late 1930s they were sent off to the North African colonies due to their worn-out state. Curiously enough, one battalion returned to France and took part in the 1940 campaign; the other battalion switched sides and served with Free French forces in Tunisia in 1943 alongside the U.S. Army.

The year 1936 was a turning point in French tank production with the start of manufacture of three new types: the Char B, the Renault R-35 infantry tank, and the Hotchkiss H35 infantry/cavalry tank. These come in at the tail end of our period here, so they will be considered in detail in the next chapter on tanks of the blitzkrieg era.

PACIFIC WAR PATH

War clouds appeared in Asia and the Pacific sooner than in Europe. Tanks were used in small numbers in the fighting in China between the warlords and the central government in the 1920s. When Japan began to intervene in China in the 1930s, tanks were used in modest numbers on both sides. Full-scale fighting broke out between China and Japan in the summer of 1937 and both countries used tanks in the fighting for Shanghai and other key locations. The fighting spread farther north with border engagements by the Japanese Kwantung Army and the Red Army. There was extensive tank use by both sides at Lake Khasan in 1938 and Khalkhin Gol in 1939.

Japanese tank development in the 1930s was largely independent, although with significant British influence. Japan acquired a Vickers Model C in 1927. One of the clearest lessons from trials was the desirability of a diesel rather than gasoline engine. The Vickers Model C helped establish the guidelines for the design and production of Japan's most important tank of the early 1930s, the Type 89 medium tank. The definitive Type 89B with diesel engine appeared in 1933. This tank was armed with a short 57mm gun for infantry support and was the backbone of the Japanese tank force through the late 1930s during the original fighting in China.[8]

WORLDWIDE TANK PROCUREMENT, 1931–36

	1931	1932	1933	1934	1935	1936	Total
United States			3	8	60	144	215
United Kingdom*	16	53	9	33	34	73	218
Italy*				~310	~400	~400	1,110
Japan	12	21	112	161	404	410	1,120
France	15	142	172	238	379	997	1,943
Germany				54	905	1,794	2,753
USSR	835	3,121	3,819	3,556	2,994	3,905	18,230

*UK figures are for British army orders; no detailed annual figures are available for Italy.

The best of the early Japanese tanks was the Type 89 that entered service in the early 1930s. This Type 89A tank was assigned to the Special Naval Landing Forces and is followed by a Carden-Loyd Mark VI tankette. The Type 89 had a short 57mm gun and a light machine gun, which in this view is positioned forward while the 57mm gun is aimed aft.

Japan also acquired Carden-Loyd tankettes, but trials led to the conclusion that these were too small and light. Instead, Japan moved in the direction of the Vickers light tanks with the indigenous Type 94 tankette. Although called a tankette, it was in fact a light tank with a machine-gun turret. Experience with the Type 89 medium tank led the Japanese army to realize that it was too slow to operate with motorized infantry. As a result, a new gun tank entered trials in 1934. It resembled an enlarged version of the Type 94 tankette in terms of suspension, but followed a more conventional layout with a rear-mounted engine and a turret with a 37mm gun in the center. This tank, the Type 95 Ha-Go, eventually supplanted the Type 89 as the Japanese army's principal tank in China in the 1930s and went on to become the backbone of Japanese tank regiments in the Pacific War of 1941–45. It was ultimately supplemented by the larger Type 97 Chi-Ha medium tank, but this did not appear in significant numbers until 1938.

In general, Japanese tanks of the mid-1930s were comparable to European tanks of the period, with an accent on the infantry support mission. The Type 95 Ha-Go was certainly comparable if not superior to the German PzKpfw I, though smaller and less capable than the Soviet T-26.

China was dependent on imports for its tanks. A number of Renault FT tanks were used by the warlords in the 1920s. The first large-scale purchases by the central government in Nanking did not take place until 1929 when an order was placed for twenty-four Carden-Loyd tankettes from Vickers. A major effort to build up the tank force took place in 1935 with the purchase of ten PzKpfw I tanks from Germany, twenty CV 33 tankettes from Italy, twenty Vickers 6-Ton tanks, and twenty-nine Vickers amphibious tanks. Many of these took part in the fighting with the Japanese army in Shanghai in 1937.

TOP TANK OF THE ROARING THIRTIES

So what was the Top Tank of the Roaring Thirties? Some tanks can be ruled out rather quickly. The little tankettes, popular in Italy and Poland, do not stack up well in any major category and so can be quickly discarded. French tanks, with the exception of the infantry's D1, were mostly light cavalry tanks with very modest firepower. Likewise, the most numerous British type during this period was the Mark VI light tank, not a world beater in firepower or armor. Germany's main tank during this period was the PzKpfw I light tank, with no significant advantages over the British Mark VI or French types such as the AMR 33 cavalry tank.

The most likely candidates for Top Tank in this era are the Soviet designs, if for no other reason than their enormous variety. The Soviet Union began a major tank production program in 1931, three or four years before most European armies. As a result, by 1936 there was a wide range of tanks available, from the T-27 tankette through the T-26 infantry tank and BT-5 cavalry tank, up to the T-35 land battleship.

In terms of sheer numbers, the T-26 and BT-5 are the most obvious contenders. In terms of firepower, they are both equivalent since they shared a common turret with its 45mm gun. This weapon was superior to the machine-gun armament common with French, British, and German tanks of the period since it offered an excellent balance of antiarmor and antipersonnel capability, supplemented by a co-axial machine gun. Armor was comparable to or better than the western European types. Between

The T-28 remained a viable design well into the early years of World War II. This particular captured Finnish example is from the final series, which had an added layer of armor and the improved L-10 76mm gun. SA-KUVA

The Red Army bought license production rights for the Christie and built them as the BT for cavalry mechanization. The BT-5 was armed with the same 45mm gun and cylindrical turret as the T-26 infantry tank. The Red Army was an early advocate of tank radios, as can be seen from the clothesline antenna. However, the early radios were delicate and unreliable. The tanks behind are the earlier BT-2 armed with twin machine guns.

the two types, the BT-5 had an edge in armor and mobility as well as thicker front hull armor than the T-26. In addition, it had a more powerful engine which gave it higher road speed, and a more elaborate suspension which gave it better cross-country performance. The Soviet T-28 medium tank is another contender, offering thicker armor and more firepower than the BT-5.

I give my nod for the Tanker's Choice of the Roaring Thirties to the T-28 for its armor and firepower. Since the BT series was over ten times more numerous than the T-28 and the basis for mechanizing the Soviet cavalry, I give my nod for Commander's Choice to the BT-5 for its mixture of technical features as well as its importance in Red Army mechanization.

COMPARATIVE TECHNICAL CHARACTERISTICS

	PzKpfw I Ausf. B	Type 95	BT-5	T-28
Army	Germany	Japan	USSR	USSR
Crew	2	3	3	6
Dimensions: L x W x H (m)	4.42 x 2.06 x 1.72	4.36 x 2.05 x 2.13	5.8 x 2.23 x 2.34	7.37 x 2.87 x 2.62
Loaded weight (tonnes)	5.8	7.4	11.9	25.2
Main gun	2 x 7.62 MG13	37mm Type 94	45mm 20K	76.2mm KT-28
Main gun ammo	2,250	130	72	69
Engine (hp)	100	120	400	500
Max. speed (km/h)	40	45	53	42
Fuel (liters)	146	131	530	660
Range (km)	170	210	160	190
Ground pressure (kg/cm^2)	0.52	0.61	0.65	0.62
Armor*				
Mantlet (mm)	15**=>15	12@0=12	15** =>15	30@0=30
Turret front (mm)	13@10=13.2	12@10=12.2	15@0=15	20@0=20
Turret side (mm)	13@22=14	12@11=12.2	15@0=15	20@0=20
Upper hull front (mm)	13@21=14	12@0=12	13@61=26.8	30@10=30.4
Lower hull front (mm)	13@25=14	12@18=12.6	13@10=13.2	30@15=31
Upper hull side (mm)	13@21=14	12@34=14.5	13@0=13	20@0=20

*Armor data provided as: actual thickness in mm @ angle from vertical = effective thickness in mm.
**Curved

33
40732
HOTCHKISS

CHAPTER 3

Blitzkrieg Tanks: 1939–40

THIS CHAPTER EXAMINES THE TANKS of the principal combatants in the early blitzkrieg years: Germany, France, and Britain. The Soviet Union was involved in the invasion of Poland in 1939, but the Red Army will be ignored in this chapter since the types used in 1939 have already been examined in the previous chapter.

At the time of the invasion of Poland in September 1939, the German army still relied very heavily on machine-gun armed light tanks. During the invasion of Poland in 1939, almost 80 percent of the German tanks were light tanks, while during the battle of France in 1940 this percentage dropped to about 65 percent. Neither the PzKpfw I nor PzKpfw II are likely contenders for Top Tank. The remaining four types include two war-booty Czechoslovak tanks, the PzKpfw 35(t), and the PzKpfw 38(t), of which the later PzKpfw 38(t) was clearly the superior of the two. This was armed with a gun similar to the German PzKpfw III, but it was a smaller tank with a two-man turret. For this reason, the PzKpfw 38(t) will be dropped from consideration, and the focus here will be on the PzKpfw III and PzKpfw IV as the most likely German contenders for Top Tank.

The French Army of 1940 had a bewildering variety of tanks in service since both the cavalry and infantry separately acquired their own types. The two most common were the Renault R35 and Hotchkiss H39, both of which stemmed from the infantry's requirement for an infantry-accompanying tank to replace the venerable Renault FT. These tanks were designed to be economical and cheap to manufacture. They had good armor and adequate mobility, but the majority were armed with the same short 37mm gun as the Renault FT. They were also

GERMAN TANK STRENGTH IN THE POLISH AND FRENCH CAMPAIGNS

	1 Sept. 1939	1 May 1940
PzKpfw I	1,445	1,077
PzKpfw II	1,223	1,092
PzKpfw III	98	381
PzKpfw IV	211	290
PzKpfw 35(t)	196	143
PzKpfw 38(t)	78	238
Command tanks	215	244
Total	***3,466***	***3,465***

limited by an exceptionally small one-man turret, so these can be quickly ruled out. The infantry also had a few other minor types in service, such as the Char D1 and Char D2, but neither was exceptional and they will be ignored here. On the cavalry side, there were a number of light tanks intended for reconnaissance, such as the Renault AMR 33 and Renault AMR 35. They were machine-gun-armed scout tanks and not exceptional in terms of firepower or armor. Of the remaining types, the two most significant French contenders were the infantry's Char B1 bis battle tank and the cavalry Somua S35.

Britain was slower than the continental great powers in ramping up tank production. By 1940, light tanks such as the Vickers Mark VI were in large-scale production, but this type was not impressive in terms of armor or firepower. As in the French and Soviet cases, the British army acquired tanks for its nascent armored divisions as well as separate designs for its infantry. The tanks for the

The best Polish tank of 1939 was the 7TP, a derivative of the Vickers 6-Ton tank but with a Saurer diesel engine and a Bofors 37mm gun. Two battalions of these, numbering about 100 tanks, served in combat in 1939.

armored divisions included a family of related cruiser tanks—the Cruiser Mark I, Cruiser Mark III, and Cruiser Mark IV. On the infantry tank side, the Matilda I was similar to the French infantry tanks for its small size, two-man crew, and thick armor. Its machine-gun armament places it at the low end of the firepower scale. Although sharing the same name, the Matilda Mark II was a much larger tank with a much-improved 2-pounder gun. So on the British side, the cruiser tanks and the Matilda II are the most likely contenders.

In terms of the small powers, there is not a lot to choose from. Poland's best tank was the 7TP light tank, a license-produced version of the Vickers 6-Ton tank. It was one of the best of the Vickers derivatives, having an excellent 37mm Bofors gun as its main armament and an Austrian Saurer diesel engine. It was comparable in combat power to tanks such as the Soviet T-26 or the Czechoslovak PzKpfw 38(t). Belgium's best tank was the French Renault ACG1 armed with a Belgian 47mm gun. It had excellent 40mm armor, a two-man turret, and good mobility.

Italy was on the fringe of the 1939–40 fighting and its best tank was the M.11/39. This was another design heavily influenced by the Vickers 6-Ton. It had an odd armament arrangement, with its main gun in a hull sponson and twin machine guns in the turret. This was awkward and quickly replaced by a more conventional turret arrangement on the M.13/40, which will be covered in a later chapter on the Desert War. Tanks such as the Polish 7TP and Belgian ACG-1 were reasonably good designs for the time, but they were not exceptional enough to warrant consideration as the era's Top Tank.

BLITZKRIEG PANZERS

Under the terms of the Versailles Treaty that ended World War I, the German army was forbidden to have tanks. Germany covertly avoided these restrictions by means of a secret cooperative program with the Soviet Union in the late 1920s. A joint training and experimental center was established at Kazan in the Soviet Union, where new German designs could be tested in secret.[1] German panzer development focused on two types: a Leichttraktor (light tractor) armed with a 37mm gun and a Grosstraktor (large tractor) armed with a short 75mm gun. The Grosstraktor resembled a smaller version of the French Char 2C with a 75mm gun in the main turret at the front of the tank and a machine-gun turret at the rear of the tank. One odd feature was that the tank commander sat in the hull to the right of the driver rather than in the turret. Two different versions of the Grosstraktor were built by Krupp and Rheinmetall and put through their paces at Kazan in 1929–33. It was fairly obvious from the tests that neither the Leichttraktor nor Grosstraktor was entirely suitable as the basis for future panzer development. Their suspension designs were archaic, and the wargames at Kazan suggested that modern tanks needed the commander in the turret along with the loader and gunner.

When Hitler and the Nazi Party came to power in 1933, they renounced the Versailles Treaty and opened the door for remilitarization. Based on the Kazan experiments, the German army's Motorization Department wanted two principal tank types, codenamed ZW and BW. The ZW (*Zugführerwagen*: Section commander's vehicle) was the follow-on to the Leichttraktor and was the principal battle tank; it emerged as the PzKpfw III. The BW (*Battalionführerwagen*: battalion commander's vehicle) corresponded to the Grosstraktor and was a fire-support tank to accompany the ZW; it emerged as the PzKpfw IV. A German army report summarized the combat roles of the two types:

> The PzKpfw III is the assault tank (*Sturmwagen*), an "armored infantryman" (*gepanzerte Infanterist*) which wins the mobile battle with the annihilating power of its machine guns. The 3.7cm gun has been added to deal with the threat of an armored opponent. The PzKpfw IV is the over-watch

The Germans introduced the modern layout for tank crews with the Krupp turrets on the PzKpfw IV seen here. The commander was free to carry out his command role while the gun was serviced by dedicated gunners and loaders.

One of the most important but overlooked advantages of German medium tanks in 1940 was the turret layout. The commander no longer served as gunner or loader, but instead could focus on his role of leading his tank in battle. In addition, he was provided an all-around vision cupola for better situational awareness. SA-KUVA

tank (*Überwachungswagen*) following immediately behind the PzKpfw III and supporting it in overcoming the enemy. The ratio of PzKpfw III to PzKpfw IV is about the same as the infantry's ratio of light machine guns to heavy machine guns.

There are several interesting points in this report. The German army saw machine guns as the main armament for the PzKpfw III, not the 37mm gun, which was intended for the secondary role of dealing with enemy tanks. In the early 1930s, there were few tanks in European armies, and tank-versus-tank combat in World War I was a rarity. The PzKpfw III armament had the 37mm gun and the twin machine guns in separate, independent mounts. Unlike later designs, the turret machine guns were not a subsidiary armament to the gun and were not locked to it in a co-axial mount. Of the two types, the PzKpfw III was the more important, with plans to build it in a ratio of about 3 to 1 in favor of the PzKpfw IV. Armor on both tanks was modest at first, in the 15mm range, enough to protect against machine-gun fire.

Even though the German army had clear ideas for their ideal tanks, the German industry did not have the capability to manufacture such complex new weapons in 1933. The best that could be hoped for was a simple, light tank. There was considerable controversy over this issue, with some panzer advocates urging the army to delay building tanks in quantity until the ZW and BW were ready. More far-sighted officers realized the importance of forming and training the revolutionary new panzer divisions as soon as possible and that it was better to have an adequate light tank now than an ideal tank sometime in the indefinite future. As a result, the PzKpfw I was designed. Like the PzKpfw III, it had a twin machine gun in the turret as its main armament. However, it was too small to accommodate a supporting 37mm gun. In addition, the PzKpfw I was too small to have a three-man turret crew, so it ended up with a two-man crew consisting of a commander/gunner and driver. It was followed by a slightly larger tank, the PzKpfw II, which had a 20mm cannon. The main advantage of this tank was that it had modest antiarmor capability.

Development of the PzKpfw III tank began in 1934, and it entered production in early 1937. It was armed with a 37mm gun for commonality of ammunition with the new infantry antitank gun. Likewise, the PzKpfw IV tank was armed with a 75mm gun sharing ammunition commonality with the standard 75mm infantry gun. Production of the PzKpfw IV began slightly later than the PzKpfw III in the autumn of 1937.

By 1936, the German army was beginning to have second thoughts about the wisdom of its lightly armored, weakly armed tanks such as the PzKpfw I. There were signs that France and the Soviet Union were adopting more powerful antitank guns and tanks with heavier armor. Early in 1936, the army chief of staff Gen. Ludwig von Beck asked the ordnance department (Waffenamt) why they were still purchasing the light PzKpfw I and PzKpfw II instead of the greatly superior PzKpfw III. The Waffenamt answered that the PzKpfw III was not yet mature enough for mass production and probably would not be ready for it until the autumn of 1938. They rationalized this by stating the units equipped only with PzKpfw I and PzKpfw II "without question . . . have a very significant combat value." However, in March 1936 the Waffenamt released a study on tank development that acknowledged that "in the future, lightly armored Panzers will be pinned down by heavy weapons' fire just as in the last war the infantry and cavalry were forced to ground and stymied by machine guns."

Initial tank fighting in the Spanish Civil War further reinforced these concerns. The gun-armed Soviet T-26 tank dominated the tank-versus-tank fighting against German PzKpfw I and Italian L.3 tankettes. Even though tank-versus-tank fighting was never very decisive in Spain, the other lesson

The PzKpfw IV commander had a vision cupola with five episcopes protected by armored visors. Unlike the French tank turrets, the German cupola had roof hatches to enable the commander to observe from outside the tank for better situational awareness, another useful practice that supported dynamic German panzer tactics. This is a PzKpfw IV Ausf. D of the *10.Panzer-Division* on exercise at the Baumholder training grounds in April 1940 prior to the Battle of France.

A PzKpfw III of *Panzer-Regiment.36* moves off the road to advance cross-country during the approach march to Hannut on the afternoon of 11 May 1940. The subsequent battles near Hannut were the largest tank-versus-tank battles in history up to that point, pitting two German panzer divisions against two French mechanized cavalry divisions.

from the fighting was that the current level of armor protection, sufficient to protect against machine-gun fire, was completely inadequate on the modern battlefield in the presence of modern antitank guns. Both the German 37mm antitank gun and its Soviet derivative, the 45mm gun, were used in significant numbers in Spain. Tank attacks against positions defended by these guns usually failed.

Tests of the early PzKpfw III were disappointing due to problems with the suspension and transmission. The PzKpfw IV proved less troublesome, but the lessons from Spain led to a decision to shift production to the improved PzKpfw IV Ausf. B in April 1938 that had its frontal armor thickened to 30mm. The next major evolutionary step was the PzKpfw IV Ausf. D that increased side armor from 15 to 20mm and added an external mantlet to the turret to better protect the main gun opening.

The PzKpfw III program continued to wallow in technical problems with a string of unsuccessful attempts to rectify its suspension. In frustration, the Waffenamt itself took over the redesign in 1937–38, resulting in the definitive PzKpfw III Ausf. E, which introduced modern torsion bar suspension to German tank design. This type of suspension would be the most common type of tank suspension during the mid- and late-war period and is still the standard form of suspension for tanks today.

Besides the suspension improvements, the PzKpfw III Ausf. E also saw an increase in armor to the 30mm level on its frontal areas. While the evolution of the PzKpfw III in 1936–39 was marked by a steady increase in armor, the German army clearly favored mobility over armored protection. Indeed, the optimum level of armored protection on the PzKpfw III at 30mm was essentially the starting point for French tank armor, which had steadily climbed since 1921 from 30mm to 40mm and finally to 60mm by 1940 for its battle tanks.

Between the two types, the PzKpfw IV had several advantages. Both were similar in terms of armor, mobility, and crew configuration, but the PzKpfw IV had a distinct advantage in terms of firepower. The 37mm gun was inadequate in dealing with the vast majority of French tanks in the 1940 campaign due to their thick armor. The PzKpfw III could penetrate the French tanks at short range and from the sides, but was very limited in head-on engagements. The short 75mm gun of the PzKpfw IV was far from ideal as a tank-versus-tank weapon, but it was a useful dual-purpose gun and far more valuable in engaging nonarmored targets than the 37mm gun. In the world's first large tank-versus-tank battles in May 1940 in the Gembloux Gap, it was the PzKpfw IV that proved invaluable in blasting the tenacious French *dragons-portées* (mechanized infantry) from their defenses in the Belgian towns. The PzKpfw IV's other advantage in 1940 was reliability; it did not have the transmission problems that plagued the PzKpfw III design. So of the German contenders, the PzKpfw IV stands out.

THE FRENCH CONNECTION

The French Army was one of the pioneers of tank warfare and regarded the tank as a vital element in its doctrine of methodical battle. French doctrine was preoccupied with the lessons of World War I; one of the most important was that the infantry needed a steel backbone of tank support to survive against the deadly firepower of the modern battlefield. Germany had strategic objectives that would be satisfied by fast-moving, offensive operations. The French, bled white by World War I, had a profoundly defensive outlook and saw their tank force within this defensive framework. As a result, the majority of French tanks were committed to the mission of infantry accompaniment.

At the same time, the French recognized the need for mobile forces to carry out other missions. The tank offered a mechanized alternative to the horse for the traditional cavalry missions of reconnaissance and exploitation. As a result, the French devoted about a quarter of their tank force to the cavalry. These light mechanized divisions (DLM: *Division Légère Mécanique*) were the closest French equivalent to the German panzer divisions, but they were far fewer in number in 1940: only three divisions compared to ten German panzer divisions. After the first demonstration of the power of the panzer divisions in Poland in 1939, the French army belatedly recognized that its maneuver force was too small. In early 1940, it began consolidating the new Char B1 bis battle tank battalions into their own embryonic armored divisions (DCR: *Division Cuirasée*). The new French DCR armored divisions were much smaller than their German counterparts and poorly organized with too many tanks and not enough motorized infantry. However, their fatal flaw was not organization but time—they were created too late to undergo proper training. Only two were fully organized at the start of the campaign in May 1940 and they lacked the practical experience of their German opponents.

French tank development was plagued by the split between infantry and cavalry, resulting in two parallel families of tanks. Infantry tanks were designated as *chars* (tanks), while cavalry vehicles were called *automitrailleuses* (motorized machine guns) regardless of their armament or chassis. Curiously enough, France concentrated its turret and armament development under the Atelier Puteaux (APX) so it was not uncommon for French infantry and cavalry tanks to share common turrets and guns.

There was no doubt about the need for infantry support tanks, which were enthusiastically backed by the French infantry. The inspector general of the infantry in 1938 remarked:

> My profound conviction is that these machines are destined to play a decisive role in a future conflict; the infantry was unable to do without tanks in the last war and will be able even less in future operations. The tank must be the preferred arm in a nation poor in personnel. War is a question of force where the advantage rests with the most powerful machine and not with the most rapid machine.

The French defeat in 1940 had more to do with poor decisions at the command level than poor performance at the tactical level. Nevertheless, the French Divisions Cuirasée (armored divisions) were raised too late and inadequately trained. They were based in part on the new Char B1 bis battle tank.

The French army sponsored many small tank programs in the 1920s and 1930s, but there was very little production until 1936. As mentioned in the previous chapter, the French infantry attempted to develop a modernized Renault FT in the late 1920s as the Char D. This ended up too large and expensive, so another program was started to build a small and inexpensive infantry tank. The new design had a two-man crew like the original Renault FT but much thicker armor to resist the German 37mm gun. Its standard armament was the same SA 18 37mm gun as the Renault FT, but with a co-axial machine gun. The winner of the infantry tank competition was the Renault R35, and large-scale production began in 1936. These were used by the separate tank battalions assigned to support the infantry divisions. One of the losing competitors, the Hotchkiss H35, later entered production for both the infantry and cavalry for political and industrial reasons. Its combat capabilities were very similar to the R35.

The French army had been working on a battle tank since the early 1920s called the Char B (*char de bataille*: battle tank). This resembled the World War I British rhomboid Landships, but the main 75mm gun was mounted in the front of the hull. It first had a small machine-gun turret on the roof, but this gradually became larger and larger and was eventually equipped with a powerful 47mm gun and co-axial machine gun. The Char B remained mired in technical development for more than a decade, in no small measure due to changing views about the role this tank would play on the battlefield. When the requirements were drafted in 1921–22, the army expected the new Char B tank would operate like other World War I tanks in a very slow and methodical fashion. Well into the mid-1930s, the role for the Char B was still being defined. The infantry began to refer to it as a "maneuver tank," but it was closer to the old Char 2C breakthrough tank, spearheading the advance of the infantry against a determined enemy defense. It was not seen as a tank for engaging in swirling tank battles but rather as a siege machine for cracking open enemy defenses in a slow and methodical fashion.

By the time the Char B was ready for production in 1936, it was a very archaic design. The

Left: The most numerous of the new tanks was the Renault R35, intended to be a replacement for the old Renault FT. To minimize costs, it was very small, with only a two-man crew. However it was well armored, with the frontal armor designed to resist the German 37mm antitank gun. **Right:** The Hotchkiss H39 was purchased alongside the R35 since Renault could not manufacture tanks fast enough. They shared a common APX-R turret. The H39 was used by both French infantry and cavalry units; these are from the 1st Cuirassiers of the 3rd Light Mechanized Division.

To provide better antitank firepower, some H39 were fitted with the more powerful 37mm SA 38 gun during 1940, as seen here in the factory yard near Paris.

hull-mounted 75mm gun had no significant traverse and there was a fatal flaw in the aiming system. Instead of having independent traverse, the gun was aimed by the driver using a special range-finding sight and a Naeder servo device attached to the transmission that permitted precision steering of the tank. While technologically ingenious, it was tactically foolish, placing too many burdens on the driver to act as both driver and gun aimer. Furthermore, it compromised the durability of the tank since the Naeder device resulted in a mechanically delicate power-train that was very prone to breakdown.

The Char B1 started out with a good 47mm gun, but its turret design was fatally flawed. The turret was originally intended as a purely secondary feature to defend the tank. The original requirement called for a simple and small one-man turret. By 1936, the turret armament had increased in importance since it gave the Char B1 the ability to defend itself from enemy tanks. However, it kept its original one-man layout. This meant that the tank commander was overburdened with responsibilities, having to direct the tank in addition to loading and aiming the 47mm gun. The turret was later dubbed a "one-man orchestra." Production of the Char B1 was limited to 100 tanks, at which point production switched to the improved Char B1 bis. This version had thicker tank armor, shifting from 40mm to 60mm frontal armor. In addition, a new and more powerful 47mm gun was adopted.

The infantry remained unenthusiastic about creating armored divisions. As late as 1936, Gen. Maurice Gamelin noted: "The problems of constituting large tank units has been studied in France since 1932; the development of the antitank weapon has caused a renunciation of this concept." By 1937, opinions were shifting and the idea emerged to concentrate the Char B1 tanks in heavy tank brigades that might be useful as a mobile counterattack force against the German panzer divisions. In 1938, the Superior War Council ordered the formation of a commission under the army's tank inspector to study a large armored unit consisting of two Char B1 battalions, a battalion of the new Char D2,

This Char B1 bis, named *Vertus*, was commanded by Lt. Jacques Hachet and served with the 41st Tank Battalion during the ferocious battle at Stonne in May 1940. The tank remained in action until 20 May when it suffered a mechanical breakdown.

The Char B1 bis suffered from clever design features that proved impractical in the chaos of combat. The hull-mounted 75mm gun was aimed by the driver, using a precision steering system. The driver was provided with an optical rangefinder, the tubular device above the steering wheel.

The crew layout in the Char B1 bis was poor. The commander was a "one-man orchestra," manning the turret gun along with his other responsibilities. As a result, tank tactics suffered. Likewise, the driver was expected to drive the tank as well as sight and aim the hull-mounted 75mm gun. This was an invitation to tactical failure in battle.

two motorized infantry battalions, and two motorized artillery battalions. Although field trials were planned, the German annexation of Austria and the Sudeten crisis prompted the French government to cancel the trials for fear of increasing international tensions. One study in late 1938 concluded there would not be enough Char B battle tanks ready to form large units until October 1940 at the earliest and perhaps not until 1941. A provisional manual on the tactical employment of armored divisions was released for comment in February 1939. French doctrine still did not envision the armored division as an autonomous force, but rather as part of an infantry corps to assist in the maneuver of infantry divisions. The French felt pressured to form their first three armored divisions in late 1939 after the German demonstration of blitzkrieg tactics in Poland; however, it would prove too late for proper organization and training, and the Char B1 bis was poorly configured for such a unit.

It was the French cavalry that was most enthusiastic for armored divisions, seeing them as a modernized form of the traditional cavalry maneuver force. World War I was the swan song of traditional French horse cavalry; by 1918, the role of the cavalry as the mobile arm of decision on the battlefield was in serious doubt. To redeem the cavalry from oblivion, senior French commanders were prudent enough to link the cavalry to a mission rather than a mode of transport. Gen. Maxime Weygand argued that "The cavalry will keep its raison d'être as long as speed and surprise are valued on the battlefield . . . The war of tomorrow will be, more than ever, a war of machines."

Weygand began to reform the cavalry in 1930 as funds became available. Serious mechanization was contemplated under a 1934 plan to fully mechanize three cavalry divisions as light mechanized divisions (DLM). These were intended for the traditional cavalry roles of reconnaissance, flank security for infantry corps, offensive exploitation of breaches in the enemy lines, and defensive responses to enemy breakthroughs. They were the closest French equivalent to the German panzer divisions, but in 1940 only three were available and the third, the 3e DLM, had only been organized in early 1940.

The cavalry wanted a powerful battle tank as the centerpiece of its DLM. However, the first attempt, the AMC 34, was insufficiently armored to defend itself against the new German 37mm gun. A new design program began at Somua in October 1934, but serial production of the Somua S35 did not begin until 1937. In the meantime, the cavalry was saddled with the Hotchkiss H35 infantry tank to start the mechanization process. The Somua was a well-armed, well-armored design. Hull construction used very advanced casting techniques and the hull armor was 40mm thick. The tank was armed with an excellent 47mm gun capable of penetrating any German tank of the 1940 period from normal combat ranges.

The main drawback of the Somua S35 was its crew configuration. The cavalry had wanted its tanks fitted with two-man turrets, recognizing that this was a more efficient arrangement for high-speed combat. However, the requirements for the Somua had called for both a low weight of only 13 tons while at the same time a high level of armor protection. In trying to accomplish the impossible, the Somua tank was very narrow to reduce overall size and weight. As a result, the turret ring was

A Somua S35 of the 29th Dragoon Regiment, 2nd Light Mechanized Division, that took part in the massive tank battles in Belgium in mid-May 1940.

TANK GUNS, 1939–40							
Caliber	**25mm**	**37mm**	**37mm**	**47mm**	**37mm**	**47mm**	**47mm**
Army	France	France	France	France	Japan	Japan	Italy
Gun	SA34	SA18	SA38	SA35	Type 94	Type 1	47/32
Tube length	L/72	L/21	L/33	L/32	L/46	L/54	L/32
Armor-piercing projectile	Cart. mle. 1934 PT	OR mle 1935 coiffé	OR mle. 1938 coiffé	BR mle.1935	Type 94	Type 1	Gr. perf. 39
Type	AP	APC	APC	APC	AP	AP	APC
Initial muzzle velocity (m/s)	920	600	700	700	701	823	630
Projectile weight (kg)	0.5	0.39	0.7	1.5	0.68	1.53	1.44
Penetration (mm; @ 500m, 30 degree)	23	14	21	33	29	54	35

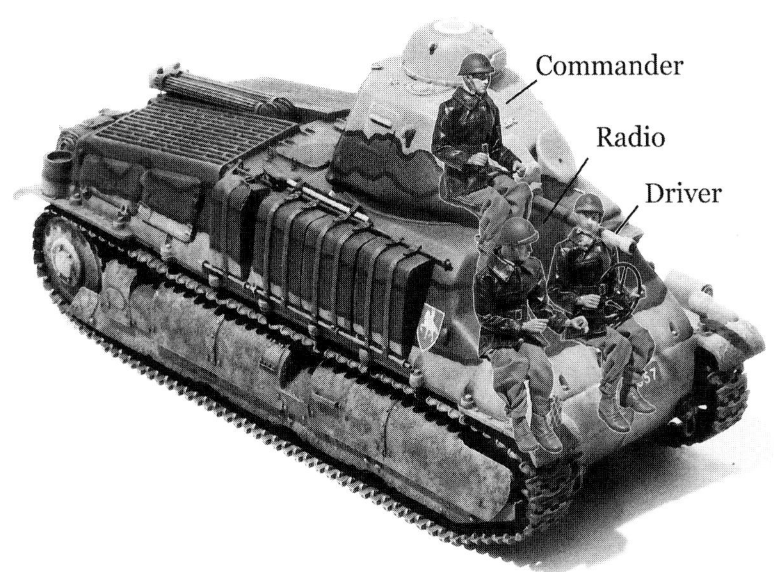

The Somua S35 had a three-man crew, with the operator in the hull having a secondary function of assisting the tank commander with loading the main gun. This was marginally better than on other French tanks but not as efficient in combat as the German layout.

narrow, permitting a "one-and-a-half-man" turret. The tank commander rode in the turret, but there was enough space on the right side of the turret to permit the radio operator to assist in loading the gun. While better than the usual French one-man turrets, it was still inferior to the German three-man turrets under actual combat conditions.

Despite this problem, the Somua S35 was a significantly better tank than the Char B1 bis. It proved to be more mechanically dependable in 1940, and its armor, while not as good as the Char B1 bis, was still adequate when facing the German 37mm antitank guns.

THE BRITISH BLITZ

Britain was at the forefront of tank design in the 1920s and early 1930s; as mentioned earlier, the Vickers 6-Ton tank largely set the stage for world tank designs in the mid-1930s. However, the British Army was third in line for industrial resources after the Royal Navy and Royal Air Force, and this lack of national priority would plague British tank design in the early years of the war. Britain was even slower than France in army mechanization, not forming its first armored division until 1939 and unhorsing its cavalry later.

Aside from reconnaissance tanks such as the Light Tank Mark VI, British tanks fell into two main categories: infantry and cruiser. The cruiser tanks were intended for the Tank Brigades and eventually the new armored divisions. The British Army had several doctrinal differences from its continental counterparts. While the Germans saw the PzKpfw III and PzKpfw IV armament primarily for engaging nonarmored targets, British doctrine placed tank-versus-tank fighting at the forefront of the mission of its cruiser tanks. Furthermore, British tactical doctrine expected tanks to fire on the move, not from the halt. These priorities had several effects on cruiser tank design: There was considerable interest in hydraulic turret traverse to enable running engagements and, like the Germans, the British also recognized the need for a three-man turret crew to conduct tank battles.

The first of the modern cruiser tanks was the Vickers A9 that entered development in 1935 and was accepted for service in the summer of 1937.[2] Its armament was the excellent new 2-pounder (40mm) gun, which could penetrate 40mm of armor at normal combat ranges. Turret traverse was hydraulic. The main drawback of the 2-pounder gun was that the high-explosive round did not have a large charge and was seldom issued to tanks in the 1939–41 period. To provide some high-explosive firepower, a close-support (CS) version of the tank was manufactured in small numbers, armed with a 3.7in (94mm) howitzer. Although called a howitzer, this weapon was actually a breech-loaded mortar, with resulting accuracy issues at longer ranges.

The A9 had its peculiarities. In view of the limitations of the 2-pounder against nonarmored targets, the A9 had two subsidiary turrets in the hull front armed with machine guns. The A9 was not well armored, with a maximum of only 15mm on the main surfaces and 7mm on other surfaces. Production began late in 1937 and by the summer of 1940, 125 series production tanks had been delivered.

There was some interest in an infantry tank version of the A9, and this was developed in parallel as the A10. The armor basis was increased to 25mm, then to 30mm, and the two front machine-gun subturrets were removed. In the event, the British army changed the infantry tank armor requirement to deal with the threat of the German 37mm antitank gun and the A10 ended up being built as a cruiser tank, with the A9 becoming the Cruiser Tank Mark I and the A10 the Cruiser Tank Mark II. Production of the A10 did not begin until 1939; a total of 170 tanks were completed by May 1941. Both of these tanks were built by the experienced firm of Vickers and proved to be dependable.

The next evolution of this family was the A13. One of Britain's main tank advocates, Gen. G. Martel, assistant director of mechanisation at the War Office, had attended wargames in the Soviet Union in 1936 and was deeply impressed by the performance of the high-speed BT-5 tanks. On returning to Britain, he instigated the development of a British equivalent using the Christie suspension. The A13 bore a strong family resemblance to the previous A9 and A10, having the thinner armor of the A9 but lacking its sub-turrets. It was powered by the same World War I Liberty aircraft engine that propelled the original Soviet BT tanks. During its development in 1939, it was appreciated that it could be penetrated by the 20mm gun on the German PzKpfw II light tank, so work began on turret appliqué to increase its protection from 14mm to 30mm on the A13 Mark IIA (later Cruiser Mark IV). Both the baseline Mark II and the unarmored Mark IIA were in service in the Battle of France. At the start of the war in September 1939, there were 77 cruiser tanks in service (35 Cruiser Mark I/A9,

The British cruiser tanks were primarily armed with the 2-pounder, but some were configured as close-support tanks with a breech-loaded mortar. This Cruiser Mark IA CS of the HQ of A Squadron, 3 RTR (Royal Tank Regiment), was lost in Calais after shedding a track.

The Matilda I infantry tank was built on a strict budget. Although well armored for its small size, it was too small and weakly armed to be a practical infantry tank. After the Battle of France, surviving tanks were retired to training units. This one is seen in the United Kingdom in 1941 with Polish troops for training.

42 Cruiser Mark III/A13). The numbers continued to increase so that there were 150 committed to France in May 1940.

Alongside the cruiser tanks, the British army also developed a family of infantry tanks. The first type, the A11, was intended to be an inexpensive two-man tank with thick armor and a single machine gun in the turret. Production began in 1938 under the code name Matilda, but second thoughts began to emerge about the wisdom of such a minimal vehicle with modest armament and a top speed of only 8 miles per hour. Fewer than 140 were completed. In its place, the A12 Matilda Senior was designed, also called the Matilda II.

The defeat of the British Expeditionary Force in France in June 1940 left Britain with very few tanks in the face of a possible German invasion. This is a Cruiser Mark III of the 3 RTR left behind at Calais.

This was a far more substantial tank, armed with a 2-pounder gun in a two-man turret and with 75mm frontal armor. Its top speed was 15 miles per hour, better than its predecessor, but no world-beater.[3] What is especially surprising about the A12 Matilda was the choice of armament. As mentioned, the 2-pounder was an excellent antitank gun for its day, but with poor high-explosive firepower. Infantry support generally depends on high-explosive firepower to deal with enemy infantry, antitank guns, and field entrenchments. British reliance on this single weapon compromised its early tank designs.

Of the British tanks that served in France in 1940, the only one to leave a lasting impression on the Germans was the A12 Matilda infantry tank, which served in the 1st Tank Brigade.[4] Although only twenty-three served in France, they took part in the counterattack at Arras on 21 May 1940, which gave the Germans a good scare. The Matilda was invulnerable to the German 37mm antitank gun at most ranges, and it usually took a 105mm field gun or an 88mm Flak gun to knock it out. However, even if it impressed the Germans, it had its share of faults. It was too slow on a mobile battlefield, its tracks offered poor traction in wet conditions, its gun lacked high-explosive firepower, and it had poor reliability.

The cruiser tanks were committed mainly with the 1st Armoured Division in its battles on the Dunkirk perimeter. The main problem with the cruiser tanks was their thin armor, which was vulnerable to the German 37mm antitank gun. The cruiser tanks had a mixed reputation with their British crews due to mechanical problems. The Liberty engines in the A13 had a running life of only about 100 hours, and suspensions and tracks had a poor reputation for durability. As in the French case, many of the problems with British tanks in France in 1940 probably had much to do with their novelty and the lack of crew experience rather than inherent design flaws. About 75 percent of the tank losses were attributed to mechanical breakdown.[5] The same tanks saw combat later in 1940 in the desert, where they displayed far greater battlefield effectiveness.[6] British tanks of 1940 do not compare well to their French or German counterparts in terms of armor, firepower, or mobility.

TOP TANK OF THE BLITZKRIEG ERA

Blitzkrieg–era tanks were extremely varied due to the lack of maturity of armored doctrine and the hasty design and manufacture of many of the types. Basic issues had not been resolved. How thick should armor be? Enough to defend against machine guns; enough to defend against antitank guns? What about the main tank armament? Was a powerful antitank gun the best solution? How important was high-explosive firepower? What about mobility? Was a slow pace better suited to infantry support? How important was high speed? Tanks of this era ran the gamut. Armor was often quite thin, only 15mm in some cases but an impressive 75mm in others. Firepower was often limited to machine guns; guns in the 37–40mm range were common and some 75mm guns were appearing. Mobility requirements ran from the arthritic 8 miles per hour of infantry tanks to the speedy 30 miles per hour of cavalry tanks.

One of the most critical battlefield ingredients in 1939–40 was mechanical reliability. The early tanks were certainly much better than tanks of World War I in this regard. However, mechanical fragility remained the main source of tank losses in

An interesting comparison of two 1940 rivals, a Somua S35 and PzKpfw IV, at the U.S. Army Ordnance Museum at Aberdeen Proving Ground. This Somua had served in the French 2nd Light Mechanized Division in 1940 and was captured by the Germans. It was later turned over to the Italians, who operated over fifty of these during the war. It was captured by the U.S. Army in 1944 near Rome and sent back to Maryland for technical evaluation.

The PzKpfw IV was intended to provide high-explosive fire support to the more numerous PzKpfw III. It was armed with a short 75mm gun, nicknamed the "cigar butt," which had excellent high-explosive firepower but very limited antitank punch.

1939–40. The German army held several advantages in this regard. German tanks were not especially impressive at this point in terms of armor or firepower; however, they were generally sound designs and benefitted from the use of reliable Maybach engines. Equally important, the German army had begun its mechanization program early and had the critical experience of the Austrian Anschluss, the occupation of Czechoslovakia, and the initial campaign in Poland to learn the mundane but essential tasks of keeping its panzers moving. The battlefield experience of the German tank crews was priceless. As Napoleon said, "In war, the moral is to the physical as three is to one."

German armored warfare doctrine was also more mature than French or British doctrine. The campaign in Poland had demonstrated that the panzer division organization was superior to the light division configuration that had been used to mechanize the cavalry. As a result, between October 1939 and the start of the France campaign in May 1940, the German army reorganized the light divisions into panzer divisions, creating a more uniform and effective force sharing a common tactical doctrine.

This discussion has condensed the Top Tank contenders to two: the French Somua S35 and the German PzKpfw IV. The Somua S35 performed very well in the tank battles of the Gembloux Gap in Belgium in the world's first large tank-versus-tank battles.[7] In the holy trinity of tank design—armor, firepower, and mobility—the S35 was an excellent design. In comparison, the PzKpfw IV scored well on two of the three basic criteria—excellent firepower and mobility—but mediocre for armor protection. From a tanker's perspective, the Somua S35 is the choice. It had excellent firepower and armor, and its main fault was its poor turret

COMPARATIVE TECHNICAL CHARACTERISTICS

	PzKpfw IV Ausf. D	Somua S35	Char B1 bis	Matilda II
Army	Germany	France	France	UK
Crew	5	3	4	4
Dimensions: L x W x H (m)	5.38 x 2.84 x 2.68	5.1 x 2.12 x 2.6	6.37 x 2.5 x 2.79	5.6 x 2.86 x 2.36
Loaded weight (tonnes)	20.0	19.5	31.5	24.0
Main gun	75mm KwK 37	47mm SA35	75mm SA35+47mm SA35	2-pounder
Main gun ammo	80	121	74+50	93
Engine (hp)	265	190	305	95+95
Max. speed (km/h)	40	45	28	24
Fuel (liters)	470	410	400	
Range (km)	200	230	180	255
Ground pressure (kg/cm^2)	.85	.85	.85	1.13
Armor*				
Mantlet (mm)	30**=>30	42**=>42	56**=>56	75**=>75
Turret front (mm)	30@10=30.4	42@0=42	56@0=56	75@10=76.1
Turret side (mm)	20@25=22	42@22=45.3	56@22=60.4	75**=>75
Upper hull front (mm)	30@7=30.3	47@21=50	60@20=63.8	75@5=75.2
Lower hull front (mm)	30@22=32.3	47**=>47	60@45=84.8	78**=>78
Upper hull side (mm)	20@0=20	40@15=41.4	55@0=55	70@10=71.1

*Armor data provided as: actual thickness in mm @ angle from vertical = effective thickness in mm.
**Curved

design. So I give it the nod for Tanker's Choice of the blitzkrieg era.

For Commander's Choice, I give the nod to the PzKpfw IV. In spite of its mediocre armor, the PzKpfw IV had better battlefield performance due to its more modern crew layout and mechanical dependability. The PzKpfw IV was a more versatile weapon and would form the backbone of the German Panzer force for the remainder of the war.

CHAPTER 4

Barbarossa: 1941

WHEN THE WEHRMACHT INVADED THE SOVIET UNION on 22 June 1941, it unleashed the largest land campaign of the Second World War. The Russian Front would dominate the European war from 1941 to 1945, encompassing the greatest number of troops and tanks. The human and material cost of this theater was equally staggering.

The Russian Front also set the pace for worldwide tank design. Innovative Soviet designs such as the T-34 established the new world standard. Germany raced to keep up with the Red Army in tank design, and so stayed ahead of contenders in other theaters such as Britain and the United States.

While it is not often recognized, the initial battles of Operation Barbarossa involved more tanks than at any other time of the war. The German panzer force in 1941 numbered over 5,000 tanks, although the actual invasion force used around 3,400 tanks. The Red Army had over 22,000 tanks, more than the rest of the world combined and the largest tank force of any army at any point during the war.

The German tank force at the outset of Operation Barbarossa was not particularly different from the Battle of France in 1940 in terms of equipment. The panzer divisions had been reorganized for a more balanced combined-arms mixture with fewer tanks but more infantry. This was done in part to create more divisions, with nearly double the divisional order of battle between 1940 and 1941. Obsolete tanks such as the PzKpfw I were far fewer in number, although there were still significant numbers of the light PzKpfw II in service.

GERMAN PANZER DEPLOYMENTS: OPERATION BARBAROSSA, 22 JUNE 1941[1]

	I	II	35(t)	38(t)	III	IV	Bef*	Total
1.Pz.Div.		43			71	20	11	145
3.Pz.Div.		58			110	32	15	215
4.Pz.Div.		44			105	20	8	177
6.Pz.Div.		47	155			30	13	245
7.Pz.Div.		53		167		30	15	265
8.Pz.Div.		49		118		30	15	212
9.Pz.Div.	8	32			71	20	12	143
10.Pz.Div.		45			105	20	12	182
11.Pz.Div.		44			71	20	8	143
12.Pz.Div.	40	33		109		30	8	220
13.Pz.Div.		45			71	20	13	149
14.Pz.Div.		45			71	20	11	147
16.Pz.Div.		45			71	20	10	146
17.Pz.Div.	12	44			106	30	10	202
18.Pz.Div.	6	50			114	36	12	218
19.Pz.Div.	42	35		110		30	11	228
20.Pz.Div.	44	31		121		31	2	229
Other		134			10		2	146
Total	***152***	***877***	***155***	***625***	***976***	***439***	***188***	***3,412***

* *Panzer Befehlswagen*: command tanks

RED ARMY TANK STRENGTH, 1 JUNE 1941[2]

T-35	KV	T-28	T-34	BT	T-26	Other Light	Total
59	504	436	891	7,433	9,792	3,587	22,702

In terms of technical quality, the panzer force had seen only modest improvements. Even before the start of the Battle of France, it was evident that the German army was falling behind in tank firepower. The PzKpfw III was woefully weak in its main gun in fighting with contemporary tanks. There had been schemes to up-arm it to a 50mm gun since the mid-1930s, but there was resistance over introducing another ammunition type. Efforts to increase both tank and antitank firepower were

GERMAN TANK STRENGTH, JUNE 1941	
PzKpfw I	877
PzKpfw II	1,074
PzKpfw 35(t)	170
PzKpfw 38(t)	754
PzKpfw III	1,440
PzKpfw IV	517
PzBefWg	330
Total	***5,162***

underway since 1939, but the new 50mm guns did not enter production until March–April 1940 and so did not take part in the French campaign. The panzer force received the 50mm KwK 38 L/42, and there were about 620 PzKpfw III with this gun with the divisions taking part in Barbarossa, or more than half of all PzKpfw III. This gun could penetrate 46mm of armor at 30 degrees at 500 meters, meaning that it was adequate to deal with French types such as the infantry tanks and the Somua S35 but only capable of defeating the Char B1 bis at closer ranges. The infantry adopted the 50mm PaK 38 with the longer L/60 barrel; there were about 850 in service by the time of invasion of Russia.

Although the 50mm gun represented an important step forward in German firepower, it would prove to be inadequate from the first days of the Russian campaign after facing the new generation of Soviet tanks such as the T-34 and KV; the 50mm gun could not penetrate these new Soviet types from the front when using the standard ammunition. Why didn't the Germans go for a more powerful gun? There was a high level of complacency about the Soviet tank threat in the late 1930s when the 50mm gun was developed. The Germans had examined both the T-26 and BT-5 tanks in Spain in 1937–38 and did not anticipate a major leap forward in Soviet tank armor. The German army had good intelligence about heavier Soviet tanks of the 1930s such as the T-28 medium tank since examples of this tank were captured by the Finnish army during the 1939–40 Winter War. The basic version had 30mm frontal hull armor and 20mm frontal turret armor that was vulnerable to the older 37mm gun. Some T-28 in Finland had additional armor appliqués added, which brought protection to 50 or 80mm. However, it is not clear if the German army was aware of these. In the event, the T-28 was an archaic design that caused little anxiety among the German tank designers. The Finnish Winter War seemed to confirm this viewpoint, since there was little evidence of any major advance in Soviet tank armor. The bulk of the Soviet tank force in Finland consisted of the standard designs of the 1930s, notably the T-26 light tank and BT-7 cavalry tank, neither of which represented a problem to the new 50mm gun.

There was some recognition that the new gun was inadequate, and one means to improve its performance was to use a new generation of high-velocity armor-piercing projectile (HVAP), the Panzergranate 40. This type of ammunition used a hard, dense tungsten-carbide core contained within a mild steel body and a light ballistic cap. This permitted a substantial increase in velocity, from 685 m/s in the case of the normal 50mm *Pz.Gr.39* projectile to 1,050 m/s for the tungsten-carbide *Pz.Gr.40* when used from the standard 500mm L/42 KwK gun on the PzKpfw III. At short range (100 meters), this had a dramatic difference in armor penetration—55mm for the old ammunition compared to 97mm with the new tungsten-carbide projectile—meaning it could penetrate the frontal armor of the T-34. This advantage dissipated quickly at range; at 500 meters the old *Pz.Gr.39* could penetrate 46mm while the *Pz.Gr.40* could penetrate 58mm, giving it marginal performance frontally against the T-34.[3] Similar tungsten-carbide ammunition was also developed for other guns such as the various 37mm tank guns. The main problem was that tungsten carbide was available in very limited amounts and reserved for use for machine tools in the defense industry. As a result, supplies were modest, with most German tanks receiving only about five rounds of this type in the summer of 1941.

In terms of armored protection, the French campaign emphasized the need for better protection on German medium tanks that were vulnerable to the

READINESS RATES OF GERMAN TANKS ON THE RUSSIAN FRONT, AUGUST–SEPTEMBER 1941

(Percentage)	PzKpfw II	PzKpfw III	PzKpfw IV	PzKpfw 38(t)
Operational	73	48	58	58
In repair	27	52	42	42

better antitank guns of the day, such as the French 25mm and 47mm and the British 2-pounder guns. The Germans were well aware of the Soviet 45mm antitank gun, having examined examples in Spain in 1937–38. The immediate solution was to reinforce the frontal hull armor of the medium tanks. As a result, when the PzKpfw III Ausf. H went into production in October 1940, it sported an additional appliqué of 30mm on the hull front and side, bringing the total to 60mm. Starting in September 1940, the PzKpfw IV Ausf. E had an additional 30mm plate on the superstructure front and side, increasing it to 60mm, and a hull front plate increase from 30mm to 50mm. The PzKpfw IV Ausf. F, which entered production in April 1941, switched from the use of 30+30mm armor to a single plate of 50mm armor. This was viewed as an adequate response to the Soviet 45mm threat since the tank and antitank gun versions could penetrate 38mm of vertical armor at 500 meters.

German tank designs were more mature and durable than their Soviet counterparts, at least during the dry summer months. Even after two months of long road marches and intense fighting, the panzer divisions still managed to keep more than half their tanks operational, as is evident from the chart above. As will be detailed below, Soviet tank units were incapable of such sustained operations in the summer of 1941.

THE RUSSIAN SURPRISE

Unknown to the Wehrmacht, the Red Army had begun a major new tank program in response to the lessons of the Spanish Civil War. The intention was to replace the T-26 infantry tank with the new T-50, the BT cavalry tank with the new T-34, and the T-28 and T-35 medium/heavy tanks with the new KV. Of these three designs, the new T-34 was by far the best and can be traced back to the prototype A-20. The main intention of this design was to increase the armor protection sufficiently to protect it against the German 37mm gun. The Soviet designers had seen photos of the new French FCM36 infantry tank and were impressed with its sharply angled hull and turret armor. Angling the armor promised to increase its protection without a major increase in weight. For example, in the case of 30mm armor plate, if angled 30 degrees from the vertical it had an effective thickness of 35mm, and if angled 60 degrees from the vertical, its effective thickness doubled to 60mm.

Aside from the redesigned hull and turret armor, the A-20 was essentially similar to the late production batch of the BT-7 cavalry tank with the same 45mm gun and M-17 engine. Despite the Red Army requirements, the designers at Plant No. 183 in Kharkov became convinced that the A-20 design was insufficiently advanced. Archaic features such as the Christie wheel-and-track feature were abandoned in favor of an all-track configuration, and a better tank gun in the 76mm range was recommended. Furthermore, they anticipated that by the time the new tank entered service, more armor would be needed since armies were likely to go from the 37–45mm guns of the late 1930s to 50–76mm guns in the early 1940s. The proposed A-32 increased the frontal armor from 20mm to 32mm, and a short 76mm gun was offered as an option to the usual 45mm gun. Trials of both types in the summer of 1939 were promising, and the A-32 proved more attractive due to its stronger armor. The T-32 tank was accepted for service in December 1939, but the state decree recognized that certain improvements were desirable before serial production began.

The next step was the A-34 design, which shifted to the 76mm L-11 gun, adopted thicker 45mm glacis armor, and switched to the new V-2 diesel engine. The new frontal armor layout with its steep angle gave protection equivalent to 90mm. Trials of this tank took place in February–April 1940, and this version was accepted for production as the T-34 tank with plans to build 200 in 1940 and 1,600 in 1941.[4]

The T-34 represented a revolutionary step forward in medium tank design. Its armor was unusually effective for a medium tank. Although about the same thickness as the latest PzKpfw IV Ausf. F, the severe sloping of the armor doubled its protective effectiveness without a corresponding increase in vehicle weight. The mobility of the T-34 also was exceptionally good. The Christie spring suspension offered a very good cross-country ride, and the wide track made the T-34 especially well-suited to operations in mud and snow. In terms of firepower, the L-11 76mm gun offered a good balance between antitank and high-explosive firepower. The new and longer F-34 gun entered production in the spring of 1941 and had even better antitank performance.

Although it has been widely written that the Germans were unaware of the existence of the T-34 before the 1941 invasion, a number of German intelligence reports mentioned it.[5] The problem was two-fold: the traditional issue of the intelligence community keeping its secrets to itself and not informing the tactical commanders, and the generally dismissive attitude of German leaders toward the Russians, especially after their own incredible victories in France in 1940 and the embarrassing performance of the Red Army in Finland in 1939–40. During the 1940 campaign, German tanks had

The initial production version of the T-34 had the shorter 76mm L-11 gun as seen here. It was replaced in 1941 with the longer and more powerful 76mm F-34.

The T-34 Model 1940 had a four-man crew, with the commander doubling as the gunner.

The prewar T-34 tanks had a much higher level of workmanship than the wartime production batches. This T-34 Model 1941 with the new F-34 gun was captured in Karelia by the Finnish army and put into their service. SA-KUVA

The T-34 had its share of teething problems. This T-34 with the initial L-11 gun had a spare transmission lashed to its rear deck when abandoned in Lvov in western Ukraine in June 1941.

Despite its many impressive features, the T-34 had its share of flaws. One of the worst was the poor turret layout, which permitted only a two-man crew. Besides the tank commander being expected to serve as gunner or loader, vision devices were inadequate and the large hatch made it impossible for the commander to peer outside in combat. SA-KUVA

A clear example of the limitations of the T-34 turret design. The commander could operate with the hatch open while traveling, but the awkward location made it impractical to remain open in combat. This is a T-34 of the 116th Tank Brigade in the Volga Military District.

been outmatched in armor and firepower by types such as the French Char B1 bis but managed to overcome them using superior training and tactics. Panzer leaders were confident they could do so again in Russia in 1941.

The Big Klim

Not all of the new Soviet tanks were equally successful. The new heavy tank, the KV, was very impressive in many respects but proved to be a disappointment. This project began as an antitank gun destroyer to help the infantry break through enemy defenses. Protective levels were able to withstand the fire of 37–45mm antitank guns at point-blank range or the fire of 75mm field guns at 1,200 meters. The new program was so important that the two premier design bureaus in Leningrad, the Bolshevik Factory and the Kirov Plant, were both assigned to develop competitive prototypes. The original requirement called for the same layout as the T-35 heavy tank with five turrets. The engineers quickly convinced the army to eliminate the "decorative" MG turrets. The Bolshevik plant called their design the T-100, or *Sotka*—Russian slang for "100." The Kirov team followed the fad for naming everything after the murdered communist party boss Sergei M. Kirov, hence SMK.

On 4 May 1938, wooden models of the designs were shown to a special meeting of the State Defense Council in Moscow. The designers questioned the utility of three turrets, which prompted Stalin to go up to one of the wooden models, break off one of the turrets, and quip: "Why make a tank into a department store!" As a result, the designs switched to a twin-turret design: a small turret with a 45mm gun up front and a large turret with a 76mm gun on a pedestal in the center of the hull. The pedestal added considerable weight to the design and a large surface area vulnerable to enemy fire. The Kirov team suggested a single-turret version of their SMK, named KV after Stalin's crony Marshal Klimenti Voroshilov, the People's Defense Commissar.

Trials of all three designs began in September 1939 and soon found that the T-100 was very sluggish and difficult to drive. The commanders in both the multi-turret tanks had difficulty coordinating the actions of both gun turrets, a not altogether surprising result since the old T-35 heavy tank was notorious for the same shortcoming. The KV emerged as the best of the three heavy tank designs.

While the tank trials were going on, the Red Army was involved in its botched invasion of Finland. The performance of the Red Army's tank force was particularly embarrassing.[6] As had been the case in Spain, the Soviet tanks could not resist 37mm antitank guns. As a result, a special experimental company of the 20th Armoured Brigade was created with new heavy tank prototypes. Manned in part by factory crews, they were used in the assault on the

German intelligence might have had their suspicions piqued by the appearance of a few photos of this monster tank knocked out by the Finnish army in 1940. This was one of the prototype T-100 Sotka heavy tanks, a competitor to the KV design, that ran over a mine while attacking the Finnish Velikan bunker complex near Summa.

The KV started out as a multi-turret monster called the SMK. This archaic configuration was rejected and replaced by a more conventional layout.

The prototype of the KV series differed in many details from the production series. It was armed with the L-11 76mm gun, which was replaced in 1941 with the longer ZIS-5.

A KV-1 with the patriotic slogan "Za Stalina!" (For Stalin) on the outskirts of Leningrad in 1941. This is from the intermediate 1941 production series with the second type of 76mm gun, the F-32.

An interior view of a KV-1 Model 1942 on the gunner's side. The ZIS-5 gun could be aimed using either the co-axial telescopic sight or the periscopic sight seen in the upper left.

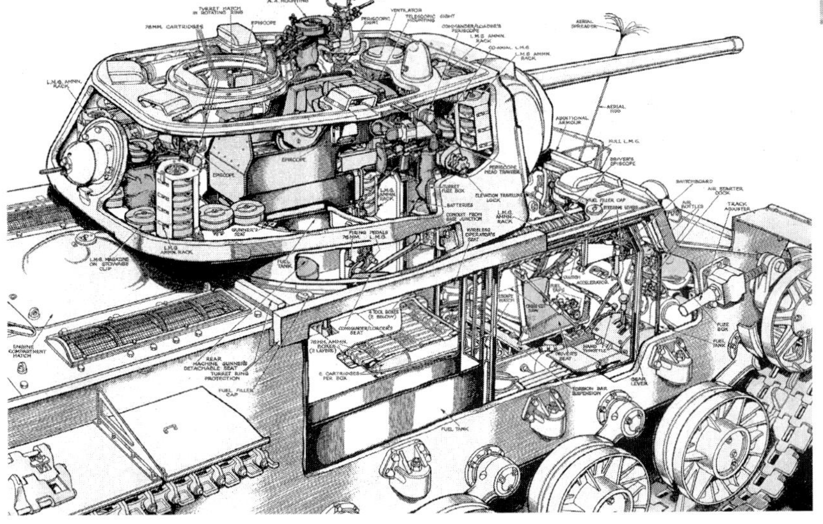

A detailed technical illustration of the interior layout of a KV-1 done by Allied intelligence in 1943, based on the two KV-1 provided to Britain and the United States.

Finnish Velikan bunker complex around Summa. The SMK drove over a large mine, which blew off one of its tracks and buckled the belly armor. The remaining KV and T-100 tanks attempted to guard the SMK while recovery attempts were made, but this proved fruitless. The Finns managed to obtain photos of the wreck, which alerted the Germans that some new monster tank was in the works.

The combat in Finland confirmed the state trials, and on 19 December 1939 the KV was accepted for service as the Red Army's new heavy tank. Problems fighting the Finnish bunkers led to a requirement for a bunker-busting version, so the first batch of KV tanks included a "small turret" KV and a "large turret" KV with a 152mm howitzer; these were later renamed as the KV-1 and KV-2. The KV tanks were the most thickly armored tanks of their day. The basic frontal armor was 75mm, but this was soon upgraded with 25mm appliqué. Unlike the T-34, this armor was not steeply angled. Nevertheless, it was more than adequate against contemporary German tank guns. In terms of firepower, the KV-1 was much the same as the T-34. It started with a short 76mm gun but by 1941 had switched to the ZiS-5, a version of the F-34 gun on the T-34 using a different gun mount. The KV was powered by the same engine as the T-34 but was less mobile because of its heavier weight. The main technical

The most powerful version of the KV fielded in 1941 was the KV-2, an artillery fire-support variant fitted with a 152mm howitzer in a massive turret. This particular example was shipped back to Germany for further inspection, and in April 1945 it was hastily put back into service for defense of the Krupp plant in Essen against the U.S. Army's 79th Division.

problem facing the KV was its very poor transmission design, which relied on 1930s American tractor technology. A German training course at Wunsdorf in early 1942 summarized the Wehrmacht's assessment of captured KVs, which largely concurred with the view of Russian commanders: "Mechanically, this tank is a poor job. Gears can only be shifted and engaged at the halt, so the maximum speed of 35 km per hour is an illusion. The clutch is too lightly constructed. Almost all abandoned tanks had clutch problems."

Little Klim

Of the trio of new Soviet tanks, the T-50 infantry tank was the greatest disappointment. It was developed by the design bureau at Plant No. 174 that had previously designed the T-26 light tank and employed a hull design patterned after the T-34 with a steeply sloped glacis plate. Its suspension was the new torsion bar type. Armor was good, with a 37mm glacis plate and turret front. Armament was the same 45mm gun as in previous light tanks. The T-50 was nicknamed "Little Klim" due to its resemblance to a smaller KV-1. The prototypes entered trials in early 1940, but production did not begin until July 1941. Due to the chaos following the German invasion, only sixty were manufactured in 1941 and fifteen more in 1942. Although it was a very good design, T-50 production was halted since it was a complicated and expensive tank. It was inferior in combat value to the T-34, and as a result the Red Army decided in late 1941 to standardize the T-34 for both the infantry and cavalry tank roles.

One of the most obscure new Soviet tanks was the T-50 infantry tank, intended to replace the ubiquitous T-26. It proved too expensive to manufacture, so the T-34 performed both the cavalry and infantry tank roles. This particular example was knocked out by the Finnish army in Karelia and later put into Finnish army service. SA-KUVA

The T-40 was a new amphibious tank, but like the T-50 its production ended after the start of war to concentrate on a smaller variety of tanks.

OPERATION BARBAROSSA

The Wehrmacht launched Operation Barbarossa on 22 June 1941. The Red Army was unprepared for the attack, as Stalin adamantly refused to believe the growing intelligence data that suggested a German attack was imminent. It was one of the greatest military disasters of all times.

In terms of tank fighting, the new T-34 and KV tanks represented only about a tenth of Soviet tank strength. The vast bulk of the Red Army tank force was made up of older T-26 light tanks and BT cavalry tanks. They were vulnerable to the German 37mm tank guns, and even more so to the new 50mm tank gun. The readiness of the older tanks varied and was their principal Achilles heel; the situation was worsened by inadequate training of the inexperienced tank crews.

The Red Army attempted to monitor the readiness of its tank force by keeping track of "motor hours," the number of hours the tank had been used. At specified times, the tanks were supposed to be sent back to military district workshops for "medium maintenance," and at another point they were to be sent back to special factories for "capital rebuilding."[7] The number of motor hours varied by tank type, as the chart below shows.

The Red Army categorized tank readiness in five categories, from 1 to 5, with 1 being new and 5 being retired for scrapping. In the western military districts that bore the brunt of the 1941 fighting, there were 12,782 tanks, of which 2,157 (17 percent) were new (Category 1), 8,383 (66 percent) were operational with minor maintenance issues (Category 2), and the rest (18 percent) in need medium maintenance or capital rebuilding.[8] The most problematic of these was Category 2. Even though the bulk of the older tanks in this category were nominally ready for action, in fact many were mechanically exhausted with excessive engine hours. Furthermore, spare parts were often lacking, meaning that even minor shortcomings such as damaged tracks left the tanks inoperable or prone to rapid breakdown. On average, Soviet tanks had already accumulated about half their engine time on the eve of the war, making them very susceptible to breakdown after typical long road marches to the battle zone.

After the fall of France in June 1940, the Red Army had reorganized its tank forces into thirty massive mechanized corps, trying to emulate the successful German Panzer Korps. The reorganization was only partly complete when the Wehrmacht struck. The new mechanized corps were too large and cumbersome in view of the available means of command and control and the poor state of senior army leadership. Stalin had purged the Soviet officer corps in 1937, leading to a profound gap in trained combat leaders. Less than a quarter of Soviet corps commanders and less than a third of Soviet division commanders had been in their positions for more than a year.[9]

SOVIET TANK MAINTENANCE (MOTOR HOURS)

Type	Medium Maintenance	Capital Rebuilding
T-27, T-37, T-38 scout tanks	200	800
T-26 light tank	150	600
BT-2, BT-5 cavalry tank	150	450
BT-7 cavalry tank	200	600
T-28 medium tank	200	400
T-35 heavy tank	150	300

The combat debut for the PzKpfw III with the 50mm gun was in Yugoslavia in April 1941, a prelude to the Russian campaign. This is a column from *11.Panzer-Division*; the second tank is a Panzerbefehlswagen command tank.

The Czech-built PzKpfw 38(t) was an essential ingredient in the mechanization of the German cavalry divisions. This is a column of *Panzer-Regiment.25*, *7.Panzer-Division*, near Kalvarija, Lithuania, at the beginning of Operation Barbarossa on 22 June 1941.

TANK STRENGTH IN RED ARMY MECHANIZED CORPS, 22 JUNE 1941[10]						
Mechanized Corps	**Tank Divisions**	**Mechanized Divisions**	**Military District**	**T-34**	**KV**	**Tanks**
1	1, 3	163	Leningrad	8	15	1,039
2	11, 16	15	Odessa	50	10	527
3	2, 5	84	Baltic	50	78	672
4	8, 32	81	Kiev	313	121	979
5	13, 17	109	Transbaikal	10	7	1,187
6	4, 7	29	Western	238	114	1,021
7	14, 18	1	Moscow	29	34	959
8	12, 34	7	Kiev	115	71	932
9	20, 35	131	Kiev			316
10	21, 24	198	Leningrad			469
11	29, 33	204	Western	28	3	414
12	23, 28	202	Baltic			730
13	25, 31	208	Western			282
14	22, 30	205	Western			518
15	10, 37	212	Kiev	91	64	749
16	15, 39	240	Kiev	65	11	608
17	27, 36	209	Western			63
18	44, 47	218	Odessa			282
19	40, 43	213	Kiev	6	5	454
20	26, 38	210	Western			94
21	42, 46	185	Moscow			175
22	19, 41	215	Kiev		31	712
23	48, 51	220	Orel	14	7	413
24	45, 49	216	Kiev			222
25	50, 55	219	Kharkov	20	4	300
26	52, 56	103	North Caucasus			184
27	9, 53	221	Central Asia			356
28	6, 54	236	Transcaucasus			869
30	58, 60	239	Far East			
Other	57, 59, 61	69, 82				
Total				***1,037***	***575***	***15,526***

A PzKpfw III with the new long 50mm gun in action with *Panzer-Abteilung 40* in Finland on 1 July 1941.

The 1940 Battle of France made clear the need for thicker frontal armor on German tanks. The PzKpfw III Ausf. H introduced additional 30mm plates on the hull front, which was proof against the Soviet 45mm tank and antitank guns. This tank served with *Panzer-Abteilung 40* on the Finnish Front in the summer of 1941. SA-KUVA

In regard to the rank-and-file Soviet tank crews, small unit training in 1940–41 was perfunctory and there was a tendency to limit small unit tank exercises and live-fire exercises for economic reasons and to reduce the wear and tear on the vehicles. Even though the Red Army had a tank force more than six times larger than the German panzer force, it was a paper tiger. It was built around mechanically fragile tanks operated by poorly trained and inexperienced crews and led by partially trained commanders whose battlefield initiative was crippled by a corrosive and brutal political system.

The border battles in June–July 1941 were an unmitigated disaster for the Red Army tank forces.

Massive tank battles broke out in the Baltic region and in Ukraine, leading to the decimation of the Soviet mechanized corps by their much more experienced panzer opponents. Nevertheless, the new Soviet T-34 and KV tanks came as a nasty surprise to the Wehrmacht, most especially to the infantrymen who were still depending on the old 37mm gun for antitank defense.

A typical encounter occurred along the Stir River in Ukraine in the first days of the war during the advance of *Schützen-Brigade.16* of the *16.Panzer-Division*. A single T-34 emerged and drove toward the position of the German 37mm antitank guns. A German account of the incident recalled the event:

> Range 100 meters. The Russian tank continued to advance. Fire! A hit. And another hit. And more hits. The men counted them: 21, 22, 23 times the 37mm rounds smacked against the steel colossus. But the projectiles simply bounced off. The gunners screamed with fury. The battery commander was pale with tension. The range was down to 20 meters. Aim at the turret ring! the lieutenant ordered. They finally had him. The tank scurried around and retreated. The turret ring was damaged and the turret immobilized but it was otherwise unscathed . . . hereafter the 37mm gun was contemptuously nicknamed "the army's door-knocker."[11]

At the same time, the T-34's impressive technical qualities were undermined by serious shortcomings in Red Army training and tactics. The T-34 also had some significant, if underappreciated flaws. As the encounter above suggests, the T-34 tank crew had very poor situational awareness on the battlefield. The tank had a two-man crew of gunner and loader. The commander could serve in either role, though often as gunner since it required a greater level of training. When serving as gunner, the commander had to concentrate on firing the gun, often limited in vision to the telescopic sight, which gave him a narrow soda-straw view of the battlefield. The optical quality of Soviet tank sights was inferior to their German counterparts after key optics factories were evacuated in 1941. A Soviet tank commander recalled, "We always recognized the high quality of the Zeiss gunsights . . . We had nothing like that."[12] The vision devices on Soviet tanks tended to be of poor quality. The German assessment from captured tanks was that "Facilities for observation are worse than in our tanks. The driver's vision is incredibly bad." The hatch on the early versions of the T-34 was supposed to be fitted with a special panoramic periscope that could be turned 360 degrees. In fact, most tanks lacked this feature. Unlike German tanks, the T-34 commander could not observe from an open hatch. The one piece "pirozhok" hatch opened forward and was so large that it exposed both turret crewmen. To operate the T-34 with the turret hatch open was to invite disaster.

The T-34 transmission and clutch, while much better than the KV, was still difficult for a poorly trained crewman to operate. A Soviet report candidly noted that:

> To avoid difficulties in shifting gears during combat, inexperienced driver-mechanics would select 2nd (starter) gear and take off the engine governor. Then the diesel would rev up to 2,300 RPM, which was good for up to 25 km/h, and maneuver the tank by means of decreasing or increasing RPM. This was done without any consideration of the engine life: of course they quickly failed as a result of this bad habit."[13]

The German panzer force had its share of one-sided encounters with the new Soviet tanks, and had to use superior tactics and training to overcome the technical shortcomings of their Panzers. One tactic that would become a hallmark of German tank fighting in the early years of the war was using combined-arms tactics when confronting heavily armored enemy tanks that could not be knocked out by the inadequate German tank guns. These tactics were first developed in France against the French Char B1 bis and British Matilda tanks. The German tanks would feign retreat but radio to German 105mm field gun batteries or 88mm Flak batteries about their withdrawal. The Soviet tanks would follow in hot pursuit, only to run into an alert gun battery that would pummel them with direct fire.

Due to mistaken intelligence about German antitank guns, there was a program in 1941 before the start of the war to reinforce the KV-1's already formidable armor with an additional 35mm plate. This example was knocked out on the Finnish Front on 1 September 1941. Several gouges from antitank rounds can be seen on the turret front.

The KV-1 underwent three changes in its main gun in 1941. Following the original short L-11 76mm gun, the intermediate version was this F-32 76mm gun. Later in the year, it was supplanted by the ZIS-5, a version of the same F-34 gun used on the T-34. This particular tank was knocked out on the Finnish Front on 19 September 1941. A very thick piece of appliqué armor has been added to the front of the turret. SA-KUVA

A pair of T-28 medium tanks in a counterattack during the summer 1941 campaign.

The KVs and T-34s also played a significant role in the fighting for "the Bloody Triangle" during the titanic tank battles around Brody-Dubno in Ukraine in the final week of June 1941.[14] The KV tanks, though prone to mechanical problems, were nearly invulnerable in tank-versus-tank combat. General Major Morgunov, the armored force commander in Ukraine in 1941, wrote in a secret report: "Special mention should be made of the good work of the 4th, 8th and 15th Mechanized Corps who showed that a single KV tank was worth 10 to 14 enemy tanks in battle."[15]

Army commanders, appreciating the near invulnerability of the KV, pleaded for more. Lt. Gen. A. Yeremenko reported that:

> Handled by brave men, the KV tanks can do wonders. In the sector of the 107th Motorized Infantry Division we sent a KV to silence an enemy anti-tank battery. It squashed the artillery, rolled up and down the enemy's gun emplacements, was hit more than 200 times, but the armor was not penetrated even though it had been the target of guns of all types. Often our tanks went out of action due to the hesitant and unsure conduct of their crews rather than direct hits. For this reason we subsequently manned the KV tanks with hand-picked crews.

In spite of the exceptional performance of the T-34 and KV tanks on many individual occasions, the overall impact of the new tanks on the 1941 campaign was disappointing. Their technical superiority could not overcome the profound tactical and operational shortcomings of the Red Army in the summer of 1941. Red Army commanders singled out several reasons for the problems with the new tanks. Most serious was the general lack of training of the crews. A report from Ukraine on 8 July 1941 noted:

> There were exceptionally great losses of KV-2 tanks in the 41st Tank Division. Of the

31 tanks available to the division, by 6 July 1941 only 9 remain. The enemy knocked out five, twelve were blown up by their own crews, and five were sent for major repairs. The heavy losses of the KV tanks are attributable primarily to the poor technical training of the crews, by their poor knowledge of the tank systems, as well as by an absence of spare parts. When the crews were unable to eliminate malfunctions on stalled KV tanks, there were many occasions when they had to blow them up.

The commander of the well-equipped 8th Mechanized Corps, Gen. Lt. D. I. Ryabyshev, echoed these views:

From 22 to 26 June 1941, we carried out movements much beyond normal forced marches without being able to observe the elementary prescribed requirements for maintaining equipment and resting personnel. The equipment arrived at the battlefield after having covered distances of 500 km. As a result of this, 40 to 50% of the tanks were broken down for technical reasons . . . and abandoned on the routes of march of the division. As the consequence of such rapid marches, the remaining tanks were technically unprepared for combat.

The lack of durability of the older Soviet tanks was evident even away from the main battle front. One of the more obscure campaigns from the summer of 1941 was Operation Compassion (*Operatsiya Sochuvstvie*), the Soviet element of the Anglo-Russian invasion of Iran in August–September 1941. The aim was to depose the pro-German Shah in order to provide a route for shipping supplies to the Red Army. The largest tank element of the Red

A T-34 Model 1941 on the Western Front moves into action under the watchful eye of a 45mm Model 1932 antitank gun crew.

Army contingent was the 28th Mechanized Corps, which contained two tank divisions, both equipped with the T-26 tank and totaling 869 light tanks and 131 flamethrower tanks. There were additional tank sub-units attached to various rifle and cavalry units. The Soviet advance was not strongly opposed, but the Red Army was plagued by repair problems. After an advance of about 700 kilometers in less than a week, about 35 percent of the tanks had broken down and required depot or factory rebuilding. In some units, for example the 24th Tank Regiment, half of the tanks were nonoperational after four days of road marches.

ASSESSING THE SUMMER CAMPAIGN

In spite of overwhelming numerical and staggering qualitative superiority, the Soviet tank force was decisively defeated by the much smaller and more modestly equipped German tank force in the summer of 1941. The roots of this defeat are connected mainly in the Red Army's lack of preparedness for war, exacerbated by the corrosive influences of the purges of the officer ranks in the late 1930s. From a technological standpoint, the defeat highlighted shortcomings in Soviet tank design philosophy, which stressed the holy trinity of tank design—armor, firepower, and mobility—to the exclusion of other key tank-fighting features. Crew layout was poor; the turret layouts prevented the commander from executing his command functions due to the distractions of serving as gunner. The commander was not provided with adequate vision devices, and the hatch designs made it impossible for him to ride

SOVIET TANK LOSSES IN 1941 BY CAMPAIGN[16]

Operation	Period	Losses	Avg. Loss Per Day
Baltic defensive operation	22 June–9 July 1941	2,523	140
Belorussian defensive operation	22 June–9 July 1941	4,799	267
Western Ukraine defensive operation	22 June–6 July 1941	4,381	292
Karelian operation vs. Finland	29 June–10 Oct. 1941	546	5
Kiev defensive operation	7July–26 Sept. 1941	411	5
Leningrad defensive operation	10 July–30 Sept. 1941	1,492	18
Smolensk operation	10 July–10 Sept. 1941	1,348	21
Donbas-Rostov defensive operation	29 Sept.–16 Nov. 1941	101	2
Moscow defensive operation	30 Sept.–5 Dec. 1941	2,785	42
Tikhvin offensive	10 Nov.–30 Dec. 1941	70	1.4
Rostov offensive	17 Nov.–2 Dec. 1941	42	3
Moscow offensive	5 Dec. 1941–7 Jan. 1942	429	13
Subtotal (listed campaigns)		18,927	
Total	***22 June–31 Dec. 1941***	***20,500***	***108***

with his head outside the tank, the German practice to gain situational awareness.

Soviet tank commanders, already hampered by inadequate training, were overwhelmed with the simple mechanics of operating the tank. They were unable to exploit terrain or determine the location and status of friend or foe around them. This meant that Soviet tank crews were hindered in carrying out cooperative battlefield tactics, making them vulnerable to the better-coordinated German tank units. The Soviets did not fully appreciate the revolutionary implications of radio technology on the command and control of tank units. This was in part due to a Soviet mistrust of radio communications stemming from the disastrous results of poor Russian radio security in the 1905 war with Japan and the 1914 battles with Germany. More Soviet tanks were fitted with radios than is generally appreciated. For example, of the 7,485 T-26 gun tanks in service in 1941, 3,440 (46 percent) had radios. However, they were often in poor repair, had fragile antennas, and depended on telegraphic communication at longer ranges in an army chronically short of skilled crews. The radio shortcomings had a synergistic effect with the poor command-and-control features of the tank, leading to abysmal tank tactics.

OPERATION TYPHOON: A SHIFTING BALANCE

By late summer, the Soviet armored force had suffered staggering losses and there were few T-34s and KVs still operational. On 15 July, STAVKA (Soviet High Command) was obliged to recognize the obvious and disband the cumbersome mechanized corps. Total Soviet tank losses during 1941 were about 20,500, of which around 15,000 had been lost in the catastrophic summer fighting. In place of the mechanized corps, the STAVKA created tank brigades as the largest tactical armored formation. These new brigades were organized around a tank regiment and a motor rifle battalion with a nominal strength of 93 tanks. The tank regiment included a company of 7 KV tanks and a company of 22 T-34 tanks; the remainder of the unit was filled out with whatever light tanks were available. For the Red Army, it was back to the basics of mechanized warfare.

By the autumn of 1941, the German panzer force had become badly worn out. From its starting strength of 3,400 tanks in June 1941, the panzer force on the Russian Front had been reduced to about 2,300 on 10 September 1941, of which only about half were actually operational and the rest in repair. Facing them on the Red Army's Western and Bryansk Fronts were only about 720 tanks, of which only 134 were T-34 tanks. In a panic, Moscow was mobilizing its reserves for the defense of the capital.[17]

The next major objective was Moscow itself, but the long summer road marches and the lack of replacement tanks and spare parts left most of the panzer divisions at only a shadow of their original strength. Exacerbating their problems was the onset of the rainy autumn weather, dubbed *rasputitsa* in Russia, the season of bad roads. Russian roads and fields turned into a morass of mud, making tank maneuver difficult and sometimes impossible. The T-34 and KV, designed to operate in Russian conditions by the use of wide tracks, were far less vulnerable to becoming bogged down in the mud. The first signs of Soviet recovery began to appear on the approaches to Moscow. New tank brigades were seen with alarming frequency. By the middle of October 1941, the Soviet tank forces on the approaches to Moscow numbered fewer than 600 tanks, but about 260 were the new T-34s and KVs. On 6 October 1941, the *4.Panzer-Division* engaged in a violent skirmish with the newly arrived 4th Tank Brigade near the town of Mtsensk on the southern approaches to Moscow. The T-34 tanks took advantage of their mobility in the mud and after a day's fighting claimed to have knocked out 43 German tanks. Gen. Heinz Guderian later recalled about the battle that:

> The enemy sent in a large number of T-34 tanks which inflicted significant losses on

> our tanks. The superiority of the material units with our tank forces which were in place at that time were also lost and taken by the enemy. This shattered the idea that we would be able to achieve quick and continuous victories.

During the summer fighting, the T-34 had been a nuisance, but the shortcomings in crew training and Soviet tactics diluted its combat effectiveness. The fighting for Mtsensk gave the clearest evidence that in the hands of better crews and unit commanders, the T-34 had become a major threat. The success of Col. Mikhail Katukov's 4th Tank Brigade led to its redesignation with the honorific title the 1st Guards Tank Brigade. Katukov would later go on to lead Soviet tank corps and tank armies and become one of the most famous Soviet tank commanders of the war.

During the Moscow Defensive Operation (30 September–5 December 1941), the Red Army lost 2,785 tanks but managed to stop the German advance on the outskirts of the city. It was the first major defeat for the Wehrmacht in Russia. The German army had demonstrated its Russian Front tactical and operational excellence against the Red Army in 1941, but by the end of 1941 Barbarossa had proven to be a strategic failure. The Red Army had not been knocked out, and the Wehrmacht now faced a prolonged war for which it was ill-prepared.

A column of T-34 tanks of Col. Mikhail Katukov's 4th Tank Brigade in action around Moscow. In November 1941, it was redesignated as the 1st Guards Tank Brigade due to its outstanding performance in stopping the German advance on Moscow.

1941 CAMPAIGN TALLY

Of the 22,000 Soviet tanks that had existed at the outset of Barbarossa, there were only 2,200 in front-line service at the beginning of 1942.[18] Total Soviet tank losses in 1941 were about 20,500. In contrast, German tank losses on the Russian Front in 1941 were about 3,000, a seven-fold difference. While there has been a tendency to attribute the high Soviet tank losses to the proficiency of German panzer divisions, this is not supported by Soviet records. Although there are no comprehensive records on the causes of Soviet tank losses in 1941, the evidence presented by the after-action reports of the Soviet mechanized corps suggests that more than half of Soviet tank losses were due to mechanical breakdowns and the abandonment of damaged or bogged-down tanks. The percentage of tanks lost to mechanical failure may have been even higher.

GERMAN AFV LOSSES ON THE RUSSIAN FRONT IN 1941 BY TYPE[19]

Type	Losses
PzKpfw I	428
PzKpfw II	424
PzKpfw III	660
PzKpfw IV	348
PzKpfw 35 and 38(t)	796
StuG III	96
PzBefelsWg	155
Other tanks	20
Total	***2,927***

GERMAN TANK LOSSES IN 1941 BY MONTH[20]

June	July	Aug.	Sept.	Oct.	Nov.	Dec.	Total
135	749	646	258	339	391	547	3,065

TOP TANK OF 1941

The laurels for Tanker's Choice and Commander's Choice on the Russian Front in 1941 undoubtedly go to the T-34 Model 1941 tank. It was such a revolutionary step forward in tank technology that it merits both awards. The battles in Russia demonstrated that the locus of tank technology had shifted from its traditional centers in England and France eastward toward Germany and the Soviet Union. The emergence of the T-34 ignited a technological arms race between Germany and the Soviet Union that set the pace for worldwide tank development throughout World War II.

While the performance of the T-34 in the summer 1941 fighting had been unimpressive, its inherent combat capabilities helped to provide the backbone for the renaissance of the Soviet tank force that started in the autumn of 1941. Without a superior tank in 1941, the Red Army would have had a difficult time reaching tactical parity with the German panzer forces on the approaches to Moscow.

Another reason that the T-34 was a clear winner in 1941 was because of the lingering mediocrity of German tank designs of this period. The German battlefield advantages were largely in crew experience and superior tactical performance despite the quality of their tanks. The best tank for tank-versus-tank fighting, the PzKpfw III, still had a gun that was barely capable of dealing with the new Soviet tanks, while at the same time its high-explosive firepower was modest. The PzKpfw IV,

The T-34 tanks fielded in the summer of 1941 had a far higher manufacturing quality than those a year later. As casting facilities became available, some of the T-34 Model 41 tanks had a cast turret in place of the more common welded turret, as seen on this example.

although having good high-explosive firepower, had poor antitank performance since that was not its role. The armor of the PzKpfw III and PzKpfw IV was adequate but unexceptional. German tank durability was better than that of Soviet tanks, but the shortage of spare parts and an overstretched logistical infrastructure left a large portion of German tanks immobile at any given time during the autumn 1941 campaign. As the hard winter weather enveloped central Russia in the winter of 1941–42, the panzer force became an icebound ghost, seldom present on the battlefield. A German report put tank strength in January 1942 at only 1,015, a third of the force starting Operation Barbarossa. Its operational strength was close to 0 due to mechanical problems.[21] Six panzer divisions reporting on operational strength in January 1942 counted barely 60 functional tanks in total.

COMPARATIVE TECHNICAL CHARACTERISTICS

	PzKpfw III Ausf. H	T-34 Model 41	KV-1
Army	Germany	USSR	USSR
Crew	5	4	5
Dimensions: L x W x H (m)	5.41 x 2.95 x 2.44	5.92 x 3.0 x 2.4	6.9 x 3.32 x 2.71
Loaded weight (tonnes)	21.5	28	47.5
Main gun	50mm KwK 39	76.2mm F-34	76.2mm ZIS-5
Main gun ammo	99	77	114
Engine (hp)	300	500	500
Max. speed (km/h)	40	55	35
Fuel (liters)	320	460 + 134	615
Range (km)	155	250	225
Ground pressure (kg/cm^2)	0.92	0.72	0.77
Armor*			
Mantlet (mm)	50**=>50	45**=>45	82**=>82
Turret front (mm)	30@15=31.1	45**=>45	82**=>82
Turret side (mm)	30@25=33.1	45@20=47.9	82@15=84.9
Upper hull front (mm)	50@9=50.8	45@60=90	75@30=86.6
Lower hull front (mm)	50@21=53.2	45@53=73.1	75@8= 75.7
Upper hull side (mm)	30@0=30	45@40=58.7	75@0=75

*Armor data provided as: actual thickness in mm @ angle from vertical = effective thickness in mm.
**Curved

CHAPTER 5

Russian Front Slug Fest: 1942

LIKE TWO PUNCH-DRUNK BOXERS, the German and Soviet tank forces staggered to their corners in early 1942 to prepare for the next round. Both sides had major technical challenges to face in the new year.

RED ARMY: QUANTITY VS. QUALITY

For the Red Army, the primary challenge was to keep the tank factories operating to provide new tanks. The two major centers of the Soviet tank industry, Leningrad and Kharkov, were out of the game. Leningrad, the center for KV production, had been surrounded and cut off from supplies of steel and other vital material. Kharkov, the center of T-34 production, had been captured by the Germans at the end of October 1941.

There had been plans underway even before the June 1941 invasion to establish new tank plants deeper inside Russia. The Stalingrad Tractor Plant (STZ: *Stalingradskiy traktorskiy zavod*) began to manufacture the T-34 in 1941 and would bear the burden in early 1942 until the Wehrmacht appeared on its doorstep. The Kharkov tank plant had established a spin-off plant in Nizhni-Tagil in the Urals region in 1941, and the T-34 design bureau along with many of the workers and machine tools had been evacuated there prior to the fall of Kharkov. Likewise, the center for KV development and production was moved from Leningrad to Cheyabinsk to a new heavy industrial facility later nicknamed Tankograd. Other plants in the Urals were also converted to tank production. Plant No. 112 in Gorkiy (now Nizhni-Novgorod) began manufacturing the T-34 in late 1941; the Uralmashzavod in

Sverdlovsk and Plant No. 174 in Omsk started in 1942. Four smaller automotive plants that could not handle medium tanks were given the task of building new light tanks such as the T-60.

To maximize tank production, the GABTU (Main Auto-Armored Technical Directorate) ruthlessly simplified production. Design changes that achieved this goal were permitted, but improvements that cost time or money were deliberately suppressed. Prior to the outbreak of the war, the Red Army had received samples of the German PzKpfw III Ausf. G during the short-lived German-Soviet alliance of 1939–41. The Red Army decided to adopt some of the better features of the PzKpfw III into a new version of the T-34 called the T-34M or A-43. This included the replacement of the T-34's Christie suspension with a modern torsion bar suspension and the redesign of the turret with an all-vision cupola and three-man crew. In the event, the T-34M design was temporarily abandoned due to the disruption it would have caused.

Another example is the original 1941 version of the F-34 76.2mm tank gun, which had 861 parts; the 1942 production version had only 614. Production time of the T-34 was cut in half and the cost was driven down from 269,500 rubles in 1941 to 193,000 in 1942. Stalingrad's STZ plant introduced new construction techniques including interlocking armor plate to simplify production. Shortages of rubber led to the design of a new road wheel that eliminated the rubber outer rim in favor of a smaller rubber shock absorber within the hub, dubbed the "steam-locomotive wheel" for its crudity. This only added to the din and noise in the fighting compartment, and even German tankers noted how it became easier to discover the approach of Soviet tanks due to the noise of the new wheels. Some plants that still had modest supplies of rubber on

After receiving a PzKpfw III from Germany in 1940 as part of the Hitler-Stalin Pact, the Red Army planned to completely revamp the T-34 in late 1941 as the T-34M with a new three-man turret and torsion bar suspension patterned after the German configuration, as shown in this model. The program was dropped in late 1941 due to the urgency to maintain high production levels.

A KV-1 Model 41 on the Southwestern Front in the spring of 1942 with a burning PzKpfw IV in the background. The political slogan on the turret is "Za Rodinu!" (For the Homeland).

The loss of the main T-34 plant at Kharkov in 1941 shifted the focus to the new Stalingrad Tractor Plant (STZ) at the end of 1941 into early 1942. This T-34, in action in the summer of 1942, was built at the STZ plant with the expedient "locomotive wheels" adopted due to a lack of rubber.

LABOR SAVINGS AT SOVIET TANK FACTORIES, 1942–43[1]

Product	Plant	Man-hours, 1 Jan. 1942	Man-hours, 1 Jan. 1943	Reduction in Man-hours (%)
T-34	No. 183	5,300	3,719	30
T-34	No. 112	9,000	5,520	39
T-34	No. 174	8,092	7,205	11
T-34 hull and turret	No. 183	1,600	1,381	14
T-34 hull and turret	No. 112	3,400	1,980	42
V-2 engine	Kirov Plant	1,933	1,420	27

hand tried to remedy the situation by putting a rubber-rimmed wheel on the first and last station, using the "locomotive wheels" only in the center; this started in March 1942 at the main Nizhni-Tagil plant and spread to some other plants as supplies of rubber resumed. The Gorkiy plant substituted the old M-17T gasoline engine for the V-2 diesel for a short time in early 1942 due to engine shortages.

The efforts to simplify production gradually paid off in reducing the effort required to manufacture the T-34 tank, as can be seen from the chart above.

One of the few improvements allowed in T-34 production was the introduction of a new hexagonal turret at the Nizhni-Tagil plant in early 1942. The original plan in November 1941 was to manufacture the Gaika (hex-nut) turret from welded armor plate. Instead, when production started in the spring of 1942, the new Gaika turret used casting since it was easier to manufacture. Stalingrad continued to manufacture tanks with the older small welded design while Gorkiy shifted to the use of a cast turret of the older small design. Uralmash had access to a large hydraulic press that had been purchased from Germany before the war and manufactured a version of the Nizhni-Tagil Gaika turret using stamping rather than casting, a process unique in World War II tank construction.

The downside of the factory simplification programs was a continuing decline in tank quality and durability. The Soviet labor force decreased in quality because experienced male employees were drafted into the army and replaced by inexperienced women and boys. The pressure to produce more and more tanks led to shortcuts that impacted quality. There was a severe decline in the quality of cast armor for T-34 turrets in 1942. The intercrystalline fractures in 1942 were damaging 50–90 percent of the turrets from the Ural Tank Factory and 20–55 percent at the Uralmashzavod. These problems were not fully overcome until the spring of 1943.[2] In mid-1942, various size cracks were found in the rolled armor plate of up to 45 percent of the armored hulls produced at Nizhni-Tagil and up to 89 percent at the Uralmashzavod. By the end of the year the size of the cracks had been reduced and the number of defective hulls was down to about 10 percent, but the problem was not completely eliminated prior to the end of the war.

During the fighting in the summer of 1942, these problems became extremely evident and led to bitter complaints from tank units at the front. The areas of greatest concern were the power-plant and transmission. The overall durability of the V-2 diesel engine fell from the prewar standard of 300 hours to only about 100 hours in 1942, and often even worse. There were reports that V-2 diesel engines operating in the dusty air of southern Russia needed repair after only 10–15 hours of operation and failed after 30–50 hours.[3] The T-34 had a nominal warranty of 1,000 kilometers of operation before failures, but the head of the GABTU tank administration, Gen. Ya. N. Fedorenko, admitted

The only changes permitted on the T-34 were those that sped up production. The Gaika (hex-nut) turret was introduced at the Nizhni-Tagil plant in early 1942. This is the first known photo of this type in combat; the one seen here was knocked out by Finnish forces in Karelia on 19 April 1942. SA-KUVA

An interior view inside a T-34 Gaika turret from the loader's side on the right. The Gaika turret was more spacious than the earlier T-34 turret but still offered poor exterior vision for the crew.

Even though Nizhni-Tagil partly switched to the Gaika turret in early 1942, other plants continued to manufacture T-34 with the earlier small turret. Plant No. 112 in Krasnoye Sormovo used this pattern of cast turret, seen here on a tank burned out during the fighting on the Southwestern Front in the summer of 1942.

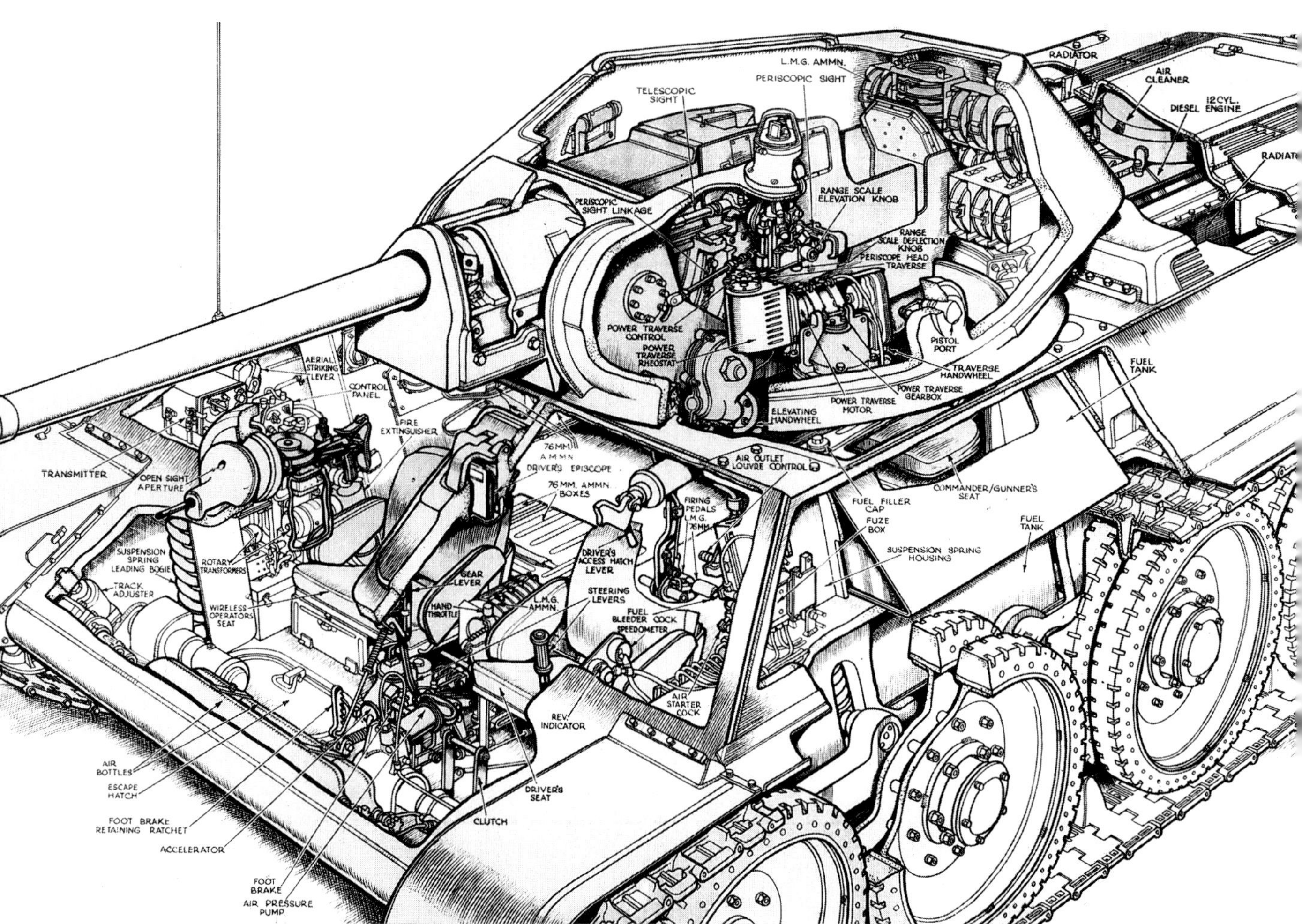

An excellent technical illustration of the T-34 interior layout. This was based on one of two Nizhni-Tagil T-34 tanks manufactured in June 1942 and delivered to Britain and the United States. Both tanks were preserved after the war, one at the Aberdeen Proving Ground Museum in Maryland and the other at Tank Museum at Bovington, United Kingdom.

that in 1942 the average was closer to 200 kilometers. A hand-picked T-34 delivered to the United States in 1942 went 343 kilometers before breaking down during trials at Aberdeen Proving Ground. Engine life for a V-2 diesel engine was 72 hours from a T-34 and 66 hours for the example from a KV-1 during the Aberdeen tests.[4]

Part of this was due to problems with quality control of the engine manufacture, but it was exacerbated by the T-34's Pomon air filter system. When examining their Soviet Union–supplied T-34 in 1942, the American tank engineers at Aberdeen found the air filter to be completely ineffective in dusty conditions and an Achilles heel of the entire power-train. The situation became so bad that Stalin personally telephoned the designers of both the T-34 and KV. The reports indicated that, on average, Soviet tanks could barely reach 50 kilometers of travel before requiring repair work, while German tanks regularly exceeded 200 kilometers in the same conditions. For all their complaints about Lend-Lease tanks, Soviet engineers testing an American M3 medium tank found that it easily covered more than 1,600 kilometers before needing repair; once the worn track was replaced, it covered another 1,200 kilometers without an issue. An American army engineer discussing tank design requirements with a Soviet officer in 1942 was surprised that he expected the gun life of the 76mm on the T-34 to be about 20 rounds, no more than 50, "because tanks don't survive long enough to fire more"; the U.S. standard was 200–300 rounds.[5]

The Red Army stuck with the 76mm gun on both the T-34 and KV-1 through 1942. Like the

Germans, the Soviets developed tungsten-carbide HVAP projectiles for their antitank guns, starting with one for the 45mm antitank gun in April 1942. The BR-350P HVAP round for the 76mm tank gun was developed during the summer of 1942. However, there was no rush to put this into production since the existing ammunition was deemed adequate. The issue changed with the appearance of the first Tiger heavy tanks at the end of 1942. As a result, production of HVAP ammunition for the 76mm gun was delayed until April–May 1943.[6]

The Soviet concentration on mass production paid off. T-34 production rose from 454 tanks in January 1942 to 1,568 in December 1942. The Soviet tank inventory rose from 7,700 tanks in January 1942 to 20,600 tanks in January 1943, despite massive combat losses in 1942. This was in part due to continued production of inferior light tanks such as the T-60 and T-70 that could be manufactured at automotive plants without the machine tools to build the larger T-34 and KV tanks.[7]

German tank inventories rose much more modestly during the same period, from 4,896 to 5,648. The year 1942 saw the German and Soviet armored forces at their most equal. In terms of medium and heavy tanks, Soviet numerical advantage was slight and its technological edge was gradually worn away by German technical improvements.[8]

The other critical ingredient in combat effectiveness was the training and experience of the tank crews. In this regard, the Red Army had little opportunity to indulge in prolonged crew training due to the high levels of crew casualties and the voracious personnel demands of the many new tank formations. The prewar practice of training the tank crews within the unit in special training companies

The Chelyabinsk plant attempted to redeem the KV tank series by developing a lighter version called the KV-1S. Although it improved the overall performance, it decreased armor protection precisely at a point when improved German tank firepower was posing a greater threat to Soviet tanks.

was largely abandoned after the start of the war. New tank training regiments were set up, many near the tank factories, to train tank crews.[9] To speed up the process, in the spring of 1942 the Red Army sent out a notice that all troops who had been tractor drivers or who had driving licenses must be transferred to the new tank training units. On paper, the training program was four months long and included basic training followed by technical training. At the end of the training, the new crews were organized into platoons and companies and dispatched to a crash-course fifteen-day unit training exercise. This consisted of five days of crew drills, a three-day platoon familiarization course, and finally a four-day company exercise to learn offensive and defensive tactics. Resources were quite limited, so during the platoon exercise, the norm was only two and a half hours of actual tank driving, three live rounds of tank gun ammunition, and fifty rounds of machine-gun ammunition. With this course complete, the crews were sent to their new units. The Soviet training program was far less extensive than in the Wehrmacht.[10]

In 1942, Soviet crew training courses were frequently cut short due to urgent demands from the front, and there were not enough crews trained to fill out all of the positions. So for example, in 1942 some 34,664 tank crewmen were trained, but the new tanks manufactured in 1942 required more than 82,000 crewmen. This required units to fill positions with untrained troops. The limited training of the tank crews led to complaints from the front, and the programs were expanded considerably in later years.[11]

GERMANY: QUALITY OVER QUANTITY

The panzer force in Russia at the start of 1942 was a shadow of its glory days in the summer of 1941. The winter campaigns had been very hard on its worn-out tanks. There were about 1,015 tanks in service in Russia in January 1942, only a third of the strength at the start of the campaign in the summer of 1941. However, most of these tanks were broken down, and day-to-day operational strength varied from none to about 300 tanks. German tanks were not well suited to severe winter conditions and suffered from a host of mechanical defects.

Aside from addressing these durability issues, the Waffenamt had to finally deal with the mediocre armor and firepower of the panzers compared to their Soviet opponents. This was a three-step effort. To address the shortage of tanks, Hitler authorized the initiation of *Panzerprogramm* 1941, which gave greater industrial priority to tank production. Hopes of a short, victorious war had evaporated and Berlin finally recognized that preparations were needed for a grinding war of attrition. Three more tank assembly plants began to operate in 1942, and in February Hitler appointed Albert Speer as Reichsminister of Armaments and War Production to rationalize and expand the armaments industry.[12] Greater priority was given to panzer production, but even by the end of 1942 it constituted only 4.7 percent of German weapons production, lagging behind aircraft (36.3 percent) and warships and submarines (10.9 percent).[13]

In the short term, the existing PzKpfw III and PzKpfw IV would be the backbone of the panzer force, so they needed to be upgraded in armor and firepower. In the long term, new tanks were needed to overmatch the T-34 and KV. Work had been underway on a variety of new tank types, most of which were scrapped in favor of new designs better suited to the Russian Front. A new heavy breakthrough tank was in the works that would emerge late in 1942 as the Tiger. A new medium tank was also started to address the T-34 threat, but it would not be ready until the summer of 1943 as the Panther.

Vociferous complaints about the inability of German tank and antitank guns to penetrate the armor of the T-34 and KV led to a crash program to field better antitank weapons. The Waffenamt had been working on more powerful antitank guns since 1939, but the programs had low priority until the summer 1940 battles with the French Char B1 bis and British Matilda tanks. Although these encounters reinvigorated the programs, the start of production of the new 50mm PaK 38 antitank gun and the 50mm KwK for the PzKpfw III in the summer of 1940 misled many German commanders to believe that the issue was being addressed. The battles against the T-34 and KV in July 1941 made it clear that both weapons were inadequate. The new 50mm KwK gun on the PzKpfw III had a shorter barrel than the towed 50mm PaK 38 antitank gun, L/42 versus L/60. This directly affected performance, with the tank gun having a muzzle velocity of only 635 m/s compared to 835 m/s for the towed gun. This translated into inferior armor penetration using the standard *Pz.Gr.39*, 46mm versus 59mm.

Inferior versions of the gun were used due to the widespread belief in tank circles in the 1930s that tank guns should not overhang the front of the chassis for fear they would be prone to accidents that would damage the gun. This viewpoint was not peculiar just to the Wehrmacht but also to many other armies of the day and was the reason for the American Sherman tank's short gun. The new 50mm KwK 39 with a lengthened L/60 barrel had been ready in the summer of 1940, and there were plans to introduce it on the PzKpfw III Ausf. J starting in March 1941. The Waffenamt was complacent about the issue, believing that the L/42 version was perfectly adequate. When Hitler attended a weapon's demonstration on his birthday in April 1941, he noticed that the new PzKpfw III Ausf. J still had the short 50mm gun. In spite of his admonitions that it be replaced by the long L/60 gun, these did not enter production until December 1941. Russian accounts claim that this version began appearing in Russia during the December 1941 fight for Moscow, but in actuality they did not appear in any significant numbers until early 1942. As was the case with the towed version of the gun, the 50mm was not capable of penetrating the T-34 or KV frontally unless using the special *Pz.Gr.40* projectile with tungsten-carbide core. This ammunition type was limited due to the scarcity of tungsten carbide and amounted to only 8 percent of ammunition production in 1942–43.

Once they recognized the effectiveness of the new German tungsten-carbide ammunition, the Soviet government asked Britain and the United States to shut down supplies of the precious metal. Portugal was one of the main sources, and Britain managed to pressure the government into cutting back supplies. German army monthly consumption peaked at 155 tons in the second quarter of 1941 and fell to only 4 tons in the first quarter of 1942.[14]

The 50mm gun in its tank and antitank versions formed the backbone of German antitank weapons in the 1942 campaign. A Soviet study of the source

50MM GUN AMMUNITION PRODUCTION (IN THOUSANDS), 1942–45[15]

Projectile	Type	1942	1943	1944	1945
SprGr 38	HE	753.8	1,138.7	684.8	11.3
Pz.Gr.39	AP	644.5	1,186.6	410.1	28.7
Pz.Gr.40	HVAP	184.6	135.9	0	0
Total		***1,582.9***	***2,461.2***	***1,094.9***	***40.0***

SOURCE OF T-34 LOSSES TO GERMAN GUNS BY CALIBER (%), JUNE 1941–SEPTEMBER 1942

20mm	37mm	50 (Short)	50 (Long)	75mm	88mm	105mm	Unknown
4.7	10.0	7.5	54.3	10.1	3.4	2.9	7.1

GERMAN TANK GUNS, 1939–42[16]					
Caliber	**37mm**	**50mm**	**50mm**	**75mm**	**75mm**
Main gun	KwK	KwK	KwK 39	KwK 37	KwK 40
Caliber	37mm	50mm	50mm	75mm	75mm
Tube length	L/45	L/42	L/60	L/24	L/43
Armor-piercing projectile	*Pz.Gr.*	*Pz.Gr.39*	*Pz.Gr.39*	*Pz.Gr.*	*Pz.Gr.39*
Type	AP	APC	APC	APCBC	APCBC
Initial muzzle velocity (m/s)	745	685	835	385	740
Round weight (kg)	1.33	4.05	4.05	8.15	11.5
Projectile weight (kg)	0.685	2.06	2.06	6.8	6.8
Propellant weight (kg)	0.175	0.498	0.498	0.351	2.4
Penetration (mm; @500m, 30 degree)	29	47	59	38	91
Armor-piercing projectile (high-velocity)	*Pz.Gr.40*	*Pz.Gr.40*	*Pz.Gr.40*	Gr.38 H1/A	*Pz.Gr.40*
Type	HVAP	HVAP	HVAP	HEAT	HVAP
Initial muzzle velocity (m/s)	1,020	1,050	1,190	450	920
Round weight (kg)	1.305	2.8	2.8	5.9	8.8
Projectile weight (kg)	0.368	0.925	0.925	4.4	4.1
Propellant weight (kg)	0.15	0.544	0.544	0.357	2.7
Penetration (mm; @500m, 30 degree)	37	55	72	70	108
High-explosive projectile	Spr.Gr.18 umg	Srp.Gr.38	Spr.Gr.38	Spr.Gr.34	Spr.Gr.34
Projectile weight (kg)	0.615	1.86	1.86	5.74	5.74
Explosive fill (g)	28	166	166	653	653

of gunfire penetrations of the T-34 tank found that the long 50mm gun accounted for more than half of all penetrations.[17]

It was pointless to employ the tungsten-carbide ammunition for the short 75mm gun on the PzKpfw IV since it did not have enough velocity to make it an efficient penetrator. Instead, two approaches were taken. As an expedient, a new shaped-charge warhead was fielded, the Gr 38 H1/A. This was a new type of ammunition based on discoveries by Egon Neumann in 1910 that a high-explosive charge shaped around a copper cone would explosively propel the copper into a narrow hypersonic stream of particles that could penetrate armor plate.[18] This type of ammunition, now called HEAT (high-explosive antitank) was first issued to tanks on the Russian Front in January 1942, but its performance was erratic. For maximum effectiveness, it depended on the fuze detonating the warhead in the microseconds before the impact of the projectile against the enemy tank's armor crushed the copper cone. Since these early HEAT projectiles used a simple impact fuze, the cone was often damaged or deformed in the microseconds after impact before the fuze triggered the explosive, thereby substantially degrading its penetration power. Still, it was better than nothing. At short range, it could penetrate 75mm of armor compared to only 41mm of armor of a conventional 75mm armor-piercing round. Improved versions such as the Gr 38 H1/C, which appeared later in 1942, could penetrate about 100mm of armor, making it lethal against the T-34's frontal armor if it detonated properly.

The HEAT round for the short 75mm tank gun was obviously only an expedient, and so a second approach was taken. A longer and more powerful 75mm gun was needed to consistently penetrate the T-34 and KV at normal battle ranges. Since the PzKpfw III had a small turret race that could not accommodate much more recoil, this meant that such a weapon would be fitted to the PzKpfw IV. Instead of being the Wehrmacht's secondary support tank, the PzKpfw IV would become its main tank in the mid-war years, replacing the PzKpfw III.

The initial plan in May 1941 was to mount a tank version of the 50mm PaK 38 on the PzKpfw IV to improve its antitank performance. The 50mm KwK 39 was a longer (L/60) gun than the weapon then in use on the PzKpfw III Ausf. J (L/42). However, the first encounters with the T-34 and KV in June 1941 put a quick end to these plans. A new 75mm PaK 40 towed antitank gun already had entered production in response to the encounters with heavily armored French and British tanks in 1940. The first PaK 40 guns were manufactured in February 1941 shortly before the start of Operation Barbarossa and first deployed in April 1941. In view of the T-34 threat, the Waffenamt awarded Krupp a contract in November 1941 to develop a 75mm tank on a crash basis in cooperation with Rheinmetall. This gun had a shorter barrel than the towed Pak 40 (L/43 versus L/46) and used a shorter propellant cartridge better suited to loading inside a tank turret. The new 75mm KwK 40 tank gun was put into production on a crash basis on the PzKpfw IV F2 starting in March 1942. This offered a major step forward in German tank firepower, and it was able to penetrate 91mm of armor at 30 degrees at 500 meters using the normal *Pz.Gr.39* round and 108mm of armor using the tungsten-carbide *Pz.Gr.40* round. The growing importance of the PzKpfw IV was reflected in its production rate, with the monthly rate going from 40 tanks per month in 1940 to 65 tanks per month by the end of 1942.

While the main focus had been on increasing firepower to deal with the T-34 threat, the Waffenamt also pursued a gradual increase in tank armor. At the beginning of 1942, the standard frontal protection on the PzKpfw III Ausf. J was 30mm on the turret front and 50mm on the hull front. With the introduction of the PzKpfw III Ausf. L in June 1942, the gun mantlet was increased to 50mm plus a spaced 20mm appliqué, and the hull likewise increased with a 20mm spaced appliqué. The PzKpfw IV Ausf. G was upgraded with an additional 30mm of armor bolted to the existing 50mm armor starting in June 1942.

THE RED ARMY TANK FORCE IN THE 1942 CAMPAIGNS

At the beginning of 1942, the Red Army tank force was still based on small formations. The tank brigades, with a nominal strength of sixty-seven tanks each, were intended for independent action in support of corps and armies. The rifle divisions were supported by separate tank battalions or regiments, often equipped with older types such as the T-26 or BT tanks or with the newly arrived Lend-Lease tanks.[19] Tank brigade strength continued to drop through the winter due to production shortfalls and heavy combat losses. The official organization in December 1941 was only forty-six tanks, down to just twenty-seven in February 1942. Many brigades didn't even reach these official figures. Once the new tank plants came on line in the late winter of 1941–42, the tank brigades began to grow again. The April 1942 table had forty-six tanks: sixteen T-34s, ten KV-1, and twenty T-60 light tanks.

The senior Red Army commanders recognized that they needed larger combined-arms formations to have a decisive impact on the battlefield. On 31 March 1942, the Red Army started the activation of four new tank corps. The name of these units was deceptive. By European and American standards, the corps were in fact weak divisions with barely 5,000 men each. They were based on two tank brigades and a motor rifle brigade, but the brigades at this point were only battalion-strength by Western standards. In mid-April 1942, the tank corps organization was enlarged again to three tank brigades with a total of about 150 tanks. In spite of their limitations, the new tank corps were the first step in reviving the Red Army's mechanized forces.

The initial use of the tank corps was disappointing due to the Red Army's lack of tactical experience, poor training, and materiel defects. Two tank

A T-34 Model 42 with the Gaika turret passes by a knocked-out PzKpfw III during the fighting on the Western Front west of Moscow in September 1942.

A trio of T-34 in action in the Ukraine in the autumn of 1942. The tank in the foreground is a Krasnoye Sormovo–built tank with the small cast turret while the two behind have the enlarged Gaika turret.

corps were committed to action in May 1942 during the offensive near Kharkov and suffered serious losses. Soviet commanders were still not very adept at using the larger tank formations, often breaking the corps up into separate subunits to support the infantry. Soviet tank losses in May alone were nearly 1,500.

One of the problems with the Soviet tank units in early 1942 was the diverse selection of equipment. For example, in the case of the 22nd Tank Corps that took part in the Kharkov fighting, one of its brigades had fifty tanks (twelve Lend-Lease Matildas, twenty Lend-Lease Valentines, and eighteen T-60 light tanks); another brigade had only twenty-three tanks (twelve T-34 and eleven BT tanks); and the third had thirty-two tanks (twelve Matildas and Valentines, fourteen BT, and six T-26).[20] This motley selection of types presented a maintenance nightmare that degraded an already-weak logistics network.

Even the units with new Soviet tanks had problems. The KV-1 heavy tanks were a frequent source of difficulty, being considerably slower than the T-34 and T-60 light tanks. The KV tanks were also so heavy that they could not use many rural bridges. Combined with their slow speed, they often became isolated from the rest of the brigade. Although the KV had emerged from the 1941 onslaught as a "wonder weapon," it was no longer invulnerable by 1942. By then the more experienced Soviet tank commanders preferred the faster and more reliable T-34 and would have preferred to see KV heavy tank and T-60 light tank production end altogether. Although plans were considered to end all light and heavy tank production, this would have disrupted the armament industry just as it was beginning to rise to the challenge of meeting the Red Army's production requirements.

The painful debut of the tank corps in the Kharkov battles led to a serious reassessment of the Red Army tank forces. There was greater effort to try to standardize tank types within units. For example, the new July 1942 tank brigade organization dropped the KV altogether and was based on

A pair of tanks of the 106th Tank Brigade, 12th Tank Corps, on the Western Front in September 1942, consisting of a T-34 Model 1942 with Gaika turret named after Molotov in the foreground and a T-34 Model 41 behind it. This unit had been decimated in a series of costly and inept attacks on Army Group Center in July–August 1942 and the tanks are seen here being reconstituted in the Moscow area.

three companies with thirty-two T-34s and one light tank company with twenty-one T-60 or T-70 tanks. The KV tanks were sequestered in the heavy tank regiments for infantry support.

These reorganization efforts had not taken hold by the time the Wehrmacht unleashed its principal summer offensive of 1942, Operation Blau, aimed at seizing the oil fields of the Caucasus in southern Russia. Even though the Red Army tank forces of the Bryansk Front substantially outnumbered the attacking German formations on the approaches to Voronezh, three Soviet tank corps and several brigades were decimated in late June 1942 without appreciably slowing the German onslaught. For example, the 17th Tank Corps was relatively well-equipped with 23 KV-1, 88 T-34, and 68 T-60 light tanks for a total of 179. It was committed against the *XXIV.Panzer-Korps* along the Olym River near Kastornoye but lost 141 of its 179 tanks in a few days of fighting.

The Bryansk Front then attempted to stem the German assault on the northern shoulder by using the Fifth Tank Army, consisting of three tank corps with 641 tanks. In less than two weeks of fighting, the three tank corps lost 341 tanks, had a further 158 broken down or battle damaged, and had only 142 (22 percent) still operational.[21] The three Soviet fronts lost over 2,400 tanks in the Voronezh-Voroshilovgrad defensive campaign from 28 June–24 July, about three-quarters of their starting strength.[22] A further 1,425 tanks were lost in the fighting farther south on the approaches to Stalingrad from July–November 1942. The fighting along the Don River in the summer of 1942 was the costliest tank fighting of the year, averaging a loss of 90 tanks per day. It showed the Red Army to be still unprepared for large-scale tank operations against their more skilled adversary. Having penetrated the Soviet defenses, the German panzers spearheaded the drive toward the Volga and Stalingrad.

The situation was not much better on other fronts. An offensive directed by Marshal Georgi Zhukov managed to overcome the German defenses on the northeast corner of the Rzhev Salient in early August 1942. The Western Front's Thirty-First and Twentieth Armies were well equipped with tanks, using them for infantry support in the initial breakthrough of the German defenses. Two tank corps were held in reserve to exploit the breakthrough. The Thirty-First Army was supported by six tank brigades numbering 274 tanks, while the Twentieth Army contained two of the new tank corps (6th and 8th Corps) along with five tank brigades with a total of 614 tanks. Following the breakthrough, both tank corps were committed, but the Germans responded by sending in the *2.* and *5.Panzer-Divisions* to staunch the gap. In less than two weeks of fighting, the two armies lost 505 of their 888 tanks. Of these losses, 223 were total losses while 282 were temporary losses due to mechanical breakdowns or battle damage. A report prepared after the battle noted that the armies did not have the spare parts to repair many of the tanks and that there were insufficient recovery vehicles. Trucks that were intended to carry the motor rifle brigades into battle were instead used to haul supplies from the rear, undermining combined-arms tactics in the inexperienced tank corps.[23]

Soviet tank casualties in the summer 1942 fighting totaled about 8,000 tanks. Not only were tank losses severe, but also the tank units were constantly short of trained and experienced tank crews. After so many tanks had been abandoned in the summer of 1941, the Red Army enacted draconian measures, sending tank crews to penal battalions if they left a tank that had been knocked out in combat but had not burned. Given the lingering mechanical difficulties with Soviet tanks, this only served to exaggerate crew casualties when crews were left exposed on the battlefield vainly waiting for evacuation by the scarce repair teams. There was also a tendency to let tank units fight until all their tanks were lost, and then absorb any surviving crews into neighboring infantry units. As the Red Army began to appreciate the critical human element in tank combat and the value of experienced tank crews, Red Army policies became less brutal and less senseless. In December 1942, Moscow ordered that all trained tank crews and wounded tank crewmen in hospitals be returned to the tank force and not serve in the other branches of the army.[24]

The German advance on Stalingrad was finally stopped in the autumn of 1942 due to exhaustion and relentless Soviet counterattacks. It was the high-water mark of the Wehrmacht's assault into Russia. The German *6.Armee* reached the outskirts of Stalingrad in late August 1942 and started a bitter battle to capture the city. Although there were extensive tank battles on the approaches to the city,

SOVIET TANK STRENGTH ON THE SOUTHWESTERN FRONT NEAR STALINGRAD[25]

	Strength	Ready	In Repair	Lost
12 Aug.	222	64	99	59
23 Aug.	220	88	110	22
31 Aug.	265	101	114	40
11 Sept.	144	80	64	
1 Oct.	73	58	15	

A T-34 Model 1942 with the Gaika turret serving with the Southwestern Front on the Middle Don during Operation Uranus in the winter of 1942–43, the operation to crush the German Sixth Army in Stalingrad. This is typical of T-34 production later in 1942, with rubber-rimmed wheels on the first and last stations to make up for the use of the metal "locomotive wheels" in the center.

the city fighting itself was a classic urban battle with tanks playing a secondary support role. The Red Army's tank force in the immediate Stalingrad area suffered heavy losses in the initial fighting, as can be seen in the accompanying chart.

The Red Army decided to envelope the *6.Armee* from the flanks under a plan code-named Operation Uranus. The attack took place after the winter weather froze the autumnal mud. One of the key elements of this attack was a lightning strike by the Fifth Tank Army through the weak Romanian Third Army on the Don River north of Stalingrad. Operation Uranus was launched on 19 November 1942 and was a stunning success. It was the first time that the Soviet tank corps had demonstrated their potential for deep operations. The Germans responded in early December 1942 with Operation Winter Storm, an attempt to relieve the trapped *6.Armee* in Stalingrad. These winter battles were extremely costly on both sides. The tank forces of the Voronezh and Southwestern Fronts in December 1942 included five tank and mechanized corps that lost 90 percent of their tanks in two weeks of fighting, mainly from mechanical breakdowns and other logistical problems.[26] Nevertheless, the German relief effort failed and *6.Armee* was finally forced to surrender in February 1943.

The Red Army had started the 1942 campaigns with 7,700 tanks and during the course of the year's fighting lost 15,000 tanks. However, tank production in 1942 totaled 24,589 tanks; added to this were a further 3,514 Lend-Lease tanks supplied in 1942, 1,689 British and 1,825 American tanks.[27] As a result, on 1 January 1943, the Red Army tank force had expanded three-fold to 20,600 tanks.[28] The Red Army tank force still had very limited battlefield experience, but the Soviet Union had won the "Battle of the Factories," survived another campaign season, and demonstrated the potential of its revived tank forces in the fighting around Stalingrad.

SOVIET TANK LOSSES BY CAMPAIGN, 1942[29]

Campaign	Period	Tank Losses	Avg. Daily Tank Loss
Kerch-Fedosiya amphibious operation	25 Dec. 1941–2 Jan. 1942	35	4
Rzhev-Vyazma offensive	8 Jan.–20 Apr. 1942	957	9
Voronezh-Voroshilovgrad defense	28 June–24 July 1942	2,436	90
Stalingrad defense	17 July–18 Nov. 1942	1,426	11
Northern Caucasus defense	25 July–31 Dec. 1942	990	6
Stalingrad offensive	19 Nov. 1942–2 Feb. 1943	2,915	38
Subtotal (listed campaigns)		**8,759**	
Total (1942)	***1 Jan.–31 Dec. 1942***	***15,000***	***43***

THE WEHRMACHT PANZER FORCE IN THE 1942 CAMPAIGNS

The Wehrmacht tank force continued to exhibit tactical superiority over their Soviet opponents through the 1942 campaign. The introduction of the long 50mm gun on the PzKpfw III and the long 75mm gun on the PzKpfw IV created a level of technical parity in tank-versus-tank fighting during the summer and autumn 1942 campaigns.

Despite the tactical excellence of the panzer force in 1942, there were alarming issues which undermined the overall effectiveness of the Wehrmacht against the Red Army. The two most serious of these were the surprisingly low rate of German tank production, exacerbated by low readiness rate of German tanks on the Russian Front.

At the start of 1942, German tank power on the Russian Front was a spent force. The Wehrmacht had 1,015 tanks on the Russian Front, most of which were broken down from mechanical exhaustion and battle damage.[30] The challenge facing the Ostheer (Eastern Army) was to rebuild the tank force sufficiently to spearhead its summer campaign. In contrast to 1941, German operational objectives in 1942 were geographically limited since it could not operate in strength along the entire Russian Front. Instead, the objectives of Operation Blau were concentrated entirely on the southern flank beyond the Don River in order to seize Soviet oil reserves in the Caucasus. Operations in the north around Leningrad and in the center around Moscow were defensive holding operations and panzer divisions in these sectors were starved of tanks.

The Wehrmacht was overextended with tanks deployed in Norway to the north, to France in the west, and to North Africa in the south. The Ostheer panzer force was the largest single element of the deployed force, averaging about 61 percent of the deployed force and about 37 percent of overall German tank strength in 1942. Production kept ahead of losses in 1942 with 4,278 tanks manufactured and 2,651 tanks lost. The difference between production and loss, some 1,627 tanks, accounts for the increase in overall German tank strength on the Russian Front, which went from 1,015 to 2,758 in 1942. However, the overall improvement of the Ostheer panzer force pales in comparison to the Soviet tank force, which grew from 7,700 at the start of 1942 to 20,600 by the end of 1942.

Obsolete does not always mean useless. Some PzKpfw I light tanks remained in use on the Eastern Front in secondary roles. This one was serving in Finland with *Panzer-Abteilung 40* and is seen in action on 15 May 1940 in support of German infantry. SA-KUVA

A PzKpfw IV Ausf. G with the long 75mm KwK 40 gun during the summer 1942 campaign.

THE GERMAN TANK FORCE IN 1942[31]

	Jan.	Feb.	Mar.	Apr.	May	June	July	Aug.	Sept.	Oct.	Nov.	Dec.
Production	320	377	330	363	408	369	339	364	325	324	309	450
Losses	382	285	64	100	66	185	345	218	280	196	391	139
Losses (East)	362	305	72	125	66	74	198	232	298	200	169	159
Overall strength	4,896	4,828	4,462	4,802	5,082	5,385	5,663	5,673	5,903	5,839	5,973	5,931
Front strength	2,758	2,695	2,468	2,718	2,946	3,251	3,471	3,473	3,736	3,760	3,941	3,939
Strength (East)	1,015	1,139	1,301	1,469	1,751	1,791	2,060	2,644	2,705	2,731	2,677	2,758
Operational (East)	0	340	643	736	1,167	1,069	1,337	1,669	1,702	1,789	1,907	1,723
In repair (East)	1,015	799	658	733	584	722	723	975	1,003	942	770	1,035

The workhorse of the panzer force in Russia remained the PzKpfw III, in this case an Ausf. J with the long 50mm gun of the *9.Panzer-Division* on 20 July 1942.

This scene may suggest North Africa but it shows the advance of SS-Division Nordland during the advance to the Caucasus in the summer of 1942. The conditions in southern Russia led to the dispatch of tropicalized tanks to some units in this sector for the summer offensive. This is a PzKpfw III Ausf. J with the long 50mm KwK 39 gun.

One reason for the German complacency about the need to match Soviet tank strength was a tendency in the early years of the war to exaggerate Soviet tank losses and underestimate Soviet productive capacity. The Wehrmacht tended to overestimate the number of tanks it had destroyed or captured in combat. To their credit, the army's Russian Front intelligence agency, the Fremde Heere Ost (FHO), usually made allowances for the exaggeration in their assessments. This resulted in reasonably accurate tallies of actual Soviet tank losses.[32] Nevertheless, the lopsided nature of the tank losses in 1942 led to a certain amount of overconfidence on the German side. The Soviet-German tank loss ratio in 1942 was 6.6:1. This is sometimes misinterpreted to suggest that German tanks were killing Soviet tanks at a ratio of more than 6 to 1. It should be kept in mind that the majority of Soviet tank losses were probably due to mechanical breakdown and abandonment and that about half of the combat losses were to weapons other than tanks.

From available figures, the panzer force on the Russian Front had a dismal durability rate. On average, only about 60 percent of the tanks were operational at any one time, while on average 40 percent were being repaired. The reasons for this included both the shortcomings of German tank design when facing harsh winter conditions in Russia and a continual shortage of spare parts. As detailed earlier, the German tank force was almost entirely derelict at the start of 1942 due to mechanical exhaustion and weather-induced problems. These were gradually overcome prior to the summer campaign season, but reappeared in the winter of 1942–43.

When viewed in the longer perspective, the operational rates of the panzer force on the Russian

GERMAN TANK AVAILABILITY RATES ON THE RUSSIAN FRONT, 1942–43[33]

1942	Jan.	Feb.	Mar.	Apr.	May	June	July	Aug.	Sept.	Oct.	Nov.	Dec.	Avg.
Strength	1,015	1,139	1,301	1,469	1,751	1,791	2,060	2,644	2,705	2,731	2,677	2,758	
Operational (%)	5	30	49	50	67	60	65	63	63	66	71	62	54

Front were cyclic, declining in winter from combat attrition and weather, improving in spring as spare parts began arriving from Germany, reaching their peak in the summer for the campaigning season, declining in the autumn due to combat losses and growing shortages of spare parts, and reaching their nadir in the winter again as weather exacerbated the problems.

One reason that the German durability rates look so bad on paper is the accounting methods used by the Wehrmacht. Units usually held on to wrecked or damaged tanks since they could be cannibalized for spare parts. There was nothing to be gained by sending tanks back to Germany for repair since this would not trigger the dispatch of a replacement. Tank replacement policy was miserly. A postwar British intelligence assessment noted that the allocation problem could be traced back to OKW (Armed Forces High Command) policy:

> The basic policy of allocation was that 90 per cent of new production was to be given to units being formed, for new setting-up, while 10 per cent went to the field to replace the losses of formations in action. The result was that veteran formations in action were chronically short of equipment, while new "green" units were committed to action with complete or near complete establishment of equipment only to lose a fantastically high percentage in their first engagement.[34]

In the case of panzer units, the new equipment was often withheld in Germany to re-equip divisions that had been decimated on the Russian Front and then sent back to the rear for reconstruction.

Part of the problems encountered by the Germans in assessing the Red Army was the very different approach to force-generation in both armies in 1942. The Soviet leadership tacitly recognized that it could not yet match the Wehrmacht in a man-for-man, tank-for-tank contest. Instead, Soviet tanks and tank units were regarded as expendable. A tank corps or tank brigade would be committed to battle, fight for a week or two until nearly annihilated, and then rebuilt from the remnants. This required a very large reservoir of tanks to sustain a desperate, attritional struggle.

The Nazi regime was notoriously inept in industrial planning in the early war years, spending vast portions of its limited resources on marginal forces such as a blue-water navy. The biggest drain on Germany's industrial resources was the Luftwaffe, directed by Hitler's paladin, Hermann Göring, which consumed the majority of the Reich's weapons procurement resources. The Wehrmacht could not match the Red Army in manpower, and the German tank industry never received the resources necessary to challenge its Soviet counterpart in sheer numbers. The Wehrmacht hoped to maintain battlefield parity by stressing quality over quantity. It was able to maintain parity in 1942, but the improving quality of the Soviet tank force in 1942 and their ruthlessly practical approach to weapons production threatened to tip the balance sometime in the not-too-distant future.

A widely overlooked consequence of the small scale of German tank production was the inability of the Wehrmacht to provide adequate tank support to the infantry divisions. Unlike the Red Army, the Wehrmacht did not deploy separate tank regiments for infantry support missions, concentrating its

In spite of opposition from senior panzer commanders such as Heinz Guderian, the Wehrmacht began to devote more industrial resources to the production of the StuG III assault gun to provide essential infantry fire support. This is a StuG III Ausf. F of *Sturmgeschütz-Abteilung 210* during the fighting in the Kuban in southern Russia in the autumn of 1942.

The StuG III Ausf. F introduced the longer L/48 gun. This is an assault gun of *Sturmgeschütz-Abteilung 210* in the port of Novorossiysk after its capture in early September 1942 during the fighting in the Kuban. The battalion was nicknamed "Tigerkopf" for its tiger-head insignia.

tanks entirely in the panzer divisions. The lack of direct tank support degraded the offensive capability of the German infantry divisions, especially when attempting to conduct breakthrough operations against the Red Army.

As an alternative, the artillery branch had attempted to build up a force of assault guns (*Sturmgeschütz*) as a mobile equivalent of the World War I infantry guns. Notoriously, Heinz Guderian accused Erich von Manstein of "treason" for his advocacy of *Sturmgeschütz* production before the war since it would impact panzer production. In the event, *Sturmgeschütz* battalions began to appear in 1940 but were so few in number that they were usually sequestered as corps or field army assets. It wasn't until 1944 that German infantry divisions began to receive a company of *Panzerjäger* and a company of *Sturmgeschütz*. The declining offensive power of the German infantry divisions often forced the army to use panzer divisions for breakthrough operations, explicitly against tactical doctrine.

Despite the many shortcomings in the German tank industry in 1942, by the winter of 1942–43 the Ostheer panzer force was in better shape than it had been in the previous winter. The industry had managed to come up with many small innovations to keep the panzer force running even in the depths of Russian winters. The introduction of new antifreeze solutions and lubricants kept them moving in the winter months. The manufacture of *Winterketten* (winter tracks) with extended end connectors gave the PzKpfw III and PzKpfw IV similar or better traction in the snow than their Soviet counterparts. But there were still not enough German tanks for the vast battlefront in Russia.

INTELLIGENCE MISJUDGMENTS

One of the mysteries of the quantity versus quality approach to tank production was the role of poor intelligence on both sides. It is possible that German underestimation of Soviet tank production led Berlin to be complacent about the need for greater panzer production in 1941–42. Likewise, Soviet overestimation of German production may have been a contributory cause in pushing for very extravagant production rates.

The German FHO badly underestimated Soviet production capacity in the early war years. In 1942, FHO estimated that Soviet tank forces had gained 19,000 tanks (14,500 manufactured plus 4,500 Lend-Lease) when in fact production had been 24,589 plus 3,914 Lend-Lease tanks for a total of 28,503, a discrepancy of almost 10,000 tanks. FHO also underestimated Soviet tank holdings at the start of 1942, so after estimating 17,330 Soviet tanks lost in 1942, they assessed the Red Army tank strength as 5,640 at the start of 1943 instead of the actual 20,600.[35]

In the Soviet case, the Red Army's GRU (Main Intelligence Directorate) grossly overestimated German tank production in the early war years by a factor of five. These exaggerated numbers may not have seemed so wildly improbable since the GRU also grossly overestimated German tank losses by more than four-fold.[36]

The impact of bad intelligence on tank production requirements has not been widely explored, and this book is the first to have even raised the issue. This is something of a "chicken-and-egg"

SOVIET ESTIMATE OF GERMAN TANK PRODUCTION VS. ACTUAL PRODUCTION[37]

	1939	1940	1941	1942	Total
Soviet estimate	4,287	12,589	17,902	16,206	50,984
German production	743	1,559	3,256	4,278	9,836

dilemma. Which came first, the bad intelligence estimate or the production requirements? It is possible that the production priorities of both armies were established by their own internal dynamics, regardless of bad intelligence. In this case, the intelligence estimates may have been fostered by one of the classic intelligence blunders—mirror imaging. The Red Army may have presumed that German production was on a scale similar to Soviet production, hence the gross exaggerations. This is a mystery that requires more research.

TOP TANK OF 1942 ON THE RUSSIAN FRONT

By 1942, the T-34 tank was slipping in combat performance compared to its German adversaries; it no longer enjoyed the same clear-cut superiority as in 1941. As detailed above, shortcuts in its manufacture degraded its performance and self-imposed restrictions on improvements doomed it to diminishing effectiveness against German tanks. In contrast, the decision to up-gun and up-armor the PzKpfw IV gave it the firepower to deal with the T-34. At the same time, German tanks still maintained an edge in the less tangible aspects of tank performance, especially crew situational awareness, command and control, and durability. The nods for Tanker's Choice and Commander's Choice both go to the PzKpfw IV Ausf. G.

For Tiger enthusiasts in the reading audience, I have not considered this type in this chapter because it appeared too late in 1942 and in too small a number to have had any measurable impact. It will be covered in detail in Chapter 7.

A PzKpfw IV Ausf. G during the fighting in the winter of 1942–43. This tank is fitted with *Ostketten*, a widened track intended to provide better traction in the snow.

COMPARATIVE TECHNICAL CHARACTERISTICS

	PzKpfw III Ausf. J	PzKpfw IV Ausf. G	T-34 Model 42
Army	Germany	Germany	USSR
Crew	5	5	4
Dimensions: L x W x H (m)	6.28 x 2.95 x 2.5	7.02 x 2.88 x 2.68	5.92 x 3.0 x 2.4
Loaded weight (tonnes)	21.5	25.0	29.1
Main gun	50mm KwK 39	75mm KwK 40	76.2mm F-34
Main gun ammo	84	87	77
Engine (hp)	300	300	500
Max. speed (km/h)	40	38	55
Fuel (liters)	320	470	465 + 1,343
Range (km)	155	210	300
Ground pressure (kg/cm^2)	0.92	0.91	0.72
Armor*			
Mantlet (mm)	50**=>50	50**=>50	45**=>45
Turret front (mm)	30@15=31	50@5=50.2	52@30=60
Turret side (mm)	30@25=33.1	33@25=36.4	52@20=55.3
Upper hull front (mm)	50@9=50.6	50@8=50.3	45@60=90
Lower hull front (mm)	50@21=56.6	50@14=51.8	45@53=73.1
Upper hull side (mm)	30@0=30	30@0=30	45@40=58.7

*Armor data provided as: actual thickness in mm @ angle from vertical = effective thickness in mm.
**Curved

CHAPTER 6

The Tank War on Other Fronts: 1941–45

ALTHOUGH THE FOCUS OF MOST TANK FIGHTING in World War II was on Europe, and especially the Russian Front, there was notable combat use of tanks in peripheral theaters. The two most important of these theaters were the North African desert in 1941–43 and the Pacific in 1941–45. This book will not devote a great deal of detail to either theater because they were relatively small scale and had marginal impact on World War II tank design.

TANKS IN THE PACIFIC WAR

Japan had an active and prolific tank program in the late 1930s to support its army in China, but after a brief use of tanks at the outset of the enlarged Pacific War in December 1941, its tank force was allowed to atrophy due to a lack of resources. By December 1941, the Imperial Japanese Army (IJA) was forming more than a dozen new tank regiments intended to act as the shock force of offensive operations. The army's ten main infantry divisions each had a tank company. In the autumn of 1941, with the Red Army crippled by Germany's Operation Barbarossa, the Imperial General Headquarters decided to shift the strategic focus of Japan's military operations from the Kwantung Army in China to the Imperial Japanese Navy and the Southern Army against objectives in the South Sea region—the possessions of United States, Britain, and the Netherlands. This bold and ambitious plan intended to seize the Philippines, Malaysia, Burma, and the Dutch East Indies (today's Indonesia) and to cripple Allied military power in the Pacific by attacks on the U.S. fleet in Pearl Harbor and Britain's main fortified

Most western armies considered the Asia–Pacific Theater to be unsuitable for the use of tanks until the Japanese demonstrated otherwise in 1941. This Type 89B medium tank of Col. Seinosuke Sonoda's 7th Tank Regiment is seen here crossing an improvised bridge erected to bypass Highway 6 north of Manila on 3 January 1942 during the fighting in the Philippines. This company used a white star as its unit insignia.

garrison in Singapore. The attacks began on 7 December 1941 with carrier-borne air strikes against Pearl Harbor followed by air attacks on the other key targets. The IJA planned to make extensive use of its burgeoning tank force during these operations even though it had no experience in jungle warfare.[1]

The British army felt that the rough terrain around Singapore made it impassable to tanks and difficult if not impossible to traverse by any large military formations. The Japanese disagreed and staged amphibious landings at the northern neck of the Malay Peninsula on 8 December 1941. Gen. Tomoyuki Yamashita's Twenty-Fifth Army deployed 211 tanks in the three tank regiments. The most important tank battle of this campaign took place on 7 January 1942 when the Japanese 6th Tank Regiment overcame the Slim River line north of Singapore. Singapore fell on 15 February, due in no small measure to the effective use of tanks.

Spearheaded by two tank regiments, the IJA struck into Burma, hoping to fight all the way into India. The British 7th Armoured Brigade had recently arrived from North Africa and was tasked with stopping the Japanese advance on India. Equipped with M3 Stuart tanks, the British 2 Royal Tank Regiment fought a series of costly rearguard actions in Burma, including several tangles with the Japanese 14th Tank Regiment. By the time the survivors reached British lines in India, only one Stuart tank remained in action.

The Japanese assault on the Philippines took place at the Lingayen Gulf on Luzon in December 1941 and included the two tank regiments. The first tank-versus-tank engagement of the Pacific War occurred on 22 December 1941 when Type 95 Ha-Go light tanks of the 4th Tank Regiment ambushed a patrol of M3 light tanks from the U.S. Army's 192nd Tank Battalion near Damortis. These two opposing tank units continued to skirmish as the U.S. forces retreated toward the Bataan peninsula. Following the fall of Bataan, a special Japanese tank unit was formed and was instrumental in overcoming the island fortress of Corregidor.

Japan's early victories in the Pacific War displayed a skillful and imaginative use of tanks in terrain that the British and American commanders thought prohibited their use. Having won critical early victories against the Allies, Japanese strategy now shifted to a defensive orientation. Industrial priority was given to the warships and aircraft that bore the brunt of the new defensive naval campaigns. In spite of their important role in the 1941–42 victories, tank production fell after its peak in 1941.

Not only did tank production suffer, new tank design stagnated as well. Japan had been dependent on European influences to help direct their technological advancement. The Allied tanks encountered in 1941–42, notably the M3 Stuart light tank, did not particularly impress the Japanese and were little better than Japan's most modern tank, the Type 97-kai Shinhoto Chi-Ha. Japan attempted to learn about newer trends in European tank design from their German allies, but technology transfer was so slow as to be almost useless. Germany sold Japan a

The most widely used Japanese tank during the Pacific War of 1941–45 was the Type 95 Ha-Go light tank. Armed with a 37mm gun, it was competitive when faced with tanks such as the M3 Stuart in 1941. However, by 1944 it was hopelessly outgunned by the M4 Sherman.

The best Japanese tank deployed outside Japan was the Type 97-kai Shinhoto Chi-Ha armed with a 47mm. It was no match for contemporary American medium tanks such as the Sherman. The largest tank-versus-tank battles of the Pacific War were fought in the Philippines in January–February 1945, pitting the Japanese 2nd Armored Division against several U.S. Army tank companies and infantry units. Here, an M4A3 tank named "Classy Peg" of the 716th Tank Battalion passes a smoldering Type 97-kai Shinhoto Chi-Ha of the 7th Tank Regiment knocked out during the fighting around Binalonan on 17 January 1945.

The Type 97-kai Shinhoto Chi-Ha used the classic three-man turret configuration and had a cupola for the commander. Japanese tanks often lacked radios, and hand flags remained in common use for inter-vehicle communication.

pair of PzKpfw III in 1943, one with the 50mm gun and one with the short 75mm gun, but by the time they arrived in Japan they were already obsolete. Germany later sold Japan a Panther and a Tiger in September 1943, but by the time they were ready in 1944 it was no longer possible to ship them to Japan due to Allied naval interdiction.

The U.S. Army and Marine Corps made extensive use of tanks in the Pacific War. Following the use of two tank battalions in the Philippines campaign equipped with M3 light tanks, the next major use occurred on Guadalcanal in 1942. There was seldom any tank-versus-tank fighting in these early campaigns since neither side had large numbers of tanks. There was some small-scale skirmishing by Marine Corps M4A2 Sherman tanks with Japanese Type 95 Ha-Go tanks on Tarawa in November 1943. The IJA committed a tank regiment on Saipan and Guam in the summer 1944 campaign, but it was overwhelmed by the growing U.S. Marine Corps tank force, which eventually numbered six battalions. By this stage of the war, the contest was unequal with the obsolete Type 97-kai Shinhoto Chi-Ha facing Army and Marine M4 Sherman tanks. During the fighting on Luzon in the Philippines in 1944–45, the IJA committed an entire armored division, but its tanks were deployed in static fashion as pillboxes and the division was overrun by the U.S. Army.[2]

The Japanese tank force was also subjected to the Red Army in 1945 when the Soviet Union entered the Pacific War in August 1945. This was the largest tank operation of the Asian war, and one of the least known outside of Russia. The Red Army overran the Kwantung Army in Manchuria in two weeks with a rapid, three-pronged pincer movement involving over 5,000 armored vehicles—more than at Kursk. There was very little tank-versus-tank fighting during this campaign, as the war ended before the Red Army reached the main defense line where the IJA tank brigades were stationed. The Red Army captured 369 Japanese tanks and 35 armored cars during the August 1945 campaign.

The Japanese ultimately developed medium and heavy tanks, but the few that were completed were kept in Japan for the final defense in 1945. The Type 3 Chi-Nu was armed with a long 75mm gun and attached to the 4th Tank Division in 1945 at the time the war ended.

TANK COMBAT IN NORTH AFRICA

The North African desert was the scene of prolonged tank combat, taking place from 1940 through 1943. However, the scale of the fighting was small compared to the Russian Front. As far as this book is concerned, its significance is further diminished by its lack of influence on world tank design. The technological momentum in much of the fighting after 1941 came from Germany, and most of the tank types used in North Africa had been based on the lessons from the Russian Front. The campaigns in North Africa were a technological backwater as far as tank development was concerned.

Italy had made extensive use of tanks in its colonial adventures in North Africa in the 1930s including Ethiopia and Libya. Most of these early campaigns were fought with the L.3 tankettes, which had been proven obsolete in European warfare as early as the Spanish Civil War in 1937.[3] By 1940, the Italian forces in North Africa had been reinforced with new medium tanks including the M.11/39 and M.13/40. These tanks were strongly influenced by the British Vickers 6-Ton tank and its foreign offshoots such as the Soviet T-26. The M.11/39 had an unfortunate layout with a hull-mounted gun supported by a small turret with machine guns. It was quickly redesigned with a more conventional turret and armed with an effective 47mm gun. By the standards of the late 1930s, it was not a bad design, with 30mm frontal armor and a 42mm gun mantlet. This was not proof against the British 2-pounder, but the armor was better than that on most British cruiser tanks of the day.[4]

In September 1940, the Italian army launched an offensive into Egypt with extensive tank support.

The Italian M.11/39 had its main 37mm gun located in the hull, supplemented by a pair of machine guns in the small turret. It fared poorly against British tanks in the fighting in late 1940 in Libya.

The M.13/40 began to arrive in Libya in late 1940. Although armed with a better 47mm gun and having a more practical configuration than the M.11/39, it did not do well in the initial 1940–41 battles. The M.13/40 and its derivatives such as the M.14/41 remained the backbone of Italian armor in the desert through 1943.

There was some expectation that it would be an easy campaign, as the Italians substantially outnumbered the British garrison in Egypt. The British armored force in Egypt included the 7th Armoured Division, and the various British formations had 175 light tanks, mainly the machine-gun-armed light tank Mark VI, 73 cruiser tanks, and about 50 Matilda infantry tanks.

The Vickers Cruiser Tank Mark I (A9) was built in two armament configurations.[5] The baseline version was armed with the 2-pounder (40mm) tank gun. Since this weapon was only issued armor-piercing ammunition, a portion of the tanks were fitted out as "close-support" tanks and fitted with a 3.7-inch (94mm) howitzer, actually a breech-loaded mortar. For reasons that remain obscure, high-explosive rounds for the 2-pounder, though available, were not issued to tanks in the Western Desert. One of the oddities of British tank doctrine at this point in the war was the use of a shoulder pad to elevate and depress the gun instead of the usual geared system. This was linked to British tactical doctrine that favored firing on the move. Although peacetime tests suggested that good results could be obtained, the results in wartime were more likely to be very poor.[6]

The Cruiser Mark I had an armor basis of 14mm, enough to protect it against light machine guns. It was followed by the Cruiser Mark II (A10) with a 30mm armor basis, enough to protect against heavy machine guns. A parallel Cruiser Tank Mark IV was built by Nuffield and used a Christie suspension and a Liberty aircraft engine. Tanks of this era had an engine life of around 100 hours in desert conditions and about 1,000 miles of travel, after which mechanical problems quickly multiplied. During the opening moves of the first battle for Tobruk, the 2nd Armoured Division lost forty-nine

A view inside a Matilda II turret on the gunner's side to the left. The leather-covered shoulder brace seen in the lower right was used to elevate and depress the 2-pounder.

cruiser tanks, of which thirty-nine were abandoned due to mechanical faults or fuel shortage.[7]

The initial tank battle of Operation Compass at Nibeiwa camp in December pitted the Matildas of the 7 RTR (Royal Tank Regiment) against most of the forward-deployed Italian armor, including 35 M.11/39 and 35 L.3/35 tankettes. The battle was entirely one-sided, with the British force overrunning the Italians and capturing or knocking out 73 tanks and tankettes. Further fighting in January pitted cruiser tanks of the British 4th Armoured Brigade against Italy's newest tanks, the M.13/40. This was less one-sided than the initial fighting against the Matildas since the cruiser tanks' armor was not proof against the Italian 47mm guns. A few cruiser tanks were knocked out, but the Italians were forced to withdraw. Britain's Western Desert Force pushed into Libya and made short work of the Italian forces, taking the vital port of Tobruk in late January 1941 along with a further 87 Italian tanks and tankettes. British tank combat losses during the campaign were light—5 cruiser tanks, 13 light tanks, and 1 Matilda—while Italian losses were heavy, about 400 tankettes and tanks.

The Matilda was the "Queen of the Battlefield." Although it was intended to be used as an infantry support tank, its excellent armor and potent 2-pounder gun proved very effective against the poorly prepared Italian forces in Libya. At the same time, the fighting also revealed the Matilda's lingering mechanical problems. On the first day at Sidi Barrani on 9 December 1940, there were 44 Matildas in use; by the third day there were only 17. At the time of the fighting for the Bardia fortress on 5 January 1941 the Matilda force was only 23, falling to 8 by the third day of fighting due to mechanical breakdowns. Days later at Tobruk, the 7 RTR started with 18 Matildas but was down to 10 by the second day. The desert was a harsh environment, but British tank forces in France in June 1940 also had experienced rapid exhaustion of their tank strength due to poor reliability. At the end of the short campaign, 7 RTR had to send all of its Matilda tanks back for rebuilding. In March 1941, British strength in the Middle East was 368 light tanks, 258 cruiser tanks, and 65 Matilda infantry tanks, but many of them were mechanically exhausted. This strength fell rapidly in March 1941 when the 1st Armoured Brigade was sent from Egypt as part of the doomed Operation Lustre to reinforce the Greek army.

Enter the Afrika Korps: March 1941

The conduct of the desert war changed dramatically in March 1941 when Hitler decided to reinforce his hapless Italian allies with the *Deutsches Afrika Korps* (DAK) led by Erwin Rommel. In its initial form in March 1941, the DAK included *Panzer-Regiment.5* with 45 PzKpfw II, 71 PzKpfw III, and 20 PzKpfw IV. It was followed later by the *10.Panzer-Division*. In comparison to the British tanks available at the time, the German 50mm gun on the PzKpfw III offered better antiarmor performance and was regularly issued with high explosive ammunition; the short 75mm gun on the PzKpfw IV could demolish any of the British tanks other than the Matilda, but its role was fire support. Many

The arrival of Rommel's Afrika Korps in early 1941 changed the course of the war in the Western Desert. Tank equipment such as this PzKpfw III Ausf. H was not well suited to desert conditions, and the German panzers had to be "tropicalized" for better performance.

The Matilda had been the "Queen of the Desert" in early 1941 against the poorly prepared Italian forces. The tide changed when faced with the Afrika Korps in the spring of 1941. In the background of this scene from the Gazala battles is a PzKpfw III Ausf. H armed with the short 50mm gun.

of the tanks arriving in Libya in 1941 had upgraded armor based on the lessons of the French campaign. German tanks had adequate reliability for the time, but the desert conditions were a maintenance nightmare. During the 700-kilometer forced march by *Panzer-Regiment.5* toward Tobruk at the end of March 1941, 83 out of 155 tanks broke down and had to be repaired. Existing air filters were inadequate; fine dust penetrated into the crankshaft, freezing the engine. Shock absorbers and transmissions were also vulnerable to desert conditions.[8]

The first major equipment improvement for British forces was the new Crusader cruiser tank, which began to arrive in the Western Desert in 1941.[9] This design could be traced back to the A13 Covenanter heavy cruiser, a new design by Nuffield aimed at providing the cruiser tanks with a higher level of armor protection. The Covenanter also aimed at fielding a more compact design than the boxy Vickers Cruiser tanks and unwisely used a horizontally opposed piston engine for the design. It was further compromised by the decision to place the radiator in the front of the tank to the side of the driver due to the small size of the engine compartment. On top of this, production of the first batch was approved before a prototype had been built because of the war crisis in 1939. At an early stage in its development, Nuffield began to have an inkling that there might be trouble ahead and offered to develop a parallel design, the Crusader, which used the same Liberty engine as the existing Cruiser Mark IV. When it finally reached production in 1940, the Covenanter proved to be an engineering nightmare. Out of desperation after the loss of so many tanks in France in the summer of 1940, production contracts continued. However, it was quickly appreciated that the Covenanter's engine and cooling system were ill suited to the desert, and all of the tanks remained in Britain for training. The Crusader began to be deployed with the 6 RTR in May 1941 and in larger numbers with the 22nd Armoured Brigade later that year. Although a significantly better tank than the earlier cruisers in terms of armored protection, it was still armed with

The early cruiser tanks were found wanting in the 1941 desert battles. The Cruiser Mark III suffered from reliability issues in the harsh desert climate, and its armor was overmatched by German tank and antitank guns.

The Crusader introduced a more modern hull design to improve armor protection compared to the earlier cruiser tanks. Its service use proved troublesome due to mechanical unreliability of the power-train. This example with the 2-pounder gun is seen on exercise in Britain in October 1942.

the same 2-pounder. Furthermore, it suffered from congenital durability problems that were exacerbated in the desert conditions.

One new arrival in late 1941 was a new Vickers design, the Valentine.[10] This was based on the earlier Cruiser Mark 1 type of suspension, but the hull and turret were new and much more heavily armored. It was an infantry tank by British definition but still plagued by a small turret, a two-man turret crew, and the 2-pounder gun. Based on a sound and mature suspension and power-train, it was the most durable of the new British tanks—some of the 40 RTR's tanks reached 3,000 miles by the time of the Tunisia campaign.[11]

The composition of the British tank force in the Western Desert began to change in the summer of 1941 with the arrival of the first American Lend-Lease M3 light tanks, a type soon called the General Stuart after Winston Churchill's earlier admonition to name British tanks in some recognizable fashion instead of the usual army gibberish. (British designations for tanks—including development designations such as A9 and army designations such as Light Tank Mark VI or Cruiser Tank Mark I—were very confusing to Churchill. As a result, in 1941 he ordered that tanks be given names such as Crusader, Covenanter, Cromwell, etc. Likewise, when Lend-Lease American tanks appeared with their equally confusing names, such as M3 light tank and M3 medium tank, these two were called Stuart and Lee.) The Stuart was an awkward fit for the British army, neither fast enough to be considered a cruiser tank nor well-enough armored to be considered an infantry tank; it was usually deployed as a cruiser tank. Its 37mm gun was inferior to the British 2-pounder in armor penetration but it was regularly

An impressive display of armored might at a training ground in Britain in December 1941. The Valentine fell between the usual infantry and cruiser tank categories, not having the speed of a cruiser nor the armor of an infantry tank, yet was the most dependable British tank of its generation.

This Valentine fell victim to a volley of antitank fire during the 1941 campaign, as is evident from the multiple hit on the sand shields and elsewhere.

The arrival of the M3 light tank in the autumn of 1941 prior to Operation Crusader was welcomed by British tank crews for its automotive reliability. It was nicknamed the "Honey" in desert service, though its official British name was the General Stuart after the Civil War cavalry commander. These two are from the 8th Hussars on a training run in September 1941.

issued with high-explosive ammunition, making it more versatile. Like the British tanks, it used a shoulder pad for gun elevation, not a geared wheel. Its profusion of machine guns did not fit British doctrine and they were removed.

The main feature in favor of the Stuart was its automotive durability. This was due both to U.S. Army policy and design maturity. The American Expeditionary Force in France in 1918 had suffered from the dreadful dependability of American trucks, and this led to a very strict policy afterward to insist on automotive reliability. U.S. tanks were subjected to rigorous testing at Aberdeen Proving Ground's automotive test tracks, and newly manufactured tanks were subjected to 50-mile trials at factory test tracks before their acceptance. The Stuart also benefited from design maturity. It was the latest iteration of a family of light tanks and combat cars dating back to the mid-1930s that used the same basic power-train and suspension. By 1941, it was a well-proven design. As tank historian David Fletcher has noted, British tank units in the desert "considered themselves lucky not to lose six Crusaders each day to mechanical problems while the Stuarts just trundled on and on."[12]

The Stuarts first saw combat in Operation Crusader, the November 1941 attempt to recapture Cyrenaica and relieve Tobruk. There were 165 Stuarts on hand at the start of the operation, and 7th Armoured Division's other two brigades were equipped with 287 tanks, mainly Crusaders, for a grand total of 452 tanks. Including the other tank units, British forces had about 700 tanks at the beginning of the offensive. The Afrika Korps's two panzer divisions (*15.* and *21.Panzer-Divisions*) at the start of Operation Crusader had 260 tanks,

German tactics stressed the need of commanders leading from the front. As a result, panzer units received specialized Panzerbefehlswagen with additional radio equipment but a dummy gun. This is a PzBefWg Ausf. H based on the PzKpfw III chassis.

including 77 light PzKpfw II, 145 PzKpfw III, and 38 PzKpfw IV, plus about 135 M.13/40 tanks with the Italian Ariete Division.

The decimation of the 7th Armoured Division in the initial fighting at Sidi Rezegh had more to do with tactical deficiencies than with technical deficiencies. The German armor units were able to overcome their more numerous opponent by superior tactics, including a skilled use of tanks in coordination with the highly effective 50mm PaK 38 antitank gun and the legendary 88mm gun. Rommel remarked to a captured British officer: "What difference does it make for me if you have two tanks to my one? You send them out and let me smash them in detail. You presented me with three brigades in succession." The British army was slow to adopt combined-arms tactics, a problem that would linger into 1944.[13]

The congenital durability problems with the Crusader had a direct impact on the battlefield. Col. Norman Berry, the chief mechanical engineer for Eighth Army, lamented:

> The lack of mechanical reliability was a very different matter and had a profound effect on the whole of the desert fighting in 1941 and 1942. Like the Matilda, the engine of the Crusader tank engine was not developed as such. It was a 12-cylinder 400 hp aero engine left over from the 1914–18 war . . . Unfortunately the cooling problems in a tank are very different from those in an aeroplane, and here the troubles began . . . In the Crusader the engine was modified by the fitting of two fans and two water-pumps driven from the engine crankshaft by a long chain.

> This was a disaster. As soon as the tank was used in the desert, sand got into the chain, the chain stretched and started to jump the crankshaft driving sprocket. It was a three-day job to change the sprocket. Worse still, the water-pump would not stand up to the sand and the heat of the desert and soon leaked very badly. A re-design was necessary but unfortunately the manufacturing facilities did not exist in Egypt. In January 1942, we had pushed Rommel right back to El Agheila and he seemed to be nearly finished. I think he would have been finished if we had not had two hundred Crusader tanks under repair . . . The reply had come back: "Regret not available in UK." If those water-pumps had been available, Rommel's counter-attack could never have succeeded and would not have been a battle of Alamein, first, second, or third.[14]

The fighting showed that the Stuart and Crusader tanks were barely adequate for tank fighting. This was not simply a matter of gun and armor. Although many accounts of the desert fighting suggest that the German tanks were better armored and had longer-ranged guns, this was not the case. The 30mm superstructure front armor of the PzKpfw III Ausf. G. could theoretically be penetrated by the Honey's gun at 1,500 meters, while the PzKpfw III Ausf. G's 50mm gun could penetrate the Stuart's 38mm superstructure front at similar ranges. Most engagements took place at closer ranges where both tanks were vulnerable to each other's fire, and shots were often against the side armor of opposing tanks, where there was no clear advantage to either side.

The German advantage was in less-appreciated factors such as tactics, training, command and control, and tank fightability. The PzKpfw III was better laid out for tank fighting than the Stuart, having a turret crew of three—commander, gunner, and loader—allowing the commander to concentrate on directing his tank and coordinating its actions with those of neighboring tanks. The German tank periscope was also superior, using an early form of stadiametric range-finding. Gun elevation was geared so that after firing the first shot, the German gunner could adjust his fire with precision.

In the Stuart, the commander had to double up as gunner. This seriously distracted him from his function of observing enemy actions and made the tank almost blind in combat. When operating the gun, the commander had no means of vision other than the tank's telescopic sight or a small pistol port. The British realized this shortcoming and, as an expedient, shifted crew functions. During combat, the commander moved to the rear of the turret while the redundant hull co-driver moved into the turret and served as gunner. To accommodate the tank commander, an armored car-pattern sling seat was added under the turret cupola. British doctrine of the time still recommended firing from the move, but Stuart crews found that the most effective tactic was to close on the enemy as quickly as possible, make a quick halt, and then fire the main gun.

In early 1942, both sides began to receive upgraded tanks. The German innovations were heavily influenced by developments on the Russian Front. There was a continual increase in tank armor, first in the form of appliqué panels on the hull and eventually with thicker integral plate. Due to the appearance of the T-34 and KV in 1941, there was a steady escalation in German firepower. Shipments in early 1942 included the first of the PzKpfw III with the new 50mm L/60 gun. The most welcome addition was the arrival of the first ten PzKpfw IV Ausf. F2 with the long L/43 gun in May 1942. Larger shipments of the PzKpfw III Ausf. L with the long L/60 gun and additional appliqué armor arrived that summer. An inspection team sent from Berlin in the late summer of 1942 concluded: "The new PzKpfw III with the 50mm KwK L/60 and the new PzKpfw IV with the 75mm KwK 40 L/43 are rated above all other weapons as the best in meeting the modern requirements in desert warfare . . . [they] are rated as superior to all enemy tanks including the American Pilot (M3 Grant/Lee). It is the opinion of the troops that the PzKpfw IV with the 75mm KwK L.24 is not usable in tank versus tank battles in this theater of war."[15]

The Crusader underwent firepower improvements with the substitution of the 6-pounder for the earlier 2-pounder. However, the Crusader turret was

An Afrika Korps PzKpfw IV on the road near Chechiban, Libya, south of Derna on 13 April 1942.

British troops recover a PzKpfw III Ausf. L with the added appliqué armor on the gun mantlet.

The Grant tank was the M3 medium tank with the British-designed turret. The new turret had a rear bustle to permit locating the radio near the tank commander, as was standard British tactical practice. This Grant belongs to the Royal Scots Greys in Egypt in September 1942.

so compact that the new gun meant the turret crew was reduced from three to two, not an ideal situation in 1942. The Crusader also had not lost its earlier reputation as mechanically unreliable, and units preferred receiving the new Lend-Lease tanks.

The most important new arrival for British forces in early 1942 was the Lend-Lease M3 medium tank. The type with the original American turret was dubbed the Lee, while the British-inspired version with the enlarged turret with radio bustle was called the Grant. The first Grant and Lee tanks arrived in the Middle East in November 1941 and were initially used for trials and training; most British records refer to both types as Grants. Shipments were slow to arrive, and the first unit equipped, the 5 RTR, had only thirty-two at the beginning of February 1942. The Grant and its dual-purpose 75mm gun was a welcome addition to the British arsenal following the serious losses endured during Operation Crusader in November 1941. This gun finally gave the British army the ability to deal both with tank threats and antitank guns. A gunnery instructor with the 3 RTR recalled that "the crews were overjoyed to be able to fire a large 14 pound shell at the Panzer tanks." The British were not keen on the Grant's archaic configuration, however. The 75mm gun was mounted in a side sponson, and there was a supplementary 37mm gun in the small turret. The location of the 75mm gun made it difficult to take advantage of hull-down positions, using terrain to protect the bulk of the tank. U.S. Army Ordnance accepted the design as a compromise until there was enough industrial capacity to manufacture a cast turret and turret ring large enough to accommodate the 75mm gun in the turret. This would emerge later in 1942 as the M4 Sherman. For the time being, the

The M3 medium tank, known as the Lee in British service, had a smaller turret surmounted by a machine-gun cupola. This is an M3 of the 1st Armoured Division on exercise in Britain in the summer of 1942 prior to its deployment to Tunisia.

Grant/Lee was the best available, even if its configuration was no one's first choice.

Like the Stuart, the Grant's other significant advantage was its automotive reliability. It was based on the earlier M2 medium tank, a mature design though even more archaic in configuration than the Grant/Lee. Overall, the Grant was well received by British tankers. A tank officer recalled that "it was fairly fast with a possible road speed of about 25 mph, well-armoured, and considered capable of out-shooting an enemy tank or anti-tank gun except the 88mm. The Grant crews also found their new tank and armament ideal and we looked forward to meeting the panzers more or less on even terms."[16]

By March 1942, there were about 340 Grants and Lees in Egypt along with American liaison teams to provide training and maintenance assistance. Prior to the Gazala battles, the Axis side had about 560 tanks, including 332 German and 228 Italian. By this stage of the war, the Italian army was depending primarily on the M.14/41 tank, a modestly improved version of the earlier M.13/40 and roughly comparable to the Stuart in technical features. Small numbers of the new Semovente 75/18, an assault gun with a short 75mm gun in a fixed casemate on an M.14/41 hull, were arriving. Although intended for infantry support, it was as often as not used as a substitute tank due to the modest firepower of the M.14/41.

At the time of the Gazala battles in May 1942, British units had 167 Grants and Lees with the 1st and 7th Armoured Divisions, with more in Egypt equipping other units or being used for training or reserve. This made it the second most common tank type in the armored divisions, compared to 257 Crusaders and 149 Stuarts. At the time, the Grant was the best tank in the desert, offering better antitank punch than the 50mm gun on the PzKpfw III and better armor protection. However, despite the new Grant tanks, the May–June Gazala battles went badly for the Eighth Army. The problems were not technical, but tactical. The Afrika Korps continued to display greater combat effectiveness despite technical and numerical shortcomings due to better combined-arms tactics. Rommel's offensive succeeded in pushing the Eighth Army back into Egypt to El Alamein. The performance of the Grant during the battle was good, and its 75mm gun proved an unpleasant surprise for the Germans in numerous encounters. A staff officer who inspected the several knocked-out tanks from the 22nd Armoured Brigade afterward commented, "It is apparent that the Grant tank can take a great deal of punishment." One Grant had been hit no fewer than 31 times with the only damage caused by two 50mm hits on the front visors and a rear hit by a 37mm gun. Another had been hit 12 times with no penetrations. Larger-caliber artillery was particularly lethal, with two of the inspected tanks penetrated and burnt out by 105mm field gun hits and another by an 88mm round that set off an internal fire.

Tank losses at Gazala were heavy on both sides, and July was spent rebuilding for the next encounter. Nevertheless, by mid-1942 Britain had an enormous advantage in tanks, having shipped almost half its tank strength to the Mid-East. The August fighting at Alam Halfa again saw the Grant as one of the mainstays of the British armored force, with 164 Grants and Lees among the 713 tanks in the forward-deployed units. The battle was fought from defensive positions and the Grants

Due to the weak firepower of the M.13/40 and M.14/41 tanks, the Italian army began to use their Semovente 75/18 assault guns as surrogate tanks. This vehicle was based on the standard tank chassis but had a fixed casemate and a short 75mm gun.

BRITISH TANK STRENGTH, 30 JUNE 1942[17]							
	Covenanter	Crusader	M3 Cruiser	Valentine	Matilda	Churchill	Total
UK	816		67	848	155	875	2,761
Middle East		582	990	300	302		2,174
New Zealand				80			80
Australia			104		104		208
India			212	183			395
Burma			114				114
Iraq			57				57
Total	***816***	***582***	***1,544***	***1,411***	***561***	***875***	***5,789***

were often emplaced with the help of engineers and bulldozers to reduce their high silhouette. On the German side, the Alam Halfa battle represented the arrival of the long-barreled 75mm gun on the PzKpfw IV Ausf. F2 tank, an echo of the arms race taking place on the Russian Front since 1941. Alam Halfa was the last of Rommel's offensives against the Eighth Army. At the time, the Afrika Korps had only 238 tanks on hand, of which 73 were the PzKpfw III with the long L/60 gun and 27 were the PzKpfw IV with the long L/43 gun. With British command rejuvenated by the arrival of a dynamic new leader, Lt. Gen. Bernard Montgomery, the initiative shifted to the British side with preparations for an offensive at El Alamein.[18]

Churchill pressured the U.S. government to speed the shipment of new tanks, especially the new M4A1 Sherman. This was essentially the same chassis as the M3 Grant/Lee but with the 75mm gun mounted in a new three-man turret. From a technical perspective, it was close to the PzKpfw IV Ausf. G in technical features, but more importantly it was available in substantially greater numbers. When the second battle of El Alamein started on 23 October 1943, Lend-Lease tanks made up the backbone of the British armored forces with 270 Shermans and 210 Grants. The Grant was still a viable battle tank in the autumn 1942 fighting since the Afrika Korps still had few of the long-barreled PzKpfw III Ausf. L or PzKpfw IV Ausf. G. British losses through 10 November included 53 Grants, of which 30 were complete write-offs. In total, 350 Grants and Lees were lost in combat in 1942. Rommel lost over 50 tanks and by November 1942 had only 126 tanks on hand.

With Rommel on the run after El Alamein, the North Africa campaign exploded in a new direction. The U.S. Army staged the Operation Torch amphibious landings on the coast of French North Africa. This led to some small-scale tank-versus-tank fighting with Vichy French forces, but this fighting was short-lived when the French army switched sides. Portions of the American forces along with Commonwealth forces formed Anderson's First Army, which set about to occupy Tunisia, striking Rommel from behind. The Germans struck first, deploying the *5.Panzer-Armee* to Tunisia before the Allies arrived. The Axis reinforcement of the Tunisian bridgehead in November 1942–January 1943 included 428 tanks, 271 German and the remainder Italian. This included the first two companies with 20 of the new Tiger tank; a third company with 11 more Tigers arrived in March–April 1943.

The U.S. armored force in Tunisia consisted of the 1st Armored Division and several separate tank battalions. The 1st Armored Division at the time still contained a mixture of M3 and M4 medium tanks, as well as the M3 light tank. In February

The T6 medium tank used the same chassis as the M3 medium tank, but with the gun in the turret. There were many changes to the T6 design before it emerged as the definitive M4A1 Sherman tank in early 1942.

The Sherman saw its baptism by fire in British hands during the second battle of El Alamein in October 1942. This is a Sherman II (M4A1) of the 9th Lancers, 1st Armoured Division, during training prior to the battle.

1ST ARMORED DIVISION TANK STRENGTH IN TUNISIA[19]

	9 Dec. 1942*	29 Jan. 1943	2 Feb.	6 Feb.	14 Feb.	19 Feb.	3 Mar.	12 Mar.	24 Mar.	8 June
Light	62	217	192	190	165	99	193	174	209	229
Medium	22	111	86	83	85	74	69	82	89	56
Total	***84***	***328***	***278***	***273***	***250***	***173***	***262***	***256***	***298***	***285***

*Includes only Combat Command B (CCB).

The Sherman tank followed the German pattern of a three-man turret crew but shifted the layout with the gunner on the right rather than left side.

1943, *5.Panzer-Armee* launched a surprise offensive, concentrating on the thinly spread and inexperienced U.S. sector near Kasserine Pass. The German offensive overwhelmed two tank battalions and a tank destroyer battalion.

The U.S. Army recovered after a change of leadership. Lt. Gen. George S. Patton took command of the U.S. II Corps and led it to its first major victory at El Guettar in March 1943.

Although the Tiger tank proved to be a deadly opponent in Tunisia, it was not available in the numbers needed to have a critical impact on the battlefield. The first two companies were seldom able to put more than ten tanks in the field at any given time due to mechanical problems and the difficulty of supporting such a heavy vehicle on a remote battlefield. The battalion claimed the destruction of more than 150 tanks during the campaign.[20]

The British also received a new heavy tank in Tunisia with the arrival of the first Churchill infantry tanks, which focused on armor over firepower. They originally had a 2-pounder, but by the time of Tunisia the Mark III was equipped with a 6-pounder. The first six Churchill saw action with Kingforce in November 1942.[21]

The conjunction of Anderson's First Army and Montgomery's Eighth Army led to the eventual rout of the German and Italian forces in North Africa, with their last stand on the Mediterranean coast near Tunis and Bizerte in May 1943.

The Churchill suffered significant teething problems in its early days before turning into one of the better British tanks. This Churchill II is in training with the Polish 65th Battalion, 16th Tank Brigade, in Scotland in 1942.

BRITISH TANK GUNS, 1940–45[22]

Caliber	2-pounder	6-pounder	17-pounder
Tube length	52	47	55
Armor-piercing projectile	AP	APCBC	APCBC
Initial muzzle velocity (m/s)	792	792	885
Projectile weight (kg)	1.1	3.2	7.7
Penetration (mm; @500m, 30 degree)	52	75	128
Armor-piercing projectile (high-velocity)	N/A	APDS	APDS
Initial muzzle velocity (m/s)		1,220	1,125
Projectile weight (kg)		1.44	3.69
Penetration (mm; @500m, 30 degree)		123	170

THE MYSTERIES OF BRITISH TANK DESIGN

This chapter raises an intriguing question: Why was British tank design so bad for so long? As British historian David Fletcher put it some years ago, "That mistakes were made is understandable; that they should be repeated on a regular basis is almost beyond belief." The title of some prominent studies of British tank development—"The Great Tank Scandal" and "Death by Design"—give a flavor of controversy.[23] This is all the more perplexing due to Britain's central role in the early development of the tank in 1916–18 and its prominence in tank development through the 1930s. It is easy enough to understand the poverty of Italian tank design in World War II: Italy suffered from wretchedly poor industrial resources. But Britain?

From a bird's-eye view, the British situation can be described as the polar opposite of Soviet tank design. Britain's premier services were the Royal Navy and the Royal Air Force. Priority went to these services in terms of engineering and production resources. Britain had some of the finest aircraft engines of World War II; British tanks received the dregs. The best British engineering resources went to warship and aircraft design. Britain was a pioneer in many technologies, but especially in aviation and aviation electronics. Britain's resources were not limitless, but Britain had a far more rational distribution of resources than Germany.

The Soviet situation was precisely the opposite. The Soviet Union excelled in tank development and production in World War II because the Red Army had the priority. Funding for the Soviet Navy in World War II was miniscule. The Soviet Air Force was funded to serve as an adjunct of the army; little money was given to heavy bombers for autonomous air force operations. Aluminum was needed for the V-2 diesel engines in the Soviet tanks; Soviet fighter aircraft were mostly built from wood and minimal amounts of aluminum.

The Covenanter cruiser tank proved so mechanically flawed that it was never sent into combat. One of its unusual design features was the radiator location in the front of the tank under the armored louvers. This example was used by elements of the Polish 1st Armored Division during training in Scotland in the summer of 1942.

The Valentine infantry tank, built by Vickers, benefited from their trademark durability and reliability. However, the design was undermined by a small two-man turret and the use of the inadequate 2-pounder gun. This example is seen on display in London in 1942 during a parade through Leicester Square.

The Crusader was improved with the substitution of the more powerful 6-pounder gun, as seen on this example in Tunisia in 1943. However, it never escaped its reputation for poor reliability.

TOP TANK OF 1941–43 ON OTHER FRONTS

The war in the Western Desert spanned two and a half years. At various points in time, different tanks were supreme: the Matilda in early 1941, the PzKpfw III later in 1941, and the Grant for a time in 1942. I would give the Tanker's Choice award to the PzKpfw IV Ausf. G. It offered a slightly better gun than the Sherman's, and its commander's cupola and telescopic sight provided better situational awareness. I am slighting the Tiger in this chapter as it was available in puny numbers and played a marginal role in the campaign.

For Commander's Choice, I would give the nod to the Sherman. At this stage in its career it had excellent firepower and armor, was available in large numbers, and was dependable.

The PzKpfw IV Ausf. G, known by the British as the Mark IV Special, was the best German tank in service in the summer of 1942 and introduced the new long 75mm KwK 40 gun. This captured example was photographed at an exhibit in Washington, D.C., in 1944 with U.S. soldiers in German uniforms.

The Sherman became the predominant Allied tank in the Mediterranean Theatre in 1943, used by the U.S. Army as well as by British and Commonwealth forces. This is an M4A1 of the 2nd Armored Division during the Operation Husky landings on Sicily in July 1943.

COMPARATIVE TECHNICAL CHARACTERISTICS

	Crusader	PzKpfw IV Ausf. F2	M3 Grant	M4A1 Sherman
Army	UK	Germany	USA/UK	USA/UK
Crew	4	5	6–7	5
Dimensions: L x W x H (m)	6.3 x 2.77 x 2.22	7.02 x 2.88 x 2.68	5.63 x 2.71 x 3.02	5.84 x 2.61 x 2.74
Loaded weight (tonnes)	17.2	25.0	28.1	30.3
Main gun	2-pounder	75mm KwK 40	75mm M3, 37mm M6	75mm M3
Main gun ammo	139	87	65+128	90
Engine (hp)	340	300	350	350
Max. speed (km/h)	44	38	39	39
Fuel (liters)	140	470	662	662
Range (km)	320	210	195	195
Ground pressure (kg/cm^2)	1.02	0.91	0.89	0.96
Armor*				
Mantlet (mm)	50**=>50	50**=>50	76**=>76	76**=>76
Turret front (mm)	49@10=49.7	50@5=50.2	76@47=107.5	76@30=87.7
Turret side (mm)	24@50=37.3	33@25=36.4	51*=>51	51@5=51.2
Upper hull front (mm)	40@0=40	80@8=80.8	51@30=58.9	51@~50=79.3
Lower hull front (mm)	34@20=36.2	80@14=82.8	51**=>51	51**=>51
Upper hull side (mm)	29@0=29	30@0=30	38@0=38	38@0=38

*Armor data provided as: actual thickness in mm @ angle from vertical = effective thickness in mm
**Curved

CHAPTER 7

Tiger Rampant: 1943

THE CAMPAIGNS OF 1943 saw the continuing contest of the Red Army's quantity approach versus the Wehrmacht's quality approach. After a gestation of two years, the German army deployed a new generation of tanks in the summer of 1943. Of the two types, the Tiger heavy tank had the most influence.

THE ADOLF HITLER PANZER PROGRAM

The continuing shortages of tanks on the Russian Front in 1942 led Hitler to demand that more resources be put into armored vehicle manufacture. In September 1942 he established a goal of 1,200 AFVs per month by the end of 1944, of which 800 were to be tanks—600 Panthers and 50 Tigers. To put this in perspective, German tank production in September 1942 was 325 tanks per month, plus a further 120 assault guns and tank destroyers, for a total of 445. The new Reichsminister for the Armaments Industry, Albert Speer, began planning the Adolf Hitler *Panzerprogramm*. One aspect of this program was the establishment of a *Hauptausschusses* (main committee) in each of the key armament industries to better coordinate production of subcomponents and final assembly. The first head of the *Hauptausschusses Panzerwagen und Zugmaschinen* was Dr. Ferdinand Porsche, who most likely was chosen for his close connections to Hitler. It was not an ideal choice, as Porsche tended to favor unorthodox designs and lacked a practical appreciation for the suitability of designs for mass production.[1] Due to his poor performance, he was relieved of this post and

The panzer force in Russia remained of mixed composition in 1943, with the PzKpfw IV and its long 75mm KwK 40 gun, as seen in the foreground, becoming the predominant type. In the background is a pair of PzKpfw III Ausf. M with the long 50mm gun. Although this gun was capable of knocking out the T-34, it was not as versatile as the long 75mm gun in high-explosive throwing power. All these tanks have the new skirts to defend them against the ubiquitous Soviet antitank rifles.

replaced by Walter Rohland, a steel industry executive, and subsequently by Stiele von Heydekampf from Henschel.

One of the main reasons for the difficulties in reaching the ambitious production goals was the decision by Hitler and the senior leadership to favor heavy tanks. Hitler was heavily influenced by Porsche in his views on optimal panzer design. Kurt Arnoldt, the chief technical engineer of Henschel and one of the principals behind the Tiger tank, later recalled that Porsche was:

> a personal friend of Hitler and Speer . . . he had more influence on German tank design policy than anyone else. Porsche traded on his great reputation as the designer of the Volkswagen to gate-crash on the AFV industry. A capable engineer in many ways, but extremely Nazi. He allowed his technical views to be influenced by his political views. He was jealous and intolerant . . . He maintained that light tanks were no good and was always urging Hitler and Speer to allow him to build an even bigger tank with an even bigger gun.

Arnoldt argued that if Hitler and the senior leadership had followed the advice of professional tank engineers such as Heinrich Kniepkamp, head of the Waffenamt's weapons testing office (*Waffenprüfwesen 6*), Germany might have taken an alternate course. Instead of shifting its limited production resources to heavy and expensive tanks, they could have had a tank force based around more

The new PzKpfw IV Ausf. H that entered production in April 1943 kept the classic German turret layout with the commander afforded a vision cupola.

sensible 30-ton tank designs that would have been better than the T-34 and more suited to mass production in large quantities.[2] What is often forgotten about the *Panzerprogramm* was the enormous sums of money needed for the capital improvements and production facilities for the new tank designs.

On 17 January 1943, Hitler held a conference with Speer and senior industry leaders, declaring that the September goal was inadequate in view of the tremendous losses around Stalingrad and insisting that the goals be increased to 1,500–2,100 armored fighting vehicles per month by the end of 1944. The program, released on 23 January 1943, provided detailed objectives from March 1943 through March 1944 and aimed to raise overall AFV production from 600 monthly in January 1943 to 1,100 by March 1944; maximum production in 1944 was expected to reach 1,500 AFVs per month. There was an underlying degree of desperation in the planning since German intelligence agencies estimated that German AFV production in 1943 would only be 12,000 versus the 68,000 of the United States, United Kingdom, and USSR. A special industrial authorization of "panzer priority" was given to the industry, which Hitler acknowledged "even if these measures adversely affect other important branches of the armament industry for a time."

German tank strength on the Russian Front continued to plummet through March 1943 due to the heavy losses suffered following the retreat from Stalingrad. From a peak strength of 2,758 tanks

PANZER INDUSTRY OUTPUT AS PERCENTAGE OF GERMAN ARMAMENT INDUSTRY[3]

	Value (RM Million)	% of Industry Output
Oct. 1942	57	4.0
May 1943	147	6.8
Dec. 1943	165	8.0
July 1944	234	7.8

(1,710 operational) in December 1942, the Ostheer tank strength fell to only 1,686 tanks (895 operational) in March 1943. The readiness rate for tanks in the Ostheer had fallen to only 41 percent in February 1943, not as bad as in 1942 but still quite alarming. A major push began in the late winter and early spring to increase the strength in Russia for the upcoming summer offensive. An important part of this effort was the plan to field a powerful new generation of tanks to face the Soviet hordes.

Another major change in 1943 was the shift to produce more AFVs other than tanks. Guderian had attempted to monopolize industrial resources for tank production to the exclusion of other AFVs aimed at infantry support, notably assault guns (*Sturmgeschütz*). Germany was the only major army in 1942 that did not have tanks assigned to the infantry support mission; they were all concentrated in the panzer divisions. The trend in all other major armies was to devote a fraction of the tank force to infantry support in order to provide these divisions with greater offensive power.

The German policy began to change after 1941 with the advent of the T-34 and KV. The new 75mm PaK 40 was a big and heavy weapon, weighing 1.4 tons. As a result, it was difficult for the crew to manhandle and required mechanized traction. Many infantry officers preferred a mechanized solution, the tank destroyer (*Panzerjäger*). This led to the construction of the first generation of Marder tank destroyers on obsolete light tank chassis: the French Lorraine (Marder I), German PzKpfw II (Marder II), and Czech PzKpfw 38(t) (Marder III).

In parallel to the *Panzerprogramm* was an *Infanterieprogramm*. It did not have as much priority as the tank effort, but did lead to greater emphasis on providing the infantry with mechanized support in the form of the StuG III assault gun due

The failed Porsche Tiger was reconfigured as a tank destroyer with a fixed casemate and deployed to the Kursk battlefield as the Ferdinand. They were rebuilt after the Kursk fighting and renamed as the Elefant after Porsche had fallen out of favor. They were deployed both on the Russian Front and in Italy. This surviving Elefant was recovered by the U.S. Army in Italy in 1944.

GERMAN AFV PRODUCTION BY TYPE, 1941–44							
	Panzer	%	*Sturmgeschütz*	%	*Panzerjäger*	%	Total
1941	3,256	85.7	540	14.2	0	0	3,796
1942	4,278	69.5	748	12.1	1,123	18.2	6,149
1943	5,966	55.5	3,406	31.6	1,375	12.7	10,747
1944	9,161	50.1	8,682	47.4	441	2.4	18,284

to its exemplary role in the Russian Front fighting. It was not only excellent for providing direct high-explosive fire support for the infantry, but also proved to be an ideal dual-role vehicle with excellent antitank capability. As a result, by 1943 it had become one of the principal types of German AFVs. Furthermore, its combat effectiveness was enhanced by its durability; it was the most reliable German AFV on the Russian Front.

The PzKpfw VI Tiger Heavy Tank

The German army was in the process of developing a variety of new tanks before 1941, but most of these projects were shelved in the face of the T-34 threat.[4] The most significant of these programs was the Henschel VK3001(H), a 1938 scheme to build a heavy tank to support the infantry on breakthrough missions. The design offered heavier armor than the contemporary PzKpfw IV tanks, with frontal armor of 50mm, and a heavier weight, going from the 20 tons of the PzKpfw IV to about 30 tons on the new design. Firepower was not especially impressive, since the short 75mm gun on the PzKpfw IV was deemed more than adequate for the mission. A short 105mm gun was also under consideration. In 1939, a Porsche design was added to the program and had the armor increased to 75–80mm. The VK3001(P) also used a novel propulsion system of two conventional gasoline engines powering electric final drives via electric generators, a concept pioneered on French tanks of 1917–18 such as the St. Chamond and Char 2C. By the time the prototypes entered testing, the Waffenamt had second thoughts about the requirement after the encounters with French and British tanks in the summer of 1940. The next iteration in May 1941, the VK3601, envisioned a tank with 100mm armor and a powerful gun capable of penetrating 100mm armor: the revolutionary new squeeze-bore 75mm Gerät 725.

On 26 May 1941, Hitler held a conference of weapons designers to discuss future requirements. Porsche promoted the idea of heavy tanks serving as the spearheads of panzer divisions, with about twenty per division. As a result, Hitler ordered the start of yet another new heavy tank program, the VK4501, with competing designs from Henschel and Porsche. The Henschel design benefited from the firm's earlier work on 30-ton tanks and relied on a conventional power-train. The Porsche design was based around their hybrid gasoline/electric drive-train. By this time, the focus of the design had shifted from a breakthrough tank to a powerful battle tank able to destroy enemy heavy tanks such as the French Char B1 bis. The first weapon examined for the design was a new long-barreled 75mm L/70 gun, but in the event a tank gun derivative of the 88mm Flak gun was chosen instead. The encounters with the T-34 and KV tanks in June 1941 put more urgency on the program. The plan was to begin production by the summer of 1942.

Development of the Henschel design was relatively quick since it was based on the earlier designs. However, the army was not happy with the pace of work and the tank program was removed from the family control of Oscar Henschel and turned over to an engineering specialist, Stiele von Heydekampf. The first serial production Tiger I tank was completed in June 1942 but the rate of production was quite slow, with only seventy-seven Tigers completed that year. The Porsche Tiger (P) design

A Tiger of *schwere 13.Kompanie*, *Grossdeutschland Division*, during the fighting around Kharkov in January 1943.

A Tiger of the *schwere 8.Kompanie*, *2.SS-Panzer-Division Das Reich* under repair during the fighting around Kharkov in the early winter of 1943.

A Tiger of *2.Kompanie, schwere Panzer-Abteilung 505*, moves to the front near Orel in the summer fighting on the northern shoulder of the Kursk bulge.

proved far more troublesome, in no small measure due to its novel power-train.

The first production Henschel Tiger I was dispatched to Kummersdorf for field trials. In three weeks of trials, the tank negotiated 960 kilometers of terrain. The tests were carefully watched by Col. Wolfgang Thomale, an experienced panzer officer and the chief of staff of Guderian's General Inspectorate of the Panzer Troops. In September 1942, there was a scheme to equip two tank detachments for service in North Africa. Thomale was quite pleased with the results, but realistic enough to recognize that lingering teething problems would delay the deployment of the first twenty-five tanks to October 1943 at the earliest.

In contrast to the Henschel Tiger, the testing of Porsche's Tiger (P) was a complete fiasco and the tank broke down repeatedly, with the engines failing by the 100-kilometer mark.[5] Work on the tank was halted in November 1942 due to lingering mechanical unreliability. In view of the tremendous resources already spent on the project, work shifted instead to creating a heavy tank destroyer based on the tank chassis but armed with a longer L/71 version of the 88mm gun in a fixed casemate. Ninety of these "Ferdinands" were completed in the spring of 1943 and earmarked for the summer offensive against the Kursk bulge.

Hitler was impatient with the slow development pace of the Tiger, and the army tried to placate him by deploying small numbers of Tigers before all their teething problems had been solved. The first company of Tigers was rushed into action to the Russian Front near Leningrad. A platoon of four tanks of *1.Kompanie, schwere Panzer-Abteilung 502* was deployed to Leningrad and saw its first action on 29 August 1942. The tanks broke down or became trapped in the boggy terrain. The first real fighting took place on 16 September 1942 against Soviet infantry units of the 2nd Shock Army of the Volkhov Front. Two Tigers were knocked out by antitank guns and one was burned out. Additional Tigers reinforced this unit through the winter of 1942–43. During the Soviet Operation Spark (Iskra) on 18 January 1943, the Tiger tank of one of the company commanders was operating along the

Schlusselburg Road when it was hit by antitank gun fire from the 18th Rifle Division and driven off the road into a bog. The crew was killed trying to escape. Senior commanders were informed of the occurrence and they ordered that the tank be recovered. This was done by tanks of the 98th Tank Brigade, and the Tiger was sent to Moscow for further examination.[6] A second Tiger was recovered later in the month. This premature deployment had little consequence for German operations on the Leningrad Front but provided Soviet intelligence with their first close look at the new tank. The next Tiger deployment was to Tunisia with elements of *schwere Panzer-Abteilung 501* arriving in December 1942, as mentioned in the previous chapter.

The Panther Medium Tank

The tank crisis that erupted in the summer of 1941 after encountering the T-34 and KV led to an army requirement for a fundamentally new tank to overmatch the T-34 in armor, firepower, and mobility.[7] A special *Panzerkommission* was assembled, headed by Col. Sebastian Fichtner of the army's Waffenamt, that included the heads of all the major tank plants. The commission traveled to the Russian Front in November 1941 to be briefed by Gen. Heinz Guderian on the requirements for a new tank. Guderian stressed the need for a new gun capable of penetrating Soviet tanks beyond the range at which the Soviet 76mm gun could penetrate German armor, along with thicker armor and wider tracks for better

German designers continued to place great importance on situational awareness for tank commanders. This is an inside view into the cupola of a Panther Ausf. G showing the layout of the vision devices.

A view inside a Panther Ausf. G turret on the loader's side to the left.

GERMAN TANK GUNS, 1943–45[8]

Caliber	75mm	75mm	88mm	88mm
Main gun	KwK 40	KwK 42	KwK 36	KwK 43
Tube length	L/48	L/70	L/56	L/71
Armor-piercing projectile	*Pz.Gr.39*	*Pz.Gr.39/42*	*Pz.Gr.39*	*Pz.Gr.39/43*
Type	APCBC	APCBC	APCBC	APCBC
Initial muzzle velocity (m/s)	790	925	780	1,000
Round weight (kg)	11.5	14.24	22.7	22.7
Projectile weight (kg)	6.8	6.8	10.2	10.2
Propellant weight (kg)	2.4	3.67	5.4	5.4
Penetration (mm; @500m, 30 degree)	91–96	117–129	110	185
Armor-piercing projectile (high-velocity)	*Pz.Gr.40*	*Pz.Gr.40/42*	*Pz.Gr.40*	*Pz.Gr.40/43*
Type	HVAP	HVAP	HVAP	HVAP
Initial muzzle velocity (m/s)	930	1,120	940	1,130
Round weight (kg)	8.8	11.42	7.2	7.2
Projectile weight (kg)	4.1	5.74	7.3	7.3
Propellant weight (kg)	2.7	3.7	2.78	2.78
Penetration (mm; @500m, 30 degree)	108–120	174–184	155	217
High-explosive projectile	*Spr.Gr.34*	*Spr.Gr.42*	*Spr.Gr.L/4.5*	*Spr.Gr.43*
Projectile weight (kg)	5.74	5.74	9.0	9.4
Explosive fill (g)	653	653	861	861

mobility in Russian conditions. Two competitive designs were ordered from Daimler Benz and MAN, with the turret developed by Rheinmetall-Borsig. The Daimler Benz design closely resembled the T-34 in layout, while the MAN design adopted sloped armor but with the turret mounted more conventionally in the middle of the hull. At first, Hitler and Reichsminister for Armaments Albert Speer favored the Daimler Benz design. However, an evaluation of the design by the engineers of the *Panzerkommission* came out strongly in favor of the MAN design. Hitler was convinced by their points and on 13 May 1942 selected the MAN design for the new tank, with the proviso that frontal armor be increased from 60mm to 80mm. The plan was to begin production in December 1942 with the aim of having about 250 tanks ready for the summer 1943 offensive. During a conference in June 1942, Hitler wanted the frontal armor increased even further, to 100mm. In the short term, 80mm was the objective and the 100mm level would have to wait for the next generation, the Panther II.

The PzKpfw V Panther tank used a new 75mm KwK 42 L/70 gun with a new generation of projectiles. This long gun was powerful enough to penetrate the T-34 tank frontally even without using tungsten-carbide HVAP ammunition. The hull armor was 80mm at 55 degrees, giving it an effective protection equivalent to 140mm of vertical armor. The gun mantlet on the turret front was a 100mm-thick semicircular cast design. These levels of armor protection made the Panther essentially invulnerable to the T-34's 76mm gun from the front at normal combat ranges. Although intended to replace medium tanks, its weight of 43 tons was about 20 tons heavier than most existing medium tanks and placed the Panther in the heavy tank category, even if it was not designated as such. The plan was to conduct Panther production at six assembly plants and to reach a monthly output of 475 tanks per month by March 1944; actual production that month was 277 tanks.

Speer was given a demonstration of some of the first serial production Panther tanks at the Grafenwöhr range on 22 February 1943. Although the demonstration went well, staff from the first Panther unit, *Panzer-Abteilung 51*, noted numerous problems encountered on the early production vehicles, including motor fires, fuel pump failures, weak final drives, transmission problems, and excessive fume buildup in the turret while firing. Speer pointed out that PzKpfw III development had taken two and a half years compared to one year for the Panther, and he thought the progress to date had been extraordinary. Although MAN set out to remedy the many teething problems in the Panther design, these faults would continue to manifest themselves when the tank saw its combat debut during the Kursk offensive in July 1944.

SOVIET TANK DEVELOPMENT IN 1943

The Soviet tank program for 1943 retained its focus on quantity over quality, but made several significant changes in the mix of designs. The KV tank was no longer invulnerable to German antitank guns and continued to be plagued with mechanical problems. As a result, its production was considerably trimmed in favor of the T-34. A program was underway to gradually replace the T-34 with a new type with thicker armor, the T-43. However, it had not entered production at the time of the Kursk battles, and the lessons from this campaign stressed the need for better firepower rather than better armor. The T-70 light tank was widely despised for its puny gun and indifferent automotive performance. However, the automotive production plants where it was assembled could not handle larger tanks. Instead, the new SU-76 assault gun armed with the standard 76mm divisional gun was built on its chassis. The Soviet plants churned out the SU-76 assault gun to the point where it became the second most numerous Soviet AFV type after the T-34. The popular Lend-Lease Valentine tank took over the light tank role.

The Decline of the KV Tank

The KV tank had fallen out of favor in 1942. One of the senior Red Army tank commanders, Gen. Pavel Rotmistrov, described the general attitude:

> The difficulty is that while there isn't much difference in speed between the light T-60 and medium T-34 on the roads, when moving cross-country the light tanks are quickly left behind. The KV heavy tank is already behind and often crushed local bridges which cut off units following behind. Under battlefield conditions, that too often meant that the T-34 alone arrived; the light tanks had difficulty fighting the German tanks anyway and the KVs were still delayed in the rear. It was also difficult to command these companies as they sometimes were

Of all the British tanks provided to the Red Army via Lend-Lease, the Valentine was by far the favorite due to its dependability. Virtually the entire Canadian production run of Valentines went to the Soviet Union. In total, some 3,591 Valentines were shipped to the Soviet Union, of which 3,184 arrived. Here a pair of Valentines with the later 6-pounder guns are seen in a barge near Tanuma, Iran, during shipment to the Soviet Union over the Iranian-Soviet frontier.

Although this is a staged propaganda photo, it shows an interesting mixture of T-34 tanks and Lend-Lease British Tetrarch airborne tanks of the 563rd Separate Tank Battalion in operation in the North Caucasus in March 1943. The Red Army received only twenty of these small tanks during the war.

By early 1943, the numerous PzKpfw III tanks captured by the Red Army around Stalingrad were no longer considered well enough armed for front-line use. Instead, Plant No. 37 converted 201 into the SU-76i (I = *innostranaya*, foreign) using the same F-34 76mm gun as the T-34 tank. The first were delivered in May 1943. This shows the original configuration; after Kursk they received an additional armor shield over the gun.

equipped with different types of radios or none at all.

In an attempt to redeem the KV, the SKB-2 design bureau at Chelyabinsk tried a two-pronged approach. A crash program began on a KV with reduced armor called the KV-1S (S=*skorostnoi*, speedy), an attempt to decrease the disparity in automotive performance between the KV and the T-34. In April 1942 work also began on the KV-13 in an effort to develop a more compact version of the KV that retained its heavy armor while improving its automotive performance. It was hoped that the KV-13 would be a true universal tank, bridging the gap between medium and heavy tanks.

The KV-1S cut 5 tonnes of weight from the KV by decreasing the side armor from 90mm to 75mm. The power-train of the tank was completely upgraded, including a new clutch, new transmission, and other improvements that helped close the gap in automotive performance with the T-34. A new, lighter turret was introduced that also adopted the German pattern of a three man crew, freeing the commander of his responsibilities as gunner. Although a vision cupola was introduced, it did not have a hatch so the commander could follow the German practice of fighting with his head outside the tank. The KV-1S was accepted for production on 20 August 1942 and began to be built later in the month alongside T-34s. In spite of its improvements, the Red Army still favored the T-34, and part of the production at Chelyabinsk shifted to the T-34.

Gen. Mikhail Katukov, the tank commander who so skillfully demonstrated the potential of the T-34 tank in the defense of Moscow in October 1941, described his view of the situation at a meeting with Stalin in September 1942:

> The T-34 fulfills all our hopes and has proven itself in combat. But the KV heavy tank . . . the soldiers don't like it. . . . It is very heavy and clumsy and not very agile. It surmounts obstacles with great difficulty. It often damages bridges and becomes involved in other accidents. More to the point, it is equipped with the same 76mm gun as the T-34. This raises the question, to what extent is it superior to the T-34? If the KV had a more potent gun or one of greater caliber, then it might be possible to excuse its weight and other shortcomings.

The KV-13 was yet another attempt to redeem the KV series by modifying it into a smaller and lighter "universal tank." In the wake of the Kursk fighting, this approach fell out of favor and both the KV-13 and its rival the T-43 were cancelled.

The other attempt to redeem the KV after Kursk was the KV-85, which mounted the D-5T 85mm gun in a turret derived from the KV-13 project. Although the KV-85 was built in small numbers in 1943, the Red Army waited for a thorough redesign before committing to large-scale production. This resulted in the renamed IS-1 tank.

As a temporary solution, KVs were removed from the tank brigades in October 1942 and used instead to form separate heavy tank breakthrough regiments for use by army commanders in assault and infantry support missions. Ironically, the KV-1S, the most nimble of the KV heavy tanks, arrived at a time when heavy armor rather than mobility would have been preferable.

A pair of KV-1 Model 41 tanks go into action on the Kalinin Front in January 1943. By this stage, most KV tanks had been relegated to separate tank regiments for infantry support missions.

Parallel to work on the KV-1S, Chelyabinsk also developed the KV-13. In reality, the KV-13 was a whole new design intended to be as well armored as the KV but as maneuverable as the T-34. The KV-1 design was clearly too large to accomplish these goals, so the designers intended to create a smaller tank. The crew was reduced from five to three: the driver, loader, and the commander/gunner. The KV-13 weighed only 31 metric tons, compared to 42.5 for the KV-1S and 47 for the basic KV-1. The KV-13 was still in development in the summer of 1943 at the time of the Kursk battles. Although it never entered production, it formed the basis for the later IS Stalin heavy tanks.

T-34: Upgrades and Alternatives

The T-34 tanks being manufactured in early 1943 were not significantly different from those manufactured in 1942. There had been several schemes to update the T-34 with significant new features, but all of them were stillborn due to government decisions to concentrate on production quantity over quality. Some modest changes that might have improved automotive and combat effectiveness were developed, but it usually took months to introduce these features into the production lines.

The Red Army recognized it had a problem with the turret layout of the T-34 and the tank commander's lack of situational awareness. Russian tank officers complained that the T-34 commander had to be a "circus performer," instructing the driver, aiming the gun, and trying to direct the crew all at the same time. In the summer of 1942, the T-34 design bureau at Nizhni-Tagil developed the T-34S, which had a new three-man turret. The commander was in the rear of the turret with a cupola, though as in the case of the KV-1S there was no hatch. Although the tests were extremely favorable and recommended serial production, this was not undertaken. The T-34S was followed by the T-34M Model 1942, which increased the armor of the tank to 60–80mm on the hull and 58–80mm on the turret. This project also fell by the wayside. In October–November 1942, GABTU instructed the designers at Nizhni-Tagil to examine a more radical improvement of the T-34 as the T-43. This was intended as a "universal tank" like the parallel KV-13 project, meant to bridge the gap between medium and heavy tanks. It continued the features of the T-34S and T-34M, such as the new three-man turret and increased armor; however, it retained the same 76mm gun of the existing T-34. The T-43 was still in the testing phase at the time of the Battle of Kursk in July 1943.

Prior to the Battle of Kursk, the T-43 was the planned replacement for the T-34. After Kursk, the Red Army wanted more firepower, not more armor.

The most common version of the T-34 in 1943 was the type with the Gaika turret. This tank from the Kalinin Front drives past an abandoned German 105mm IFH 18 howitzer. The logs carried on the side of the tank were unditching beams used to extract the tank from deep mud.

The Uralmash tank plant had an enormous press purchased from Germany before the war and used it to produce a different version of the T-34 Gaika turret that was stamped out of armor plate. This particular example is configured as an OT-34 flamethrower tank with the flamethrower nozzle in place of the usual hull machine gun.

The poor ergonomics in the T-34 turret might have been helped by adding better vision devices to the existing Gaika hex-nut turret. A commander's vision cupola had already been developed in June 1942 but not authorized for production. In the autumn of 1942, the Red Army began steps to copy the British traversable tank periscope, designated as the Mk-4 after the Churchill Mark IV on which it was based. A final version of the commander's cupola with the Mk-4 was accepted for production at Nizhni-Tagil on 7 June 1943, but the Mk-4 production line was not yet ready. As a result, the new cupola didn't go into widespread production until the autumn of 1943 after the Kursk battles overwhelmingly demonstrated its urgent need.

One of the worst automotive features of the T-34 was its poor transmission system, which included a clutch in the driver's compartment connected to a four-speed transmission in the rear via a set of long actuating rods.[9] This system was difficult and tiring to operate, and the driver often required the assistance of the radio operator to help work the clutch, especially on long drives. In 1942, a new clutch and five-speed transmission was developed to improve the drive-train and make it easier to operate. This went into production in 1943 at the Chelyabinsk and Sverdlovsk plants but not at the main Nizhni-Tagil plant, which lacked the necessary new machine tools. Eventually Nizhni-Tagil began assembling tanks with the five-speed gearbox when supplies became available from other plants, but Nizhni-Tagil T-34 tanks continued to receive four-speed gearboxes when the improved five-speed version was not available.

Another critical improvement was the replacement of the Pomon oil-bath air cleaner with the improved *Tsiklon* (Cyclone) air filter. Although it was approved on 12 June 1942, it was not fitted to new tanks at the main Nizhni-Tagil plant until December 1942 and at Chelyabinsk until January 1943. While better than the Pomon, it still required careful crew attention. During the famous march of the 5th Guards Tank Army to Prokhorovka during the Kursk campaign, tanks had to stop every three to five hours to clean out accumulated dust from the filters. A postwar American report was far more critical:

> Wholly inadequate engine intake air cleaners could be expected to allow early engine failure due to dust intake and the resulting abrasive wear. Several hundred miles in very dusty operation would probably be accompanied by severe power loss . . . Centrifugal separation of dirt from air was abandoned several decades ago in America as being very ineffective in motor vehicle operation.[10]

A quick method of improving the firepower of the T-34 would have been to provide it with tungsten-carbide HVAP ammunition. Priority had been given to the manufacture of HVAP for the 45mm antitank gun, and as a result the 76mm BR-354P round was not completed until April–May 1943. A few rounds may have been issued at the time of the Kursk battles, but it was not in widespread service until October 1943 after the Kursk battles had demonstrated its urgent need.[11]

Despite the slow pace of introducing long-overdue design improvements, a greater effort was made in 1943 to impose quality control at the tank plants. A new policy was adopted that all T-34 tanks had to undergo a 30-kilometer test at the plant, followed by a 50-kilometer test by military inspectors before the tank would be accepted by the army. In addition, one tank from every hundred was subjected to a 300-kilometer test run, the nominal warranty endurance of the T-34 in 1943. The initial 300-kilometer tests conducted in April 1943 disclosed appalling results—only 10.1 percent of the tanks passed the test. The June 1943 tests were even worse, with only 7.7 percent completing the test.

The technical faults varied from plant to plant. In May 1943, the five plants producing the T-34 were instructed to provide five new T-34 tanks for endurance trials near Kazan. Of the five plants, the T-34s from the UZTM plant in Sverdlovsk had the best results, reaching 1,001 kilometers in 4.9 days of operation before breakdowns; the worst were the T-34s from the Chelyabinsk plant, which reached only 409 kilometers in 2.8 days of operation. The average was 710 kilometers.[12] Technical improvements such as the new transmission and air filters, as well as greater attention to quality control, significantly improved the durability of new T-34 tanks, and by December 1943, 83.6 percent of the tanks tested completed the 300-kilometer run.[13]

The quality control improvements were evident on the battlefield. Combat losses due to mechanical breakdowns decreased from 8.6 percent in 1942 to about 2 percent in the Kursk campaign.[14] In the days before the tank clash at Prokhorovka, the 5th Guards Tank Army executed a three-day forced march on 7–9 July totaling 330–380 kilometers, a distance that would have proved debilitating a year earlier.

THE 1943 CAMPAIGNS

The early winter of 1943 was dominated by two large campaigns. The final phase of the Stalingrad campaign ended in early February with the surrender of the German *6.Armee*. During the course of this operation, the Red Army launched a series of subsidiary attacks including winter offensives that recaptured Kharkov. The Wehrmacht responded with their Donets campaign that led to the recapture of Kharkov by the *1.SS-Panzer-Division*.

The front quieted briefly after early March 1943 as both sides recovered from the heavy winter losses. The Kharkov battle led to the creation of a large salient in the center of the Russian Front around the city of Kursk. For the Germans, this presented an opportunity to encircle a large portion of the Red Army in one of their predictable summer offensives. For the Red Army, the Kursk bulge offered a chance to finally defeat the "summer Germans." The Red Army had won two substantial

THE GERMAN TANK FORCE IN 1943[15]													
	Jan.	Feb.	Mar.	Apr.	May	June	July	Aug.	Sept.	Oct.	Nov.	Dec.	Total
Production	257	320	370	306	689	484	511	458	591	662	561	757	5,966
Losses	431	1,596	502	416	306	19	645	572	353	450	524	548	6,362
Overall strength	5,648	5,463	4,149	3,797	3,643	4,001	4,536	4,379	4,328	4,991	5,157	5,158	N/A
Front strength	4,364	4,261	3,177	2,540	2,504	2,900	3,452	2,547	2,672	2,986	3,227	3,355	N/A
Strength—East	2,803	2,422	1,686	1,742	1,837	2,209	2,584	2,274	2,202	1,953	2,198	2,287	N/A
Operational—East	1,475	981	902	1,052	1,371	1,846	2,287	1,176	821	605	962	817	N/A
Operational (%)*	53%	41%	53%	75%	84%	89%	52%	41%	31%	44%	36%	51%	54%

*Monthly average

2.SS-Panzergrenadier Division Das Reich used the captured Soviet tank plant in Kharkov to rebuild a number of T-34 tanks to reinforce their antitank battalion. These were used during the battle of Kursk.

winter victories in the defense of Moscow in 1941 and Stalingrad 1942–43, but had been unable to defeat the two German summer offensives. The Kursk option was apparent to both sides, and the Red Army decided to remain on the defensive in the opening stage after creating a dense defensive belt on the northern and southern shoulders of the salient. Through the early summer, the Red Army built up a substantial tank reserve behind the Kursk salient with an aim toward launching a series of massive, mechanized counteroffensives in the wake of a defense of the Kursk bulge.

Operation Citadel: The Kursk Campaign

Operation Citadel, the German plan to cut off the Kursk salient, was a two-pronged attack. Army Group Center would attack the northern shoulder of the bulge using 8 Panzer divisions with 747 tanks, 31 new Tigers, and 89 Ferdinand assault guns, plus a variety of assault guns and other armor, bringing the grand total to about 1,375 AFVs. The heaviest concentration of German armor faced the southern shoulder of the bulge, and Army Group South included 5 panzer divisions and 4 panzergrenadier divisions with some 1,035 panzers, plus 45 Tigers, 200 Panthers, and a variety of supporting armor for a grand total of about 1,420 AFVs.[16]

By this stage of the war, German offensive tactics had evolved into a combined-arms process. Gone were the days of blitzkrieg when panzer divisions could rampage through terrorized infantry formations with impunity. The Red Army had become a far more formidable adversary than in 1941, and the fight to secure a breakthrough needed a stalwart infantry attack. The main armored support for the infantry breakthrough came from the 11 assault gun battalions (*Sturmgeschütz-Abteilungen*), totaling about 345 StuG III, that were attached at corps level and doled out to the infantry divisions that formed the *Schwerpunkt* (focal point) of the

A tank attack by the *20.Panzer-Division* during the summer of 1943 from the perspective of a PzKpfw III commander. To the right is a PzKpfw IV with the new side skirts and in the background are the dismounted panzergrenadiers. This division fought on the northern sector of the Kursk salient.

The Tiger won a reputation in the Red Army after Kursk far out of proportion to its actual combat record. This was in no small measure due to identity confusion with the new and ubiquitous PzKpfw IV Ausf. G and Ausf. H that had been fitted with side skirts for protection against Soviet antitank rifles.

A pair of Tigers of the *schwere Panzer-Abteilung 505* during the operations on the northern flank of the Kursk salient around Orel in the summer of 1943.

assault. In the case of Kursk, these were further reinforced by the Tiger battalions, as well as the Ferdinands where available. German tactical doctrine discouraged use of the panzer divisions in the opening days of the offensive for fear that they would simply become trapped in the Soviet infantry defenses and ground down by attrition. Instead, they would wait until the infantry divisions won the breakthrough battle, then be committed to the break-out battle and exploit the gain by a rapid race deep into the Soviet rear area to trap and destroy any units remaining in the Kursk bulge. In reality, German infantry divisions were no longer strong or numerous enough to penetrate the toughest of Soviet defenses. They had not been modernized sufficiently since 1941 and lacked the armored support to grind through a heavily fortified defense belt. As a desperate expedient, the Wehrmacht was forced to use panzer divisions in some sectors to accomplish the breakthrough, which led to premature attrition. This would result in the downfall of German panzer tactics at Kursk.

Facing Army Group North was the Red Army's Central Front with about 1,785 tanks, while Army Group South faced the Voronezh Front with 1,704 tanks. Although tanks formed an ingredient in the Soviet defenses, they were not the main element. The Red Army was very well aware of German combined-arms tactics and responded with an unprecedented defense scheme of multiple defensive lines intended to defeat the German infantry attacks and exhaust any German attempt to penetrate the defense using tanks. The core of the antitank defense was the antitank strongpoint (PTOP: *Protivo-tankoviy oboroniy punkt*), usually battalion-sized defenses consisting of a series of echeloned entrenchments with carefully sighted antitank rifles and regimental artillery. Behind the PTOP were special antitank reserves (PTR) consisting of the 76mm guns of the divisional artillery used in a direct-fire antitank role, sometimes supplemented with 85mm antiaircraft guns in an improvised antitank role. The defense network was shielded by minefields with a density of 2,400 antitank and 2,700 antipersonnel

A scene near the village of Gremuchiy of two Panthers of *Panzer-Regiment.39* during the Kursk fighting in July 1943. The tank to the right, number 101, ran over mines and was abandoned.

mines per kilometer. Most infantry divisions had an attached tank battalion or regiment, often dug in with only the turret exposed.

A typical example was the 375th Rifle Division, which held a 16-kilometer-wide front in the 6th Guards Army sector of the Voronezh Front. It had 7 PTOP and 3 PTR strongpoints equipped with 134 of the 14.5mm antitank rifles, 39 of the 45mm antitank guns, 12 of the 76mm regimental guns, and 68 of the 76mm ZiS-3 divisional guns. It was supported by the 61 tanks of the 96th Tank Brigade. Soviet antitank weapons, like the tank force, had focused on quantity over quality. By 1943, the 14.5mm antitank rifle was ineffective against the frontal armor of nearly all German tanks, barring a lucky hit on the tracks. It was still effective against the thin side armor of tanks such as the PzKpfw III and PzKpfw IV; however, prior to Kursk, the Wehrmacht had begun to introduce armor skirts to the sides of their tanks specifically to defeat the Soviet antitank rifles. Therefore, the most numerous Soviet antitank weapons were rendered ineffective by this innovation prior to the start of the battle.

The Soviet 45mm antitank gun had been improved in 1942 by the development of a new version with a longer gun-tube and also enhanced with the new HVAP tungsten-carbide ammunition. An excellent 57mm antitank gun had also been introduced, but its use was largely confined to a few specialized antitank regiments at corps level. Despite these shortcomings, Soviet antitank defenses were formidable due to their density and depth. The Wehrmacht had largely overlooked the potential to develop combat engineer tanks to rapidly breach

One of the specialized versions of the PzKpfw III was the Pz.Beob.Wg (Panzerbeobachtungswagen). This was an artillery forward observer vehicle to support self-propelled artillery units in the panzer divisions and converted from older, obsolete tanks. This one is moving forward during the summer 1943 fighting.

A view of several Panther tanks of *Panzer-Regiment.39*, also called *Panzer-Regiment von Lauchert* after its commander. The unit's two battalions fought on the southern shoulder of the Kursk salient in July 1943. In this view, a few Soviet prisoners can be seen in the foreground.

minefields or overcome antitank ditches, even though the British army had demonstrated the value of these innovations in 1942 in the desert campaigns.

The German attack began on 5 July 1943 with a series of vicious artillery duels and air strikes. The assault by Army Group Center against the northern shoulder managed to overcome the first Soviet defense belt in three days of battle, but became bogged down and exhausted.

The assault against the southern shoulder by Army Group South made far better progress. By the third day of the battle, the *II.SS-Panzer-Korps* had penetrated both the first and second defense belts and seemed to be on the verge of breaking out toward the rail junction at Prokhorovka. However, in the process of using the SS panzer divisions to secure the breakthrough, these divisions had become badly weakened. The Red Army poured in reinforcements, and for the next three days the campaign became a slow battle of attrition. Soviet tank counterattacks evaporated in the face of the new German guns. The Tiger and Panther tanks were able to engage and destroy T-34 tanks at 1,500 meters or more and were essentially invulnerable to T-34 fire except at close ranges from the side. The exchange ratio in these battles was often around 8 to 1 in the Germans' favor.

The turning point came on 10 July 1943. This date was critical for two reasons. First, the Red Army began committing its theater reserve, Gen. Pavel Rotmistrov's 5th Guards Tank Army, to staunch the German advance toward Prokhorovka. Second, in the Mediterranean Theater the Allies began Operation Husky, the amphibious invasion of Sicily. Hitler

The M3 medium tank was not one of the more popular Lend-Lease types in Soviet service, grimly nicknamed "the Grave for Seven Brothers." About 170 served on the Central Front in July 1943; this example was knocked out during the fighting.

had already expressed misgivings about the Italian theater since an Italian withdrawal from the war would subtract eighty divisions from the Axis order of battle. While the Italian divisions did not have the equivalent combat value of German divisions, about forty divisions were on occupation duty in Greece, the Balkans, and southern France. Their sudden removal would require replacement with German divisions; the Russian Front would inevitably be drained of forces. Hitler's decision to abandon Operation Citadel following Operation Husky is sometimes explained as a face-saving measure in response to the approaching failure of Citadel. A more cogent assessment was that Citadel was a last-ditch gamble to restore German strategic initiative on the Russian Front after the Stalingrad debacle, but a gamble that could not be sustained due to Germany's declining military resources.[17] Hitler called off Citadel on 13 July following the crucial battle near Prokhorovka.

The counterattack by Rotmistrov's 5th Guards Tank Army on 10–11 July 1943 involved nearly 830 AFVs facing just over 400 German AFVs in the Prokhorovka sector. Although it is often described as the largest tank battle of World War II, this is a considerable exaggeration.[18] The German and French tank fighting on 13–15 May 1940 in the Gembloux Gap involved as many tanks, and the battle for the "Bloody Triangle" of Brody-Dubno in Ukraine in the last week of June 1941 certainly involved far more.

Regardless of whether it was the largest tank battle or not, Prokhorovka is significant for both its dramatic action and its decisive results. In a massive engagement fought over the course of several days, Rotmistrov's 5th Guards Tank Army stopped the forward momentum of the German attack. On 12 July, the Red Army began to launch large-scale counterattacks that marked the change of the tide of

The crew of a PzKpfw IV Ausf. G conducts repair on the KwK 40 gun with the help of a recovery vehicle based on the PzKpfw 38(t) light tank.

A column of PzKpfw IV Ausf. H move forward during the fighting in the summer of 1943.

This Lend-Lease Churchill IV served with the 10th Guards Heavy Breakthrough Tank Regiment of the 23rd Tank Corps during their ill-fated attack on the Voronezh Front on 21 July 1943.

The Tiger's legend stemmed from its performance during the Kursk campaign in the summer of 1943. The legend was inflated by Soviet misperceptions, labeling nearly any of the new tanks as Tigers, including the PzKpfw IV, due to their changed appearance with side skirts.

war on the Russian Front. The Wehrmacht had lost the strategic initiative in the conflict and was irrevocably doomed to a defensive posture for the rest of the war.

The battle of Prokhorovka was a Pyrrhic victory for the Red Army. Casualties on both sides were heavy but fell disproportionately on the Soviet tank force. The 5th Guards Tank Army lost 340 tanks and 19 assault guns, of which 207 were total losses.[19] The *II.SS-Panzer-Korps* and *III.Panzer-Korps* lost about 150 AFVs, although most of these were recovered and not written off yet as total losses.

Total German AFV losses in July 1943 on all fronts were 932 AFVs (645 tanks, 207 StuG, and 80 *Panzerjäger*), of which the vast majority were suffered during Operation Citadel. Their peak strength of 2,609 tanks in the east earlier in July had fallen to 2,274 by the end of the month. More critically, operational strength fell from 2,287 to only 1,178 tanks due to extensive battle damage suffered during Citadel.

DYNAMICS OF SOVIET TANK STRENGTH, 1943	
Tank strength, 1 Jan. 1943	20,600
Total losses	22,400
Tank production	19,907
Lend-Lease tank deliveries	2,990
Tank strength, 1 Jan. 1944	21,100

SOVIET TANK AND AFV LOSSES BY CAMPAIGN, 1943[20]

Campaign	Period	Losses	Avg. Daily Tank Loss
Stalingrad offensive operations	19 Nov. 1942–2 Feb. 1943	2,915	38
Northern Caucasus offensive operations	1 Jan.–4 Feb.	220	6
Leningrad offensive	12–30 Jan.	41	2
Voronezh-Kharkov offensive	13 Jan.–3 Mar.	1,023	20
Kharkov defensive operations	4–25 Mar.	322	15
Kursk defensive operations	5–23 July	1,614	85
Orlov offensive operations	12 July–18 Aug.	2,586	68
Belgorod-Kharkov offensive operations	3–23 Aug.	1,864	89
Smolensk offensive operations	7 Aug.–2 Oct.	863	15
Donbass offensive operations	13 Aug.–22 Sept.	886	22
Chernigov-Poltava offensive operations	26 Aug.–30 Sept.	1,140	32
Novorossiysk-Taman offensive operations	10 Sept.–9 Oct.	111	4
Nizhnedneprovsk offensive operations	26 Sept.–20 Dec.	2,639	31
Kiev offensive operations	3–13 Nov.	271	25
Subtotal (listed campaigns)		**16,495**	
Total tank and AFV losses, 1943		***22,400***	***64***

GREAT EXPECTATIONS

Hitler had great expectations that the new Tiger, Panther, and Ferdinand tanks would throw the battle in favor of the Wehrmacht. The results in retrospect were quite mixed. Of the new types, the Tiger was clearly the standout performer and the only tank that could claim to have had decisive tactical impact in the various skirmishes during the campaign.

At the start of the campaign, there were about 147 Tiger tanks assigned; 5 replacements were later received during the fighting.[21] The heaviest concentrations were in two army battalions: *schwere Panzer-Abteilung 503* in the south and *schwere Panzer-Abteilung 505* in the north, with a nominal strength of 45 Tiger tanks each. The *Grossdeutschland Division* had a reinforced Tiger company and the three *SS-Panzer-Divisions* had a Tiger company, each with a nominal strength of 14 tanks. A total of 133 Tiger tanks were available at the start of Citadel, but only 97 were ready on the first day because of lingering mechanical problems and difficulties moving such heavy tanks to the front without adequate tactical bridging.

Tiger strength fell quickly due to combat attrition. Although very few were written off as total losses, many were disabled in the first days of fighting after encountering minefields. In the case of one of the Tiger battalions, an entire company was disabled by mines in one day. The Tiger's thick armor offered it excellent protection except against the heaviest of Soviet antitank weapons. Most Tiger tanks withstood multiple hits against their frontal armor; the few penetrations that did occur were usually to the more vulnerable side and rear armor. The only effective Tiger killers were the relatively rare

The first glimpse of the Panther tank by British and American intelligence was this Panther Ausf. D captured by the Red Army during the Kursk fighting that was put on display in Gorkiy Park in Moscow. Due to its mechanical woes, the Panther did not leave as strong an impression in 1943 as the Tiger did, and it was underestimated as a result.

TIGER STRENGTH DURING OPERATION CITADEL, JULY 1943

July	4	5	6	7	8	9	10	11	12	13	14	15	16	17	18	19	20
Ready	133	97	56	58	56	77	60	57	52	47	49	51	52	64	63	62	71
Losses			1	5			2	1	1		3			2			1

57mm antitank guns or overmatching weapons such as heavy field guns or 85mm antiaircraft guns in a direct-fire mode.[22] For example, a number of Tigers were knocked out when their commander cupolas were completely blown off by a direct field gun hit.

The Tiger's 88mm gun proved to be a formidable weapon against the Soviet tanks. The two army Tiger battalions claimed 182 Soviet tanks up to 16 July 1943 when the offensive was called off; these claims were undoubtedly exaggerated. As mentioned earlier, the German FHO intelligence organization regularly discounted claims due to the problems of double-counting, especially in long-range engagements. Furthermore, German claims of Soviet tank kills covered any Soviet tank knocked out in combat, whether it was a total loss or later recovered and put back into action, while German Tiger losses included only total losses and no temporary losses.[23] So for example, the two battalions recorded only 8 Tiger total losses during the fighting up to 16 July, but by that date they had suffered 58 temporary losses due to combat damage and mechanical breakdowns and had only 24 Tiger tanks operational. While some of these damaged tanks were later repaired in the field or sent back to Germany for repair, others eventually were stricken off.[24]

While the Tiger tank was undoubtedly a formidable tank killer at Kursk, its actual combat effectiveness was far less than might be suggested by its legend. Soviet accounts of the Battle of Kursk are filled with reports of battles with Tigers when undoubtedly most of the skirmishes involved more mundane types such as the PzKpfw IV. The enormous scale of Soviet tank losses seemed slightly less embarrassing if they could be credited to this invulnerable new monster. As was the case later in Normandy in 1944, "Tiger" simply became the Red Army soldier's nickname for virtually any German tank. Likewise, every lowly StuG III was described as a "Ferdinand" in Russian accounts despite their rarity.

The Tiger's greatest moment of glory during the Kursk fighting was on 5 July 1943 when the *schwere Panzer-Abteilung 505* was able to penetrate the initial defensive belt of the Soviet 15th Rifle Division near Butyrki in the Army Group Center sector. However, the rapidity of this breakthrough was unanticipated and follow-on panzer divisions were not ready to exploit the success. In the Army Group South sector, *schwere Panzer-Abteilung 503* proved far less effective. Against doctrine, it was split up into its three constituent companies and used piecemeal with little tactical effect. Within the first three days of fighting, the combat effectiveness of the Tiger units had been diluted by poor tactical employment, the ubiquitous Soviet minefields, and mechanical breakdowns. On average, only about 38 percent of the Tiger force was operational on any given day, though the readiness rate varied considerably from day to day. Overall, the army and Waffen-SS Tiger units reported total losses of only 13 Tiger tanks by 16 July 1943, but they had suffered temporary losses of 87 tanks and had just 52 tanks ready for action. The technical superiority of the Tiger was almost meaningless in view of the tiny number of tanks available from day to day, especially when so thinly spread across such a large front.

The combat debut of the new Panther tank at Kursk was a major disappointment, especially when compared to the Tiger. It was technically immature and had a host of mechanical problems, which were aggravated by inadequate training of the crews when the tank was rushed into service.[25] Although the Panther had very thick frontal armor, its side armor was vulnerable to a variety of Soviet antitank weapons. Following the battle, Soviet tank specialists conducted a detailed examination of thirty-one knocked-out Panther tanks, twenty-two of which had been knocked out by gunfire.[26] There were no penetrations of the front of the tanks; they were all to the hull side (59 percent), rear (23 percent) and turret (18 percent), often with multiple hits. Of these, seventeen were knocked out by 76mm tank or antitank guns, four by 85mm antiaircraft guns used in an antitank role, and one by a 45mm antitank gun.

Although more vulnerable to Soviet antitank fire than the Tiger, the new 75mm gun on the Panther was quite lethal against Soviet tanks. The Panther units fighting at Kursk claimed to have destroyed 263 Soviet tanks up to the end of the offensive on 16 July 1943; as mentioned earlier, these claims were overstated. Of the 200 Panther tanks available at the start of Citadel, 65 were written off as total losses following the battle and 42 were sent back for repair. Of the 105 tanks remaining in Russia at the start of the withdrawal, 76 were lost or abandoned during the retreat, many having suffered battle damage at Kursk. Only 29 remained in service in Russia on 12 August 1943.[27]

TANK TECHNOLOGY IN THE WAKE OF OPERATION CITADEL

The Battle of Kursk marked another technological watershed in tank development, particularly in the case of Soviet tank technology. The poor performance of the T-34 at Kursk created a crisis in the autumn of 1943. Post-combat Soviet assessments stressed the impact of the Tiger and Ferdinand.[28] In fact, the whole panoply of German innovations—including the PzKpfw IV with skirts and the long L/48 gun and the large-scale use of the new StuG III Ausf. G—had all upset the technological balance. As mentioned earlier, Soviet tankers inevitably identified nearly all the new German tanks as Tigers and all the new assault guns as Ferdinands.

After the war, the main Soviet tank research institute, VNII Transmash in Leningrad, used its standard computer modeling program to examine the combat effectiveness of the major tank types used in the Kursk. The PzKpfw III with the long 50mm gun was chosen as the baseline and valued at 1.

For the first time during the war, tank panic set in amongst the Soviet units, and the tank force demanded tanks with a "longer arm" to be able to deal with the new German designs. Gen. Pavel Rotmistrov wrote an impassioned letter to Marshal Georgi Zhukov, pleading for the development of tanks to restore the technological balance on the battlefield. The T-34 had proven to be woefully inadequate at Kursk. The primary problem was the poor performance of its 76mm gun against the thickly armored German tanks. By this stage, even the PzKpfw IV had 80mm frontal armor.

The trajectory in Soviet tank development through the summer of 1943 was movement from a medium/heavy tank mix toward a "universal tank" such as the T-43 or KV-13. The emphasis of both these designs was thicker armor than the baseline T-34, but their firepower was the same 76mm F-34 gun in use since 1941. In the wake of the Kursk battle, this approach was abandoned entirely.

In the case of the T-34, a crash program was instituted in the late summer of 1943 to field a better gun. There was a scheme in the summer of 1943 to fit the existing Gaika turret with the long 57mm ZiS-4 gun, which had far superior antiarmor performance over the 76mm F-34. Since it had poor high-explosive capability compared to the 76mm gun, the plan was to issue it on a scale of about one in five tanks. This would have been a quick way to restore some firepower balance in 1943 and would have paralleled the British pattern of 75mm Shermans and Sherman 17-pounders in Normandy. Another option was to lengthen the existing 76mm gun, but tests of the L/50 F-34M gun found that it improved antiarmor penetration by only 20–30 percent. A derivative of the 76mm antiaircraft gun with a long barrel, the S-54, was also examined, but its performance fell short of other alternatives and it would have required a new family of ammunition.

COMPARATIVE COMBAT VALUE, 1943–44[29]				
PzKpfw III	**T-34**	**PzKpfw IV**	**T-34-85**	**Panther**
1.0	1.16	1.27	1.32	2.37

SOVIET TANK GUNS, 1939–45[30]							
Caliber	**45mm**	**57mm**	**76mm**	**76mm**	**85mm**	**100mm**	**122mm**
Gun type	20-Km	ZIS-4	L-11	F-34, ZIS-5	ZIS-S-53	D-10	D-25
Tube length	L/46	L/73	L/30.5	L/41.6	L/52	L/53.5	L/48
Armor-piercing projectile	BR-240SP	BR-271	BR-350	BR-350A	BR-365	BR-412B	BR-471B
Type	APC	APC	APC	APCBC	AP	APC	APC
Initial muzzle velocity (m/s)	757	990	612	662	792	1,000	795
Projectile weight (kg)	1.43	3.14	6.3	6.3	9.02	15.9	25.0
Penetration (mm; @500m, 30 degree)	31	83	54	59	90	125	122
Armor-piercing projectile (high-velocity)	BR-240P	BR-271P	N/A	BR-350P	BR-365P	N/A	N/A
Type	HVAP	HVAP		HVAP	HVAP		
Initial muzzle velocity (m/s)	1,065	1,270		965	1,030		
Projectile weight (kg)	0.85	1.75		3.02	4.99		
Penetration (mm; @500m, 30 degree)	54	101		77	90		
High-explosive projectile	O-240	O-271	O-350A	O-350A	O-365	OF-412	OF-462
Projectile weight (kg)	2.1	3.68	6.2	6.2	9.57	15.5	21.7
Explosive fill (g)	120	218	490	490	775	1,460	3,460

As a stopgap until a new weapon was selected, a series of minor improvements were quickly put in the field. The 76mm BR-350P HVAP tungsten-carbide projectile entered series production and became available in significant quantities in the autumn of 1943. Belatedly, a commander's cupola was added to the Gaika turret to provide the commander with better situational awareness.

A comparison of a standard T-34 on the left and the T-43 universal tank on the right.

The T-34 with the Gaika turret began to receive commander's cupolas starting in the autumn of 1943, a long-delayed upgrade that provided the tank commander with better situational awareness. This is the command tank of Lieutenant Colonel Vaynovskiy of the 1st Baltic Front during Operation Bagration in Belorussia in the summer of 1944.

In the wake of the Kursk fighting, Soviet tank commanders asked Moscow to give them "a longer arm." The initial version of the T-34-85 built at the Gorkiy plant used the D-5T 85mm gun seen in this early production example.

The next step forward in tank firepower was expected to be an 85mm gun; such a weapon was already in development as the D-5S for the new SU-85 tank destroyer and the D-5T for the new KV-85 tank. The KV-85 heavy tank was rushed into service as a stopgap. It consisted of a new turret mounting the D-5T 85mm gun on a modified KV-1S hull. It was accepted for service on 8 August 1943 and entered limited production in September 1943, with only 148 manufactured.

It was widely recognized that the T-34 needed a better gun to remain viable on the battlefield. One of the new 85mm guns was mounted in a Gaika turret, but the weapon was so large it could not be efficiently serviced by the loader. Besides this, there was widespread recognition that the two-man Gaika turret was one reason for the inferior performance of the T-34 in combat against German tanks with three-man crews. A new cast turret with a three-man crew had been developed for the T-43 tank and was large enough to accommodate an 85mm gun, as demonstrated in September 1943. Furthermore, it had substantially better armor than the existing Gaika turret and would not overburden the T-34 hull since it only added 1.3 tons to the tank's weight. A number of technical issues had to be resolved in the design, including an increase in the turret ring diameter from 1.46m to 1.6m to accommodate the new turret and the desire to develop an improved 85mm gun with features better suited to a tank turret than the bulky D-5T. The Soviet tank industry had a very limited capacity to make machine-wide turret rings.

Due to the urgency of the requirement, a version of the T-34-85 tank developed at the Krasnoye Sormovo No. 112 plant was accepted for production on 15 December 1943. A total of 255 of these were built through April 1944.[31] This version was armed with the initial D-5T 85mm gun. Its combat debut was with the 38th Independent Tank Regiment, serving with the Fifty-Third Army in Ukraine in March 1944. This is covered in more detail in the next chapter.

TOP TANK OF 1943

By 1943, the T-34 had become obsolete. Its performance was inferior not only to the new Tigers and Panthers, but also even to its old nemesis, the PzKpfw IV. Of the new German tanks, the Tiger was the superior of the two. It had better firepower since its 88mm gun fired both an excellent armor-piercing round and an excellent high-explosive round. The Panther's 75mm gun had an excellent armor-piercing round, but its high-explosive firepower was mediocre. Both tanks had excellent armor, but the Tiger was less vulnerable to side penetrations than the Panther. In terms of reliability, neither type was very good. Their average reliability in the last half of 1943 was about the same: 37 percent for the Panther and 36 percent for the Tiger. The Tiger gets the nod for Tanker's Choice.

A case can be made that the real rivals to the Tiger and Panther in 1943 were the humble PzKpfw IV Ausf. H and the StuG III Ausf. G. Neither could compare to the Tiger and Panther in armor protection, but both had reasonably good protection at longer ranges. In terms of firepower, the 75mm L/48 gun that armed both types did not have the penetrating power of the Panther's 75mm L/70 or the Tiger's 88mm gun. However, it really didn't matter in 1943. Less than 15 percent of Soviet tank losses in 1943 occurred at ranges over 1,000 meters. About 60 percent occurred at 200–600 meters, and

A Tiger of *schwere Panzer-Abteilung 505* with the unit's distinctive charging bull insignia evident on the front plate above the driver's visor.

A shortfall of conventional tanks prompted an increasing use of assault guns in lieu of tanks. This StuG III Ausf. G served in *Panzer-Abteilung 103* and was lost near Cori, Italy, in May 1944.

10 percent under 200 meters. At these ranges, the 75mm L/48 gun was lethal against the front of the T-34 and most other Soviet tanks.

The main advantage of the PzKpfw IV and StuG III was their availability. They were much cheaper and easier to build and so manufactured in much more substantial numbers. The PzKpfw IV and StuG III were not only much more numerous, but also much more reliable. In the second half of 1943, the PzKpfw IV had an average reliability rate of 48 percent; the StuG III had a rate of 65 percent—double that of the Tiger or Panther. It is not widely appreciated, but the high reliability of the StuG III meant that assault guns became the most numerous operational German AFV on the front in the latter half of 1943. At the time of the Kursk fighting on 5 July 1943, there were 1,870 operational tanks and 860 assault guns. The switchover occurred at the end of August when Russian Front AFV strength totaled 524 assault guns and only 484 operational tanks. In most cases, the numbers of tanks on hand on the Russian Front outnumbered the assault guns, but the number of functional assault guns outnumbered tanks on the Russian Front through the end of 1944.[32] Indeed, the shortage of the expensive Panther and Tiger tanks prompted the *Generalinspekteur der Panzertruppe*, Heinz Guderian, to authorize a special table of equipment in October 1943 for a panzer StuG company. This was to be used as a substitute in panzer units when there were shortages of Panther and Tiger tanks. By the end of 1943, only about half (54

COMPARATIVE TECHNICAL CHARACTERISTICS

	StuG III Ausf. G	PzKpfw IV Ausf. H	Tiger I	KV-1S
Army	Germany	Germany	Germany	USSR
Crew	4	5	5	5
Dimensions: L x W x H (m)	6.77 x 2.95 x 2.16	7.02 x 2.88 x 2.68	8.45 x 3.7 x 2.93	6.9 x 3.25 x 2.53
Loaded weight (tonnes)	23.9	25.0	57.0	42.5
Main gun	75mm StuK 40	75mm KwK 40	88mm KwK 36	76.2mm ZIS-5
Main gun ammo	54	87	92	114
Engine (hp)	300	300	650	600
Max. speed (km/h)	40	38	38	43
Fuel (liters)	310	470	534	880
Range (km)	155	210	140	225
Ground pressure (kg/cm^2)	0.93	0.91	1.5	0.8
Armor*				
Mantlet (mm)	80@0=80	50**=>50	110@0=110	82**=>82
Turret front (mm)	N/A	50@5=50.2	100@0=100	82**=>82
Turret side (mm)	N/A	33@25=36.4	80@0=80	75@15=77.6
Upper hull front (mm)	80@10=81.2	80@8=80.8	100@8=101	75@10=76.1
Lower hull front (mm)	80@21=85.1	80@14=82.8	100@27=110.3	75@30=86.6
Upper hull side (mm)	30@0=30	30@0=30	80@0=80	60@0=60

*Armor data provided as: actual thickness in mm @ angle from vertical = effective thickness in mm.
**Curved

percent) of the assault guns were in the assault gun battalions. More than a quarter (25.3 percent) were assigned to panzer divisions and the rest to the Waffen SS and Luftwaffe.

The antitank performance of the StuG III was reinforced by the crews' excellent artillery training and better fire-control sights compared to conventional tanks. The sights on the StuG III were more powerful than those on the tanks, and the StuG III commander had a special binocular periscopic sight that improved range-finding. A report by the Waffenamt in September 1943 reported that "The kill rates of assault gun batteries are frequently higher than those of Panzer units even though both are equipped with the same [75mm L/48] main gun." A report to Hitler in August 1943 after the Kursk battles indicated that "the reports from the front submitted to the Führer highlight the exceptional value of the assault gun which in several cases under the prevailing combat conditions proved superior to the Panzer IV."

The presence of the StuG III provided a major boost to the combat power of German infantry units during the increasingly difficult combat operations in 1943. The StuG III became the Wehrmacht's infantry tank. Even though it was not intended for tank fighting, by 1943 this became an increasing portion of its mission. From the start of Operation Barbarossa in June 1941 through August 1944, *Sturmgeschütz* units claimed 18,261 kills against Soviet AFVs; propaganda reports rounded this to 20,000. Total German claims against Soviet AFVs during this period totaled 100,748, so the StuG claims represented nearly one-fifth (18 percent) of all claims. Nevertheless, the main mission of the StuG III was direct-fire support of the infantry, and about 85 percent of its ammunition consumption was high-explosive projectiles for this mission.

From a purely technical standpoint, the Tiger tank was clearly superior to the StuG III. But from a cost perspective, the Wehrmacht could have bought ten StuG III or three Tiger tanks. Taking this equation one step further and factoring in reliability, the Wehrmacht could have had seven operational StuG III for one operational Tiger tank. For the badly outnumbered and overstretched Wehrmacht in Russia, I would argue that seven operational StuG III tanks represent far greater combat power than one operational Tiger. So my nod for the Commander's Choice on the Russian Front in 1943 is the StuG III "infantry tank."

CHAPTER 8

The 1944 Tank Contest

WITH THE ALLIED LANDINGS IN NORMANDY ON D-DAY, 6 June 1944, the war in Europe became a true two-front battle. By May 1944, German tank strength in the west exceeded that on the Russian Front as the Wehrmacht prepared for the invasion. The Wehrmacht became badly overextended and suffered a crushing series of defeats. The Red Army's Operation Bagration offensive in late June 1944 crushed Army Group Center and propelled the Red Army out of the Soviet Union and into Poland. Further offensives to the south put the Red Army into Romania by late summer and so sealed Germany's fate by cutting off its principal source of oil.

In the West, the U.S. Army's Operation Cobra offensive started the Normandy breakout. Hitler responded by launching a futile and costly counterattack at Mortain. The panzer divisions for this counterattack had been resisting the relentless British armor attacks around Caen. With the Caen Front weakened and the Mortain counterattack crushed, the Wehrmacht's precarious defenses collapsed. In August 1944, much of the German army in the west was trapped in the Falaise pocket and the subsequent pockets on the Seine River, and around Mons in Belgium. With the panzer force grossly evaporating, Hitler had to decide whether to put the focus on East or West. He gambled on a last-ditch offensive in the west, while at the same time trying to hold back the Red Army in the east. The majority of new tanks went to the West to rebuild for the Ardennes offensive.

TANK BATTLES IN THE EAST: RED ARMY UPGRADES

By 1944, the Red Army was deploying a substantial and powerful armored force. On 1 January 1944 it totaled 23 tank and mechanized corps, 46 tank and other armored brigades, and 106 tank and other armored regiments, with 24,400 tanks and assault guns. There were numerous tactical improvements in the mechanized force. On the personnel side, the Red Army had moved away from its wasteful early war practices and made a greater effort to preserve specialized tank crews in the wake of costly battles for the reconstitution of the tank formations rather than expending them as surrogate riflemen and starting from scratch with new tank crews. A cadre of well-trained officers had gradually been created, even if the Red Army still lacked a modern NCO corps. The mechanized force had deepened the motorization of the motor-rifle troops of the tank and mechanized corps, thanks to the influx of Lend-Lease American all-terrain trucks.

On the equipment side, the German introduction of the Panther and Tiger tank at the Battle of Kursk led to a crash program in late 1943 to rejuvenate the Soviet tank force. The previous policy of favoring quantity over quality was abandoned. By this stage, the Soviet tank factories were on much sounder footing. A largely unheralded U.S. effort to provide industrial support included a stream of scarce materials and machine tools. More than half of the Soviet Union's aluminum, a vital component of Soviet tank engines, came from U.S. supplies. The U.S. supply

Leningrad remained isolated due to the blockade and so had some very old types of tanks in service in 1944. This column of T-34 Model 41 tanks have been upgraded with appliqué armor by one of the local plants during the course of the siege and are seen on the rain-slicked streets of the city in January 1944.

A T-34 Model 1943 named "Leningradets" of the 30th Guards Tank Brigade enters Krasnoye Selo outside Leningrad in January 1944. This unit converted to IS-2 heavy tanks later in the year.

of cross-country trucks not only helped motorize the Red Army but also freed up Soviet automotive plants to manufacture light armored vehicles such as the ubiquitous SU-76M assault gun.

As mentioned in the previous chapter, in the autumn of 1943, the Red Army dropped the planned T-43 in favor of adding a more powerful gun to the existing T-34. The first batch of tanks had the D-5T, the same gun as on the SU-85 tank destroyer. The definitive version developed at the main T-34 plant at Nizhni-Tagil used the ZiS-S-53, an improved weapon better suited to mounting in tank turrets. This entered production in March 1944 and started later at plant No. 174 in Omsk and at Krasnoye Sormovo as well. Production of the BR-365P tungsten-carbide HVAP ammunition began in February 1944 and the standard combat load was five to six rounds per tank. Although its gun was not as effective as either the Panther's long 75mm gun or the Tiger I's 88mm gun, it restored a measure of balance in the technological arms race since it could defeat either tank under the right circumstances. Furthermore, since it was based on a virtually unchanged T-34 chassis it did not upset production to the extent that the costly new Panther had done to German industry. Work on a next generation tank, the T-44, began in late 1943.

The shift to the T-34-85 had two other important consequences for the Soviet tank force beyond its better firepower. The T-34-85 finally introduced a three-man turret crew and a commander's vision cupola. The retention of two-man turrets on the T-34 had been a lingering dead weight on Soviet tank tactics. Tank commanders were overburdened with their command responsibilities and gunnery chores. Combined with the abysmal optics in Soviet tanks and the tendency to fight "buttoned-up," the Soviet tank commanders had poor situational awareness. The result was sluggish, bumbling, and uncoordinated tank tactics. Commander's cupolas began to be added to the T-34 Gaika turret in the autumn of 1943, but this was only a temporary palliative. The

A T-34 Model 1943 with tank riders of the 1st Ukrainian Front drives past a burning Tiger during the savage battles in southeastern Ukraine in March 1944. The Red Army had begun to receive HVAP ammunition for the 76mm gun, which gave it the capability to knock out the Tiger from the side at less suicidal ranges than in the battles in the summer of 1943.

A T-34 Model 43 fitted with the yoke for a PT-34 mine roller passes by a scout detachment with Lend-Lease GPA amphibious jeeps during the liberation of the Lithuanian capital of Vilnius on 13 July 1943. This T-34 has the commander's cupola fitted, as of the autumn of 1943.

A T-34 Model 42 with Gaika turret of the 2nd Baltic Front advances toward Revel during the summer 1944 campaign. The turret tactical number is D003.

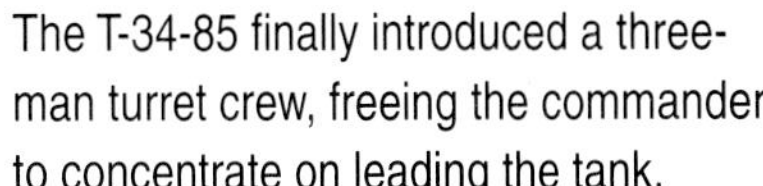
The T-34-85 finally introduced a three-man turret crew, freeing the commander to concentrate on leading the tank.

commander had somewhat better situational awareness than in the earlier types of two-man turrets, but his tasks had not been reduced. The T-34-85 solved both problems with the three-man crew layout and the commander's cupola. Another important change was the shift of the radio from the bow gunner's station to the commander's station. This allowed the tank commander to coordinate the actions of his tank with those of the neighboring tanks.

Another key ingredient in the rejuvenation of the Soviet tank fleet was the improvement in quality control. Through 1943, output quantity had remained the emphasis; quality control was weak, as mentioned in the previous chapter. The Nizhni-Tagil design bureau had been pressing the GABTU to allow them to impose greater uniformity on the several plants manufacturing the T-34-85 and to put more emphasis on quality control at the

A view from the commander's station in the T-34-85 looking forward toward the gunner's station.

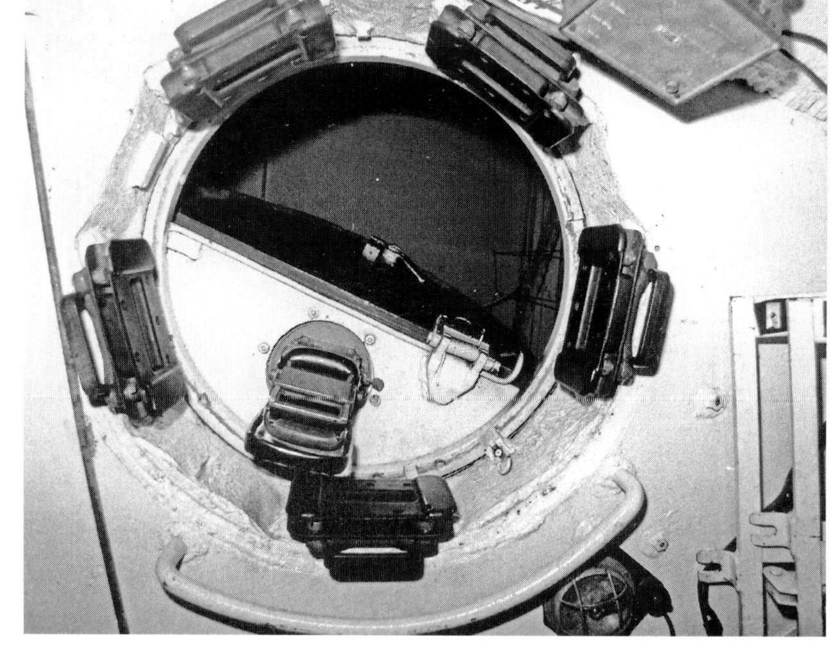

One of the most important upgrades in the new T-34-85 was providing the commander with a vision cupola. This view, looking up toward the cupola, shows that it had five view slits around the base as well as a traversable MK-4 periscopic sight.

subcontracting plants. This began to pay off in 1944. The policy of testing new T-34 tanks on a test track in 1943 found that only a small fraction could run the minimum requirement of 300 kilometers before breaking down. By early 1944, this dismal record had been overcome, and T-34 reliability finally reached acceptable levels. During February 1944 tests, 79 percent of tanks reached 300 kilometers, and of the test batches 33 percent reached 1,000 kilometers. This became immediately apparent to the tank troops. The deputy commander of the 1st Guards Tank Army, P. G. Dyner, commented that tanks in 1943 would reach only 75 percent of their guaranteed life span in engine hours and mileage, but in 1944 they reached 150 percent.[1]

The decision to simply rearm the existing T-34 hull, rather than move to the production of a more thoroughly improved tank such as the T-44, is

PERCENTAGE OF T-34 TANKS REACHING 330 KILOMETERS DURING FACTORY TRIALS[2]

Apr. 43	May	June	July	Aug.	Sept.	Oct.	Nov.	Dec.	Jan. 44	Feb.
10.1	23.0	7.7	28.6	43.0	46.0	78.0	57.0	83.6	83.4	79.0

illustrative of Soviet tank design philosophy during the war. The German programs were willing to incur a continual string of production and logistics difficulties to acquire modest—and in many cases irrelevant—technical improvements. The Soviet designers were forced to compromise in order to ensure ease of production, high production rates, and logistical harmony with the supply system. Although German industrial resources were greater than those of the Soviet Union, the incredible muddle of German industrial policy meant that the Red Army would outnumber the Wehrmacht in nearly all major categories of combat arms, but especially in tanks.

The arrival of the T-34-85 in March 1944 did not reverse the German technical advantage in tank technology but it did level the playing field. The T-34-85 was superior to the most common German tank, the PzKpfw IV Ausf. J, in armor and firepower, though it was still not evenly matched against the Panther. The Panther could penetrate the T-34-85 frontally at 1,200 meters against the gun mantlet and turret front, and from 300 meters against the glacis plate. The T-34-85's improved BR-365P tungsten-carbide HVAP core could penetrate 138mm of armor at 500 meters at 60 degrees, finally giving it the capability

The T-34-85 with the early D-5T gun saw its combat debut in the early winter of 1944. These served with the 119th Rifle-Tank Regiment in March 1944.

A tank attack by a T-34 Model 43 of the 24th Tank Regiment, 46th Mechanized Brigade, with the 1st Baltic Front on 18 July 1944 during Operation Bagration. Although Soviet combined-arms tactics improved through the war, the Red Army never fielded an infantry half-track to mechanize its motor rifle troops.

of penetrating the Panther frontally, though not at ranges as far as the Panther.

The T-34-85's real advantage was in numbers. At the end of May 1944, the Wehrmacht had only 304 Panthers on the whole Eastern Front. Production of the T-34-85 was running at about 1,200 per month in the spring of 1944, and there were about 7,200 produced by the time the summer 1944 offensives started. It was largely irrelevant whether the T-34-85 was evenly matched against the Panther the summer of 1944 because there were few confrontations with Panthers. The focal point of the Soviet Bagration offensive in June 1944, Army Group Center, had no Panther tanks at all at the start of the campaign.[3] The T-34-85's gun was very effective against the PzKpfw IV and StuG III that made up the bulk of the German armored force on the Eastern Front. In the postwar years, the Soviet Army developed a computer modeling program to assess relative combat performance of various types. Some historical examples were also run. The table below shows the Soviet assessment of major types in 1944, using the PzKpfw III with 50mm L/60 gun as the baseline tank.

The other major new tank to arrive on the scene in 1944 was the IS-2 heavy tank. By the summer of 1944, the KV-1 tank was regarded as obsolete. Its armor was insufficient to protect it against common German antitank weapons such as the 75mm PaK 40 antitank or the 75mm KwK 40 gun of the PzKpfw IV Ausf. G and Ausf. H. It had no firepower advantage over the T-34 since they shared the same gun. As a temporary expedient, the KV-85 was manufactured on a limited basis in August–October 1943 with only 148 built. This tank consisted of the KV-1S chassis with a new turret armed

COMPARATIVE COMBAT VALUE, 1943–44[4]

PzKpfw III	T-34	PzKpfw IV	T-34-85	IS-2M	Panther
1.0	1.16	1.27	1.32	1.66	2.37

with the D-5T 85mm gun. These saw their combat debut in November 1943, starting in Ukraine.[5]

In the summer of 1943, the heavy tank design bureau in Chelyabinsk was working on a new KV-13 "universal tank" to compete with the T-43. Even though this program was canceled, the KV-13 served as the basis for a new heavy tank to replace the KV family. The armor level was raised to 100mm on the bow and turret front. By this time, the old defense minister Klimenti Voroshilov was no longer in favor, so the new tank was named IS for Iosef Stalin. Although classified as a heavy tank by the Red Army, the IS was in fact about the same size and weight as the German Panther medium tank. There was some debate within the Red Army about the weapon needed for the new heavy tank. At first, the consensus was to arm the tank with an 85mm gun. This had performance similar to the German 88mm gun, and its ammunition was already in widespread production for both the SU-85 tank destroyer and the 85mm antiaircraft gun. The original version of the IS heavy tank with this gun, the IS-85, entered production at Chelyabinsk in December 1943. It was redesignated as the IS-1 shortly afterward.

However, before the IS-1 was issued to the troops, this matter was reconsidered. To begin with, the new T-34-85 tank would be armed with the same gun, so it made sense to give the IS a heavier weapon. The primary role of the new IS heavy tank was not tank fighting—they were to be issued to special Guards heavy tank regiments. The role of these regiments was to assist in breaking through German defenses during offensive operations. It is worth noting that this was the original tactical role of the German Tiger I; however, the Wehrmacht went onto the strategic defensive by the time the Tiger I was available in significant numbers, so as

The KV-13 project was reorganized and the focus switched to heavier firepower. The result was the IS-85m, later called the IS-1. A small number were sent into combat in early 1944, but large-scale production awaited the 122mm gun version.

Since the T-34 was scheduled to receive the 85mm gun, it made more sense to arm the new IS heavy tank with a more powerful gun. The 122mm D-25T was selected. This version was first called the IS-122 and later the IS-2.

often as not it was used in its secondary defensive role of combating Soviet tanks.

The Stalin tank's tactical role had significant repercussions in the selection of a main gun. The best tank gun for the IS series from a tank-versus-tank standpoint would have been the new D-10 100mm gun being developed for the new SU-100 tank destroyer. Although the IS was experimentally fitted with 100mm guns, this option was rejected. Production of 100mm ammunition was inadequate to support the new tank. The other option was a 122mm gun derived from the common A-19 field gun. This was attractive for two reasons. It offered good, though not great, antitank performance due to the sheer size of its projectile rather than the projectile speed. But more importantly, it was a fearsome direct-fire weapon, firing a massive 25kg (55lb) high-explosive projectile. This was six times heavier than the Panther's puny 4kg round and three times heavier than the Tiger's 9kg round. This was an important feature since the primary role of the IS tank was not to fight German tanks but to smash through German infantry defenses where good high-explosive firepower was essential. The A-19 gun was adapted for tank use by the addition of a

A view inside an IS-2m from the commander's cupola on the left side of the turret, looking down toward the gunner's station with the massive gun breech on the right.

fast-action tank-type breech and a muzzle brake, and the new gun was designated D-25T. The main drawback of the 122mm gun was its ammunition. It was a conventional two-piece field artillery type, which reduced the rate of fire and limited the on-board ammunition to only twenty-eight rounds.

A total of 67 IS-1 tanks were completed by the end of 1943, and 40 more at the beginning of 1944. However, the decision was to proceed with the IS-122, later designated IS-2. The first 35 IS-2s were finished in December 1943, followed by 360 through April 1944. The first separate Guards heavy tank regiments (OGvTTP: *otdelniy gvardeiskiy tyazheliy tankoviy polk*) began to be formed in February 1944. These regiments had a total of 21 IS-2 tanks formed into four companies with 5 tanks each. Heavy tank regiments not given the Guards honorific were designated as separate breakthrough tank regiments (*otdelniy tankoviy polk proryva*). These first saw widespread use during the summer campaigns of 1944.

Despite the importance of the T-34-85 and IS-2 in the summer campaigns, it should not be forgotten that light tanks constituted the bulk of the Soviet tank force even in 1944. This consisted of the T-70 light tank as well as Lend-Lease types such as the Valentine. So for example on 1 January 1944, of the 21,100 tanks on hand, 10,300 (49 percent) of the force was made up of light tanks. The end of light tank production in the Soviet Union was due in no small measure to the escalation in firepower on the Eastern Front. A study of T-34 tank losses in early 1945 showed the Wehrmacht's shift to more powerful guns between 1943 and 1944.

One of the major changes in Soviet force structure in 1944 was the addition of an enormous mass of self-propelled guns. These had begun to enter service in the summer of 1943, but became

After the stunning victories in Belorussia and Poland in the summer, the Soviet tank force began to run into stiffer opposition in the autumn. This new T-34-85 of the 25th Guards Tank Brigade, 2nd Guards Tank Corps, was knocked out in October 1944 during the bitter fighting in East Prussia, the first Soviet attack on German soil.

T-34 LOSSES TO GUNFIRE (PERCENTAGE), 1943–44[6]				
	Up to 50mm	50mm	75mm	88mm
1943	10.4	19.8	33.3	26.4
1944	-	-	59.2	33.2

increasingly important in 1944–45. The predominant type was the SU-76M, a light SP gun consisting of the standard 76mm ZiS-3 divisional gun on an extended T-70 light tank chassis. This was employed as an assault gun, comparable in role, though not in configuration, to the German StuG III. The SU-76M was much more weakly protected than the StuG III, with the gun mounted in an open rear compartment. It was never a very popular vehicle in service, called "Suka" (bitch), a word play on its designation, or "golozhopy Ferdinand" (bare-ass Ferdinand). Nevertheless, it provided the Soviet infantry with a measure of armored support. The other assault guns were the ISU-122 and ISU-152, which were the IS-2 tank chassis fitted with a fixed superstructure and a 122mm gun or 152mm gun-howitzer. These powerful assault guns were intended for direct-fire support during breakthrough operations, though they had a secondary antitank role. The only dedicated tank destroyer was the

Both sides made occasional use of captured tanks. This Panther Ausf. A served with Lieutenant Sotnikov's company of captured Panthers, part of the 62nd Guards Heavy Tank Regiment, 8th Guards Tank Corps, during the fighting on the east bank of the Vistula near Warsaw in the late summer of 1944.

SU-85, which combined the T-34 tank chassis with a D-5S 85mm gun in a fixed superstructure. At the beginning of 1944, self-propelled guns numbered 3,300, or 13 percent of Soviet AFV inventory. By the end of the year, they numbered over 10,000 and constituted 29 percent of the Soviet AFV inventory. This was largely due to the decision to end T-70 light tank production at the automotive plants in favor of the cheap but powerful SU-76M.

TANK BATTLES IN THE EAST: GERMAN OPTIONS

For the Wehrmacht, 1944 was a year of desperation. The year started out with a continuation of savage tank battles in Ukraine that lasted into the spring. There was a short respite in May and early June as both sides regrouped and prepared for the inevitable summer battles.

The likelihood of an Allied invasion of France prompted Berlin to begin shifting panzer divisions from the Russian Front to France precisely at a time when the Red Army was becoming its strongest and most competent. By the summer of 1944, the Ostheer was grossly overextended on the Russian Front, with an average tank strength of only 1,500 tanks through the first half of the year. As mentioned above, Red Army tank strength during this period was in excess of 20,000. Generally, about half of the total Soviet inventory was deployed at the front and the remainder split between reserves, military districts in the interior for training and reconstitution of new units, and the rebuild plants.

Through the summer of 1943, the Germans had been able to maintain a combat equilibrium on the Russian Front by offsetting their numerical weakness with modest technological advantages and superior crew and small unit performance. In 1943, the Red Army lost four Soviet tanks for every German tank lost, thereby dulling the impact of Soviet numerical advantages. However, in 1944 the Germans were not able to maintain the equilibrium due to the revival in Soviet tank design, substantial

GERMAN EASTERN FRONT TANK STRENGTH, 1944[7]

	Jan.	Feb.	Mar.	Apr.	May	June	July	Aug.	Sept.	Oct.	Nov.	Dec.
Overall tank strength	5,266	5,543	5,883	6,479	6,478	7,141	7,447	7,059	7,180	5,189	5,396	6,036
Deployed strength—all fronts	3,544	3,868	4,207	4,816	4,823	5,481	5,807	5,486	5,605	4,594	4,793	5,423
Deployed strength—Eastern Front	1,403	1,346	1,346	1,463	1,044	1,244	1,511	1,619	1,485	1,607	1,644	1,536
Operational strength—Eastern Front	730	722	574	748	1,015	1,336	1,207	1,071	1,180	1,404	1,317	1,778

A PzKpfw IV Ausf. H in action early in 1944. The turret number starting with 5 indicates the fifth company of a panzer regiment. In 1944, panzer regiments typically consisted of a first battalion with four companies of Panthers and a second battalion, number 5 to 8, with PzKpfw IV.

armor transfers to Western Europe in the spring of 1944 to deal with the forthcoming Allied invasion of France, and a diminishing disparity in German-versus-Soviet tank crew tactical skills.

On the positive side, the reforms of the German defense industry under Albert Speer ramped up German AFV production to its highest level of the war. This did not translate into enhanced combat power on the Russian Front, since attrition ate up much of the gains and more and more tanks were diverted to France. In addition, the German army suffered from a muddled and odd procurement process that left it saddled with dozens of types of tanks and assault guns, resulting in a needlessly complex logistics train. As the chart on page 219 shows, overall German tank strength on the Russian Front grew very modestly in 1944 despite the massive production increases.

In the area of medium tanks, the process of switching from the PzKpfw IV to the Panther was well underway but far from complete. There were still not enough Panther tanks in inventory to replace the PzKpfw IV. As a result, the standard panzer regiment of 1944 had one battalion of Panthers and one of PzKpfw IV tanks.

Production of the PzKpfw IV was halted at all of the plants but the Nibelungenwerk, which continued to manufacture the PzKpfw IV Ausf. H and Ausf. J. The other plants switched to various assault guns and tank destroyers on the PzKpfw IV chassis. To improve firepower and cut costs, the Jagdpanzer IV tank destroyer was recategorized as the Panzer

IV/70 and used as an interim tank. This had the long 75mm gun of the Panther tank but mounted in a less versatile, fixed casemate.

After the awful teething problems of 1943, the automotive performance and reliability of the Panther improved dramatically in 1944, first with the Panther Ausf. A and later with the Ausf. G. Availability rates went from an average of 37 percent in 1944 to an average of 54 percent by that summer. While the Panther still had its issues, by the summer of 1944 it was at its peak performance and widely regarded as the most formidable tank on the battlefield, east or west.

Production of the Tiger I halted in August 1944 after some 1,343 had been manufactured. It was still one of the most formidable tanks on the battlefield, but also complicated and expensive to manufacture. While it had been nearly invulnerable on the battlefield in 1943, by 1944 it was starting to face real opposition for the first time in the shape of the T-34-85 and the Sherman 17-pounder Firefly. A perfect example is the fate of the famous Tiger ace Michael Wittmann. He scored about 120 of his 135 tank kills on the Russian Front in 1943 when his tank was nearly invulnerable in a frontal engagement against almost all Soviet tanks. After transfer to France, he survived less than two months of combat and was ambushed and killed on 8 August 1944 by a Sherman 17-pounder Firefly.

Captured Wehrmacht documents reflected the new reality for the Tiger:

> When Tigers first appeared on the battlefield, they were in every respect proof against enemy weapons. They quickly won for themselves the title of "unbeatable" . . . But in the meantime, the enemy has not been asleep. Anti-tank guns, tanks, and mines have been developed that can hit the Tiger hard and even knock it out. Now, the Tiger, for a long time regarded as a "Life insurance policy" is relegated simply to the ranks of a heavy tank . . . No longer can the Tiger prance around, oblivious to the laws of tank tactics. They must obey these laws, just as every other German tank must.[8]

The power of the 88mm gun allowed longer engagement ranges against Soviet tanks, as is evident from the Soviet data below based on operational research on 735 medium and heavy tanks that had been knocked out.

DISTANCES AT WHICH SOVIET TANKS WERE KNOCKED OUT, 1943–44[9]

Distance (Meters)	75mm gun (%)	88mm gun (%)
100–200	10.0	4.0
200–400	26.1	14.0
400–600	33.5	18.0
600–800	14.5	31.2
800–1,000	7.0	13.5
1,000–1,200	4.5	8.5
1,200–1,400	3.6	7.6
1,400–1,600	0.4	2.0
1,600–1,800	0.4	0.7
1,800–2,000	0	0.5

The combat debut of the King Tiger on the Russian Front was far from auspicious when a column was ambushed by T-34-85 tanks in August 1944 in Poland. This King Tiger was sent back to the Soviet Union for tests and is now preserved at the Kubinka Tank Museum outside Moscow.

Even if the Tiger was not as omnipotent in 1944 as it was in 1943, it was still one of the best tanks on the battlefield. The same cannot be said for its successor, the Tiger II or King Tiger. This was another example of the excessive influence of Ferdinand Porsche on Hitler and his inner circle. The King Tiger ramped up the firepower by adopting a longer and more powerful 88mm gun. Likewise, its armor was significantly upgraded. Serial production began in January 1944, but none reached service until the summer of 1944 due to the usual teething problems. While the Tiger I had weighed 57 metric tons, the King Tiger came in at 68 metric tons. This was not a practical weight for the automotive technology of the day, nor was it a practical weapon given the limitations of railroad transport, roads, or bridges in most of the combat areas.

This became painfully evident on its combat debut on the Eastern Front. The *schwere Panzer-Abteilung 501* was delivered by train to Kielce in occupied Poland. The unit had forty-five King Tigers when it left the station, but after a 45-kilometer drive to the battlefield it was reduced to only eight functional tanks due to mechanical breakdowns, mainly reduction gear failures. By the following day, four more tanks limped to the front lines, bringing the strength to twelve. When the small number were sent on a mission on 13 August 1944 near the village of Ogledow, they were ambushed at close range by a T-34-85 of the 53rd Guards Tank Brigade, 6th Guards Tank Corps, which knocked out three with close-range side shots using HVAP ammunition. Several more were hit and lost in scattered encounters with IS-2 tanks in the same area.

GERMAN TANKS AND AFVS, 1944[10]

	Jan.	Feb.	Mar.	Apr.	May	June	July	Aug.	Sept.	Oct.	Nov.	Dec.	Total
nk oduction	718	641	704	750	792	831	840	865	720	679	800	821	9,161
uG oduction	381	442	423	478	529	671	689	682	683	813	949	881	7,621
Jg oduction	102	151	147	195	170	132	146	141	79	70	68	97	1,498
FV oduction	**1,201**	**1,234**	**1,274**	**1,423**	**1,491**	**1,634**	**1,675**	**1,688**	**1,482**	**1,562**	**1,817**	**1,799**	**18,280**
nk ength	5,266	5,543	5,883	6,479	6,478	7,141	7,447	7,059	7,180	5,189	5,396	6,036	N/A
uG/PzJg ength	3,882	4,069	4,619	4,601	4,614	5,210	5,543	5,000	5,238	5,374	5,619	6,210	N/A
FV rength	**9,148**	**9,612**	**10,502**	**11,080**	**11,092**	**12,351**	**12,990**	**12,059**	**12,418**	**10,563**	**11,015**	**12,246**	**N/A**
nk losses	531	339	191	690	226	528	1,068	769	775	546	254	517	6,434
uG sses	290	259	258	345	139	194	1033	428	520	545	194	117	4,322
zJg sses	88	82	54	166	40	127	358	75	169	20	35	9	1,223
FV osses	**909**	**680**	**503**	**1,201**	**405**	**849**	**2,459**	**1,272**	**1,464**	**1,111**	**483**	**643**	**11,979**

GERMAN AFV READINESS RATES ON THE RUSSIAN FRONT BY TYPE, 1944[11]

	Jan.	Feb.	Mar.	Apr.	May	June	July	Aug.	Sept.	Avg.
StuG III	60	56	57	65	76	85	75	65	71	**68**
Pz III	34	38	38	50	60	69	68	63	60	**53**
Pz IV	49	45	46	54	76	84	73	60	63	**61**
Panther	52	38	26	39	70	80	73	51	60	**54**
Tiger	43	45	54	40	64	75	60	48	64	**55**

A pair of Panthers on the Eastern Front in 1944. Reliability issues with the Panther had improved markedly since its combat debut at Kursk the previous summer.

A Panther Ausf. A lost during the fighting in Poland in the summer of 1944 after it slipped into an irrigation ditch. Such mishaps were not an uncommon fate for tanks in the chaos of battle.

An even more absurd design was the 188-metric-ton super-heavy tank, ironically called the Mäuschen (little mouse) and later "Maus."[12] Manufacture was expected to consume 264 metric tons of steel compared to 39 tons for a PzKpfw IV and 77.5 tons for a Panther. Production was scheduled to begin in November 1943, but Allied bombing raids managed to demolish critical production machine tools so no serial production took place. A completed prototype was sent into action around Berlin in 1945 but was blown up by its crew.

During the 1944 fighting, the Wehrmacht was seldom outfought by the Red Army at the tactical level, but it was outfought at the operational and strategic level. In the summer of 1944, Hitler was again successfully deceived by Stalin. The Red Army conducted an active and successful deception campaign to convince German commanders that their summer offensive would fall in other sectors.[13] The Wehrmacht concentrated its heaviest panzer forces in northern Ukraine, expecting the Red Army to attack across the Ukrainian plains into the flat tank country of central Poland. Instead, the Red Army executed the unexpected Operation Bagration offensive through the marshy and wooded reaches of Belarus, encircling and annihilating Army Group Center in the worst German defeat of the war. The German infantry held a wide front of reinforced trenches, supported mostly by StuG III assault guns and towed antitank guns.

A view from the commander's seat in a Panther Ausf. G, looking forward toward the gunner's station. In spite of its overall excellence, the Panther did have its foibles. The gunner was limited to the telescopic sight with no other viewports, which tended to increase the time needed to acquire and engage targets compared to tanks such as the Sherman and T-34-85, which gave the gunner periscopic sights.

The Panther retained the classic German layout with a three-man turret. It was German practice to leave the radio in the hull for operation by the bow gunner.

For the attack, the Red Army had 2,715 tanks and 1,355 assault guns, with roughly 40 percent located in tank and assault gun units for infantry support in the breakthrough phase and about 60 percent in the tank, mechanized, and cavalry corps for the breakout and exploitation phase. Of the 3,035 German tanks and AFVs on the Russian Front in June 1944, Army Group Center had only 85 operational tanks and 404 StuG assault guns.[14] There were none of the new Panthers and only 29 Tigers. The Ostheer was anticipating a continuation of the winter–spring fighting in the sector of Army Group North Ukraine, and so the bulk of its operational resources were there, some 830 operational tanks and 480 StuG assault guns. This force included most of the new Panther tanks. The success of the Red Army's deception campaign gave the Soviets an 8 to 1 advantage in AFV strength in the Bagration sector. Once the Red Army pushed through the initial German defenses in the first few days of the attack, the Germans had no reserves in the region to stem the rapid Soviet tank advances. The capital city of Minsk fell to a Soviet tank corps that hardly encountered any German armor whatsoever in a week of fighting. The rout of Army Group Center in June–July 1944 unhinged German defenses in the Soviet Union and led to the advance of the Red Army across the borders into occupied Poland, up to the gates of Warsaw.

Soviet AFV losses in this campaign were the highest of the year but also the most consequential in terms of the campaign's success. It was followed by the Lvov-Sandomierz offensive in Poland, which saw significant setbacks when the Germans staged a large panzer counterattack on the east bank of the Vistula River near Warsaw, bringing the offensive to a close.[15] By this time, opportunities beckoned elsewhere. The Red Army launched attacks into Romania, knocking the Romanian army out of the war and taking over the vital oil fields near Ploesti in August 1944. Fuel starvation would eventually cripple the Wehrmacht.

During the late autumn of 1944, fighting on the Eastern Front was concentrated on the northern and

A lingering weak spot in German defenses on the Russian Front was the poor state of equipment of its allied forces. The Germans wanted to charge the Hungarians an exorbitant price to license-manufacture the Panther tank, so the Hungarians instead designed their own equivalent, the Tas tank seen in this illustration. Only a single example was completed before Allied bombing destroyed the factory in 1944, ending the program.

SOVIET TANK AND AFV LOSSES BY CAMPAIGN, 1944[16]

Campaign	Total Losses	Avg. Daily Loss
Liberation of the right bank of the Ukraine: 24 Dec. 1943–17 Apr. 1944	4,666	40
Leningrad-Novgorod offensive: 14 Jan.–1 Mar.	462	10
Crimean offensive: 8 Apr.–12 May	171	5
Vyborg-Petrozavodvsk offensive: 10 June–9 Aug.	294	5
Operation Bagration: 23 June–29 Aug.	2,857	43
Lvov-Sandomierz offensive: 13 July–29 Aug.	1,269	26
Jassy-Kishinev offensive: 20–29 Aug.	75	7.5
Eastern Carpathian offensive: 8 Sept.–28 Oct.	478	9
Baltic offensive: 14 Sept.–24 Nov.	522	7
Belgrade offensive: 28 Sept.–20 Oct.	53	2
Petsamo-Kirkenes offensive: 7–29 Oct.	21	1
Budapest offensive: 29 Oct. 1944–3 Feb. 1945	1,766	16
Subtotal: losses in listed campaigns	12,634	~14
Total 1944 tank losses	**16,900**	**48**
Total 1944 SU losses	**6,800**	**19**
Total 1944 AFV losses	***23,700***	***67***

GERMAN KILL CLAIMS AGAINST SOVIET TANKS AND AFVS, 1944[17]

Claims	Jan.	Feb.	Mar.	Apr.	May	June	July	Aug.	Sept.	Oct.	Nov.	Dec.	Total
Army	4,479	2,154	1,997	2,643	399	838	3,875	4,373	2,339	4,433	1,186	1,361	30,077
Luftwaffe	200	25	317	280	176	46	417	257	135	247	26	54	2,180
Subtotal	**4,679**	**2,179**	**2,314**	**2,923**	**575**	**884**	**884**	**4,630**	**2,474**	**4,680**	**1,212**	**1,415**	**32,257**
Adjusted*													
Army	3,140	1,510	1,400	1,850	280	590	1,940	2,190	1,640	3,100	830	950	19,420
Luftwaffe	100	10	160	140	90	20	210	130	70	120	10	30	1,090
Total	***3,240***	***1,520***	***1,560***	***1,990***	***370***	***610***	***2,150***	***2,320***	***1,710***	***3,220***	***840***	***980***	***20,510***

*Estimated claims after adjustment by Fremde Heere Ost intelligence agency.

GERMAN AFV LOSSES IN THE EAST, DECEMBER 1943–NOVEMBER 1944[18]

	Dec. 1943–Mar. 1944	Apr.	May	June	July	Aug.	Sept.	Oct.	Nov.	Total
PzKpfw II	40	18	4	0	65	5	15	1	1	149
PzKpfw III	142	54	0	0	0	0	8	0	0	204
PzBefWg/ Beo III	204	57	6	1	39	14	0	1	3	325
PzKpfw 38(t)	10	0	0	0	0	0	2	2	0	14
PzKpfw IV	816	257	73	10	256	309	134	117	47	2,019
PzKpfw IV/70	0	0	0	0	0	0	0	14	5	19
Panther	362	243	114	17	241	246	136	263	55	1,677
Tiger I	158	96	20	11	166	76	57	40	17	641
Tiger II	0	0	0	0	0	0	0	5	3	8
Panzer subtotal	**1,732**	**725**	**217**	**39**	**767**	**650**	**352**	**443**	**131**	**5,056**
StuG III	1,146	342	128	79	887	293	321	270	109	3,575
StuG IV	0	0	0	0	0	0	30	47	8	85
Sturmpz IV	0	0	0	0	5	0	2	0	0	7
StuG subtotal	**1,146**	**342**	**128**	**79**	**892**	**293**	**353**	**317**	**117**	**3,667**
Marder I	1	8	3	2	6	0	1	0	0	21
Marder II	73	37	2	2	49	7	7	2	6	185
Marder III	195	128	30	11	264	44	67	10	14	763
JgPz 38	0	0	0	0	0	0	65	36	9	110
JgPz IV	0	0	0	0	0	0	0	55	4	59
Nashorn	85	9	1	36	34	7	32	5	0	209
PzJäg subtotal	**354**	**182**	**36**	**51**	**353**	**58**	**172**	**108**	**33**	**1,347**
Total	***3,232***	***1,249***	***381***	***169***	***2,012***	***1,001***	***877***	***868***	***281***	***10,070***

Not all tank battles of 1944 were fought with the most modern equipment. *Panzer-Abteilung 211* serving in Finland was still equipped with the old war-booty French Somua S35 tank. When Finland switched sides, the German units retreated north into Lapland and Norway. Finnish tank units, equipped with war-booty Soviet T-34 tanks, caught a rearguard on this road and knocked out these two German tanks on 29 October 1944. SA-KUVA

southern flanks. The Red Army continued to struggle against the Germans' tenacious defense of East Prussia and the Baltic coast, while in the south fierce battles erupted in Hungary around Budapest. By this stage of the war, the Red Army was irresistible. It was no longer a matter of whether the Red Army would defeat the Wehrmacht, it was simply a question of when and with how many casualties.

TANK BATTLES IN THE WEST: THE ALLIED PROSPECTS

Tank fighting in the west did not reach the proportions of the Russian Front until the summer of 1944. Although there was some tank fighting on Sicily in July 1943 and on the Italian mainland in September 1943–June 1944, it was on a relatively small scale, as can be seen from the chart below covering the period of the fighting around Anzio and Monte Cassino in early 1944. It is also interesting to note that German AFVs in Italy had a far better availability rate than in Russia, perhaps due to better spare parts supply.

As can be seen, the polarity of German tank strength began to shift westward in May 1944, a process which continued into the summer. However, the Russian Front continued to account for the majority of tank and AFV losses, especially due to the large numbers of StuG assault guns in the east, as seen from the comparative chart below.

GERMAN TANKS AND AFVS IN ITALY, 31 JANUARY 1944[19]

	Operational	Operational (%)	In Repair	Total
PzKpfw III	75	71	31	106
PzKpfw IV	124	73	47	171
Befehls/Beo.Pz.*	8	67	4	12
StuG	108	77	33	141
Hornisse	43	96	2	45
Total	***358***	***75***	***117***	***475***

*Command and artillery forward observer tanks

GERMAN TANK STRENGTH, 1944[20]

	Jan.	Feb.	Mar.	Apr.	May	June	July	Aug.	Sept.	Oct.	Nov.	Dec.	Avg.	Avg. (%)
East	1,403	1,346	1,346	1,463	1,044	1,244	1,511	1,691	1,485	1,607	1,644	1,536	1,443	40.1
OKW*	483	690	1,027	1,199	1,654	1,797	2,014	1,723	1,534	721	819	960	1,218	33.8
Homeland	740	1,021	1,027	1,064	1,157	1,011	983	874	846	826	878	778	933	25.9
Total	***2,626***	***3,057***	***3,400***	***3,726***	***3,855***	***4,052***	***4,508***	***4,288***	***3,865***	***3,154***	***3,341***	***3,274***	***3,595***	***100***

*OKW (Armed Forces High Command) includes theaters other than the Eastern Front: for example, France, Italy, and occupied countries such as Denmark and Norway.

GERMAN AFV LOSSES IN 1944, EAST VERSUS WEST[21]

	June	July	Aug.	Sept.	Oct.	Nov.	Total
Panzer losses—East	39	767	650	352	443	131	2,382
Panzer losses—West	227	297	114	1,371	74	95	2,178
StuG losses—East	79	892	293	353	317	117	2,051
StuG losses—West	27	68	112	383	109	52	751
PzJäg losses—East	51	353	58	172	108	33	775
PzJäg losses—West	29	15	24	244	48	43	403
AFV losses East—total	***169***	***2,012***	***1,001***	***877***	***868***	***281***	***5,208***
AFV losses West—total	***283***	***380***	***250***	***1,998***	***231***	***190***	***3,332***

ALLIED TANK DEVELOPMENTS: THE U.S. ARMY

The principal tank of the U.S. Army in 1944 remained the M4 and M4A1 Sherman. A number of improvements were introduced between the Mediterranean Campaign in 1943 and the Battle of France. Due to British pressure, a telescopic gun sight was added to supplement the periscopic sight, along with a new mantlet as the M34A1 gun mount. The British also complained about the vulnerability of ammunition stowed in the sponsons. As a short-term solution, appliqué armor was added. As a midterm solution, "wet" stowage was introduced that placed the ammunition in bins surrounded by water or antifreeze to reduce the probability of ammunition ignition. The more important aspect of the program was moving the ammunition from the sponson into the floor to make it less likely to be hit; this required a redesign of the fighting compartment and turret basket. The "wet stowage" Shermans began appearing in the summer of 1944. The appliqué armor and M34A1 gun mount became part of a "Quick Fix" program in 1943–44. Kits were manufactured in the United States and shipped to Britain as a "Blitz" upgrade prior to the Normandy landings.

A quick fix that could have improved the Sherman's antitank performance would have been to lengthen the gun tube as the Germans had done on the PzKpfw IV during the production of the Ausführung G from L/43 to L/48. The M3 75mm gun on the Sherman had a relatively short length of L/40 largely based on prewar conceptions that looked with disfavor on the barrel projecting beyond the front of the tank, which allegedly made it vulnerable to accidents. Extending the barrel could have increased muzzle velocity, and hence penetration, without the need for a new family of ammunition. This was never seriously considered since the Army was working on the 76mm gun and there was never much clamor from tank crews in the Mediterranean Theater for better antitank performance. There simply wasn't much tank-versus-tank fighting in Italy in 1943–44 to spur demands for improved gun performance.

After much argument, the U.S. Army began to manufacture a new 76mm gun for the Sherman family, starting with the M4A1 (76mm) in January 1944. The first batch of 120 tanks arrived in the United Kingdom in April 1944 and quickly became orphans. Although the gun offered better antiarmor performance than the 75mm gun, its high-explosive round was inferior. The 76mm HE charge was only

The first M4A1 (76mm) arrived in Britain in April 1944 but attracted little enthusiasm due to the poor high-explosive performance of its new gun. After encountering the Panther in Normandy in July 1944, attitudes changed and the 2nd and 3rd Armored Divisions received over fifty each for the Operation Cobra breakout late in July.

The M4A3 (76mm) used the standard three-man turret. The new turret included an excellent all-around vision cupola of modern design with thick, armored glass that did not require the commander to operate levers to open up each view slit.

.86 pounds of explosive while the 75mm round contained 1.47 pounds of explosive. From experiences in the Mediterranean theater, the U.S. Army viewed high-explosive firepower as more important than antitank performance; they had not yet faced the Panther tank.[22]

The British demonstrated their 17-pounder to the U.S. Army in 1943. U.S. officers who had seen the gun fired in Britain were surprised by its substantial muzzle flash and the unnerving tendency for flashback at the breech, which hinted at design problems.[23] A variety of U.S. guns were in development, including both the 76mm M1A1 and a new 90mm gun, which were believed to be more than adequate to handle the German threat. The British first proof-tested the 17-pounder in a Sherman turret in late December 1943. In late October 1943, a British officer from the Washington office tried to convince Lt. Gen. Jacob Devers of the benefits of the 17-pounder over the American guns. Devers wanted evidence to back up the claims, and a comparative shoot of the 90mm and 17-pounder was conducted at Aberdeen Proving Ground in the United States on 25 March 1944, followed by a similar trial at Shoeburyness in Britain on 23 May 1944. The British offered to provide 200 guns and ammunition per month to the United States within three months' notice. The 17-pounder had two principal antiarmor rounds, a conventional APCBC and a new APDS.

The comparative trials did demonstrate that the 17-pounder had superior short-range performance to the American 90mm gun slated for new tank destroyers, to say nothing of the 76mm tank gun. At longer ranges, its performance when using the new

U.S. TANK GUNS, 1939–45[24]

Caliber	37mm	75mm	75mm	76mm	90mm
Gun type	M5A1	M2	M3	M1	M3
Tube length	L/53	L/31	L/40	L/52	L/50
Armor-piercing projectile	M51B1	M61	M61	M62A1	M82
Type	APCBC	APCBC	APCBC	APCBC	APCBC
Initial muzzle velocity (m/s)	884	587	617	792	814
Projectile weight (kg)	0.87	6.78	6.78	7.0	10.9
Propellant weight (kg)	0.24	0.98	0.98	1.64	3.31
Penetration (mm; @500m, 30 degree)	51	55–66	62–72	92–96	110–118
Armor-piercing projectile (high-velocity)	N/A	N/A	N/A	T4 (M93)	T30E16 (M304)
Type				HVAP	HVAP
Initial muzzle velocity (m/s)				1,036	1,020
Projectile weight (kg)				4.3	6.9
Penetration (mm; @500m, 30 degree)				137	194
High-explosive projectile	M63	M48	M48	M42A1	M71
Projectile weight (kg)	0.73	6.7	6.7	5.8	10.6
Explosive fill (g)	38	665	665	390	925

APDS ammunition was erratic due to problems with the sabot separation. However, by the time these assessments were made, both the 76mm and 90mm tank guns and ammunition were already in production in the United States, and the 17-pounder would not be available until well after the Normandy landings. Ordnance was not keen on adopting the British gun for a variety of reasons. Its performance was slightly better than the 90mm gun, but Ordnance was developing the T4 high-velocity, armor-piercing (HVAP) ammunition that would boost 76mm gun performance to near the level of the 17-pounder without the need to switch to yet another new gun and ammunition. There was also concern that British arsenals could not meet U.S. quantities for either guns or ammunition. But the real problem was that the U.S. Army in general did not have a realistic appreciation of the future tank threat. Attitudes about the 17-pounder option would change after the Normandy fighting in June 1944.

As a result of these various developments, all U.S. tank units arriving in Normandy after D-Day were still equipped with the standard 75mm version of the M4 and M4A1 Sherman medium tank. Contrary to the mythology, the lack of a powerful tank gun didn't matter very much in the first two months of U.S. Army fighting in Normandy. There were no Panther tanks in the American sector in June 1944, nor, for that matter, many German tanks at all. The initial AFV fighting in June 1944 was against the StuG III, StuG IV, and Marder 3, all armed with the 75mm gun. The most common adversary was the 75mm PaK 40 antitank gun of the infantry divisions in this sector. During the advance on Cherbourg in June 1944, there were only two German tank battalions, both equipped with obsolete war-booty French tanks.

The Sherman's main problem in the Normandy fighting was its poor armor. The M4 was a good tank in 1942 and early 1943 when the main German antitank weapon was the 50mm PaK 38. But the new 75mm PaK 40 had begun to appear in Tunisia in early 1943, and by the summer of 1944 it was the predominant antitank gun in the German army. It could penetrate the Sherman frontally at any normal combat range. The Sherman design was robust enough to receive additional frontal armor, but units in Italy were adamant that they did not want more armor if it compromised mobility. The tank battalions in Italy were very sensitive to mobility issues since they were often used in mountainous areas such as the areas around Monte Cassino. In late 1943, the Army Service Forces dispatched a "New Weapons Board" to the Mediterranean Theater of Operations (MTO) and European Theater of Operations (ETO) with the dual mission of collecting information on the performance of existing U.S. Army weapons as well as informing units deployed overseas of planned improvements in weapons. Their report, published in April 1944, provides some insight into the general attitude within the U.S. Army toward the performance of the M4 and M4A1 tanks prior to the Normandy campaign. Overall, the report concluded:

> The medium tanks of the M4 series are well liked by the using personnel . . . The M4 tank is good and well liked by everyone . . . Opinion of proper armor thickness was divided. Armored Force troops generally regard the present armor as adequate. They do not want to sacrifice maneuverability, speed, or floatation to gain additional armor protection.

This opinion would be quickly reversed after the first few weeks of fighting in Normandy.

ALLIED TANK TACTICS IN 1944: THE U.S. EXPERIENCE

The U.S. Army did not begin to face serious German tank opposition until after the fall of Cherbourg in late June 1944. This shifted the focus of the U.S. Army attacks southward to Saint-Lô. The First U.S. Army had more tanks than Montgomery's British/Canadian armies in the Caen sector, but only a small fraction of these saw combat from D-Day until Operation Cobra in late July 1944. For example, in mid-July 1944 the U.S. First Army had about 3,770 tanks deployed to France, but only 1,390 were in units actually committed to the front. U.S. Army doctrine was that the infantry would be supported by the separate tank battalions but the armored divisions would not be used until the infantry had secured the breakthrough. U.S. armored divisions were designed for exploitation, not for grinding breakthrough battles, and certainly not in congested hedgerow terrain. There was a single misbegotten use of a combat command of the 3rd Armored Division around Villiers-Fossard on 29 June 1944 which only proved the point.

When the focus of U.S. attacks shifted to the Saint-Lô sector in early July 1944, the Germans began reinforcing the American sector with more

The U.S. Army had developed the M6 heavy tank early in the war, but by 1944 it was widely regarded as too cumbersome and insufficiently armored or armed for its size. Its main gun was the same 3-inch gun as in the M10 tank destroyer, but with a co-axial 37mm gun. This example was on display in Washington in February 1944, but none were deployed overseas.

tanks. The *Panzer-Lehr Division* and *2.SS-Panzer-Division Das Reich* were moved into the American sector. By this stage, the *Panzer-Lehr Division* was down to less than half of its original tank strength after a month of fighting in the British sector. A spoiling attack by four *Kampfgruppen* (battle groups) on 11 July 1944 against U.S. encroachments over the Vire River was a shambles, with one of the battle groups—including its company of Panther tanks—surrounded and wiped out. The *Panzer-Lehr Division* commander, Fritz Bayerlein, complained that the Panther was ill-suited for use in the bocage country as its long barrel was difficult to traverse on the narrow country roads.

Aside from the extensive tank losses on D-Day, U.S. tank losses in the bocage fighting were relatively modest until the combat intensified on 25 July 1944 with the launch of Operation Cobra, the breakout from the Saint-Lô sector. By this stage, the First U.S. Army was fielding nearly 1,000 M4 Sherman tanks and 880 M10 and M18 tank destroyers against a German opponent with only 154 tanks and AFVs, including 57 Panthers, a 10 to 1 advantage. Furthermore, the main fighting took place in the *Panzer-Lehr* sector, and that division had only 16 Panthers at the time of the Cobra attack, about half of which were smashed during the preliminary carpet bombing.

The first large-scale use of the U.S. armored divisions during Operation Cobra started on 26 July 1944 after the infantry had secured the breakthrough. Two armored divisions, the 2nd and 3rd, began the exploitation phase, followed a few days later by two more divisions, the 4th and 6th. After Operation Cobra succeeded in gaining a breakout, new armored divisions were gradually fed into the battle, with ten committed by the end of 1944.

Tank-versus-tank fighting intensified in the American sector in early August when the U.S. units were counterattacked by the *2.Panzer-Division* and *116.Panzer-Division*, followed by the Operation Lüttich panzer counteroffensive around Mortain. The initial fighting with the two panzer divisions consisted of very small scale skirmishing, with typical engagements comprised of fewer than a half dozen tanks on either side; the Mortain counteroffensive was borne mainly by U.S. infantry divisions.[25]

Over the years, a myth has developed that it took five Shermans to knock out a Panther or a Tiger. The U.S. Army encountered no Tiger tanks in combat in Normandy.[26] The encounters with Panther tanks were very small scale and not as lopsided as the myth would suggest. Part of the problem stems from the widespread misidentification of German AFVs by U.S. troops. Virtually all German tanks and AFVs—PzKpfw IV, StuG III, and Panthers—were indiscriminately identified as "Tigers," just as every German antitank gun and field howitzer was an "88mm." More often than not, the Normandy duel of Sherman versus panzer depended on the skirmish conditions. A PzKpfw IV or StuG III waiting in ambush could make fast work of two or three Shermans. But there were also numerous occasions when a small group of Panthers would stumble into a hidden 57mm antitank gun or Sherman tank in ambush and take disproportionate losses. The myth has also been inflated by legends such as "Barkmann's Corner," when a single Panther tank of the *2.SS-Panzer-Division* allegedly shot up nine Shermans and halted a major U.S. advance.[27] It's worth noting that the month with the highest tank casualties for the U.S. Army in 1944 was August, at a point in time when German tank strength in the west was threadbare. The high tank losses in August were typical of armies engaged in fast offensive operations regardless of the amount of armored opposition. Operational research has shown that armies engaged in pursuit and exploitation often have a high tank casualty rate caused by insufficient time for maintenance and increasing mechanical failures. Some studies from the Normandy period suggest that under these conditions, tank losses due to mechanical failures and other noncombat causes outnumber combat casualties about 4 to 1.[28]

The first large-scale tank-versus-tank fighting by the U.S. Army in France occurred in September 1944 in Lorraine. Hitler planned the so-called "Vosges panzer offensive" as a means to cut off the most threatening spearheads of Patton's U.S. Third Army. Several of the new panzer brigades, intended for combat on the Russian Front, were instead sent west. Instead of a concentrated attack, local commanders committed the panzer brigades in piecemeal fashion and they were ground up in encounters

U.S. FIRST ARMY TANK LOSSES IN NORMANDY: D-DAY–5 AUG. 1944[29]

	6–16 June	17–24 June	24 June–1 July	2–8 July	9–15 July	16–22 July	22–29 July	30 July–5 Aug.	Total
M4 (75mm)	129	37	21	21	75	33	79	68	**463**
M4 (105mm)	0	0	0	3	0	0	1	0	**4**
M4A1 (76mm)	0	0	0	0	0	0	12	6	**18**
M4 Dozer	0	3	4	1	2	4	0	4	**18**
M5A1	28	8	8	2	18	9	38	33	**144**
Total	***157***	***48***	***33***	***27***	***95***	***46***	***130***	***111***	***647***

U.S. THIRD ARMY TANK COMBAT LOSSES, SEPTEMBER 1944

	3–9 Sept.	10–16 Sept.	17–23 Sept.	24–30 Sept.	Total
M5A1 Light	7	7	15	8	**37**
M4 medium	1				**1**
M4 (105mm)	2				**2**
M4A1	1	17	7	13	**38**
M4A1 (76mm)			1		**1**
M4A3	21	5	30	4	**60**
M4A3 (76mm)			5	4	**9**
Total	***32***	***29***	***58***	***29***	***148***

with the French 2nd Armored Division at Dompaire and with U.S. infantry divisions. The panzer brigades were amply equipped with Panther and PzKpfw IV tanks, but the crews were new and inexperienced. During the climax of the fighting around Arracourt, a few panzer brigades and divisions were committed against the 4th Armored Division. The battle was a classic meeting engagement with neither side enjoying any advantage. It was a lopsided victory for the U.S. Army, and a clear example of where superior crew quality outweighs technological advantages. Of the 616 panzers and assault guns committed to the Lorraine fighting in September, there were only 127 operational by 1 October.[30] Total losses amounted to 101 PzKpfw IV, 118 Panthers, and 221 assault guns and tank destroyers; 148 armored vehicles were damaged and inoperable. Third Army AFV losses for the whole of September were 200 tanks and tank destroyers.

The subsequent tank fighting in the autumn of 1944 was on a small scale compared to the summer. German tank strength in the west, as shown on the chart on the next page, fell from around 1,500 in September to about 700 in October. This was due to both the heavy losses suffered in Normandy and Lorraine and Hitler's decision to husband his panzer force for a last-ditch gamble in the Ardennes in the early winter of 1944. The Waffen-SS panzer

GERMAN AFV STRENGTH IN LORRAINE, SEPTEMBER 1944							
	Panther	**PzKpfw III**	**PzKpfw IV**	**JagdPz IV**	**StuG III/IV**	**FlakPz IV**	**Total**
Pz-Brig. 106	36			11		4	51
Pz-Brig. 111	45		45		10	8	108
Pz-Brig. 112	45		46		10	8	109
Pz-Brig. 113	45		45		10	8	108
11.Pz-Div.	30	4	16		1	7	58
21.Pz-Div.					5		5
Pz.Gr.Div.3				31	37		68
Pz.Gr.Div.15			42	34			76
SS Pz.Gr.17				4	17	12	33
Total	***201***	***4***	***194***	***80***	***90***	***47***	***616***

GERMAN AFV STATUS IN LORRAINE, 1 OCTOBER 1944							
	Panther	**PzKpfw III**	**PzKpfw IV**	**JagdPz IV**	**StuG**	**FlakPz IV**	**Total**
Peak strength	201	4	194	80	90	47	616
On hand, 1 Oct. 1944	83	3	93	63	12	21	275
Operational, 1 Oct. 1944	26	2	28	46	6	19	127
Total losses in September	***118***	***1***	***101***	***17***	***78***	***26***	***341***
U.S. claims	***186***	***421***	***607***				

divisions were pulled back into Germany for rehabilitation; the battered army panzer divisions remained in the field but at greatly reduced strength until withdrawn in the weeks before the Battle of the Bulge for hasty reequipment.

A clear example of the reduced scale of the tank fighting was the campaign around Aachen, the first German city under siege in the west. During the attack north of Aachen on 2 October 1944 by the U.S. Army's XIX Corps, there were 320 armored vehicles consisting of about 200 M4 medium tanks, 50 M5A1 light tanks, and about 70 M10 tank destroyers. The German Corps in this sector only had about 80 armored vehicles, mostly StuG III or StuG IV assault guns.

The scale of tank fighting waxed and waned until the start of the Ardennes offensive in mid-December 1944, as can be seen from U.S. tank casualties, which fell markedly after their summer high point. The Battle of the Bulge will be covered in the next chapter.

U.S. ARMY ETO TANK AND AFV STRENGTH, 1944[31]

	June	July	Aug.	Sept.	Oct.	Nov.	Dec.
M5A1	1,489	1,545	1,693	1,695	1,643	1,800	2,206
M4 (75, 76mm)	2,202	2,093	2,557	2,423	2,464	2,832	4,076
M4 (105)	114	132	156	163	238	312	459
Tank subtotal	**3,805**	**3,770**	**4,406**	**4,281**	**4,345**	**4,944**	**6,741**
M18	146	141	176	170	189	252	306
M10	691	743	758	763	486	573	790
M36	0	0	0	0	170	183	236
TD subtotal	**837**	**884**	**934**	**933**	**845**	**1,008**	**1332**
Total	***4,642***	***4,654***	***5,340***	***5,214***	***5,190***	***5,952***	***8,073***

U.S. ARMY ETO TANK AND AFV LOSSES, 1944[32]

	June	July	Aug.	Sept.	Oct.	Nov.	Dec.	Total
M5A1	52	26	201	116	156	83	134	768
M4	167	121	557	436	237	257	495	2,270
M4 (105)	4	3	2	11	10	11	28	69
Tank subtotal	**223**	**150**	**760**	**563**	**403**	**351**	**657**	**3,107**
M18	0	0	6	6	14	7	44	77
M10	1	17	28	40	71	45	62	264
M36	0	0	0	0	2	5	21	28
TD subtotal	**1**	**17**	**34**	**46**	**87**	**57**	**127**	**369**
Total	***224***	***167***	***794***	***609***	***490***	***408***	***784***	***3,476***

ALLIED TANK DEVELOPMENTS: THE BRITISH ARMY

The British army was so favorably impressed by the performance of the Sherman tank since its combat debut in the autumn of 1942 at El Alamein, and so discouraged by the mediocre performance of most British tank types to date, that the Sherman was adopted as the standard British cruiser tank. At the same time, the more heavily armored Churchill tank had proven to be excellent for the infantry support role.

Development of a new cruiser tank had continued in Britain through 1943, concentrating on the related Centaur and Cromwell tanks. The early tests of these tanks revealed continuing reliability and maintenance problems, the traditional bane of British tank design in World War II. Examples sent to the United States were tested at Aberdeen Proving Ground. The U.S. test reports were particularly harsh about their low mechanical reliability and their excessive maintenance demands, 199 man-hours for the Cromwell compared to 39 man-hours for an M4A3 subjected to the same test.[33] A British observer at the tests sent back a note that read: "These tanks have made us a laughing stock out here . . . The Americans are politely indifferent to what happens to them."

The British Army conducted its own tests, code-named Exercise Dracula, comparing the Cromwell and Centaur against Shermans. A major of the Westminster Dragoons commented after the tests that:

> The outstanding lesson of this exercise has been to me the exceptional reliability of the American machines. All my ideas, based on 2½ years of experience with an armoured regiment equipped with British machines, have had to be revised, and though before the exercise started I was inclined to think that perhaps the Sherman was somewhat overrated, I am completely convinced of the superiority of this machine over anything that this country has produced to date. It is evident that the commander of a unit equipped with Shermans can be confident of taking 99% of his tanks into battle, at any rate during the first 2,000 miles of their life. On the other hand, if he were equipped with Cromwells or Centaurs he would be in a continuous state of anxiety as to whether enough of his tanks would reach the battlefield to carry out the normal tasks expected of the unit.[34]

These tests only served to reinforce a predilection of British leaders to rely on U.S. tank production due to their reliability, the known problems with British tank design, and the recognition that British industry was badly overstretched. Resources diverted from tank production could be used for other vital war materiel. In the summer of 1943, the British government began to take steps to trim back planned Centaur production in favor of further Lend-Lease acquisition of Sherman tanks.[35] Work on the Cromwell continued, but the lingering reliability problems encountered in 1943 curtailed deployment to the British army units earmarked for France in 1944. Although it was intended to be the principal cruiser tank of the armored divisions, it seldom exceeded a third of the strength of the Sherman with the units of Montgomery's 21st Army Group in Northwest Europe in 1944–45. Aside from addressing reliability issues, the Cromwell was rearmed. It was originally fitted with the usual 6-pounder, a gun with excellent antitank performance but poor high-explosive firepower. Instead it received a 75mm gun similar in performance to the Sherman's.

Even if the British army went into France in 1944 with the Sherman tank, the configuration of its Sherman force was markedly different from their American allies. The British army had a fundamentally different view of tank armament than the Americans, resulting from their more extensive experience in tank combat. Britain had started the war in 1939 with most tanks still armed with machine guns. By the time of the Battle of France in 1940 a transition was underway to the 2-pounder (40mm) antitank gun, roughly similar in performance to the contemporary U.S. Army 37mm tank gun. British experiences fighting panzers in

The new Cromwell cruiser tank had some of the features deemed essential in British tank doctrine, but mechanical teething problems in 1943 forced the British army to maintain their dependence on the Sherman tank as the mainstay of their armored units.

The Cromwell command tank, named "Hela," of 1st Polish Armoured Division Commander Gen. Stanislaw Maczek, which took part in the Normandy campaign and the fighting for Falaise.

France and in the North African desert led to yet another shift to the 6-pounder (57mm) tank gun, and by the battle at El Alamein in the autumn of 1942, the American 75mm tank gun had been introduced into service.

The constant escalation of German tank armor and firepower, largely propelled by the tank arms race on the Russian Front, had forced the British army into a continual series of improvements in tank firepower. Having been caught unprepared on so many occasions and forced to catch up to German developments, on 9 March 1943 the British General Staff established a new "Policy on Tanks" that noted:

> Fulfillment of their normal role necessitates that the main armament on the greater proportion of tanks of the medium class should be an effective HE weapon and at the same time as effective a weapon as possible against enemy armour of the type so far encountered during in this war. The smaller proportion of tanks of the medium-class require a first-class anti-tank weapon for the engagement, if necessary, of armour heavier than that against which the dual-purpose weapon referred to above is effective.

In practice, this meant that the British tank force slated for operations in France was based around tanks with a dual-purpose 75mm gun, especially Shermans, while two tanks per troop would be fitted with the new 17-pounder antitank gun. In contrast to the American 76mm gun program, which was pushed along by the development agencies

British regiments in Normandy were equipped with a mixture of 75mm Shermans and some with the long 17-pounder, seen here to the left. This is a unit from the Polish 1st Armoured Division that served with the Canadian First Army during the fighting to close the Falaise Gap.

The Challenger was an attempt to adapt the 17-pounder gun to the Cromwell chassis by lengthening the hull. The design never proved entirely satisfactory, though it did see combat service in Europe in 1944–45.

The Churchill became the mainstay of British tank brigades for the infantry support role. A portion retained the 6-pounder gun even in 1944 due to its superior antiarmor performance compared to the American 75mm gun. This example is seen parading in front of Buckingham Palace in London in 1944.

The Sherman Firefly with its 17-pounder gun was a major step forward in dealing with the threat of more heavily armored German tanks such as the Panther and Tiger. However, the new APDS discarding sabot ammunition did not become widely available until late in the summer of 1944.

with little enthusiasm from either the Armored Force or the Army Ground Forces, the British 17-pounder program was started earlier and enjoyed broad and official support from the development agencies, the tank force, and the general staff. It was optimized for tank fighting, and its poor high-explosive performance was simply ignored as irrelevant to its mission.

A similar effort was made in connection with the Cromwell cruiser tank. The basic Cromwell could not accommodate the 17-pounder gun due to its small turret ring. The Challenger, a lengthened version of the Cromwell with the 17-pounder, was designed to supplement the Cromwell. The Challenger suffered from serious reliability and mobility issues, and as a result was deployed in very small numbers.

After World War II, the British Army Operational Research Group (AORG) attempted to calculate the technical effectiveness of British and German tanks in tank-versus-tank engagements using both theoretical parameters and data collected from the 1944–45 campaigns. Effectiveness was defined as "the reciprocal of the number of tanks required per enemy tank to achieve parity in battle." A summary of the results are contained in the chart on the next page. The study suggested that the Cromwell was the least effective of the major tank types and the Sherman Firefly was the most effective in tank-versus-tank fighting. The Churchill was

GERMAN VERSUS BRITISH TANK COMBAT EFFECTIVENESS[36]				
	Range (Yards)	Cromwell	Sherman 75mm	Sherman 17-pounder
PzKpfw IV Ausf. H	1,000	1.35	1.1	0.9
	1,500	1.5	0.9	
Panther Ausf. G	300	1.85	1.55	1.2
	600	1.85	1.55	1.2
	1,000		2.0	
Tiger I	300	1.9	1.65	
	600	1.9	1.6	0.9
	1,000			0.9
King Tiger	300	3.2	2.7	
	600	3.2	2.7	1.55
	1,000			1.75

not considered since tank fighting was not considered its principal mission. The data suggests that the PzKpfw IV Ausf. H was about 10 percent more efficient than the normal 75mm Sherman and about 10 percent less efficient in battle than the Sherman 17-pounder Firefly in an engagement at 1,000 yards. By the study's definition, this meant that it would take eleven 75mm Shermans to reach parity with ten PzKpfw IV tanks in an engagement at 1,000 yards.

ALLIED TANK TACTICS IN 1944: THE BRITISH EXPERIENCE

The Allied tank strength in Normandy was concentrated in the British/Canadian sector during the June–July 1944 fighting, largely due to terrain difference. The countryside in the British sector around Caen was mostly open farmland that was much more suitable for tank fighting. The terrain in the American sector, both on the Cotentin peninsula and around Saint-Lô, was primarily bocage, a substantial type of hedgerow. The charts below refer to "British" tank strength as a shorthand for tank units of Montgomery's 21st Army Group. Of the six armored divisions and eight brigades committed to the Normandy fighting, one armored division and one armored brigade were Canadian and one armored division was Polish. These units were equipped and organized in British fashion. One of the British divisions, the 79th Armoured Division was a specialized unit with a variety of armored engineer vehicles, flamethrower tanks, and other "Funnies." It did not fight as an armored division, but managed and deployed its specialized vehicles to support other formations.

British armored divisions were organized into three brigades, one each of tanks, infantry, and artillery. The principal difference between these divisions and the U.S. armored divisions was tactical doctrine. The U.S. Army favored combined-arms tactics at the brigade level, and each division

The Churchill infantry tank served as the basis for the Churchill Crocodile flamethrower tank, which towed a special trailer for the fuel and compressed air. This was one of the types employed by the 79th Armoured Division "Hobart's Funnies" and is seen here near Sterkrade, Germany, on 31 March 1945.

had three combat command headquarters, essentially a brigade headquarters. Units were not permanently assigned to these, but rotated depending on the circumstances. Combat Command A and B (CCA, CCB) were intended to be the fighting force while Combat Command R was intended to serve as the reserve and for rehabilitation of exhausted units. The British armored divisions lacked these combined-arms headquarters and tended to fight the combined-arms battle at divisional level, not at brigade level. This proved deficient in Normandy. The Guards Armoured Division took their own approach and did combine tanks, infantry, and artillery in combined-arms teams; the 11th Armoured Division and the Polish 1st Armoured Division also adapted their structure to fight the combined-arms battle at brigade level by the late summer of 1944.

The independent brigades were intended to support the infantry; each had three regiments and therefore tank strength comparable to an armored division. The plan was to equip these brigades with the thickly armored Churchill infantry tank. However, there were not enough Churchills produced, so the "tank" brigades were based on Churchill tanks while the "armored" brigades received the Sherman. These units were used in the same fashion as the U.S. Army's separate tank battalions, with individual regiments allotted to the support of infantry divisions during particular missions. Of the independent brigades in Normandy, three were Churchill tank brigades and five were Sherman armored brigades.

From a broader operational perspective, the British army in Normandy suffered from a distinct shortage of infantry. The British armed forces were grossly overextended with heavy commitments to the Royal Navy and Royal Air Force; the army usually took the short end of the stick in manpower allotments. British armored doctrine was similar to all the major armies and saw the main mission of armored divisions as the exploitation of breakthrough won by the infantry supported by independent brigades. However, the available infantry divisions were too small in number and short of replacements once heavy casualties were incurred in the first few weeks of fighting. Under these circumstances, Montgomery began using the armored divisions against doctrine to win the breakthrough. Although not publicly stated, British army commanders had already expected to face this dilemma and had planned accordingly. British tank reserves in Normandy were massive, often totaling 50 percent of the deployed strength. By way of comparison, U.S. tank reserves in Normandy were only 7 percent.[37] The British commanders appreciated that using the armored divisions to win breakthroughs would prove costly in vehicles, but they made a calculated choice to sacrifice machines over men to win the Normandy campaign.[38]

The British Second Army in Normandy faced the bulk of Panzergruppe West, the main German armored force, for the first six weeks of fighting in Normandy. Montgomery launched a series of offensive operations to secure key road junctions at Tilly-sur-Seulles and Caen, and then to break out farther south. These operations proved very costly in tanks as the Germans skillfully repulsed attack after attack. The reasons for these difficulties have been very controversial and the subject of innumerable historical arguments. A technological answer has been a popular explanation, blaming the thin armor and weak antitank performance of the Sherman. Indeed, complaints of the Sherman's poor performance in 1944 largely originate in the British debates over the performance of British armored units in Normandy, not the performance of the Sherman in the U.S. Army.[40]

Recent studies have offered a more nuanced portrait of the problems facing Montgomery's forces in the Normandy battles. The British army was slow to adopt combined-arms tactics below divisional level. The expedient use of armored divisions rather than infantry divisions to secure breakthroughs inevitably resulted in heavy tank losses. Another factor worth mentioning is the relative density of German defenses. The British Second Army was facing four German panzer divisions by the middle of June, with a combined strength of more than 675 German tanks and AFVs on a front about 20 miles wide. By way of comparison, the Wehrmacht's Army Group Center, the target of the Red Army's Operation Bagration offensive in late June 1944, had about 500 tanks and AFVs on a sector about 250 miles wide. In other words, Montgomery's forces were facing an opponent with an armored density about fifteen times greater than the key summer battle fought by the Red Army. Even Army Group North Ukraine, the most heavily defended sector of the Russian Front in June 1944, had a German armor density that was more than six times less than that faced by the British in late June 1944. The successful U.S. Army breakout from Normandy, Operation Cobra, faced about four times less German armor than the British.

British armor losses in Normandy, while heavy, were not unusually severe. By way of comparison, British losses in the first two months of fighting in Normandy were 1,142; Soviet losses during the two months of Operation Bagration were 2,857. The Normandy campaign was more costly than subsequent British campaigns, as is suggested by the chart on page 249.

In the British sector, the principal source of British tank kills was other armored vehicles. The chart on page 249 shows German kill claims by type of weapon based on the data from several panzer divisions. This underestimates the number

BRITISH TANK STRENGTH IN NORTHWEST EUROPE, 1944 (UNIT HOLDINGS)[39]

	June 1944	Dec. 1944
Stuart	427	435
Sherman	1,990	1,449
Sherman 17-pounder	318	605
Cromwell	142	577
Challenger	18	21
Comet	0	31
Churchill	138	562
Total	***3,033***	***3,680***

MAJOR PANZER UNITS IN BRITISH SECOND ARMY SECTOR, MID-JUNE 1944*							
	Light Tanks	Pz IV	Panther	Tiger	StuG III	JgPz IV	Total
2.Panzer		26	4			18	48
21.Panzer	32**	104			47		183
Panzer-Lehr		99	89		8	41	237
12.SS-Panzer	2	98	50			13	163
s.SS-Pz-Abt. 101				45			45
Total	***34***	***327***	***143***	***45***	***55***	***72***	***676***

*Does not include separate StuG brigades or infantry division *Panzerjäger* battalions.
**Obsolete French tanks

AVERAGE GERMAN ARMOR DENSITIES, SUMMER 1944–MAY 1945						
Allied Force	**Operation**	**German Force**	**Time Frame**	**Frontage**	**AFVs**	**Density***
British 2nd Army	Caen	*Panzergruppe* West	Mid-June 1944	20 miles	675	33.8
U.S. First Army	Cobra	*84.Korps*	26 July	20 miles	155	7.8
Four Soviet fronts	Bagration	Army Group Center	June 1944	250 miles	500	2.0
1st Ukrainian Front	Bagration	Army Group North Ukraine	June 1944	250 miles	1,350	5.4
Three Soviet fronts	Berlin	AG Weichsel & Center	April 1945	185 miles	810	4.3

*Tanks and AFVs per mile

BRITISH TANK LOSSES IN NORTHWEST EUROPE, 1944[41]

	Through 5 Aug. 44	6 Aug.–5 Nov.	Total
Stuart	79	140	219
Sherman	717	365	1,082
Cromwell	193	87	280
Challenger	1	6	7
Churchill	152	52	204
Total	***1,142***	***650***	***1,792***
Avg. loss per day	**19.0**	**7.2**	**8.5**

GERMAN CLAIMS OF ALLIED TANK LOSSES IN NORMANDY, D-DAY–5 AUG. 1944

	UK	U.S.	Total
6–15 June	104	57	161
16–25 June	528	161	689
26 June–5 July	546	68	614
6–25 July	279	268	547
26 July–5 Aug.	478	282	760
Total claims	***1,935***	***836***	***2,771***
Actual losses*	**1,042**	**647**	**1,689**

*Actual figure is based on British/U.S. records.

ALLIED CLAIMS OF GERMAN TANK LOSSES, D-DAY–AUGUST 1944[42]

	Pz III	Pz IV	Panther	Tiger	Unidentified	Total
Canadian First Army		16	13	10		39
British Second Army	12	211	249	122	260	854
U.S. First Army		82	34	27	52	195
Total	***12***	***309***	***296***	***159***	***312***	***1,088***

U.S. claims through 6 Aug., Canadian through 11 Aug., British through 12 Aug.

A Panther knocked out by Canadian troops with a PIAT antitank launcher during the fighting in the Caen sector in June 1944.

of tanks knocked out by antitank guns and rockets since it does not include the claims by these divisions and supporting elements.

German armored vehicle losses in 1944 exceeded the entire previous four years of war. Statistics on German tank losses in the west in 1944 are misleading and probably incomplete. The German army had a habit of keeping knocked-out tanks on strength as "repairable" if they were recovered. In the event they were transported back to Germany for rebuilding, they do not appear to have been counted as a loss, since the records only cover "total losses." In the case of the Normandy fighting, the many tanks knocked out but still in German hands were not written off until September 1944 after the debacles at Falaise, the Seine River, and the Mons pocket. This creates a misleading impression of tank combat losses in June–August.

GERMAN KILL CLAIMS VERSUS ALLIED TANKS BY WEAPON TYPE, D-DAY–3 JULY 1944

	Quantity	Percent
Tank	227	42.2
StuG and *Panzerjäger*	61	11.3
Antitank and Flak guns	105	19.5
Field artillery	36	6.7
Close-combat weapons	108	20.1
Total	***537***	***100***

After the August debacle in France, in early September 1944 the Wehrmacht's High Command West (OB West) had only thirteen infantry divisions, three panzer divisions, and two panzer brigades rated as combat effective. A further forty-two infantry divisions and thirteen panzer divisions had been rendered ineffective for combat, and of the infantry divisions seven were simply disbanded. There were barely a hundred tanks still available on the Western

GERMAN AFV LOSSES IN THE WEST, JUNE–NOVEMBER 1944[43]

	June	July	Aug.	Sept.	Oct.	Nov.	Total
PzKpfw II	1	7	4	14	7	0	33
PzBefWg/Beo III	1	2	1	72	0	0	76
PzKpfw IV	126	149	53	612	21	30	991
PzKpfw IV/70	0	0	0	17	6	0	23
Panther	80	125	41	540	35	55	876
Tiger I	19	14	15	93	0	2	143
Tiger II	0	0	0	23	5	8	36
Panzer subtotal	**227**	**297**	**114**	**1,371**	**74**	**95**	**2,178**
StuG III	27	68	98	379	98	34	704
StuG IV	0	0		2	4	18	24
Sturmpz IV	0	0	14	2	7	0	23
StuG subtotal	**27**	**68**	**112**	**383**	**109**	**52**	**751**
Marder I	9	0	0	55	0	0	64
Marder II	5	10	24	23	2	1	65
Marder III	15	5	0	71	1	2	94
JgPz 38	0	0	0	71	26	16	113
JgPz IV	0	0	0	0	13	8	21
Jagdpanther	0	0	0	24	6	16	46
PzJäg subtotal	**29**	**15**	**24**	**244**	**48**	**43**	**403**
Total	***283***	***380***	***250***	***1,998***	***231***	***190***	***3,332***

Front. On 4 September, the new Army Group B commander, Field Marshal Walter Model, warned Hitler that unless ten infantry and five or six panzer divisions were available by September 15, "the door to north-west Europe would stand open." German officers called the last weeks of August and first weeks of September 1944 "the Void" due to the collapse of German defenses.

The rapid pursuit to the German frontier created problems for the Allies. On 11 September 1944, the first day that U.S. Army troops entered Germany near Aachen, the Allies were along a phase line that the Operation Overlord plans did not expect to reach until D+330, 2 May 1945, some 233 days ahead of schedule. Logistics had failed to keep pace with the unexpectedly rapid victories of August–September 1944. Until the supply situation could be remedied, Allied operations along the German frontier would inevitably be constrained.

COMPARATIVE TECHNICAL CHARACTERISTICS				
	Cromwell	**M4A3**	**T-34-85**	**Panther Ausf. A**
Army	UK	USA	USSR	Germany
Crew	5	5	5	5
Dimensions: L x W x H (m)	6.46 x 3.04 x 2.34	6.27 x 2.61 x 2.74	8.1 x 3.0 x 2.7	8.86 x 3.42 x 2.98
Loaded weight (tonnes)	24.9	31.5	32.2	44.8
Main gun	75mm	75mm M3	85mm ZIS-S-53	75mm KwK 42
Main gun ammo	64	104	60	79
Engine (hp)	550	450	500	600
Max. speed (km/h)	62	42	55	46
Fuel (liters)	525	635	815	720
Range (km)	265	160	300	200
Ground pressure (kg/cm^2)	1.03	1.0	.83	.88
Armor*				
Mantlet (mm)	76@0=76	90**=>90	90**=>90	100**=>100
Turret front (mm)	76@0=76	51@30=58.9	90**=>90	100@5=100.4
Turret side (mm)	64@0=64	51@5=51.2	45@5=45.2	45@25=49.6
Upper hull front (mm)	64@0=64	51@45=72.1	45@60=90	80@55=139.4
Lower hull front (mm)	64@22=68.1	51@50=79.3	45@60=90	65@55=113.3
Upper hull side (mm)	44@0=44	38@0=38	45@53=73.1	40@40=52.2

*Armor data provided as: actual thickness in mm @ angle from vertical = effective thickness in mm.
**Curved

Germany did manage to hang on. The risky Operation Market Garden airborne operation in the Netherlands failed. The fuel shortage caused by the U.S. Army Air Force oil campaign and the loss of the Romanian oil fields to the Red Army in August 1944 put an end to most Luftwaffe and Kriegsmarine operations. The young air force technicians and navy crew were unceremoniously transferred as infantry fodder along the German frontier. The sudden rebirth of the Wehrmacht in September 1944 was dubbed the "Miracle on the Westwall."

TOP TANK OF 1944

My Top Tank choices for 1944 are fairly obvious. Tanker's Choice is the Panther, which redeemed itself after its messy introduction into service in 1943. In the summer of 1944, the Panther was at its peak since it still had excellent crews. Its performance would start to falter later in the year due to the heavy attrition in trained and experienced crews. The most likely Allied contender would be the Sherman Firefly 17-pounder, but it had unimpressive armor compared to the Panther.

Commander's Choice for 1944 goes to the T-34-85. This was an excellent and much-belated upgrade to the T-34 that was too long in coming. But when it did arrive, it came at an opportune moment to assist in the Soviet victories of the summer and autumn of 1944. As in the case of other Commander's Choices, it combined good technical capabilities with decent durability and large production quantities. The most likely U.S. contender would be one of the Sherman variants, but the M4A3 (76mm) was not quite up to its peak in the autumn of 1944, with too little HVAP ammo available and mediocre floatation in soft ground.

A Panther on the prowl during the battles in Hungary in the autumn of 1944. Hungary would be the focus of German panzer operations through early 1945.

A column from the 2nd Guards Tank Corps enters Vilnius, Lithuania, on 13 July 1944 following a week of fighting with the *3.Panzer-Armee.* Behind the T-34-85 on the left is an improvised Flak truck, consisting of a GAZ-AA mounting a war-booty German 20mm antiaircraft gun

Wasser-Anlagen
führt aus
Gas-Anlagen
führt aus
64

CHAPTER 9

The Final Campaigns: December 1944–May 1945

THE FINAL SIX MONTHS OF FIGHTING in the European war shifted in intensity from front to front. In view of the desperate imbalance of forces against Germany, Hitler decided on a desperate gamble in December 1944, hoping to strike hard in the west while holding in the east. As a result, precious panzer reinforcements were concentrated near the Ardennes in December 1944 for the "Watch on Rhine" offensive. Technically, the composition of armored forces in these campaigns was very similar to the situation in the summer of 1944. There were few dramatic technical innovations in the final six months of the war.

GERMANY'S LATE-WAR PANZERS

The German panzer force in the last months of the war still relied on a mix of PzKpfw IV and Panthers in most of its panzer regiments. The primary emphasis of the German tank industry was simply aimed at maximizing production. Rather surprisingly, the Allied bombing offensive had not paid much attention to the German tank industry until the autumn of 1944. An RAF raid in the autumn of 1943 had struck the Alkett plant, but there were few raids on the main tank plants until the autumn of 1944. Although panzer production continued to increase through the summer of 1944, it began to suffer from the fortunes of war, losing access to metal alloys critical in steel armor production. In February 1944, the Wehrmacht lost control of the Soviet manganese mines at Nikopol and Krivoy Rog in Ukraine. Access to molybdenum was cut off by Allied bomber attacks on the Knaben mine in Norway as well as by the end of supplies from Finland and Japan. As a result, the

The Allies did not begin a serious campaign against the German tank factories until the autumn of 1944, and even then the effort was short-lived. It most seriously affected King Tiger production, but did not have as much impact against the dispersed Panther tank plants.

molybdenum content in thick armor plate fell from a high of about 0.55 percent in 1943 to 0.25 percent in mid-1944 to none at all in 1945, leading to declining shock properties in German tank armor.[1] Combined with declining industrial quality control in the quenching process, German tank armor, though still very hard, was increasingly brittle, prone to fracturing and decreased impact resistance. By some estimates, as much as half of the Panther armor was flawed, losing about 10–20 percent of its effectiveness. Quality control was further undermined by the extensive use of foreign forced labor in the panzer plants. Recent museum restorations have revealed some evidence of deliberate sabotage of fuel and lubrication lines in Panther tanks.[2]

In August 1944, the RAF and USAAF began the first systematic air campaign against the German tank and vehicle industry.[3] The main Panther plant, MAN at Nurnberg, was hit hard on 10 September 1944, costing the Wehrmacht the equivalent of over four months' production, or about 645 tanks. Daimler-Benz was hit as well, but the second most important Panther plant, the MNH (Maschinenfabrik Niedersachsen) in Hanover was spared until March 1945. The greatest success of the air attacks were the raids against Henschel King Tiger plant in Kassel, which resulted in the loss of nearly three months' worth of production, or about 700 King Tiger tanks.[4] The Allies were unhappy with the results of the raids and they petered out in October, only to be resumed in the wake of the Battle of the Bulge.

While the air raids may not have had the dramatic results expected by Allied bomber chiefs, they had insidious effects on the panzer force. Speer was able to keep panzer production at adequate levels through the end of 1944 by shifting plant resources away from other products such as trucks and focusing on tanks. More critically, the panzer plants dramatically cut production of spare parts that in 1943 had constituted as much as 25–30 percent of the tank contracts. By the summer of 1944, only about 15 percent of Maybach engines were put aside as spares, and by the autumn of 1944 this had been halved again to only about 8 percent. This hidden cost of the air campaign would have dire consequences for the panzer regiments during the Battle of the Bulge due to the confluence of the continuing unreliability of some key components such as final drives and the growing decline in spare parts. The situation became so acute during the Ardennes campaign that some new tanks brought forward as replacements were cannibalized for parts to repair tanks at the front.[5]

The most critical loss of resources occurred in the summer of 1944 with the end of oil supplies from Romania, Germany's main source of fuel. The strict rationing of fuel limited driver training. In the wake of the catastrophic loss of trained panzer crews in 1944, the lack of adequate driver training combined with lingering power-train problems in some of the designs such as the Panther and King Tiger led to frequent breakdowns, which contributed to poor operational readiness in the units. Some German accounts suggest that as many as half of all German panzer losses in the Ardennes were due to the abandonment in combat when they could not be quickly repaired or retrieved.

During 1944, the plants assigned to manufacture the PzKpfw IV gradually shifted away from the standard tank configuration to other options. The Jagdpanzer IV, a tank destroyer version of the PzKpfw IV, had already been in production. This was modified to carry the long 75mm gun of the Panther tank, called the Pz IV/70, and used as a substitute tank in panzer regiments in place of the turreted version. Only one plant, the Nibelungenwerk, continued to manufacture the turreted version of the PzKpfw IV Ausf. J, and even this plant shifted part of its production to the Pz IV/70.[6]

Panther production was mainly focused on simplifying the design to maximize production. The Panther Ausf. G that had entered production in March 1944 remained the standard model through the end of the war with only modest detail changes. Likewise, the King Tiger with the Henschel turret configuration remained the production type from

By the time of the Ardennes fighting, the Panther regiments had been reequipped with the new Panther Ausf. G, which featured an improved hull. This is an example from the September 1944 production at MAN in Nuremburg using steel-rimmed road-wheels, an uncommon variant of the series.

The final production version of the Panther was the Ausf. G with the simplified hull. By this stage, the gun mantlet had been revised with a "chin" below since Allied tank crews had discovered that Panthers could be knocked out by hitting the lower half of the original mantlet, bouncing the round through the thin armor of the hull roof. This was abandoned near Hosingen, Germany, in mid-February 1945.

There has been considerable fascination in recent years about possible "Paper Panzers" entering service later in 1945. In reality, designs such as the E-50 seen in this illustration were very far from production.

The decline in the offensive power of German infantry divisions forced the Wehrmacht to employ panzer divisions for breakthrough missions for which they were not well suited. The *12.SS-Panzer-Division Hitlerjugend* tried using its Panther regiment to break through U.S. infantry defenses around the twin villages of Krinkelt-Rocherath in the opening phase of the Battle of the Bulge, only to have the regiment smashed in violent close-quarter combat.

A trio of Panther Ausf. G of *Panzer-Regiment.9* are burned out in a field outside Humain, Belgium, on 28 December 1944 after a battle with the U.S. 2nd Armored Division on 27 December 1944 during the Battle of the Bulge.

the summer of 1944 through the end of the war. Some idea of the combat potential of the King Tiger can be gathered by the tactics employed by Kampfgruppe Peiper, the spearhead of the *1.SS-Panzer-Division* in the Ardennes offensive. This battlegroup was allotted a battalion of new King Tiger tanks for the attack. Peiper stuck them in the rear, following up the Panther and PzKpfw IV spearheads, realizing that these clumsy monsters were not well suited to offensive operations.

While there has been a fair amount of attention paid to various futuristic "Paper Panzer" designs, German production plans through the summer of 1945 envisioned manufacturing much the same assortment of tanks that had been in production since the summer of 1944. PzKpfw IV Ausf. J production was scheduled to finally end at Nibleungenwerk in July 1945 in order to switch completely to the Pz IV/70 and other variants. The only new type scheduled to enter production was the Pz 38D, an upgraded version of the chassis used for the Jagdpanzer 38 (Hetzer), slated to replace other types at the two Czech plants. Besides the assault gun version, a scout tank and Kugelblitz antiaircraft tank were also scheduled to enter production. There were no plans to build any of the "E-series" of future tanks, which remained a "make-work" project for German tank engineers rather than a serious production scheme. The noted panzer historian Tom Jentz wryly commented that the German engineers wasting time on these fanciful tanks found it "preferable to being drafted and sent off to a muddy foxhole on the Eastern Front."[7]

PLANNED GERMAN TANK AND AFV PRODUCTION, MAY–AUGUST 1945[8]

	May	June	July	Aug.
PzKpfw IV	200	150	50	0
Pz IV/70	310	260	200	200
Panther	310	322	335	342
Tiger II	90	105	115	125
Jagdpanther	110	110	110	120
Jagdtiger	5	15	25	25
StuG III	400	300	200	100
StuG IV	80	70	40	20
JgPz 38	700	700	700	700
JgPz 38D	50	100	200	300
Total	***2,255***	***2,132***	***1,975***	***1,932***

ALLIED ARMOR IN THE EUROPEAN THEATER OF OPERATIONS: LATE ARRIVALS

With very modest exceptions, the final campaigns in the European Theater of Operations (ETO) in February–May 1945 were fought with the same types of tanks as the campaigns in late 1944. Some new and improved tank types appeared, but they were very modest in number.

The most significant new U.S. tank type was the M26 Pershing, which began arriving in February–March 1945 under its original experimental designation of T26E3. The U.S. Army's Ordnance department had been working on a follow-on tank for the Sherman since 1942, but with little sense of urgency. The most important innovation in the design was that the transmission was shifted from the front of the tank back to the rear engine compartment. This removed the need for a power-shaft through the center of the fighting compartment. The power-shaft in the Sherman took up considerable space and led to the tank's excessive height, so the new design had a lower, sleeker hull. However, there was no consensus about what features were important, and the design went through numerous variations as the T20, T22, T23, and T25. These various designs examined different power-plants, types of suspension, and armaments. By late 1943, two of these were favored. The T25 was fitted with 3-inch (75mm) frontal armor, weighed 36 tons, and was armed with a 90mm gun. The T26 was essentially similar but with 4-inch (100mm) frontal armor, weighing 40 tons. A total of 40 T25E1 and 10 T26E1 prototypes were completed from February to May 1944.

In the autumn of 1943, Lt. Gen. Jacob Devers was commander of U.S. forces in the ETO, a placeholder position until Dwight Eisenhower's appointment at the beginning of 1944. Devers had previously headed the Armored Force and was well aware that U.S. forces had encountered Tigers again on Sicily in July 1943 and in Italy in 1943–44. He wanted to make certain that U.S. forces could better deal with this threat. Devers requested that development of the T26E1 be accelerated and that 250 of these be manufactured as quickly as possible so that it would be possible to deploy them on the scale of one per every five M4 medium tanks. The head of Army Ground Forces, Lt. Gen. Lesley McNair, flatly turned down the request on the grounds that there was no demand from troops in the field and that the new Sherman with its 76mm gun was perfectly adequate. Devers continued to press the case for the T26E1, and on 16 December 1943 the War Department issued a directive that authorized the production of 250 T26E1 tanks by April 1945. The army's opinion about the need for new tanks changed abruptly after the Normandy landings in

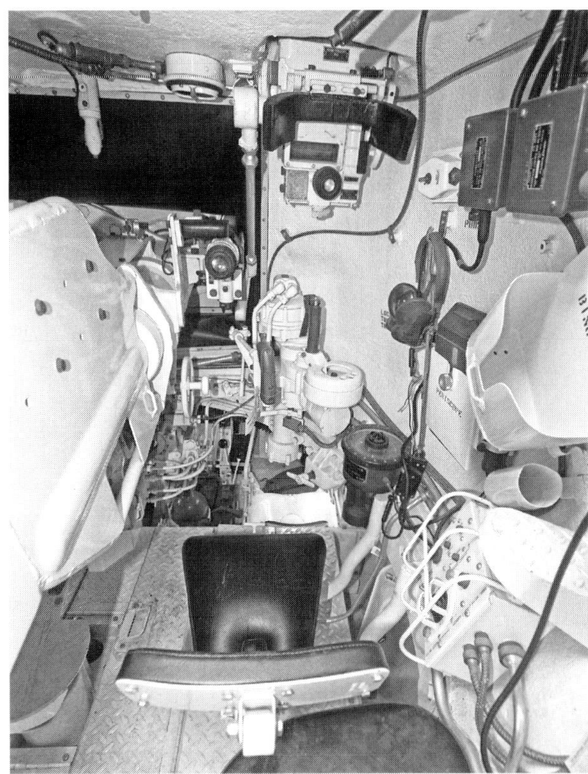

A view inside an M26 Pershing on the gunner's side to the right. The gunner in American medium tanks could use either the telescopic sight to the left or the periscopic sight above to aim the gun. The periscopic sight also gave U.S. gunners better situational awareness than Panther tank gunners, who lacked such a sight. This extra sight facilitated rapid engagements.

The M26 Pershing began to arrive in Europe in small numbers in early 1945 as part of the Zebra Mission. By the time they had arrived, the German tank threat had largely evaporated and they saw very little tank fighting.

The most powerful U.S. tank to see service in the ETO was a single "Super Pershing." This was a unique test tank based on the original T26E1 pilot tank but rearmed with the more powerful T15E1 version of the 90mm gun designed to offer performance comparable to the German 88mm KwK 43 on the King Tiger. It was not U.S. Army practice to send prototypes into combat, but in February 1945 Ordnance decided to ship the pilot tank to the European theater for a trial by combat.

June 1944. Widespread encounters with the Panther in Normandy in June–July 1944 led to an outcry about the poor armor and firepower of the Sherman.

Trials of the prototype T26E1 tanks in the summer of 1944 were successful enough that on 15 June 1944 the War Department decided that the 1945 tank production program would be changed to permit production of 6,000 T26 tanks. Nevertheless, the testing program uncovered a substantial number of significant modifications that would be needed before series production of the improved T26E3 started. By the end of 1944, forty T26E3 tanks had been completed. There was pressure to do something in response to the growing criticism coming from Europe; the tank fighting in the Ardennes in December 1944 increased the volume of complaints. The head of Ordnance research, Maj. Gen. G. M. Barnes, suggested sending half of the new tanks to Europe for impromptu combat trials while the other twenty went to Ft. Knox for the usual tests. The first batch of twenty T26E3 tanks arrived at the port of Antwerp in January 1945 and were assigned to General Bradley's 12th Army Group. They were split into two groups, with ten each going to the 3rd and 9th Armored Divisions. Training for the new tank crews concluded by late February 1945 and the tanks went into action in March. Those with the 9th Armored Division attracted the most attention when they took part in the capture of the Rhine River bridge at Remagen. Additional batches of T26E3 tanks arrived in late March and early April and were issued to the 2nd Armored Division (twenty-two), the 5th Armored Division (eighteen), and the 11th Armored Division (thirty).

The T26E3 tanks saw little tank-versus-tank combat due to the miniscule size of the panzer force in the west in April 1945. By the end of the war, 310 T26E3 had been delivered to Europe, of which 200 were issued to tank units. However, it was only the tanks supplied in February 1945 that saw extensive combat. The Pershing experience can best be summed up as "too little, too late." A postwar report by First Army assessed the combat trials of the Zebra Mission: "Unfortunately for this test, the German armor had been so crippled as to present a very poor opponent and the cessation of hostilities so soon after forming these companies precluded the gaining of any real experience." The main complaint about the M26 was that its automotive performance was sluggish compared to the M4A3 Sherman, since they both were powered by the same engine but the M26 was nearly 10 tons heavier. U.S. Army operational research after the Korean War concluded that the M26 Pershing was about three times more effective than the M4A3E8; combat effectiveness was assessed as the ratio of tank losses versus tank kills along with the relative number of enemy and friendly tanks.

Another newcomer to the ETO was the M24 Chaffee light tank. This was a thoroughly modern design intended to replace the obsolete M5A1 Stuart light tank. It was armed with a lightweight 75mm gun with performance the same as the 75mm on the Sherman tank. It was the best light tank of World War II.

The Sherman underwent some significant improvements in the final months of the war. A new horizontal volute suspension system (HVSS) was introduced, permitting the use of wider 23-inch tracks. This substantially improved the mobility of the Sherman in soft soil. The first examples were fielded by the 4th Armored Division in the Bastogne area around Christmas 1944. They are generally called M4A3E8, although the U.S. Army actually had no formal designation distinguishing the VVS from HVSS Sherman types.

In the wake of the Ardennes fighting, many tank units began to introduce local innovations in protection and firepower. One of the most common local initiatives was the extensive use of sand bag or concrete appliqué to provide better protection against the *panzerfaust* and other German antitank weapons. Many Ordnance officers felt these improvisations offered little or no additional protection, but the efforts were tolerated, if for no other reason than the psychological value to the embattled tank crews. The most effective of these appliqué programs was undertaken by Patton's Third Army, which began cutting up the tank wrecks in the Ardennes and welding the salvaged armor plate onto their Sherman tanks. This program was judged to be so successful that Bradley's 12th Army Group sent back photos of the conversion to the United States, urging this to become the standard configuration for

An M4A3 (76mm) of Company C, 774th Tank Battalion, passes by a knocked-out Panther tank near Bovigny on 17 January 1945 while supporting the 83rd Division during the drive to seal the Bulge.

The best Sherman variant for the infantry support mission was the M4A3E2, which had an increased armor basis thicker than the Tiger tank. The gun mantlet was 7 inches thick (180mm) and the turret front sides were 6 inches (150mm). In early 1945, about 100 were rearmed with spare 76mm guns, such as this example with the 3rd Armored Division in Cologne.

An M4A1 of Company F, 33rd Armored Regiment, Combat Command B, 3rd Armored Division, passes by a knocked-out PzKpfw IV Ausf. G, probably from the *11.Panzer-Division*, in Bad Marienburg on 28 March 1945 during the breakout from the Remagen bridgehead. The M4A1 is a survivor from the Normandy campaign and has a large steel plate added to the hull front, a modification on many 3rd Armored Division tanks following the capture of Cologne earlier in the month. By this stage of the war, there were barely a dozen PzKpfw IV in service on the entire Western Front.

The lingering inadequacy of the Sherman's frontal armor led Patton's U.S. Third Army to devise the most practical solution: They cut armor plate off knocked-out American and German tanks in the Ardennes area and bolted it to their tanks like on this M4A3E8 of the 11th Armored Division.

the U.S. Army in Europe. It also included a few changes in machine-gun armament, substituting a .50-cal heavy machine gun for the usual .30-cal coaxial machine gun and adding a .30-cal machine gun in front of the commander's cupola.

In the British case, 1945 saw the first widespread deployment of the new Comet cruiser tank.[9] This was an evolutionary break from the Centaur/Cromwell/Challenger family, with the redesign of nearly all of the critical features. The Comet was designed from the outset to carry a new 77mm high-velocity gun that used the same projectiles as the 17-pounder but a more compact propellant casing. The suspension was completely redesigned, and the tank used a wider track to get away from some of the mobility issues suffered in the Cromwell. Much as was the case with the M26 Pershing, few Comets arrived before war's end and they saw very little tank-versus-tank combat since there were so few German tanks operational in the west in the last months of the war. In the wings was a completely new tank design, the Centurion, but it did not enter service use prior to the end of the war. A postwar British study concluded that the Comet was more effective than the T-34-85 but slightly less effective than the IS-3 Stalin heavy tank.

EFFECTIVENESS OF THE COMET VS. SOVIET TANKS[10]

Comet	T-34-85	IS-3
600 yards	1.3	0.9
1,000 yards	1.1	0.9

Undoubtedly the best British tank of the war was the Comet. The 29th Armoured Brigade began converting to the new type in January 1945, and there was at least one duel between a Comet and a Tiger on 12 April 1945, with the Comet winning in this rare encounter.

A total of about 100 American M4 and M4A3 tanks were rearmed with 17-pounder guns by British arsenals in the spring of 1945, but they did not arrive in the ETO until April 1945 and never saw combat. The smaller tanks in the foreground are M22 Locust airborne tanks. GEORGE BRADFORD

The Churchill infantry tank continued in service through 1945 with the Guards Armoured Brigade. This one, named "Essex," supported troops of the U.S. 17th Airborne Division during the Rhine operations in March 1945.

THE ENDGAME: FINAL GERMAN OPTIONS

In view of Germany's desperate circumstances in late 1944, Hitler convinced himself that a success in the west could change the course of the war. In his fevered mind, the alliance between Britain and the United States was fragile, and if their forces could be separated by an assault to the North Sea, the Allied front would collapse. Hitler dreamed that a third to a half of the Allied divisions on the Western Front could be destroyed. In September 1944, he began to chart the strategic course for Germany in the final phase of the war. The basic premise was "Hold in the East, attack in the West." The Ardennes offensive was a final gamble concocted out of desperation.

Given the disparity of forces, the precious panzer forces had to be allotted with the utmost care—a powerful panzer force was essential to the success of an Ardennes attack. As a result, the panzer units in combat on the front line in the west were kept to a minimum through the autumn of 1944. Panzer units destroyed in Normandy were rebuilt in Germany and held in reserve along the frontier. Due to the priority given the Ardennes offensive, panzer allotments favored the West over the East through December 1944, as is evident in the chart on the next page.

The panzer units withdrawn from France in September 1944 were quite weak, and many did not receive their full complement of tanks until four to six weeks before the start of the Ardennes offensive, as seen in the same chart.

From a technical perspective, the tank fighting in the Ardennes that started on 16 December 1944 did not differ greatly from the fighting in Normandy.

Production of the PzKpfw IV tank shifted to the PzKpfw IV/70 late in 1944. This was armed with the long 75mm gun of the Panther tank, but in a fixed casemate. This is a late-production example with the mesh "Thoma" skirts. This particular vehicle was captured by the 78th Division during the fighting near Ückerath on 28 March 1945.

DELIVERY OF GERMAN AFVS BY THEATER, OCTOBER 1944–MARCH 1945[11]

	Nov. 1944	Dec. 1944	Jan. 1945	Feb. 1945	March 1945	Total
Pz IV	205	47	58	0	0	310
Pz IV Lg (A)	49	0	25	0	0	74
Panther	281	191	85	1	0	558
Tiger	26	6	6	0	13	51
StuG	382	361	82	0	88	913
Pz IV Lg (V)	135	128	17	0	0	280
Jagdpanther	20	49	36	20	5	130
Jagdpanzer 38	218	137	24	40	0	419
Jagdtiger	9	16	6	6	14	51
Sturmpanzer	20	17	4	0	14	55
West subtotal	**1,345**	**952**	**343**	**67**	**134**	**2,841**
Pz IV	10	65	120	194	55	444
Pz IV Lg (A)	0	24	37	49	16	126
Panther	83	48	154	178	50	513
Tiger	20	46	55	45	13	179
StuG	102	231	431	382	122	1268
Pz IV Lg (V)	0	82	98	227	28	435
Jagdpanther	0	0	42	48	0	90
Jagdpanzer 38	73	135	327	332	83	950
East subtotal	**288**	**631**	**1,264**	**1,455**	**367**	**4,005**
Total	***1,633***	***1,583***	***1,607***	***1,522***	***501***	***6,846***

The principal tank types on both sides were largely similar. In the case of the U.S. Army, the most important shift from June 1944 to December 1944 was the arrival of more M4A3 tanks with the 76mm gun. In June 1944, no U.S. tank units in Normandy had the 76mm gun tanks, but by the time of the Ardennes a third of all Sherman tanks in the Ardennes were the 76mm version. In addition, there were small but significant supplies of HVAP ammunition. In the case of German units, the mix was similar to Normandy, with the panzer regiments roughly equal in PzKpfw IV and Panther tanks; however, there were some changes, for example the growing numbers of Pz IV/70 being used as substitute tanks in some units.

The outcome of the Ardennes fighting had far more to do with tactical circumstances than with technical factors. There was little tank-versus-tank

By 1945, the Panther was no longer invulnerable to frontal attack. This one was knocked out during the fighting for Festung Posen in the city of Poznan, Poland, in February 1945. There are two gouges on the upper glacis plate and two large penetrations, most likely from 122mm projectiles.

U.S. Army encounters with the Tiger I in the ETO were very rare. This Tiger from *4.Kompanie, schwere Panzer-Abteilung 506*, knocked out a T26E3 Pershing named "Fireball" of the 3rd Armored Division on 26 February 1945 near Elsdorf, Germany, but while attempting to withdraw was immobilized and abandoned. "Fireball" was repaired and put back into action. Another Tiger from this unit was knocked out the following day in an encounter with another Pershing.

BUILDUP OF PANTHER UNITS FACING THE ARDENNES, AUTUMN 1944

Date (1944)	5 Sept.		1 Oct.		1 Nov.		16 Dec.	
	Panthers	Troops (%)	Panthers	Troops (%)	Panthers	Troops (%)	Panthers	Troops (%)
Pz.Rgt. 3 (2.Pz.Div.)	**3**	43	**0**	68	**5**	67	**64**	96
Pz.Rgt. 33 (9.Pz.Div.)	**26**	76	**53**	85	**45**	97	**60**	100
Pz.Rgt.16 (116.Pz.Div.)	**1**	68	**28**	83	**44**	92	**64**	96
Pz.Rgt. 130 (Pz.Lehr-Div.)	**13**	54	**0**	85	**16**	99	**29**	95
SS-Pz.Rgt. 1 (1.SS-Pz.Div.)	**4**	74	**3**	81	**25**	95	**42**	100
SS-Pz.Rgt. 2 (2.SS-Pz.Div.)	**6**	58	**1**	79	**1**	100	**58**	100
SS-Pz.Rgt. 9 (9.SS-Pz.Div.)	**5**	35	**19**	54	**2**	100	**58**	124
SS-Pz.Rgt.12 (12.SS-Pz.Div.)	**4**	29	**3**	75	**23**	89	**41**	100
Total (average %)	***62***	55	***107***	75	***161***	92	***416***	101

fighting in the first few days of the battle, since the U.S. units stationed in the Ardennes were four infantry divisions with a small number of supporting tank battalions and tank destroyer battalions. The first few days of the campaign occurred in early winter weather with soggy ground, rain, and evening snow. The German tanks were obliged to stay on the roads, and each little stone village was contested.

The *Schwerpunkt* (focal point) of the attack was in the northern sector by Sepp Dietrich's *6.Panzer-Armee* consisting of two *SS-Panzer-Korps*. The infantry divisions in the northernmost sector failed to win a breakthrough, so the *12.SS-Panzer-Division* was committed to this role; it was ground down in these struggles and failed to penetrate the U.S. infantry defenses. The neighboring *1.SS-Panzer-Division* plunged into the weakly held Losheim Gap, encountering little resistance from the scattered U.S. mechanized cavalry units. Although it pushed as far as La Gleize, the U.S. Army brought up infantry reinforcements that encircled and destroyed the German spearhead, Kampfgruppe Peiper. The failure of the *6.Panzer-Armee* attack was a reminder of the Wehrmacht's declining offensive power due to its weak infantry and panzer divisions' inability to penetrate a stout infantry defense.

Farther south, Manteuffel's *5.Panzer-Armee* showed much greater prowess than the Waffen-SS and managed to encircle and break through the newly arrived and inexperienced 106th Infantry Division. This created a significant breakout opportunity, especially once the weather changed and the

WEHRMACHT AFV STRENGTH IN THE ARDENNES, DECEMBER 1944–JANUARY 1945[12]

	16 Dec. 1944	26 Dec. 1944	6 Jan. 1945	16 Jan. 1945
PzKpfw IV	317	219	169	172
Panzer IV/70	171	130	97	99
Panther	341	219	173	170
Tiger	14	14		
King Tiger	52	39	13	35
Tanks subtotal	**895**	**621**	**452**	**476**
StuG III	304	281	229	264
StuH (105mm)	42	42	26	37
Hetzer	99	110	73	68
Jagdpanther	21	18	17	17
AFV subtotal	**466**	**451**	**345**	**386**
Tanks and AFVs total	***1,467***	***1,167***	***860***	***915***

The U.S. Army had a series of encounters with the King Tiger in March and April 1945 in the areas near Kassel where the tank was manufactured. This one from *schwere Panzer-Abteilung 507* was knocked out by Task Force Kane, Combat Command A, 3rd Armored Division, in front of Hotel Kaiserhofen in the fighting in Osterode on 10 April 1945.

U.S. TANK STRENGTH IN THE ARDENNES, DECEMBER 1944–JANUARY 1945*

Type	16 Dec. 1944	26 Dec. 1944	6 Jan. 1945	16 Jan. 1945
M4 (75mm) medium tank	490	649	1,190	1,205
M4 (76mm) medium tank	297	237	558	511
M4 (105mm) assault gun	104	128	249	247
M5A1 light tank	501	617	1,016	945
M8 75mm HMC	60	94	137	131
Total	***1,452***	***1,725***	***3,150***	***3,039***

*Data for 6 and 16 January 1945 includes Third Army minus its XX Corps units.

ground froze. The gap near St. Vith was exploited both by the army panzer divisions that raced toward Bastogne and by the remaining *II.SS-Panzer-Korps* that pushed toward Liège. The problem facing the Wehrmacht at this point was that the U.S. Army had far greater reserves as well as the capability to move them far more quickly than the German reserves. The *II.SS-Panzer-Korps* advance was halted around Manhay upon the arrival of the 3rd Armored Division with substantial infantry and artillery support. The army panzer advance beyond Bastogne was crushed in the days around Christmas by the 2nd Armored Division in the Celles pocket.

By this stage, the offensive had failed since the U.S. Army could continue to reinforce the Ardennes while the Wehrmacht's momentum was already spent. Hitler would not accept defeat and insisted that Bastogne be taken as a consolation prize for his ill-conceived gamble. In the face of Patton's spectacular counterattack, even this minor prize eluded him.

At the end of two weeks of intense fighting, the panzer regiments in the Ardennes were shattered. The best units, the 8 Panther battalions, had only about 105 tanks operational out of the starting force of about 415 Panthers; 180 were total losses and the remainder were battle damaged or broken down. The Panther was again suffering from durability issues, especially with the power-train's final drives. Its strained transmission was functional in the hands of an experienced driver, but the inexperienced crews in the Ardennes had received insufficient training due to the late arrival of their new tanks and the lack of fuel for practice. German accounts suggest that as many as half of the tank losses in the Ardennes were due to mechanical breakdowns.

U.S. tank losses in the Ardennes were numerically greater than German losses simply because the U.S. Army had so many more tanks. In the case of the U.S. First Army, which bore the brunt of the Ardennes fighting, by the end of December it had lost about 320 Sherman tanks, of which about 90 were M4A1/A3 (76mm), equivalent to about a quarter of its average daily strength that month. Due to continual reinforcements, First Army had about 1,085 Shermans on hand at the end of December 1944 with about 980 operational and only 9 percent sidelined with mechanical problems or battle damage. Maj. (Dr.) P. E. Schramm, historian of the German High Command, concluded that "the Battle of the Bulge finally demonstrated the armored superiority of the U.S. Army over the Wehrmacht."

There was a sharp flare-up of fighting in Alsace when German Army Group G launched Operation Nordwind on New Year's Eve. This sector was starved of armor due to the priority afforded the Ardennes offensive; there were only about 260 tanks and AFVs, of which about 200 were operational.

On the U.S. side, the Seventh Army had one French and two U.S. armored divisions: 2e Division Blindée, 12th and 14th Armored Divisions, plus

GERMAN AFVS, OPERATION NORDWIND, 1 JANUARY 1945[13]

	17.SS-Pz.Div	*21.Pz.Div.*	*25.Pz.Gr.Div.*	Other
BefPz III	3			
PzKpfw IV		34		
Panther		38	6	
StuG III	76		14	20
Flamm.Pz.38				20
JgPz.38				28
Jagdpanzer IV	2	4	5	
Jagdtiger				9
Marder III	1			

GERMAN TANK STRENGTH, EAST VERSUS WEST, 1 FEBRUARY 1945[14]

	Strength	Operational	% Operational
West	2,013	1,162	58
East	2,550	1,323	52
Total	***4,563***	***2,485***	***54***

STRENGTH OF PANZER UNITS, 15 MARCH 1945[15]

	Pz IV	Pz IV/70	Panther	Tiger	StuG	FlakPz	Total*
West	19+40=59	33+44=77	49+103=152	6+22=28	67+59=126	19+22 =41	193+290 =483
Italy	108+23=131	0	22+4=26	32+4=36	57+10=67	19+3=22	238+44 =282
Total— West	***127+63=190***	***33+44=77***	***71+107=178***	***38+26=64***	***124+69=193***	***38+25= 63***	***431+334 =765***
East	345+248 =593	189+168 =357	387+389 =776	125+87=212	314+231 =545	50+47=97	1,410+1,170 =2,580

*(Operational + In Repair = Total)

GERMAN TANK AND ASSAULT GUN STRENGTH, 10 APRIL 1945[16]

	Tanks	StuG	Total
East (strength)	1,297	1,802	3,099
East (operational)	768	1,213	1,981
West (strength)	67	206	273
West (operational)	47	131	178
Total (strength)	***1,713***	***2,347***	***4,060***
Total (operational)	***1,124***	***1,636***	***2,760***

One of the more absurd German projects was the 180-ton Maus super-heavy tank. The project was abruptly ended by Allied bombing attacks against its plant, but one tank was hurriedly put into action in the Berlin area in 1945. It was demolished by its crew, but the Red Army pieced together a hybrid using the combat-damaged hull and the turret from a second prototype. It is now preserved at the Kubinka Tank Museum outside Moscow.

U.S. ARMY ETO TANK AND AFV STRENGTH, JANUARY–MAY 1945[17]

	Jan.	Feb.	Mar.	Apr.	May
M5A1	2,970	3,479	2,981	3,427	4,119
M4 (75, 76mm)	4,561	5,297	6,249	5,727	6,336
M4 (105)	620	804	612	612	636
Tank subtotal	**8,151**	**9,580**	**9,842**	**9,766**	**11,091**
M18	312	448	540	427	427
M10	768	686	684	427	427
M36	365	826	684	1,054	1,029
TD subtotal	**1,445**	**1,960**	**1,908**	**1,908**	**1,883**
Total	***9,596***	***11,540***	***11,750***	***11,674***	***12,974***

U.S. ARMY ETO TANK AND AFV LOSSES, 1945[18]

	Jan.	Feb.	Mar.	Apr.	May	Total
M5A1	208	93	136	190	112	739
M4	585	320	463	554	207	2,129
M4 (105)	29	62	0	13	5	109
Tank subtotal	**822**	**475**	**599**	**757**	**324**	**2,977**
M18	27	16	21	55	21	140
M10	69	106	27	37	37	276
M36	26	18	21	34	25	124
TD subtotal	**122**	**140**	**69**	**126**	**83**	**540**
Total	***944***	***615***	***668***	***883***	***407***	***3,517***

BRITISH TANK STRENGTH IN NORTHWEST EUROPE, 1945 (UNIT HOLDINGS)[19]

	27 Jan. 1945	5 May 1945
Stuart	446	601
Sherman	1,247	1,373
Sherman 17-pounder	636	709
Cromwell	603	549
Challenger	25	30
Comet	35	237
Churchill	535	742
Total	***3,527***	***4,241***

BRITISH CUMULATIVE TANK LOSSES IN NORTHWEST EUROPE THROUGH 1945[20]

	Through 31 Jan. 1945	Through 30 June 1945
Stuart	281	433
Chaffee	0	2
Sherman	1,855	2,712
Cromwell	464	609
Challenger	1	39
Comet	0	26
Churchill	365	656
Cumulative total	***2,965***	***4,477***

five separate tank battalions and five self-propelled tank destroyer battalions with a total of 376 light tanks and 704 M4 medium tanks. The French 1st Army in the Colmar area had substantial armor but was not involved in the initial Nordwind fighting. The Nordwind attacks were beaten off with heavy German losses; this was the last major use of German armor in the west. By 1 February 1945, overall German tank and AFV strength was 2,013 (1,162 operational) in the west and 2,550 (1,323 operational) in the east.

Since the Russian Front had priority, replacements to the West fell to a trickle. By 15 March 1945 the Wehrmacht had only 765 tanks and AFVs in the west, of which just 431 were operational. With the destruction of Army Group B in the Ruhr pocket in April 1945, on 10 April the Wehrmacht in the west had 273 tanks and AFVs, with only 178 operational. At this point, the American and British forces had in excess of 15,000 tanks and AFVs operational. Encounters with German tanks and assault guns continued through the end of the war but on a greatly diminished scale.

RED ARMY TANK INNOVATIONS: 1945

The Red Army's tank units fought the 1945 campaign with the same tank types used during the latter half of 1944. There were some improvements in the T-34-85 and IS-2, but new types such as the T-44 and IS-3 arrived too late for combat use. Quality control at the tank plants continued to improve, significantly reducing attrition through mechanical breakdown. Out of 18,346 tanks and AFVs from the 1st Belorussian and 1st Ukrainian Fronts participating in the Berlin Operation, 212 vehicles failed for mechanical reasons, or a bit more than 1 percent.[21]

Following the cancellation of the T-43 universal tank and the adoption of the T-34-85, the Soviet medium tank design bureau at Nizhi-Tagil turned their attention to an entirely new medium tank design that emerged in 1944 as the T-44. The new layout would form the basis for nearly twenty years of Soviet medium tank production, through the T-62 of 1962. The T-44 used a turret and gun system virtually identical to that on the T-34-85. The main departure in the design came in the hull. The hull form was extremely simple, its compact size made possible by a radically different transverse engine layout. The power-plant was a derivative of the wartime V-2 diesel that powered the T-34, KV, and IS, but mated to a new transmission. The suspension externally resembled the T-34, but inside torsion bars had replaced the Christie–style spring suspension in order to provide more internal volume. The first trial series of the tank entered production in

The Red Army made extensive use of Lend-Lease Sherman tanks in the final campaigns. This M4A2 (76mm) is seen in Grabow, Germany, in May 1945 shortly before war's end.

Although the T-34 went out of production in 1944 in favor of the T-34-85, there were still some in service in the 1945 campaigns, such as these two examples in Leipzig, Germany, at the end of the war.

Design of the T-44 began after cancellation of the T-43. It used a turret very similar to the T-34-85, but the hull was a completely new design with torsion bar suspension and a transversely mounted engine. Although a number of training regiments received the T-44 before war's end, it never saw combat use during World War II.

COMPARATIVE COMBAT VALUE OF SOVIET AFVS, 1944–45					
SU-76M	T-34	T-34-85	T-44	IS-2M	IS-3
0.74	1.0	1.14	1.71	1.62	1.92

1944. No large-scale production was undertaken during World War II due to severe teething problems with the design, especially its new power-train. This tank represented an impressive mixture of design simplicity and high combat effectiveness for a 30-ton tank. The T-44 came very close to the combat capabilities of the German Panther in a design that weighed only about 65 percent as much. Although some Soviet tank training regiments were equipped with the T-44 during 1945, none of the tanks saw combat use due to their technical immaturity.

Following the completion of the IS-2 design in 1943, the Soviet heavy tank design bureau at Chelyabinsk began design of IS-3 heavy tanks based on the lessons of the Kursk battle.[22] Soviet engineers concluded that hits on the turret front were most often the cause of tank loss, followed by hits on the hull front. The IS-3 design placed the emphasis on a radical new turret with 200mm armor and a new hull front design. However, the thick, new armor proved difficult to manufacture, and the first series production examples did not begin to roll

Among the armament options for the T-44 was the same 122mm D-25T gun used in the IS-2 heavy tank. Although the gun was successfully mounted in a prototype as seen here, the ammunition was too large and the gun breech too massive to make this a practical alternative.

off assembly lines until May 1945 and did not see combat use against Germany. The IS-3 was first publicly displayed at a victory parade in Berlin on 7 September 1945, which involved fifty-two IS-3 tanks from the 2nd Guards Tank Army. Aside from a very small number of IS-3s produced in 1945, large-scale production did not take place until 1946.

Although the Red Army did not conduct a comparative evaluation of the various types of tank present on the 1945 battlefield, it was done after the war as part of a computer modeling effort.[23]

January 1945: Red Deluge

The Russian Front at the beginning of 1945 was quiet in the center around Warsaw while fighting continued to rage in the northern sector in East Prussia and in the southern sector around Budapest. Berlin had no doubt that the Red Army was planning a major campaign into central Germany sometime in the New Year, and on 12 January 1945 the Vistula-Oder offensive was unleashed. In about three weeks' time, the Red Army swept from Warsaw all the way to the Oder River, swamping the threadbare German defenses. The Soviet formation at the heart of the offensive, Marshal Georgi Zhukov's 1st Belorussian Front, had nearly a third of the armor deployed by the Red Army at the time.

By the beginning of February 1945, the 1st Belorussian Front had reached Kustrin, 50 miles from the heart of Berlin. The Soviet penetration at this point was narrow, so the neighboring fronts began assaults to widen the penetration at its shoulders. In the north, the 3rd Belorussian Front began its attack toward the Prussian port of Königsberg while the 2nd Belorussian Front pushed into Pomerania, aiming for the Baltic port of Danzig. On Zhukov's southern flank, Marshal Ivan Koniev's 1st Ukrainian Front pushed through southern Poland toward Dresden.

At the beginning of February 1945, the German tank balance between East and West was fairly similar. The tank imbalance between the Wehrmacht

A T-34-85 of the 3rd Belorussian Front during the fighting with the *3.Panzer-Armee* in Prussia in January 1945.

The most numerous Soviet armored vehicle after the T-34 was the SU-76M assault gun. It was put into production at smaller automotive plants as a more useful weapon than the previous T-70 light tank. It was used primarily for infantry fire support. Two are seen here in action in the Carpathian Mountains in January 1945.

A snow-camouflaged Panther Ausf. G moves forward toward a tactical bridge during the fighting in the Gran bridgehead in February 1945.

TANK AND AFV STRENGTH, 1ST BELORUSSIAN FRONT, 14 JANUARY 1945[24]

	IS-2	T-34	Lend-Lease Tanks	SU-57	SU-76M, SU-85	Heavy ISU	Total
1st Guards Tank Army	42	511	0	94	85	21	753
2nd Guards Tank Army	42	432	195	15	130	42	856
Other front units	176	778	87	23	843	144	2,051
Total	***260***	***1,721***	***282***	***132***	***1,058***	***207***	***3,660***

OPERATIONAL PANZER STRENGTH, ARMY GROUP SOUTH*, 5 MARCH 1945[25]

Pz IV	Panther	King Tiger	PzJg.	StuG	Total
135	249	104	94	176	758

*A further 167 tanks and 99 StuG/*Panzerjäger* in repair

TANKS AND AFVS OF THE 3RD UKRAINIAN FRONT, 5 MARCH 1945[26]

	T-34	M4A2	IS-2	SU-76	SU-100	ISU-122	ISU-152	Total
Operational	157	47	4	95	78	23	9	413
In repair	4	1	0	0	2	1	1	9
Total	***161***	***48***	***4***	***95***	***80***	***24***	***10***	***422***

and the Red Army was grotesquely skewed in favor of the Red Army, with Zhukov's forces alone having about double the entire German tank strength on the Eastern Front. With the Red Army now in striking distance of Berlin and the Ardennes operation a costly flop, Hitler ordered another strategic change of course. Tank reinforcements to the West dried to a trickle, and most armored resources were directed to the East. Dietrich's *6.SS-Panzer-Armee* was pulled out of the Ardennes in mid-January, partially refitted in Germany, and sent east to Hungary.

Hitler had little confidence that defensive measures against Zhukov's force on the Oder River would have any appreciable effect. However, the southern flank in Hungary seemed to offer more lucrative prospects since the Red Army had concentrated the bulk of its offensive strength in the center in the drive through Pomerania and Silesia. The available panzer reserves were moved into the Lake Balaton region of Hungary for Hitler's last major panzer offensive of the war. The aim was to strike southeastward from the area between Lake Balaton

A pair of IS-2m tanks of the 29th Guards Heavy Tank Regiment, 4th Guards Tank Corps, 1st Ukrainian Front, during the fighting near Wislica, Poland, during the January Vistula-Oder offensive.

and Budapest and cut off a bulge in the Soviet line to the western edge of Balaton.

Operation Frühlingserwachen ("Spring Awakening") was launched by Army Group South on 6 March 1945. The main strike force was Dietrich's *6.SS-Panzer-Armee*, modestly reequipped since the Ardennes debacle. For this offensive, the corps's four panzer divisions had a total of 278 tanks and AFVs, including 87 PzKpfw IV, 61 Panthers, 9 King Tigers, and 80 PzIV/L70. This was only about half the strength the corps had at the start of the Ardennes offensive.

Facing this offensive was the 3rd Ukrainian Front. The Red Army was concentrating its resources in the central sector toward Berlin, and local commanders were warned that they would have to make do with available resources. Therefore, defensive preparations were based heavily on antitank artillery. This was one theater where the Germans had a decided advantage in armor strength.

The Spring Awakening offensive penetrated nearly 30 kilometers into Soviet lines but quickly floundered on the Soviet antitank defenses. The Wehrmacht's offensive energy was largely spent in a week of fighting. The 3rd Ukrainian Front claimed 324 tanks, StuG, and *Panzerjäger* at the end of the offensive, about half of the attacking force. This was the last major German panzer operation of the war. By this stage, whatever tactical and technological edge the Wehrmacht may have enjoyed was impotent in the face of the growing proficiency of the Red Army and its substantial advantage in armored force.

Enemy guns still remained the main adversary of Soviet tanks. A survey of knocked-out and disabled tanks detailed the causes of incapacitation. Of the tanks listed as disabled in the top chart on the next page, 34 percent of the February figures and 26 percent of the March figures were total losses.

The final month of fighting saw the Red Army conducting massive armored offensives along

SOVIET TANK AND ASSAULT GUN CASUALTIES BY CAUSE, FEBRUARY–MARCH 1945[27]

	Gunfire	Mines	Aircraft	RPG	Drowning	Swamps	Ditches	Technical	Total
February (#)	4,286	295	125	N/A	21	370	60	604	5,761
February (%)	74.2	5.1	2.2	N/A	0.4	6.4	1.2	10.5	
March (#)	4,994	281	42	181	47	658	90	799	7,092
March (%)	71	4	0.6	2.5	0.6	9.1	1.2	11	

SOVIET TANK AND AFV LOSSES BY CAMPAIGN, 1945 [28]

Campaign	Total Losses	Avg. Daily Loss
Budapest offensive: 29 Oct. 1944–13 Feb. 1945	1,766	16
Vistula-Oder offensive: 12 Jan.–2 Mar.	1,267	55
Western Carpathian offensive: 12 Jan.–18 Feb.	359	9
East Prussian offensive: 13 Jan.–25 Apr.	3,525	34
Eastern Pomeranian offensive: 10 Feb.–4 Apr.	1,027	19
Vienna offensive: 16 Mar.–8 May	603	19
Berlin offensive: 16 Apr.–8 May	1,997	87
Prague offensive: 6–11 May	373	62
Subtotal—AFV losses during listed campaigns	**10,917**	
Total tank losses in 1945	8,700	
Total SU losses in 1945	5,000	
Total AFV losses in 1945	***13,700***	***105***

several axes. Although the final operation against Berlin is certainly the most famous, there were also large-scale operations in the direction of Prague and Vienna. There were four entire tank armies taking part in the Berlin campaign: the 3rd and the 4th Guards Tank Armies advancing from the southeast, and the 1st and 2nd Guards Tank Armies advancing from the Kustrin area from the east. Although called "armies" by the Red Army, they were closer in strength to American or British corps. For example, the 3rd Guards Tank Army had 606 tanks and AFVs on 15 April 1945, including 386 T-34-85, 23 IS-2, and about 190 assault guns and tank destroyers.[29] The three Soviet fronts (1st Ukrainian, 1st

A column of IS-2m heavy tanks on the approaches to Berlin in the spring of 1945.

A classic view of an IS-2m prowling the streets of Berlin in the final campaign of the war. This is from the later production series with the simplified, thicker nose armor.

GERMAN OPERATIONAL PANZER STRENGTH ON THE BERLIN FRONT, 10 APRIL 1945[30]

	AG Center	AG Vistula	Total
PzKpfw III	3	2	5
PzKpfw IV	71	102	173
Pz IV/70	113	10	123
Panther	116	83	199
Tiger	1	46	47
StuG III	215	202	417
StuG IV	29	20	49
StuH	15	38	53
JagdPz 38	198	187	385
Nashorn	39	0	39
Jagdpanther	5	0	5
Total	***805***	***690***	***1,495***

SOVIET AFV DEPLOYMENT AT WAR'S END[31]

	Front	Reserve	Military Districts	Rebuilding Plants	Total
Unidentified	0	0	43	256	299
T-26	35	0	213	176	424
Other types	265	269	1,750	676	2,960
Foreign light tanks	207	109	295	303	914
T-34 + IS	5,640	963	1,677	2,032	10,312
Foreign med. tanks	877	219	275	446	1,817
Tanks subtotal	**7,024**	**1,560**	**4,253**	**3,889**	**16,726**
SU-57	250	66	10	14	340
SU-76	3,546	999	688	670	5,903
ISU-122/-152	1,196	340	129	336	2,028
SU subtotal	**4,992**	**1,405**	**827**	**1,020**	**8,271**
Total AFV	***12,016***	***2,965***	***5,080***	***4,909***	***24,997***

Does not include holdings of Far Eastern or Baikal fronts.

COMPARATIVE TECHNICAL CHARACTERISTICS					
	M4A3E8	**IS-2m**	**King Tiger**	**Pershing**	**Comet**
Army	USA	USSR	Germany	USA	UK
Crew	5	4	5	5	5
Dimensions: L x W x H (m)	5.89 x 2.61 x 2.74	9.8 x 3.1 x 2.73	10.3 x 3.7 x 3.1	8.6 x 3.5 x 2.7	7.6 x 3.0 x 2.65
Loaded weight (tonnes)	33.6	46	69.8	41.8	29.6
Main gun	76mm M1A1	122mm D-25T	88mm KwK 43	90mm M3	77mm HV
Main gun ammo	71	28	84	70	61
Engine (hp)	450	520	600	450	550
Max. speed (km/h)	42	37	41	48	51
Fuel (liters)	635	820	860	693	527
Range (km)	160	150	170	160	200
Ground pressure (kg/cm^2)	.963	.81	1.02	.879	.973
Armor*					
Mantlet (mm)	90@5=90.3	105**=>105	100**=>100	102**=>102	102@0=102
Turret front (mm)	51@30=58.9	105**=>105	180@10=182.8	102@7=103	102@0=102
Turret side (mm)	51@5=51.2	95@12=97.1	80@20=85.1	76@0=76	64@0=64
Upper hull front (mm)	51@45=72.1	120@65=132.4	150@50=233.3	102@43=139.5	74@0=74
Lower hull front (mm)	51@50=79.3	100@35=122.1	120@50=186.7	102@35=124.5	64@22=69
Upper hull side (mm)	38@0=38	95@12=97.1	80@25=88.3	76@0=76	46@0=46

*Armor data provided as: actual thickness in mm @ angle from vertical = effective thickness in mm.
**Curved

Belorussian, and 2nd Belorussian) totaled 6,250 tanks and assault guns in mid-April 1945.[32]

The two German army groups, Mitte (Center) and Weichsel (Vistula) faced the three Soviet fronts from the Baltic to Dresden, covering a battleline about 185 miles wide. Army Group Center, the main group defending Berlin, had about 1,190 tanks and AFVs, of which 805 were operational on 10 April, as detailed in the chart on page 287. This was about half of total German panzer strength on the Russian Front at the time. Soviet accounts usually credit the Wehrmacht with 1,519 tanks and assault guns for this campaign, though this total probably includes other categories of armor such as armored cars that are excluded from the table. Army Group Vistula, covering the northern German sector, was smaller but in better working order with a total of 770 tanks and AFVs, of which 690 were operational. In total, both army groups fielded 547 tanks, 904 assault guns, and 44 tank destroyers in the opening phase of the campaign. It's interesting to note that the three Soviet fronts later claimed to have knocked out or captured 4,183 German tanks and assault guns in the Berlin operation. The number of tanks and armored vehicles actually involved in the storming of Berlin is considerably smaller than these figures suggest since these numbers cover the entire front line.

The Soviet assault lasted for about three weeks and was enormously costly on both sides. The Red Army's final assault made lavish use of armor and artillery. In the main sector, the 1st Guards Tank Army deployed 138.5 tanks per kilometer; the 2nd Guards Tank density was 130.1 tanks per kilometer. By the time the Red Army reached the outskirts of Berlin, most of the Wehrmacht tank force had been overcome, but there were a small number of tank-versus-tank engagements within the city. Soviet armor losses were substantial, amounting to about a third of the attacking force in a three-week battle.

TOP TANKS OF 1945

Picking the Top Tanks of 1945 is difficult since there were a number of late arrivals and "might have beens." For example, if the T-44 had actually seen service, it would be a serious contender. But it did not, as was the case with Britain's excellent Centurion.

The German tanks were contenders, but the performance of the Panther in the Ardennes was shaky due to both mediocre crew training and declining technical quality. The King Tiger had impressive armor and firepower but its excessive weight and cranky automotive performance rule it out. For Tanker's Choice, I would pick the M26 Pershing. It had an excellent gun, which offered both antitank and high-explosive firepower. Furthermore, the quality of the design is evident in its longevity. The M26 formed the basis for the postwar generation of U.S. battle tanks from the M46 through the M47, M48, and M60 series. The Pershing also had advantages in armor. Other contenders such as the British Comet had excellent antitank firepower but less-potent high-explosive firepower. Possible Soviet contenders such as the IS-2M had significant issues, especially the meager ammunition stowage and slow rate of fire.

Commander's Choice is more difficult. Top contenders would include the M4A3E8, especially with the U.S. Third Army upgrades. Its most likely rival was the T-34-85 for its widespread availability and generally good technical qualities. The winning combination for me is the M4A3E8, specifically the U.S. Third Army version with HVAP ammunition. By this stage, the M4A3E8 had excellent dependability and was available in large numbers, and the upgrades significantly improved both survivability and firepower.

TOP TANK ROUND-UP		
	Tanker's Choice	**Commander's Choice**
The Roaring Thirties	T-28	BT-5
Blitzkrieg era	Somua S 35	PzKpfw IV Ausf. D
Barbarossa: 1941	T-34 Model 41	T-34 Model 41
Russian Slug Fest: 1942	PzKpfw IV Ausf. G	PzKpfw IV Ausf. G
Other Theaters	PzKpfw IV Ausf. G	M4A1 Sherman
Kursk: Summer 1943	Tiger	StuG III Ausf. G
Normandy: Summer 1944	Panther	T-34-85
War's End: 1945	M26 Pershing	M4A3E8+

The M26 Pershing continued to serve in Europe in the years after the war, in this case during Exercise Rainbow in Germany in September 1950.

Aggravated by the failure of Ordnance to address the Panther threat, U.S. tank units in the ETO took measures into their own hands. The 12th Army Group offered this configuration as their solution to the problem, refitting an M4A3E8 with extra armor plate on the hull front and making a number of other changes such as a co-axial .50-cal machine gun and an additional machine gun for the commander.

APPENDIX 1

Soviet AFV Production: 1941–45

SOVIET TANK PRODUCTION, 1939–45[1]								
	1939	1940	1941	1942	1943	1944	1945*	Total
T-38	154							154
T-30, T-40		41	668					709
T-26	1,396	1,601	116					3,113
T-50			60	15				75
T-60			1,388	4,477	55			5,920
T-70, T-80				4,883	3,423			8,306
BT-7	1,346	780						2,126
T-34		115	3,016	12,661	15,710	3,986		35,488
T-34-85						10,662	9,510	20,172
T-44						25	545	570
T-28	131	13						144
T-35	6							6
KV	1	243	1,323	2,553	617			4,737
IS					102	2,250	2,015	4,367
Total	***3,034***	***2,793***	***6,571***	***24,589***	***19,907***	***16,923***	***12,070***	***85,887***

*To September 1945

SOVIET SELF-PROPELLED GUNS, 1941–45

	1941*	1942	1943	1944	1945*	Total
ZIS-30	101					101
SU-76		25	1,908	7,155	2,966	12,054
SU-85		761	1,578	315		2,654
SU-100				500	1,060	1,560
SU-122		26	612			638
ISU-122				1,170	740	1,910
SU-152			668	2		670
ISU-152			35	1,340	510	1,885
Total	***101***	***812***	***4,801***	***10,482***	***5,276***	***21,472***

*July 1941–September 1945

SOVIET ARMORED VEHICLE PRODUCTION, 1939–45

	1939	1940	1941	1942	1943	1944	1945*	Total
Tanks	3,034	2,793	6,571	24,589	19,907	16,923	12,070	85,887
SP Guns			101	812	4,801	10,482	5,276	21,472
Armored cars	1,239	1,380	1,564	2,623	1,820	3,000	868	12,494
Total	***4,273***	***4,173***	***8,236***	***28,024***	***26,528***	***30,405***	***18,214***	***119,853***

*To September 1945

LEND-LEASE TANK AND AFV DELIVERIES TO THE SOVIET UNION, 1941–45[2]

	1941	1942	1943	1944	1945	Delivered*	Sent*
Matilda II	145	626	147			918	932
Valentine	216	959	1,776	381		3,332	3,275
Churchill		84	179			263	258
Cromwell				6		6	6
Tetrarch		20				20	20
M3 Stuart		977	255			1,232	1,676
M5A1 Stuart			5			5	5
M24 Chafee					2	2	2
M3 Lee		812	164			976	1,386
M4A2 Sherman		36	469	2,345	814	3,664	4,102
M26 Pershing					1	1	1
M10 3-inch GMC				52		52	52
M18 76mm GMC			5			5	5
T48 57mm GMC			241	409		650	650
M31 ARV			41	86		127	115
Total	***361***	***3,514***	***3,282***	***3,279***	***817***	***11,253***	***12,485***

*"Delivered" counts vehicles received by USSR; "Sent" includes those dispatched, some of which were sunk in transit by sea.

APPENDIX 2

German Armored Vehicle Production

GERMAN TANK PRODUCTION, 1939–45[3]								
	1939	**1940**	**1941**	**1942**	**1943**	**1944**	**1945**	**Total**
PzKpfw I				70				70
PzKpfw II	246	9	236	322				813
PzKpfw 38t	150	370	698	193				1411
PzKpfw III	206	858	1,713	2,608	235			5,620
PzKpfw IV	141	278	467	994	3,013	3,126	385	8,404
Panther					1,768	3,749	459	5,976
Tiger I				89	647	623		1,359
King Tiger						377	112	489
PzBefWg	44	34	132	131	14	4		359
Flame tanks		44	39	29	100	20		232
Total	***787***	***1,593***	***3,285***	***4,436***	***5,777***	***7,899***	***956***	***24,733***

GERMAN ARMORED VEHICLE PRODUCTION, 1939–45								
	1939	**1940**	**1941**	**1942**	**1943**	**1944**	**1945**	**Total**
Tanks	787	1,593	3,285	4,436	5,777	7,899	956	24,733
StuG		184	548	789	3,042	4,999	988	10,550
StuH/M				34	270	1,118	112	1,534
PzJäger		2	9	835	1,498	3,721	1,766	7,831
Arm. artillery	1	262	617	7	1,794	926	81	3,688
SP Flak					86	259	42	387
Engineer		22			85	342	111	560
Arm. half-track	232	337	813	2,574	7,153	9,486	1,285	21,880
Armored cars	324	189	618	982	826	555	113	3,607
Total	***1,344***	***2,589***	***5,890***	***9,657***	***20,531***	***29,305***	***5,454***	***74,770***

APPENDIX 3

American Armored Vehicle Production

U.S. TANK PRODUCTION[4]							
	1940	1941	1942	1943	1944	1945	Total
M2A4 light	325	40	10				375
M3 light		2,551	7,841	3,425			13,817
M5 light			2,858	4,063	1,963		8,884
LVT(A) amtank			3	288	1,708	670	2,669
Other light			240	680	150		1,070
M24 light					1,930	2,801	4,731
M3 medium		1,342	4,916				6,258
M4 (75mm)			8,017	21,245	3,504	651	33,417
M4 (76mm)					7,135	3,748	10,883
M4 (105mm)					2,286	2,394	4,680
M26*				1	339	2,374	2,714
Other med, heavy	6	88	4	39			137
Total	***331***	***4,021***	***23,889***	***29,741***	***19,015***	***12,638***	***89,635***

*Includes T23 and T25.

U.S. ARMORED VEHICLE PRODUCTION, 1940–45							
	1940	**1941**	**1942**	**1943**	**1944**	**1945**	**Total**
Tanks	331	4,021	23,889	29,741	19,015	12,638	89,635
Tank destroyers			639	6,879	1,882		9,400
SP arty (tracked)			2,461	2,156	1,239	1,315	7,171
SP arty (half-track)		87	2,880	9,356	1,974		14,297
Armored car	825	1,908	7,205	19,023	6,450	1,671	37,082
Half-track APC		5,424	9,846	21,585	3,394	920	41,169
LVT(A) amtrac				277	1,265	295	1,837
Other (armored tracked)		4	4,083	6,455	8,493	1,407	20,442
Total	***1,156***	***11,444***	***51,003***	***95,472***	***43,712***	***18,246***	***221,033***

APPENDIX 4

British and Commonwealth AFV Production in World War II

UK TANK/AFV PRODUCTION, 1939–45[5]								
	1939*	1940	1941	1942	1943	1944	1945*	Total
Light tanks	180	175	68	12	33	58	9	535
Cruiser Mark 1–IV		66	464	17				547
Covenanter		7	762	957	27			1,753
Crusader		2	655	2,249	1,097			4,003
Cavalier					319	182		501
Centaur				2	1,261	145		1,408
Cromwell				1	593	1,935	79	2,608
Challenger						145	56	201
Comet						143	984	1,127
Matilda I	41	33						74
Matilda II	24	356	1,038	1,330	143			2,891
Valentine		345	1,621	1,939	1,531	35		5,471
Churchill			690	1,700	1,325	1,062	702	5,479
SP Guns				163	36	354	377	930
Total	***245***	***984***	***5,298***	***8,370***	***6,365***	***4,059***	***2,207***	***27,528***

*War months only

BRITISH AND COMMONWEALTH ARMORED VEHICLE PRODUCTION, 1939–45								
	1939*	**1940**	**1941**	**1942**	**1943**	**1944**	**1945***	**Total**
Tanks and AFVs (UK)	245	984	5,298	8,370	6,365	4,059	2,207	27,528
Tanks and AFVs (Cmn)			100	2,065	1,965	1,236	462	5,828
Armored Cars (UK)	22	3,110	2,211	6,617	7,246	5,488	1,497	26,191
Armored Cars (Cmn)	150	887	1,368	4,692	4,374	1,180	185	12,836
Carriers (UK)	1,187	5,336	8,662	15,880	18,866	17,275	1,865	69,071
Carriers (Cmn)		160	5,206	13,375	14,176	8,806	3,093	44,816
Total	***1,604***	***10,477***	***22,845***	***50,999***	***52,992***	***38,044***	***9,309***	***186,270***

*War months only

APPENDIX 5

Japanese Armored Vehicle Production

JAPANESE TANK PRODUCTION, 1941–45[6]						
	1941	**1942**	**1943**	**1944**	**1945**	**Total**
Type 97 tankette	3	35	5	15		58
Type 95 light tank	705	655	239			1,599
Type 98 light tank	1	24	79			104
Type 2 light tank				29	5	34
Type 97 medium tank	507	28				535
Type 97-kai medium tank		503	427			930
Type 1 medium tank			15	155		170
Type 3 medium tank				55	89	144
Type 3 gun tank				15	16	31
Type 2 amphibious tank			112	70		182
Type 3 amphibious tank				12		12
Type 1 75mm SP gun		26				26
Type 1 105mm SP gun			14	20	20	54
Other AFV	181	124	631	554	126	1,616
Total	***1,397***	***1,395***	***1,522***	***925***	***256***	***5,495***

Notes

CHAPTER 1

1. E. Benn and R. Shephard, *Tank Effectiveness: A Comparison of the Theoretical Measure with Observed Battle Performance* (AORG Report No. 6/52; Byfleet, UK: 1952).
2. *Wehrmacht* actually means "armed forces," not "army." In German the army is *Heer*. I will use "Wehrmacht" in this book since it is the more familiar term to most English-speaking readers and also helps avoid the need for clumsy phrases such as "Heer and Waffen-SS panzer units."
3. Steven Zaloga, *Panzer IV vs. M4A1 Sherman: Normandy 1944*, Duel (Oxford: Osprey, 2015).
4. One of the Russian accounts comparing German and Soviet tank aces found that most of the Soviet aces were from 1941 when the T-34 was clearly superior to German tanks of the day. Most of the German aces were Tiger commanders in the year from the summer of 1943 to 1944 when the Tiger was largely invulnerable to Soviet guns. There are a few outliers including Nashorn and StuG III commanders, but these too are "bushwhacker" weapons. Aleksandr Smirnov, *Tankovye asy: SSSR i Germanii 1941–1945g* (Moscow: Frontovaya Illyustratsiya, 2006).
5. Alvin Coox, *US Armor in the Anti-Tank Role: Korea 1950* (Washington, D.C.: Operations Research Office, July 1952); H. W. McDonald, et al., *The Employment of Armor in Korea* (Washington, D.C.: Operations Research Office, April 1951); Vincent McRae and Alvin Coox, *Tank-vs.-Tank Combat in Korea* (Washington, D.C.: Operations Research Office, September 1954).
6. Alvin Coox and L. Van Loan Naisawald, *Survey of Allied Tank Casualties in World War II (ORO-T-117)*, Figure 13 (Operations Research Office, Johns Hopkins University, March 1951), hereafter "Coox, *Tank Casualties*."
7. For discussions about armor plate and armor testing, there have been a variety in the pages of *AFV News* over the years. For example: Giuseppe Finizio, "Armour Plate: Hardness and Toughness Tests," *AFV News*, Vol. 26, No. 3 (September–December 1991): 10–13; Hal Hock, "Projectile Perforation of Hardened Armor," *AFV News*, Vol. 26, No. 2 (May–August 1991): 11–15.
8. Armor hardness is usually measured on the Brinell hardness scale. The U.S. Army preferred "normally hard" armor in the 280–320 Brinell range and argued that "Competitive ballistic trials which have been conducted at Ordnance proving grounds on both very hard and normally hard domestic armor and Soviet armor have established beyond question of doubt that in many cases, representative of actual battlefield attack, very hard armor is distinctly inferior in resistance to penetration as compared to armor of more conventional hardnesses." A. Hurlich, Review of Soviet Ordnance Metallurgy (Watertown Arsenal, April 1956). The opposing Russian viewpoint on this controversy can be found in the official T-34 history by the Uralvagon tank plant: Sergey Ustyantsev and D. Kolmakov, *Boevye mashiny uravagonzvoda tank T-34* (Nighni-Tagil: Media-Print, 2005), 67.
9. Coox, *Tank Casualties*, Table 1.
10. Didier Laugier, *Sturmartillerie, Tom I* (Bayeux: Heimdal, 2011), 115.
11. Maksim Kolomiets, *Proslaveniy T-34* (Moscow: Yauza, 2012), 476. Hereafter "Kolomiets, *T-34*."
12. Kolomiets, *T-34*, 470.
13. An explanation of APDS technology in World War II can be found in the report of the Office of Scientific Research and Development in chapter 35, "The Quest for Hypervelocity," in John Burchard, ed., *Rockets, Guns and Targets* (Boston: Little, Brown, 1948).
14. Peter Müller and Wolfgang Zimmermann, *Sturmgeschütz III: Development, Production, Deployment* (Andelfingen, Switzerland: History Facts, 2009), 206.
15. Thomas Jentz, *Dreaded Threat: The 8.8cm Flak 18/36/37 in the Anti-Tank Role* (Boyds, MD: Panzer Tracts, 2001), 50.
16. In recent years, Russian historians have taken great delight in pointing to examples of German distortions and exaggerations in tank kill claim records. See for example the website Archive Awareness (tankarchives.blogspot.com), "Cheating at Statistics: Part 3" (31 July 2014) or "Cheating at Statistics, Part 7: Korner the Conjurer."

17. Coox, *Tank Casualties*, 44.
18. Ibid., 14.
19. The author is not aware of any thorough account of German tank radio development, but there are some good accounts of the technical aspects of German radios. Pierre Metsu, *Les Materiels radio de la Wehrmacht 1935–1945* (Bayeux: Heimdal, 2004).
20. Simon Godfrey, *British Army Communications in the Second World War: Lifting the Fog of Battle* (London: Bloomsbury, 2013).
21. P. Lyet, "L'evolution des Matériel de Transmissions de 1920 à 1939," *Revue Historique de l'Armée*, Vol. 23, No. 1 (1967): 57–78.
22. James Butler, "Individual Tank-Infantry Communications," *Armored Cavalry Journal* (July–August 1947): 43–45.
23. The layout of the new radio system was described in the technical bulletin issued to panzer troops: "Nachrichtenwesen-leicht gemacht!" *Nachrichtenblatt der Panzertruppen*, No. 8 (February 1944): 19–26.
24. John Horan, "The Interphone System in Armored Vehicles," *Armored Cavalry Journal* (July–August 1946): 25–27.
25. Steven Zaloga, "Technological Surprise and the Initial Period of War: The Case of the T-34 Tank in 1941," *Journal of Slavic Military Studies*, Vol. 6, No. 4 (December 1993): 634–46.
26. Harry Yeide, *Steel Victory: The Heroic Story of America's Independent Tank Battalions at War in Europe* (New York: Presidio, 2003), 17–18.
27. Yu. P. Kostenko, *Tanki (taktika, tekhnika, ehkonomika)* (Moscow, 1992), 13.
28. Soviet data on the use of the T-26 in Spain comes from numerous reports in the collection of documents obtained from the Russian State Military Archives (RGVA) by Yale University and currently housed at the Manuscript and Archives branch of Sterling Memorial Library in the Russian State Military Archive Collection (RSMAC-Group 1670).
29. Janusz Magnuski and Maksim Kolomiets, *Czerwony Blitzkrieg wrzesien 1939: Sowieckie wojska pancerne w Polsce* (Warsaw: Pelta, 1994).
30. The French website www.chars-francais.net has histories of most of the Char B and Char B1 bis tanks that saw combat in 1940, including their fates. This data was compiled along with unit histories to prepare a summary for my book: Steven Zaloga, *Panzer IV vs. Char B1 bis: France 1940*, Duel 33 (Oxford: Osprey, 2011), 75.
31. South African National Defence Forces archive, Technical Orders, via William Marshall.
32. Benjamin Coombs, *British Tank Production and the War Economy 1934–1945* (New York: Bloomsbury, 2013), 95.
33. "Ersatzteil-Auslieferung für Panzer-Kampfwagen in to," NARA RG242, T-78, R-146, F-077457.
34. The German *Panzerkampfwagenprogramm* 41 was based on an initial tank requirement to which was added 10 percent for the Replacement army for training purposes plus 10 percent for the supply chain; an additional 15 percent was added for both spares and for the repair system. "Panzerkampfwagenprogramm 41: Umwandlung der Forderungen (Stck.Zahl) in fabrikatorische 18 to Einheiten," NARA RG 242 T-78, R-146, F-077291.
35. This data was compiled from the war diaries (*Kriegstagebuch*) of the *3.* and *4.Panzer-Divisions*, located in the microfilm collection at NARA II in Record Group 242, T315, principally Rolls 112, 113, and 192.
36. Bantz Craddock, *Effects of Cold Weather upon Armored Combat Vehicles during the First Winter Campaign, Eastern Front, World War II* (Fort Leavenworth, KS: U.S. Army Command and General Staff College, 1985).
37. Walter Spielberger, *Panther & Its Variants* (Atglen, PA: Schiffer, 1993), 232.
38. Panzer-Montage, Adolf Hitler *Panzerprogramme*, NARA II, RG 242, T-78 R619, F107 et passim.
39. The difficulties in assessing German wartime costs are covered in various supporting documents collected by the U.S. Strategic Bombing Survey (USSBS) for their 1947 "(German) Tank Industry Report." A typical example was the interrogation of Dr. Karl-Otto Saur on 4 June 1945. Saur pointed out the enormous difficulties in calculating comparative prices or a common base price. For example, the tank plants were subject to three different tax structures, with varying degrees of government compensation for these costs. This can be found at NARA II in Record Group 243, Entry 6: Records of the USSBS-European Survey.
40. Mikhail Svirin, *Bronevoy shchit Stalina: Istoriya sovetskogo tanka 1937–1943* (Moscow: Yauza, 2006), 440.
41. These are the prices charged to the allied Polish and Czechoslovak armies in 1943–45. "Otchet o kolichestve otruzhennykh tankov s zavodov promyshlennosti inostrannym armiyam" (25 January 1945), *GABTU Collection, Vol. V*, 349.
42. A. Yu. Yermolov, *Gosudarstvennoe upravlenie voennoy promyshlennostyu v 1940-e gody: Tankovaya promyshlenost* (St. Petersburg: Aleteyya: 2012), 324.
43. "Ministry of Supply Ledger with Information on Tank Costs," The Tank Museum, Bovington, UK.
44. The basic price and price with GFE comes from the Raritan Arsenal technical bulletin ORD-5-3-1, Section 3, Major Items of Group G. The Lend-Lease prices come from the Monthly Progress Reports, Army Service Forces: International Aid, Section 2G (various numbers from 1942 to 1945).
45. Vincent Bernard, "Panzer Produktion," *Blindées & Batailles*, No. 99 (June–July 2012): 32–33.

CHAPTER 2

1. Christopher Foss and P. McKenzie, *The Vickers Tanks: From Landships to Challenger* (Somerset: Patrick Stephens, 1988).
2. Janusz Magnuski, *Karaluchy przeciw panzerom* (Warsaw: Pelta, 1995).
3. Charles Kliment and Vladimir Francev, *Czechoslovak Armored Fighting Vehicles 1918–1948* (Atglen, PA: Schiffer, 1997), 276.
4. Ralph Riccio, *Italian Tanks and Combat Vehicles of World War II* (Fidenza: Roadrunner, 2010), 79.
5. Ian Walker, *Iron Hulls, Iron Hearts: Mussolini's Elite Armoured Divisions in North Africa* (Wiltshire: Crowood, 2003), 36–37.
6. Steven Zaloga, *Spanish Civil War Tanks: The Proving Ground for Blitzkrieg* (Oxford: Osprey, 2010), 16.
7. A. Yu. Yermolov, *Gosudarstvennoe upravlenie voennoy promyshlennostyu v 1940-e gody: Tankovaya promyshlennost* (Saint Petersburg: Aleteyya, 2012), 66.
8. Steven Zaloga, *Japanese Tanks 1939–45* (Oxford: Osprey, 2007).

CHAPTER 3

1. Willi Esser, *Dokumentation uber die Enteicklung und Erprobung der ersten Panzerkampfwagen der Reichswehr* (Munich: Krauss-Maffei, 1979).
2. The most thorough account of the Vickers Cruiser tanks is a series of articles by Peter Brown in *Military Modelling* magazine. The A9 was covered in Vol. 36, No. 2 (2006); the A10 in Vol. 37, No. 3 (2007); and the A13 in Vol. 40, No. 12 (2010) through Vol. 41, No. 4 (2011).
3. David Fletcher, *Matilda Infantry Tank 1938–1945* (Oxford: Osprey, 1994).
4. The most thorough account of the Matilda in France is the three-part series by Peter Brown: "1 ATB in France 1939–40," *Military Modelling* Vol. 44, No. 4–6 (2014).
5. Kenneth Macksey, *A History of the Royal Armoured Corps 1914–1975* (Beaminster, UK: Newtown, 1983), 79–80. This figure presumably comes from the remarks by Brigadier Vyvyan Pope of the Armoured Reconnaissance Brigade. A. J. Smithers, *Rude Mechanicals: An Account of Tank Maturity during the Second World War* (London: Grafton, 1989), 79.
6. David Fletcher, *The Great Tank Scandal: British Armour in the Second World War, Part 1* (London: HMSO, 1989).
7. Steven Zaloga, *Panzer III vs Somua S35: France 1940*, Duel (Oxford: Osprey, 2014).

CHAPTER 4

1. Thomas Jentz, *Panzertruppen vol. 1: The Complete Guide to the Creation and Combat Employment of Germany's Tank Force 1933–1942* (Atglen, PA: Schiffer, 1996), 190–93.
2. A. G. Solyankin, et al., *Otechestvennye bronirovannye mashiny XX vek: Tom 2 1941–45* (Moscow: Eksprint, 2005), 24. Hereafter, "Solyankin, *Vol. 2*." The numbers were somewhat higher if counting tanks in factories, in which case the total was 23,767 including 1,383 T-34 (of which 388 were in factories). K. A. Kalshnikov, et al., *Krasnaya armiya v iyune 1941 goda: statisticheskiy sbornik* (Novosibirsk: Sibirskiy khronograf, 2003), 146–47.
3. These penetration figures are for armor angled at 30 degrees from the vertical. NARA RG242, T-78, R-144, F 74634.
4. A. Makarov, et al., *Opytnye obrastsy tank T-34* (Moscow: Magalion, 2010).
5. For example, an OKW report on Soviet military industrial capacity prepared in March 1941, "Der wehrgeographischen der UdSSR," mentions the production of the new T-32 medium tank. NARA RG-242 microfilm T-84 R 122, EAP 66-c-12-22/275.
6. Maksim Kolomiets, *Tanki v zimney voyne 1939–40* (Moscow: Frontovaya Illyustratsiya, 2002).
7. N. P. Zolotov and S. I. Isayev, "Boegotovy byli . . . Istoriko-statisticheskoe issledonvanie kolichestvenno-kachestvennogo sostoyaniya tankovogo parka Krasnoy Armii nakanune VOV," *Voenno-istoricheskiy zhurnal*, #11 (1993): 75–77.
8. Ibid. and Solyankin, *Vol. 2*, 23.
9. G. F. Krivosheyev, ed., *Rossiya i SSSR v voynakh XX veka: Kniga poter* (Moscow: Veche, 2010), 203.
10. Compiled from various sources including Evgeniy Drig, *Mekhanizirovannye korpusa RKKA v boyu* (Moscow: Transitkniga, 2005), and Kalshnikov, et al.
11. Paul Carell, *Hitler Moves East 1941–43* (New York: Ballantine, 1971), 30–31.
12. Artem Drabkin and Oleg Sheremet, *T-34 in Action* (Barnsley, UK: Pen & Sword, 2006), 37.
13. Ustyantsev, *T-34*, 48.
14. For an English-language account of these battles, see Victor Kamenir, *The Bloody Triangle: The Defeat of Soviet Armor in the Ukraine, June 1941* (Minneapolis: Zenith, 2008).
15. Report by the head of tank forces, Southwestern Front, General Major Morgunov, 3 July 1941, in P. I. Pinchuk, et al, ed., *Sbornik boevykh documentov VOV, Vypusk 33: Bronetankoviy i mekhanizirovanniy voisk* (Moscow: Voenno-nauchnoe upravlenie Generalniy Shtab, 1957), 133.
16. Krivosheyev, *Rossiya*, 520–21.
17. Maksim Kolomiets, *Bitva za Moskvu* (Moscow: Frontovaya Illyustratsiya, 2002).
18. A total of 4,867 new tanks had been built from 1 July to 31 December 1941.There were a total of 7,700 tanks in the Red Army on 1 January 1941, but many of these were in the Far East or in rear areas for training and mobilization. Krivosheyev, *Rossiya*, 510.
19. Fritz Hahn, *Waffen und Geheimwaffen des deutschen Heeres 1933–1945 Band 2* (Koblenz: Bernard & Graefe, 1987), 220. The total here for command tanks (Pz.Befelswagen) also includes other types of command vehicles (Pz.Funkwagen and Pz.Beobachtungswagen).

20. "Verbrauch an PzKpfWg: Totalverluste" (Generalinspekteur der Panzerwaffe), NARA RG 242, T-48, R-146, F 77218. These figures include losses in North Africa, which totaled 229 (42 PzKpfw II, 135 PzKpfw III, 34 PzKpfw IV, and 18 PzBefelsWg).
21. Jentz, *Panzertruppen Vol. 1*, 252.

CHAPTER 5

1. A. Yu. Yermolov, *Gosudarstvennoe upravlenie voennoy promyshlennostyu v 1940-e gody: Tankovaya promyshlennost* (Saint Petersburg: Aleteyya, 2012), 188.
2. Ustyantsev, *T-34*, 66.
3. Ibid., 50.
4. These findings were contained in a report in August 1943, stamped top secret and sent to only three senior Soviet leaders: Stalin himself, the head of the tank industry, Vyacheslav Malyshev, and the head of the GABTU, General Fedorenko. The report was prepared by the GRU (*Glavnoe razvedyvatelnoe upravlenie*), the military intelligence directorate, equivalent to the U.S. Army's wartime Military Intelligence Division or today's DIA. The report was based on conversations between Soviet liaison officials and U.S. Army personnel at Aberdeen Proving Ground regarding the U.S. Army tests on the two Soviet tanks in early 1942. The full report has appeared on Russian websites, but a shortened version is in print and often mistakenly reported to be a U.S. Army summary. The U.S. Army Ordnance reports on the T-34 and KV are actually much more lengthy, running hundreds of pages, and do not contain an overall summary of this type. They are available at NARA II, although the author read them many years ago when they were at the NARA facility at Suitland, Maryland.
5. G. B. Jarrett Papers, Archives and Manuscripts, U.S. Military History Institute, Carlisle Barracks, PA, 150.
6. Solyankin, *Vol 2*, 55.
7. A total of 9,375 light tanks were built in 1942 or about 38 percent of total tank production that year. In conjunction with the supply of Lend-Lease tanks in 1942 and the large holdings of obsolete light tanks in the Far East, light tanks made up 53 percent of Soviet tank inventory at the end of 1942.
8. The Red Army had about 9,600 medium and heavy tanks at the end of 1942.
9. V. Zalenskiy, "Podgotovka mladshikh tankovikh spetsialistov v gody VOV," *Voenno-Istorichesskiy Zhurnal*, No. 9 (September 1981): 69–73.
10. A veteran Soviet tanker visited one of the German tank training grounds in Austria in 1945 and noted that the gunnery ranges were much more sophisticated. Vasily Bryuchov, *Red Army Tank Commander: At War in a T-34 on the Eastern Front* (Barnsley, UK: Pen & Sword, 2013), 21.
11. A survey of Soviet wartime tank crew training can be found in chapter 3, "Podgotovka kadrov dlya tankovikh voisk," in O. A. Losik, ed., *Stroitelstvo i boevoe primenenie sovetskikh tankovikh voisk v godi VOV* (Moscow: Voenizdat, 1979), 79–95.
12. The three new plants were Vomag at Plauen, MNH at Hanover, and the new state-owned Nibelungenwerke at St. Valentin. *(German) Tank Industry Report*, U.S. Strategic Bombing Survey, Munitions Division, January 1947.
13. Panzer production in 1942 went from 3.8 percent of German weapons production at the beginning of 1942 to 4.7 percent at the end of 1942, while aircraft production fell from 46.1 percent to 36.3 percent. The largest category after aircraft was ammunition, which accounted for 30.6 percent of German weapons production at the end of 1942. *(German) Tank Industry Report*, 12. Panzer production as a fraction of the army expenditures managed by the *Heereswaffenamt* went from 11.5 percent in December 1941 to 31.1 percent by December 1942. *Bauvolumen Heer*, NARA RG 242, T-78, R-146, F077707.
14. The German consumption of tungsten (*Wolfram*) peaked at 355 tonnes in the second quarter of 1941 and fell to 164 tonnes by the first quarter of 1942; however, much of this was directed by a quota system to the arms industry due to its widespread use in machine tools. "Wolfram: Wehrmacht, Wirschaft and Ausfuhr ingesamt," NARA II, RG 242, R-146, F. 77671; 77711.
15. Fritz Hahn, *Waffen und Geheimwaffen des deutschen Heeres 1933–1945 Band 2* (Koblenz: Bernard & Graefe, 1987), 36. There is some reason to believe that production of the Pz.Gr.40 production may have continued on a limited scale in 1944, but documentation so far is lacking.
16. Wolfgang Fleischer, *Gepanzerte Feuerkraft: Die deutschen Kampwagen-, Panzerjäger- und Sturmkanonen, Sturmhaubitzen und Mörser bis 1945* (Wolfersheim: Podzun-Pallas, 2004); *German Ammunition* (Ordnance Service ETOUSA, November 1944); *German Explosive Ordnance, OP1666* (U.S. Navy, June 1946).
17. Aleksandr Shirokorad, "Bronya krepka i tanki nashi vystry," *Tekhnika i Oruzhie*, No. 1 (1997): 10.
18. In the United States, this was called the "Munroe effect" after its American inventor, and it formed the basis of American inventions such as the bazooka antitank rocket.
19. For an examination of the role of British supplied tanks in 1941, see: Alexander Hill, "British Lend Lease Tanks and the Battle of Moscow November–December—A Research Note," *Journal of Slavic Military Studies*, Vol. 19, No. 2 (2006): 289–294; "British Lend Lease Tanks and the Battle of Moscow November–December—Revisited,"*JSMS*, Vol. 22, No. 4 (2009): 574–87.
20. For further examples of the tank strength in the units participating in the Kharkov battles, see Andrei Galushko and Maksim Kolomiets, *Boy za Kharkov v mae 1942 goda* (Moscow: Frontovaya Illyustratsiya, 2000).

21. Maksim Kolomiets and Aleksandr Smirnov, *Boy v izluchine Dona 28 iyunya–23 iyulya 1942 goda* (Moscow: Frontovaya Illyustratsiya, 2002), 41.
22. Robert Forczyk, *Tank Warfare on the Eastern Front 1941–42* (Barnsley, UK: Pen & Sword, 2014), 207; Krivosheyev, *Rossiya*, 519.
23. "Dokladnaya zapiskia nachniku shtaba GABTU ka po rezultatam proverki tankovikh soedineniy zapadnogo fronta" (27 August 1942), reprinted in *GABTU Collection, Vol. II*, 352–55.
24. Artem Drabkin and Oleg Sheremet, *T-34 in Action* (Barnsley, UK: Pen & Sword, 2006), 4.
25. Figures for 1 October are for the renamed Stalingrad Front. Ilya Moschanskiy and Sergey Smolinov, *Oborona Stalingrada 17 iyulya–18 noyabr 1942 goda* (Moscow: Voennaya Letopis, 2001).
26. David Glantz, *Colossus Reborn: The Red Army at War, 1941–1943* (Lawrence: University Press of Kansas, 2005), 243.
27. M. Kolomiets and I. Moshchanskiy, *Tanki lend-liza 1941–1945* (Moscow: Eksprint, 2000), 12–13.
28. This included 2,000 heavy tanks, 7,600 medium tanks, and 11,000 light tanks. The latter category included the various British Lend-Lease types such as Matilda and Valentine, as well as U.S. Lend-Lease types such as the M3 light tank. Krivosheyev, *Rossiya*, 512.
29. Ibid., 519–20.
30. Figures for the number of operationally ready tanks vary. Bob Forczyk puts operational strength on 1 January 1942 at 300 (Forczyk, *Tank Warfare*, 161), while Tom Jentz puts it at zero (Jentz, *Panzertruppen Vol. 1*, 252).
31. The starting point for German tank statistics—including monthly strength, loss, and production—are the tables that first appeared in the Foreign Military Study P-059 by *Generalmajor* Burkhart Müller-Hillebrand, *German Tank Losses* (U.S. Army, 1950). These were republished in his later multivolume study, *Der Zweifrontkrieg: Das Heer vom Beginn des Feldzuges die Sowjetunion bis zum Kriegsende, Band III* (Frankfurt: E. S. Mittler & Sohn, 1969).
32. For example, in 1942 various Wehrmacht troop reports claimed Soviet tank losses as 21,367, which FHO downgraded to 16,200. The actual Soviet losses were 15,000, of which more than half were due to mechanical breakdowns and accidents. Wehrmacht claims in 1943 were 34,659, which FHO downgraded to 17,330; actual losses were 22,400. FHO report, 26 January 1944, "Feindliche Panzer Verluste 1941–43," NARA II, RG 242, T-78, R552.
33. Thomas Jentz, *Panzertruppen Vol. 2* (Atglen, PA: Schiffer, 1996), 43, 110, 252.
34. Paul Winter, *Defeating Hitler: Whitehall's Secret Report on Why Hitler Lost the War* (London: Continuum, 2012), 232.
35. These figures come from various OKH/Abt. Fremde Heere Ost (IID) files at NARA II including "Feindliche Panzer- und Sturgeschutze Producktion un Einfuhr 1941–1944"; "Entwicklung der Panzerlage in der S.U. seit 1.1.42/Stand 31.10.43"; and "Geschatzer Ist-Panzerbestand der bekannten Pz.Verbande vom 30.9.42 bis 31.3.44," NARA RG 242, T-78, R552. FHO estimates in 1943 and after included a more accurate appraisal by encompassing large reserves behind the front as well as deployments elsewhere.
36. The Red Army claimed to have destroyed 70,336 German tanks from the start of the war until 31 December 1944, when in fact German losses to date had been 15,673 tanks, or 23,802 AFVs if StuGs and *Panzerjägers* were included. Winter, *Defeating Hitler*, 233–34.
37. "Svedeniya Glavrazvedupravleniya nachalniku shtaba BT i MV KA o proizvodstve tankov i gruzovykh avtomashin v Germanii v 1939–1942 goda," 23 July 1943, in Polonskiy, *GABTU Collection, Vol. III*, 297.

CHAPTER 6

1. Steven Zaloga, *Tank Battles of the Pacific War 1941–45* (Hong Kong: Concord, 1995).
2. Steven Zaloga, *M4 Sherman vs Type 97 Chi-Ha: The Pacific 1945*, Duel (Oxford: Osprey, 2012).
3. Steven Zaloga, *Spanish Civil War Tanks: The Proving Ground for Blitzkrieg*, New Vanguard (Oxford: Osprey, 2010).
4. The most thorough account of Italian tank design is Ralph Riccio, *Italian Tanks and Combat Vehicles of World War II* (Fidenza: Roadrunner, 2010). The semi-official Italian history is the massive two-volume study: Nicola Pignato, et al., *Gli autoveicoli da combattimento del'Esercito Italiano, Volume primo dalle origini fino al 1939; Volume secondo 1940–1945* (Roma: Stato Maggiore del'Esercito, 2002). There are numerous monographs on specific Italian tank types in the Italian literature.
5. The most thorough history of the early cruiser tanks can be found in Peter Brown's series of articles "British Cruiser Tanks," published in 2006–11 in *Military Modelling* magazine: (A9) Vol. 36, No. 2 (2006); (A10) Vol. 37, No. 3 (2007); (A13) Vol. 40, No. 12 (2010); Vol. 41, Nos. 1, 2, 4, 6 (2011).
6. Thomas Jentz, *Tank Combat in North Africa: The Opening Rounds February 1941–June 1941* (Atglen, PA: Schiffer, 1998), 59.
7. Ibid., 101.
8. Jentz, *Panzertruppen Vol. 1*, 160.
9. Peter Brown, "The First Crusaders," *Military Modelling*, Vol. 37, No. 8 (2007): 24–33.
10. Dick Taylor, *Into the Valley: The Valentine Tank and Derivatives 1938–1960* (Sandomierz: MMP, 2012).
11. Bryan Perrett, *British Tanks in North Africa 1940–42*, Vanguard 42 (Oxford: Osprey, 1981), 16.
12. David Fletcher, *Crusader Cruiser Tank 1939–1945*, New Vanguard 14 (Oxford: Osprey, 1995), 20.

13. There are numerous discussions of the problems of British tank tactics in the desert. A succinct example can be found in P. G. Griffith, "British Armoured Warfare in the Western Desert 1940–43," in J. P. Harris and F. N. Toase, eds.), *Armoured Warfare* (London: Batsford, 1990), 70–87.
14. Daniel Hahn, *The Process of Change: The British Armoured Division, Its Development and Employment in North Africa during World War II*, Master's thesis (Fort Leavenworth, KS: U.S. Army Command and General Staff School, 1985), 163–64.
15. Jentz, *Panzertruppen Vol. I*, 183.
16. Maj. Bill Close, *A View from the Turret: A History of the 3rd RTR in the Second World War* (London: Dale & Bredon, 1998).
17. *Tank Equipment Situation of British Empire Forces, Dominions, Home Defence and Allies, 30th June 1942* PRO (Now National Archives), WO193/580.
18. Montgomery's important role in improving British tank employment is the focus of Hahn's Master thesis listed in note 14.
19. II Corps G-3 Journal, NARA, RG 407; Steven Zaloga, *US Armored Units in the North African and Italian Campaigns 1942–45*, Battle Orders 21 (Oxford: Osprey, 2006).
20. The claims vary from 150 to 250. Christopher Wilbeck, *Sledgehammers: Strengths and Flaws of Tiger Tank Battalions in World War II* (Wilford, PA: Aberjona, 2004), 57.
21. David Fletcher, "Kingforce," *Military Illustrated*, No. 114 (November 1997): 33–37.
22. Data comes from a U.S. Ordnance sheet entitled "Penetration Performance of British, American, German, and Japanese A/T Guns against Homogenous Armor at 30 degrees of Attack." The data came from British tests from Inclosure No. 1 Military Attaché Report No. 2473-44. The firing tests were conducted in England and the data was based on 50 percent success. Data has been converted to metric for commonality with other charts in this book.
23. David Fletcher, *The Great Tank Scandal: British Armour in the Second World War, Part 3* (London: HMSO, 1989); Peter Beale, *Death by Design: British Tank Development in the Second World War* (London: Sutton, 1998).

CHAPTER 7

1. "Interrogation of Herr Stiele von Heydekampf," Combined Intelligence Objectives Sub-Committee Evaluation Report No. 153, 28 June 1945, 1.
2. "Interrogation of Herr Kurt Arnoldt, Chief Technical Engineer Henschel AFV Research and Experimental Establishment at Haustenbeck," 21 Army Group Technical Intelligence Report No. 5, 28 May 1945.
3. *The Effects of Strategic Bombing on the German War Economy*, U.S. Strategic Bombing Survey, Overall Effects Division, 31 October 1945, 145.
4. Walter Spielberger and Hilary Doyle, *Tigers I and II and their Variants* (Atglen, PA: Schiffer, 2007).
5. Thomas Jentz and Hilary Doyle, *Panzerkampfwagen VI P (Sd.Kfz. 181)* (Darlington, MD: Darlington Productions, 1999).
6. An account of the first Tigers on the Russian Front is detailed in Maksim Kolomiets, *Pervye Tigry* (Moscow: Frontovaya Illyustratsiya, 2002).
7. Thomas Jentz, *Germany's Panther Tank: The Quest for Combat Supremacy* (Atglen, PA: Schiffer, 1995).
8. Wolfgang Fleischer, *Gepanzerte Feuerkraft: Die deutschen Kampwagen-, Panzerjäger- und Sturmkanonen, Sturmhaubitzen und Mörser bis 1945* (Wolfersheim: Podzun-Pallas, 2004); *German Ammunition* (Ordnance Service ETOUSA, November 1944); *German Explosive Ordnance, OP1666* (U.S. Navy, June 1946). It should be noted that different German documents give different penetration values for these guns. For example, a General Inspector of the Panzer Troops document from June 1944 lists the Pz.Gr.39 from the L/48 gun at 500 meters as 91mm vs. the 96mm figure here, but 129mm for the L/70 gun vs. the 124mm given here. NARA RG 242, T-78, R622, F576. Another data table provides other values: RG 242, T-78, R-144, F074634. As a result, a range of values is given for some of the projectiles here.
9. This flaw is frequently mentioned in the memoirs of T-34 crews; see Artem Drabkin and Oleg Sheremet, *T-34 in Action* (Barnsley, UK: Pen & Sword, 2006).
10. This evaluation was based on the later and improved 1944 Multitsyklon air filter; these filters were apparently based on imported U.S. tractor designs. *Engineering Analysis of the Russian T34/85 Tank* (Chrysler Corp., September 1951), 9, 18.
11. Ustyantsev, *T-34*, 78.
12. Maksim Kolomiets, *Proslavlenniy T-34* (Moscow: Yauza, 2012), 251–54.
13. "Doklad nachalnikka GBTU KA voennomu sovetu BT i MV KA o resultatakh probegovykh ispytaniy seriynykh tankov i samokhodnykh artstanovok, 24 marta 1944 g.," in Polonskiy, *GABTU Collection, Vol. III*, 700.
14. Ustyantsev, *T-34*, 104.
15. Production, strength, and loss figures from Burkhart Müller-Hillebrand, *German Tank Losses*, Foreign Military Study P-059 (U.S. Army, 1950). Tank strength in Russia from Jentz, *Panzertruppen Vol. 2*, 110. Operational rates from "Einsatzbereite Pz u. Stu.Gesch. Ost.," Gen. Qu. Insp.d.Panzertruppen, NARA II, RG 242, T-78, R-145, F 76020.
16. Tank strength figures are from David Glantz and Jonathan House, *The Battle of Kursk* (Lawrence: University Press of Kansas, 1999), 65–75; and Jentz, *Panzertruppen, Vol. 2*, 74–87.
17. I have made this argument in more detail in Steven Zaloga, *Sicily 1943: The Debut of Allied Joint Operations* (Oxford: Osprey, 2013).

18. This myth has been addressed in several excellent studies in recent years, such as Niklas Zetterling and Anders Frankson, *Kursk 1943: A Statistical Analysis* (London: Frank Cass, 2000); and Valeriy Zamulin, *Demolishing the Myth: The Tank Battle at Prokhorovka, Kursk, July 1943* (Solihull, UK: Helion, 2011).
19. Zamulin, *Demolishing the Myth*, 536.
20. Krivosheyev, *Rossiya*, 519–20.
21. Figures on Tiger strength and losses come from several sources including: Thomas Jentz, *Germany's Tiger Tanks: Combat Tactics* (Atglen, PA: Schiffer, 1997); Wolfgang Schneider, *Tigers in Combat, Vols. 1 & 2* (Winnipeg: Fedorowicz, 1994, 1998); and Christopher Wilbeck, *Sledgehammers: Strengths and Flaws of Tiger Tank Battalions in World War II* (Wilford, PA: Aberjona, 2004).
22. There were only three special antitank regiments with the 57mm ZiS-2 on the Central Front at Kursk, and none on the Voronezh Front. Mikhail Makarov and Andrey Pronin, *Protivotankovaya artilleriya krasnoy armii 1941–1945g* (Moscow: Frontovaya Illyustratsiya, 2003), 65.
23. In a 26 January 1944 report on Soviet tank losses, *Fremde Heere Ost* discounted German tactical claims by 50 percent due to double-counting and Soviet recovery and repair of temporary battlefield losses. For example, German tank claims in July 1943 of 7,300 Soviet tanks destroyed was reduced to 3,650 in the FHO assessment. "Feindliche Panzer Verluste 1941–1943," NARA RG 242, T-78, R-552.
24. During July–December 1943, German units reported total losses of 192 Tiger tanks (176 Eastern Front and 16 on Sicily). However, the army loss statistics for the same period were 256 Tiger tanks. This sizeable discrepancy, about a quarter of the losses, was presumably due to writing off some of the damaged tanks sent back to Germany for repair. The most detailed compilation of Tiger losses can be found in Ronald Klages, *Trail of the Tigers* (self-published, 2002).
25. Robert Forczyk, *Panther vs. T-34: Ukraine 1943* (Oxford: Osprey, 2007).
26. One had been knocked out by a 100kg aircraft bomb; the remainder had been abandoned. Maksim Kolomiets, *Pantery na kurskoy duge* (Moscow: Frontovaya Illyustratsiya, 2002), 49–54.
27. Of these, fifteen were sent back to Germany for repair and twenty-seven to the tank repair facility at Dnepropetrovsk in Ukraine. "Anlage 2: Panzer-kampfwagen V- Lage der Pz. Brigade 10 Stand 12.8.43," in Führer Vortrag der Gen. Insp. d.Pz.Tr., 26.8.43; NARA RG 242, T-78, R-720, not paginated.
28. The Soviet General Staff study of Kursk completed in 1944 did not even mention the Panther tank, but both the Tiger and Ferdinand figure prominently in the assessment. In some respects, this was due to common misidentifications of other types of German tanks and assault guns. David Glantz and Harold Orenstein, trans./ed., *The Battle of Kursk 1943: The Soviet General Staff Study* (London: Frank Cass, 1999), 229.
29. Ustyantsev, *T-34*, 75.
30. Soviet penetration data is frequently given in a range starting with the category NP (*Nachalnoe probitie*: initial penetration), meaning a 20 percent chance of penetrating the armor, to the GP (*garantirovannoe probitie*: guaranteed penetration), meaning an 80 percent probability of penetrating based on empirical tests. GP figures are given here. Mikhail Svirin, *Artilleriyskoe vooruzhenie sovetskikh tankov 1940–1945* (Moscow: Eksprint, 1999); "Sravnitelnaya tablitsa broneprobivyemosti artilleriiskikh snyardov—13 avgusta 1943g.," in *GABTU Collection, Vol. III*, 329.
31. Ilya Moshchanskiy, *Sovetskiy sredniy tank T-34-85: rannie versii zavoda No. 112* (Moscow: Voennaya Letopis, 2006).
32. "Einsatzbereite Pz. u. Stu.Gesch.-Ost-," Generalinspekteur der Panzertruppen, 8 December 1944, NARA RG242, T-78, R-145, F75855-75856.

CHAPTER 8

1. Ustyantsev, *T-34*, 105.
2. "Doklad nachalnikka GBTU KA voennomu sovetu BT i MV KA o resultatakh probegovykh ispytaniy seriynykh tankov i samokhodnykh artstanovok, 24 marta 1944 g.," in Polonskiy, *GABTU Collection, Vol. III*, 700.
3. Of the 226 operational Panther tanks on 15 June 1944, 175 were with Army Group Nord-Ukraine, 46 with Sud-Ukraine, and 5 with Nord. *Panzerlage und Sturmgeschützlage den 15.6.1944*, Anlage zu Gen. Qu.Nr. III/012076/44 g.Kdo; NARA RG 242, T-78, R624, F485 et passim.
4. The Central Intelligence Agency obtained a copy of one of the Soviet army studies in 1980; it was declassified under the Freedom of Information Act in 2012. "Combat Potential of the Armament and Combat Equipment of the Ground Forces and Aviation of the USSR and of the Armies of the Probable Enemy," CIA Memorandum from Deputy Director of Operations John McMahon, 25 August 1980.
5. Maksim Kolomiets, *Modernizirovannye tanki Klim Voroshilov KV-1S i KV-85* (Moscow: Yauza, 2014).
6. Ustyantsev, *T-34*, 86.
7. This chart is based on the Burkhart Müller-Hillebrand data for overall tank strength (*Bestand*) and deployed strength (*Frontfähigen*). The figures for the Russian Front come from reports by the *Generalinspekteur der Panzertruppen*; Russian Front deployed strength comes from the chart "Panzerbestand Ost, OKW, Heimat (28 December 1944), NARA RG 242, T-78, R145, F75865; and the operational strength comes from the chart "Einsatzbereite Pz. u. Stu.Gesch.-Ost-, NARA RG 242, T-78, R-145, F 75855-56. It should be noted that there are some anomalies when comparing the two Russian Front data lines, for example the December numbers where deployed strength exceeds operational strength. This is presumably due to differences in the data source (including or not including fringe types such as Befelspanzer) and/or discrepancies in the data dates (1 January 1944 versus 30 January 1944) that are not explained on the charts.

8. "Panthers and Tigers: A German View: First Canadian Army Intelligence Summary ISUM 12, 7 July 1944," in Donald Graves, *Blood and Steel—The Wehrmacht Archive: Normandy 1944* (London: Frontline, 2013), 148.
9. Aleksandr Shirokorad, "Bronya krepka i tanki nashi vystry," *Tekhnika i oruzhie*, No. 1 (1997): 9.
10. These numbers are derived from tables prepared by Gen. Maj. Hermann Burkhart Müller-Hillebrand and can be found in his book *Das Heer 1933–1945. Entwicklung des organisatorischen Aufbaues. Band 3: Der Zweifrontenkrieg. Das Heer vom Gebinn des Feldzuges gegen die Sowjetunion bis zum Kriegsende, Band III* (Frankfurt: E. S. Mittler & Sohn, 1969); and in his U.S. Army Foreign Military Studies report, P-059: *Tank Losses*, 1959.
11. "Einsatzbereite Pz u. Stu.Gesch.Ost in % (Nach Gen.Qu)," Records of the OKH, Generalinspekteur der Panzertruppen, NARA RG 242 T-78, R145, F76020 et passim.
12. Adolf Hitler Panzerprogramm, Band 1: Pz-Kpfw, Stu-Gesch. u. Sfl, January 1943, NARA II RG 242, T-78, R619, F78 et passim.
13. Steven Zaloga, *Bagration 1944: The Destruction of Army Group Centre*, Campaign 42 (Oxford: Osprey, 1996), 38–41.
14. Panzerlage und Sturmgeschutzlage den 15.6.1944, Anlage zu Gen.Qu. Nr. 111/012076/44 g.Kdo, NARA RG 242, T-78, R624, F487.
15. Norbert Baczyk, *Warsaw 1944 Vol. 2: The Battle for Praga July–September 1944* (Manchester: Leandoer & Ekholm, 2007).
16. Krivosheyev, *Rossiya*, 520–21.
17. The German Eastern Front intelligence agency, *Fremde Heere Ost*, adjusted the claims to account for double counting and recovered tanks. They reduced army claims by 30 percent, except for 50 percent in July–August. They reduced all Luftwaffe claims by 50 percent due to the prevalence of overcounting. *Panzer und Sturmgeschütz-Verluste 1944*, Fremde Heere Ost (IIc), NARA RG 242, T-78, R552.
18. This chart was compiled from several appendices in OKH files that can be found at NARA in RG 242, T-78, R-145, F76029 et passim. A more convenient compilation can be found in the article: Norbert Baczyk, "Goracy rok Panzerwaffe," *Poligon* (May–June 2009): 22–32.
19. *Panzerlage O. B. Sudwest Stand 31.1.44*, NARA RG 242 T-78, R720.
20. "Panzerbestand Ost, OKW, Heimat" (data is for the first of each month), records of the OKH, Generalinspekteur der Panzertruppen, NARA RG 242 T-78, R145, F75865 et passim.
21. This chart was compiled from several appendices in OKH files that can be found at NARA in RG 242, T-78, R-145, F76029 et passim. A more convenient compilation can be found in the article: Norbert Baczyk, "Goracy rok Panzerwaffe," *Poligon* (May–June 2009): 22–32.
22. Steven Zaloga, *M4 (76mm) Sherman Medium Tank 1943–65*, New Vanguard 73 (Oxford: Osprey, 2003).
23. There is a substantial amount of documentation on the 17-pounder controversy in the U.S. Army records at NARA II, most notably in the ETO Armored Fighting Vehicles and Weapons Section records in Record Group 338.
24. Data on APCBC and HE rounds comes primarily from *Catalog of Standard Ordnance Items* (Washington, D.C.: Chief of Ordnance Technical Division, 1944). Variation in penetration for APCBC ammunition is due to the difference in homogenous versus face-hardened plate. Data for HVAP comes from various War Department Technical Bulletins. The 76mm T4 and 90mm T30E16 were chosen since they were the most common HVAP in the ETO, with 96,000 rounds of HVAP delivered August 1944–April 1945 (33,000 of the 3 in, 63,000 of the 76mm) and 43,000 T30E16 delivered January 1945–August 1945. The improved 90mm T33 had 71,000 rounds delivered March–July 1945 according to *Official Munitions Production of the United States* (Washington, D.C.: U.S. War Production Board, 1947).
25. The clearest description of the scale of the Normandy tank fighting in early August by the U.S. and German units can be found in a recent French account of the Panther battalion of the *116.Panzer-Division* detailing every single engagement that month: Frédéric Deprun, *Panzer en Normandie: Histoire des équipages de char de la 116.Panzer-division juillet–août 1944* (Louviers: Ysec, 2011). A good account of the *2.Panzer-Division* in this fighting can be found in Didier Lodieu, *La Big Red One face à la 2 Pz.-Div* (Louviers, Ysec, 2014).
26. This is very evident when examining histories of Tigers in combat; see, for example, the two volumes by Wolfgang Schneider, *Tigers in Combat* (Winnipeg: Federowicz, Vol. I, 1994; Vol. II, 1998). A few damaged Tiger tanks were encountered aboard a transport train near Braines, France, on 8 September 1944 by the 468th AAA Battalion; antiaircraft fire from a M15A1 drove away a few crewmen. The first actual combat encounter took place in late August 1944 between some U.S. Army M10 tank destroyers and a few King Tiger tanks of *3./s. Pz.-Abt. 503* (3rd Company, Heavy Tank Battalion 503) in the Mantes bridgehead north of Paris. A small number of abandoned King Tigers of *Pz.Kp. (Fkl) 316* were found around Châteaudun in France in late August, but there was no fighting.
27. The Barkmann legend was created in Eric Lefevre's book, *Panzers in Normandy Then and Now* (London: After the Battle, 1983). The problem is that U.S. records show no evidence at all of any such encounter, allegedly a column from the 3rd Armored Division. The author examined the after-action reports of the 3rd Armored Division at NARA in RG407, as well as the detailed accounts in the "Combat Interview" collection about this incident. The closest event that day that even vaguely resembles Barkmann's claims was the loss of a couple of M5A1 light tanks and jeeps of a mechanized cavalry scout patrol. This was hashed out on

the web on the Axis History forum by Rich Anderson, forum.axishistory.com/viewtopic.php?p=1360781. These legends were further reinforced by the propaganda efforts of the Waffen-SS. The German historian Peter Lieb gave an interesting presentation of this issue at the "1944: Seventy Years On" history conference at the Royal Military Academy—Sandhurst on 16 April 2014. Comparing army and Waffen-SS panzer divisions in Normandy, both types of divisions received similar numbers of the common German military awards such as the Iron Cross. However, the Waffen-SS received a disproportionate number of the high awards such as the Knight's Cross, with little evidence to suggest any exceptional difference in their actual combat performance.

28. Leonard Wainstein, *The Relationship of Battle Damage to Unit Combat Performance*, IDA Paper P-1903 (Institute for Defense Analyses, April 1986), 75.
29. Annex No. 2 to Annex 14, "Action Against the Enemy A/Action Report, Hq. First US Army, 31 August 1944: Days of Combat, Number of Tanks Operative and Losses for Periods 6–30 June and 1–31 July 1944," NARA II, RG 338, ETO AFV & Weapons Section.
30. Steven Zaloga, *Lorraine 1944: Patton vs. Manteuffel*, Campaign Series 75 (Oxford: Osprey, 2000).
31. Data is from the twentieth of each month. *Final Historical Report*, AFV & Weapons Section, HQ ETOUSA, NARA Record Group 338.
32. Ibid.
33. From Nicholas Moran's "The Chieftain's Blog," forum.worldoftanks.com/index.php?/topic/337361-testing-the-british-cruisers.
34. "The Chieftain's Blog," forum.worldoftanks.com/index.php?/topic/370649-exercise-dracula
35. Benjamin Coombs, *British Tank Production and the War Economy 1934–1945* (London: Bloomsbury, 2013).
36. The figures in the chart here are those given for engagements using rangefinders since this was found to be more representative of actual combat experiences. E. Benn and R. Shephard, *Tank Effectiveness: A Comparison of the Theoretical Measure with Observed Battle Performance*, Appendix A (Byfleet, UK: AORG Report No. 6/52, 1952), 7.
37. The depth of British AFV reserves was extensively discussed within the U.S. Army due to dissatisfaction over the 7 percent-per-month authorized reserve. U.S. tank casualties in August 1944 began to approach 20 percent per month, and local U.S. commanders started using the British example to get Washington to authorize deeper reserves. This discussion is contained in many documents of the AFV&W Section, HQ ETO, found at NARA, Record Group 338, especially under the 470.8 files.
38. The most thorough examination of these issues can be found in John Buckley, *British Armour in the Normandy Campaign 1944* (London: Frank Cass, 2004), 46 et passim.
39. Figures are for unit holdings. The 21st Army Group also had substantial holdings of reserve tanks in depots. Figures are from various 21st Army Group AFV Status reports provided by the British historian Peter Brown, or from U.S. reports in NARA Record Group 331, SHAEF G-3 (Box 182).
40. Buckley, *British Armour*, chapter 5, "The Tank Gap," 105–34.
41. Figures cover tanks of all units in 21st Army Group and so include Canadian and Polish units as well as British. Figures for August 1944 from *Appendix G to 21 Army Group RAC Liaison Letter No. 2: Operation Overlord Net Tank Wastage*; figures for November 1944 from *Appendix A to 21 Army Group RAC Liaison Letter No. 3*.
42. *Appendix C to 21 Army Group RAC Liaison Letter No. 2: Estimated Enemy Tank Casualties Since D-Day*.
43. This chart was compiled from several appendices in OKH files that can be found at NARA in RG 242, T-78, R-145, F76029 et passim. A more convenient compilation can be found in the article: Norbert Baczyk, "Goracy rok Panzerwaffe," *Poligon* (May–June 2009): 22–32. There are small discrepancies between both sources, mainly in regard to sub-variants such as command tanks.

CHAPTER 9

1. There are numerous reports in various archives detailing Allied intelligence assessments of German armor: *PzKpfw V Panther Preliminary Report on Armour Quality and Vulnerability* (Chobham, UK: Department of Tank Design (Armour Branch) Report No. M 6815A/3 No. 1, May 1944); *Metallurgical Examination of a 3¼" Thick Armor Plate from a German PzKpfw V Panther Tank* (Watertown Arsenal Lab Experimental Report 710/715, January 1945); *Metallurgical Examination of Armor and Welded Joints from the Side of a German PzKpfw V Panther Tank* (Watertown Arsenal Lab Experimental Report 710/750, May 1945).
2. The restoration of a Panther tank of the Jacques Littlefield collection revealed strong evidence of deliberate sabotage of fuel and oil lines.
3. *Tank Industry Report* (U.S. Strategic Bombing Survey, Munitions Division, January 1947). In addition to the survey report itself, there are individual reports on most of the major plants. Besides the published reports, the USSBS files at NARA in Record Group 243 contain a series of unpublished technical memos which amplify the technical details about the German panzer industry and its tribulations in 1944–45.
4. *Henschel & Sohn, Kassel, Germany* (U.S. Strategic Bombing Survey, Munitions Division, 6 October 1945).
5. General der Panzertruppen Horst Stumpff, *Tank Maintenance in the Ardennes Offensive*, ETHINT-61, U.S. Army Center for Military History, August 1945. Stumpff at the time was the panzer inspector for OB West at Rundstedt's headquarters.

6. Michael Winninger, *OKH Toy Factory—The Nibelungenwerk: Tank Production in St. Valentin* (Andelfingen, Switzerland: History Facts, 2013).
7. Conversation with author.
8. *Vorschau für Panzerrustungprogramm Stand 30.1.1945*, reprinted in "The German Tank Industry (Including Armored Fighting Vehicles), Technical Memo, USSBS Tank Industry Files, NARA, Record Group 243.
9. David Fletcher, "Britain's Best Tank of the War," *Military Illustrated*, No. 104 (January 1998): 43–47.
10. *Assessment of Forms of Anti-tank Defence: Effectiveness of British and Russian Tanks* (AORG Report No. 11/51, August 1951).
11. "Anlage.4 zu Gen. Insp. d Pz Tp/Führ St Nr F 129/45 g.Kdos vom 10.3.45," *Führer-Vorträge Der Generalinspekteur der Panzertruppe Abteilung Organization H.16/159*, NARA RG 242 T-78, R-720.
12. Overall panzer and AFV strength in the west on 10 December 1944 was 2,986, of which 2,329 were assigned to Army Group B, only a portion of which was committed to the units in the Ardennes offensive. Charles V. von Luettichau, *Armor in the Ardennes Offensive: A Comparative Study of the Potential, Authorized and On-Hand Strength of Panzer Units in the West, November 1944–February 1945* (U.S. Army Chief of Military History, June 1952). The data on this table was compiled primarily from the U.S. Army's Ardennes Campaign Database. During the early 1990s, Trevor Depuy's Institute compiled a large database on the Ardennes campaign known as the Ardennes Campaign Simulation (ARCAS) for the U.S. Army Concepts Analysis Agency to test the agency's Stochastic Concepts Evaluation Model. The D-Base 4 database compiled for this study was used to create this table.
13. Steven Zaloga, *Operation Nordwind: Hitler's last offensive in the West 1945* (Oxford: Osprey, 2010).
14. *Führer Vorträge* H.16/159 Der Generalinspekteur der Pz.Tr.Abt.Org. (10 March 1945), NARA RG 242, T-78, R720.
15. Derived from data in Jentz, *Panzertruppe Vol. 2*, 247–248.
16. *Panzerlage Zusammenstellung, Stand 10.4.45*, OKH Records NARA II RG 242, T-78, Roll 621, F530.
17. Data is from the twentieth of each month. *Final Historical Report*, AFV & Weapons Section, HQ ETOUSA, NARA Record Group 338.
18. Ibid.
19. Figures are for unit holdings. The 21st Army Group also had substantial holdings of reserve tanks in depots. G Figures are from various 21st Army Group AFV Status reports provided by the British historian Peter Brown, or from U.S. reports in NARA Record Group 331, SHAEF G-3 (Box 182).
20. Figures cover tanks of all units in 21st Army Group and so include Canadian and Polish units as well as British. Figures for August 1944 from *Appendix G to 21 Army Group RAC Liaison Letter No. 2: Operation Overlord Net Tank Wastage*; figures for 1945 from *Half-Yearly Reports of the Progress of the Royal Armoured Corps: Total Tank Losses 21st Army Group*.
21. Ustyantsev, *T-34*, 104.
22. Mikhail Baryatinskiy, *IS-3: Posledniy tank Vtoroy mirovoy* (Moscow: Yauza, 2010).
23. The Central Intelligence Agency obtained a copy of one of the Soviet army studies in 1980. It was declassified under the Freedom of Information Act in 2012. "Combat Potential of the Armament and Combat Equipment of the Ground Forces and Aviation of the USSR and of the Armies of the Probable Enemy," CIA Memorandum from Deputy Director of Operations John McMahon, 25 August 1980. On the chart here, the values have been recalculated with the T-34 serving as the baseline with a value of "1."
24. Ilya Moshchanskiy and Ivan Khokhlov, *Vpered Germaniya! Visla-oderskaya strategicheskaya nastupatelnaya operatsiya 12 yanvarya–3 fevral 1945 g.* (Moscow: Voennaya Letopis, 2005), 13.
25. Aleksei Isaev and Maksim Kolomiets, *Tomb of the Panzerwaffe: The defeat of the Sixth SS Panzer Army in Hungary 1945* (Solihull, UK: Helion, 2104) 114.
26. Ibid., 139.
27. "Doklad voennomu sovetu BT i MV KA ob eksplutatsii tankov i SAU v bronetankovykh i mechanizirovannykh voyskakh, 4 maya 1945 g.," in *GABTU Collection, Vol. IV*, 482.
28. Krivosheyev, *Rossiya*, 520–21.
29. Dmitriy Shein, *3-ya gvardeyskaya tankovaya armiya v boyakh za Berlin* (Moscow: Frontovaya Illyustratsiya, 2007), 7.
30. *Panzerlage Zusammenstellung, Stand 10.4.45*, OKH Records NARA II, RG 242, T-78, Roll 621, F530.
31. "Spravka komanuyushchego BT i MV KA v upravlenie operativnogo okruzhnogo tyla GSh KA o sostoyanii tankovogo parka, 3 yunya 1945g.," in *GABTU Collection, Vol. IV*, 536.
32. Figures for the size of the Soviet force depend on what elements of the fronts are counted, so numbers tend to run from 6,070 to 6,300. A. B. Shirokorad, *Tankovaya voyna na vostochnom fronte* (Moscow: Veche, 2009), 386.

APPENDICES

1. A. G. Solyankin, et al. *Otechestvennye bronirovannye mashiny XX vek: Tom 1: 1905–1941; Tom 2 1941–45* (Moscow: Eksprint, 2002, 2005).
2. Soviet data on tanks delivered found in Mikhail Kolomiets and Ilya Moshchanskiy, *Tanki Lend-liza 1941–1945* (Moscow: Eksprint, 2000); data on tanks and AFVs sent from official U.S. and British records.
3. Peter Chamberlain, et al., *Encyclopedia of German Tanks of World War II* (London: Arms & Armour, 1978); Burkardt Müller-Hillebrand, *Der Zweifrontkrieg: Das Heer vom Beginn des Feldzuges die Sowjetunion bis zum Kriegsende, Band III* (Frankfurt: E. S. Mittler & Sohn, 1969); T. Jentz and H. Doyle, *Panzer Production from 1933 to 1945*, Panzer Tracts No. 23 (Germantown, MD: Panzer Tracts, 2011).
4. *Summary Report of Acceptances, Tank-Automotive Materiel 1940–1945* (Army Service Forces, December 1945). Data on LVT(A) amphibious tanks and LVT(A) armored Amtracs is from *Report on LVT through 31 Sep 1945* (U.S. Navy Bureau of Ships, 1945).
5. Data compiled from Leland Ness, *World War II Tanks and Fighting Vehicles: The Complete Guide* (London: Harper Collins, 2002).
6. Japanese data is by fiscal year rather than calendar year; Ness, *World War II Tanks*, and the technical memos in the files of the U.S. Strategic Bombing Survey at NARA II on the Japanese ordnance industry during the war.

Bibliography

Baadstöe, Christer, ed. *Svenskt pansar under beredskapstiden 1939–1945*. SPFH: 1992.

Backstein, G., et al. *Handbook on Weaponry*. Düsseldorf: Rheinmetall, 1982.

Bailey, Charles. *Faint Praise: American Tanks and Tank Destroyers during World War II*. Hamden, CT: Archon Books, 1983.

Barbanson, Éric. *Le 1e DLM au Combat*. Paris: Histoire & Collections, 2011.

Baryatinskiy, Mikhail. *IS-3: Posledniy tank Vtoroy mirovoy*. Moscow: Yauza, 2010.

———. *Legkiy tank T-26*. Modelist Konstruktor: 2002.

———. *Vse tanki SSSR*. Moscow: Yauza, 2012.

Baschin, Joachim. *Der Panzerkampfwagen 35(t)*. Stuttgart: Motorbuch Verlag, 2001.

Beale, Peter. *Death by Design: British Tank Development in the Second World War*. London: Sutton, 1998.

Becze, Csaba. *Magyar Steel: Hungarian Armor in WWII*. Cornwall: Stratus, 2006.

Bernage, Georges. *The Panzers and the Battle of Normandy: June 5th–July 20th 1944*. Bayeux: Heimdal, 2000.

Bird, Lorrin, and Robert Livingston. *World War II Ballistics: Armor and Gunnery*. Albany: Overmatch, 2001.

Bonnaud, Stéphane. *Chars B au combat: Hommes et materials du 15e BCC*. Paris: Histoire & Collections, 2002.

Buckley, John. *British Armour in the Normandy Campaign 1944*. London: Frank Cass, 2004.

Burchard, John, ed. *Rockets, Guns and Targets*. Boston: Little, Brown, 1948.

Cappellano, F., and P. P. Battistelli. *Italian Medium Tanks 1939–45*. New Vanguard 195. Oxford: Osprey, 2012.

Chamberlain, Peter, et al. *Encyclopedia of German Tanks of World War II*. London: Arms & Armour, 1978.

Citino, Robert. *Quest for Decisive Victory: From Stalemate to Blitzkrieg in Europe 1899–1940*. Lawrence: University Press of Kansas, 2002.

Clarke, Jeffrey. *Military Technology in Republican France: The Evolution of the French Armored Force 1917–40*. UMI, 1970.

Close, Bill. *A View from the Turret: A History of the 3rd RTR in the Second World War*. London: Dale & Bredon, 1998.

Coombs, Benjamin. *British Tank Production and the War Economy 1934–1945*. London: Bloomsbury, 2013.

Danjou, Pascal. *Le Char B1*. Trackstory No. 13. Les Corvées Les Yys: Barbotin, 2012.

———. *Les Chars B: B1, B1 bis, B1 ter*. Trackstory No. 3. Les Corvées Les Yys: Barbotin, 2005.

———. *FCM 36*. Trackstory No. 7. Les Corvées Les Yys: Barbotin, 2007.

———. *Hotchkiss H35/H39*. Trackstory No. 6. Les Corvées Les Yys: Barbotin, 2006.

———. *Juin 40, L'impossible sursaut*. Trackstory No. 5. Les Corvées Les Yys: Barbotin, 2006.

———. *Renault D1*. Trackstory No. 8. Les Corvées Les Yys: Barbotin, 2008.

———. *Renault D2*. Trackstory No. 9. Les Corvées Les Yys: Barbotin, 2008.

———. *Renault FT*. Trackstory No. 10. Les Corvées Les Yys: Barbotin, 2009.

———. *Renault R35/R40*. Trackstory No. 4. Les Corvées Les Yys: Barbotin, 2005.

———. *Somua S35*. Trackstory No. 11. Les Corvées Les Yys: Barbotin, 2010.

Deprun, Frédéric. *Panzer en Normandie: Histoire des équipages de char de la 116.Panzerdivision juillet–août 1944*. Louviers: Ysec, 2011.

Dimitrijevic, Bojan, and Dragan Savic. *Oklopne jedinice na jugoslovenskom ratistu 1941–45*. Belgrade: Institut za savremenu istoriju, 2011.

DiNardo, Richard. *Germany's Panzer Arm in WWII*. Mechanicsburg, PA: Stackpole Books, 2007.

Doughty, Robert. *The Seeds of Disaster: The Development of French Army Doctrine, 1919–1939*. Hamden, CT: Archon Books, 1985.

Doyle, Hilary, and Tom Jentz. *Sturmgeschütz III & IV*. New Vanguard 37. Oxford: Osprey, 2001.

Drabkin, Artem, and Oleg Sheremet. *T-34 in Action*. Barnsley: Pen & Sword, 2006.

Drig, Evgeniy. *Mekhanizirovannye korpusa RKKA v boyu: istoriya avtobronetankovykh voysk krasnoy armii v 1940–1941 godakh.* Moscow: Tranzitkniga, 2005.

Esser, Willi. *Dokumentation uber die Enteicklung und Erprobung der ersten Panzerkampfwagen der Reichswehr.* Munich: Krauss-Maffei, 1979.

Estes, Kenneth. *Marines under Armor: The Marine Corps and the Armored Fighting Vehicle, 1916–2000.* Annapolis: Naval Institute Press, 2000.

Ferrard, Stephane. *France 1940: L'armement terrestre.* Paris: ETAI, 1998.

Fleischer, Wolfgang. *Gepanzerte Feuerkraft: Die deutschen Kampwagen-, Panzerjäger- und Sturmkanonen, Sturmhaubitzen und Mörser bis 1945.* Wolfersheim: Podzun-Pallas, 2004.

Fletcher, David. *Crusader Cruiser Tank 1939–1945.* New Vanguard 14. Oxford: Osprey, 1995.

———. *The Great Tank Scandal: British Armour in the Second World War Part 1.* London: HMSO, 1989.

———. *Matilda Infantry Tank 1938–1945.* Oxford: Osprey, 1994.

———. *Mr. Churchill's Tank: The British Infantry Tank Mark IV.* Atglen, PA: Schiffer, 1999.

———. *The Universal Tank: British Armour in the Second World War Part 2.* London: HMSO, 1989.

———, and Richard Harley. *Cromwell Cruiser Tank 1942–50.* New Vanguard 104. Oxford: Osprey, 2006.

Forczyk, Robert. *Panther vs. T-34: Ukraine 1943.* Oxford: Osprey, 2007.

———. *Tank Warfare on the Eastern Front 1941–42.* London: Pen & Sword, 2014.

Foss, Christopher, and P. McKenzie. *The Vickers Tanks: From Landships to Challenger.* Somerset: Patrick Stephens, 1988.

Francev, Vladimir. *Československé Tankové Síly 1945–1992.* Prague: Grada, 2012.

———. *Exportní Lehké Tanky Praga.* Minneapolis: MBI, 2007.

———. *Exportní Tančíky Praga.* Minneapolis: MBI, 2004.

———. *PzKpfw 38(t) Ausf. A-D in Detail.* Wings and Wheels, 2006.

———, and Charles Kliment. *Praga LT vz. 38.* Minneapolis: MBI, 1997.

Freiser, Karl-Heinz. *The Blitzkrieg Myth: The 1940 Campaign in the West.* Annapolis: Naval Institute Press, 2005.

Friedli, Lukas. *Repairing the Panzers: German Tank Maintenance in World War 2.* 2 vols. Monroe, NY: Panzerwrecks, 2010–2011.

Glantz, David. *Colossus Reborn: The Red Army at War, 1941–1943.* Lawrence: University Press of Kansas, 2005.

———, and Jonathan House. *The Battle of Kursk.* Lawrence: University Press of Kansas, 1999.

Glantz, David, and Harold Orenstein, trans./ed. *The Battle of Kursk 1943: The Soviet General Staff Study.* London: Frank Cass, 1999.

Godfrey, Simon. *British Army Communications in the Second World War: Lifting the Fog of Battle.* London: Bloomsbury, 2013.

Graves, Donald. *Blood and Steel—The Wehrmacht Archive: Normandy 1944.* London: Frontline, 2013.

Habeck, Mary. *Storm of Steel: The Development of Armor Doctrine in Germany and the Soviet Union 1919–1939.* New York: Cornell University, 2003.

Hahn, Fritz. *Waffen und Geheimwaffen des deutschen Heeres 1933–1945 Band 2.* Koblenz: Bernard & Graefe, 1987.

Harper, David. *Tank Warfare on Iwo Jima.* Carrollton, TX: Squadron Signal, 2006.

Harris, J. P., and F. N. Toase, eds. *Armoured Warfare.* London: Batsford, 1990.

Hayward, Mark. *The Sherman Firefly.* (Tiptree: Barbarossa Books, 2001).

Hunnicutt, Richard. *Firepower: A History of the American Heavy Tank.* Novato: Presidio, 1988.

———. *Pershing: A History of the Medium Tank T20 Series.* Berkeley: Feist, 1971.

———. *Sherman: A History of the American Medium Tank.* Belmont: Taurus, 1978.

Isaev, Aleksei, and Maksim Kolomiets. *Tomb of the Panzerwaffe: The Defeat of the Sixth SS Panzer Army in Hungary 1945.* Solihull, UK: Helion, 2014.

Jakl, Tomas. *May 1945 in the Czech Lands: Ground Operations of the Axis and Allied Forces.* Prague: MBI, 2004.

Jentz, Thomas. *Germany's Panther Tank: The Quest for Combat Supremacy.* Atglen, PA: Schiffer, 1995.

———. *Germany's Tiger Tanks: Combat Tactics.* Atglen, PA: Schiffer, 1997.

———. *Panzerkampfwagen I No. 1–2.* Boyds, MD: Panzertracks, 2002.

———. *Panzertruppen: The Complete Guide to the Creation and Combat Employment of Germany's Tank Force 1933–1942 (Vol. 1), 1943–45, (Vol. 2).* Atglen, PA: Schiffer, 1996.

———. *Tank Combat in North Africa: The Opening Rounds February 1941–June 1941.* Atglen, PA: Schiffer, 1998.

———, and H. Doyle. *Panzer Production from 1933 to 1945.* Panzer Tracts No. 23. Germantown, MD: Panzer Tracts, 2011.

Jentz, Thomas, and Hilary Doyle. *Panzerkampfwagen 38(t).* Boyds, MD: Panzer Tracts, 2007.

———. *Panzerkampfwagen III Ausf. A–D.* Panzer Tracts No. 3-1. Boyds, MD: Panzer Tracts, 2007.

———. *Panzerkampfwagen III Ausf. E–H.* Panzer Tracts No. 3-2. Boyds, MD: Panzer Tracts, 2007.

Jeudy, Jean-Gabriel. *Chars de France.* Paris: ETAI, 1997.

Johnson, David. *Fast Tanks and Heavy Bombers: Innovation in the U.S. Army 1917–1945.* New York: Cornell University, 1998.

Kululnikov, K. A., et al. *Krasnaya armiya v iyune 1941 goda: statisticheskiy sbornik.* Novosibirsk: Sibirskiy khronograf, 2003.

Kamenir, Victor. *The Bloody Triangle: The Defeat of Soviet Armor in the Ukraine, June 1941*. Minneapolis: Zenith, 2008.

Karpenko, A. V. *Obozrenie otechestvennoy bronetankovoy tekhniki 1905–1995 g*. St. Petersburg: Nevskiy Bastion, 1996.

Klages, Ronald. *Trail of the Tigers*. Self-published, 2002.

Kliment, Charles, and Vladimir Francev. *Czechoslovak Armored Fighting Vehicles 1918–1948*. Atglen, PA: Schiffer, 1997.

Kolomiets, Maksim. *Bitva za Moskvu*. Moscow: Frontovaya Illyustratsiya, 2002.

———. *Modernizirovannye tanki Klim Voroshilov KV-1S i KV-85*. Moscow: Yauza, 2014.

———. *Pantery na kurskoy duge*. Moscow: Frontovaya Illyustratsiya, 2002.

———. *Pervye Tigry*. Moscow: Frontovaya Illyustratsiya, 2002.

———. *Proslavlenniy T-34*. Moscow: Yauza, 2012.

———. *T-26: tyzhelaya sudba legkogo tanka*. Moscow: Eksmo, 2007.

———. *T-28: tyzheliy monstr Stalina*. Moscow: Eksmo, 2007.

———. *Tanki v zimney voyne 1939–40*. Moscow: Frontovaya Illyustratsiya, 2002.

———, and I. Moshchanskiy. *Tanki lend-liza 1941–1945*. Moscow: Eksprint, 2000.

Kolomiets, Maksim, and Mikhail Svirin. *T-26 legkiy tank*. Moscow: Frontovaya Illyustratsiya, 2003.

Kostenko, Yu. P. *Tanki (taktika, tekhnika, ehkonomika)*. Moscow, 1992.

Krivosheyev, G. F., ed. *Rossiya i SSSR v voynakh XX veka: Kniga poter*. Moscow: Veche, 2010.

Laugier, Didier. *Sturmartillerie*. 2 vols. Bayeux: Heimdal, 2011.

Lefevre, Eric. *Panzers in Normandy Then and Now*. London: After the Battle, 1983.

Lenskiy, A. G. *Tank otechestva: bronya i bronirovanie*. St. Petersburg: self-published, 2008.

Lindström, Rickard, and Carl-Gustaf Svantesson. *Svenskt Pansar: 90 ar av svensk stridsfordonsutveckling*. Stockholm: SMBF, 2009.

Lodieu, Didier. *La Big Red One face à la 2 Pz.-Div*. Louviers: Ysec, 2014.

Losik, O. A., ed. *Stroitelstvo i boevoe primenenie sovetskikh tankovikh voisk v godi VOV*. Moscow: Voenizdat, 1979.

Macksey, Kenneth. *A History of the Royal Armoured Corps 1914–1975*. Beaminster, UK: Newtown, 1983.

Magnuski, Janusz. *Karaluchy przeciw panzerom*. Warsaw: Pelta, 1995.

———, and Maksim Kolomiets. *Czerwony Blitzkrieg wrzesien 1939: Sowieckie wojska pancerne w Polsce*. Warsaw: Pelta, 1994.

Makarov, A., et al. *Opytnye obrastsy tank T-34*. Moscow: Magalion, 2010.

Makarov, Mikhail, and Andrey Pronin. *Protivotankovaya artilleriya krasnoy armii 1941–1945g*. Moscow: Frontovaya Illyustratsiya, 2003.

Mary, Jean-Yves. *Mai–juin 1940—Les blindés français*. Bayeux: Heimdal, 2012.

Matev, Kaloyan. *Bronetankova tekhnika 1935–45*. Sofia: Angela, 2000.

McLean, Donald, ed. *Japanese Tanks, Tactics, & Anti-Tank Weapons*. Wickenburg, AZ: Normount, 1973.

Michulec, Robert, and Miroslaw Zientarzewski. *T-34: Mythical Weapon*. Mississauga, Ontario: Air Connection, 2004.

Moore, Perry. *Panzerschlacht: Armoured Operations on the Hungarian Plains: September–November 1944*. Solihull, UK: Helion, 2008.

Moshchanskiy, Ilya. *Sovetskiy sredniy tank T-34/85: rannie versii zavoda No. 112*. Moscow: Voennaya Letopis, 2006.

———, and Ivan Khokhlov. *Vpered Germaniya! Visla-oderskaya strategicheskaya nastupatelnaya operatsiya 12 yanvarya–3 fevral 1945 g*. Moscow: Voennaya Letopis, 2005.

Muikku, Esa, and Jukka Purhonnen. *Suomalaiset Panssarivaunet 1918–1997*. Tampere, Finland: Apali, 1997.

Muller, Peter, and Wolfgang Zimmermann. *Sturmgeschütz III: Development, Production, Deployment*. 2 vols. Andelfingen, Switzerland: History Facts, 2009.

Müller-Hillebrand, Hermann Burkhart. *Der Zweifrontkrieg: Das Heer vom Beginn des Feldzuges die Sowjetunion bis zum Kriegsende, Band III*. Frankfurt: E. S. Mittler & Sohn, 1969.

Ness, Leland. *World War II Tanks and Fighting Vehicles: The Complete Guide*. London: HarperCollins, 2002.

Nevenkin, Kamen. *Fire Brigades: The Panzer Divisions 1943–1945*. Winnipeg: Federowicz, 2006.

Ogorkiewicz, Richard. *Design and Development of Fighting Vehicles*. Garden City: Doubleday, 1968.

Perrett, Bryan. *British Tanks in North Africa 1940–42*. Vanguard 42. Oxford: Osprey, 1981.

Pignato, Nicola, et al. *Gli autoveicoli da combattimento del'Esercito Italiano, Volume primo dalle origini fino al 1939; Volume secondo 1940–1945*. Rome: Stato Maggiore dell'Esercito, 2002.

Polonskiy, V. A., ed. *Glavnoe avtobronetankovoe upravlenie: Lyudi, cobytiya, fakty v dokumentakh*. 5 vols. Russian Federation: Defense Ministry, 2005.

Postnikov, Mikhail. *Bronezashchita srednikh tankov T-34 1941–1945*. Moscow: Eksprint, 2005.

———. *Bronezashchita tyazelykh tankov KV i IS 1941–1945*. Moscow: Eksprint, 2005.

Riccio, Ralph. *Italian Tanks and Combat Vehicles of World War II*. Fidenza: Roadrunner, 2010.

Saint-Martin, Gérard. *L'arme blindée française, Tome 1: Mai–Juin 1940, Les blindés français dans la tourmente*. Paris: Economica, 1998.

Sallaz, Kurt, and Peter Riklin. *Bewaffnung und Ausrüstung der Schweizer Armee seit 1817: Panzer und Panzerabwehr*. Dietikon: Stocker-Schmid, 1982.

Scafes, Cornel, et al. *Trupele Blindate din Armata Romana 1919–1947*. Bucharest: Muzeul Militar National, 2005.

Schneider, Wolfgang. *Tigers in Combat*. Winnipeg: Federowicz, Vol. I, 1994; Vol. II, 1998.

Shein, Dmitriy. *3-ya gvardeyskaya tankovaya armiya v boyakh za Berlin*. Moscow: Frontovaya Illyustratsiya, 2007.

Shirokorad, A. B. *Tankovaya voyna na vostochnom fronte.* Moscow: Veche, 2009.

Showalter, Dennis. *Hitler's Panzers: The Lightning Attacks that Revolutionized Warfare.* New York: Berkley Caliber, 2010.

Smirnov, Aleksandr. *Tankovye asy: SSSR i Germanii 1941–1945g.* Moscow: Frontovaya Illyustratsiya, 2006.

Smithers, A. J. *Rude Mechanicals: An Account of Tank Maturity during the Second World War.* London: Grafton, 1989.

Solyankin, A. G., et al. *Otechestvennye bronirovannye mashiny XX vek: Tom 1: 1905–1941; Tom 2 1941–45.* Moscow: Eksprint, 2002, 2005.

———. *Sovetskie ognemetnye i khimicheskie tanki 1929–1945.* Tseygauz, 2007.

Spielberger, Walter. *Panther & Its Variants.* Atglen, PA: Schiffer, 1993.

———. *Panzer IV and its Variants.* Atglen, PA: Schiffer, 1993.

———. *Panzers 35(t) and 38(t) and their Variants 1920–1945.* Atglen, PA: Schiffer, 2008.

———. *Sturmgeschütz & Its Variants.* Atglen, PA: Schiffer, 1993.

———, and Hilary Doyle. *Tigers I and II and their Variants.* Atglen, PA: Schiffer, 2007.

Spielberger, Walter, et al. *Panzerkampfwagen IV and its Variants 1935–1945—Book 2.* Atglen, PA: Schiffer, 2011.

Strasheim, Rainer, John Prigent, et al. *Panzerwaffe: The Evolution of the Panzerwaffe to the Fall of Poland 1939.* Shepperton, England: Ian Allen, 2007.

Svirin, Mikhail. *Artilleriskoe vooruzhenie sovetskikh tankov 1940–1945.* Moscow: Armada, 1999.

———. *Bronevoy shchit Stalina: Istoriya sovetskogo tanka 1937–1943.* Moscow: Yauza, 2006.

———. *Pervaya polnaya entsiklopediya tankovaya moshch SSSR.* Moscow: Yauza, 2009.

———, and Maksim Kolomiets. *T-26 Legkiy Tank.* Moscow: Frontovaya Illyustratsiya, 2003.

Taylor, Dick. *Into the Valley: The Valentine Tank and Derivatives 1938–1906.* Sandomierz, Poland: MMP, 2012.

Touzin, Pierre. *Les engins blindés français 1920–1945.* Vol. 1 Paris: SERA, 1976.

———. *Les véhicules blindés français 1900–1944.* Paris: EPA, 1979.

Ustyantsev, Sergey, and D. Kolmakov. *Boevye mashiny uravagonzvoda tank T-34.* Nizhni-Tagil, Russia: Media-Print, 2005.

Vasilyev, Larisa, et al. *Pravda o tanke T-34.* Moscow: Moskovskie uchebniki, 2005.

Vauvillier, Francois, and J. M. Touraine. *L'automobile sous l'uniforme 1939–40.* Paris: Massin, 1992.

Walker, Ian. *Iron Hulls, Iron Hearts: Mussolini's Elite Armoured Divisions in North Africa.* Wiltshire: Crowood, 2003.

White, B. T. *British Tanks and Fighting Vehicles 1914–1945.* London: Ian Allen, 1970.

Wilbeck, Christopher. *Sledgehammers: Strengths and Flaws of Tiger Tank Battalions in World War II.* Wilford, PA: Aberjona, 2004.

Winninger, Michael. *OKH Toy Factory—The Nibelungenwerk: Tank Production in St. Valentin.* Andelfingen, Switzerland: History Facts, 2013.

Winter, Paul. *Defeating Hitler: Whitehall's Secret Report on Why Hitler Lost the War.* London: Continuum, 2012.

Wood, M., and J. Dugdale. *Waffen SS Panzer Units in Normandy 1944.* Farnborough: Books International, 2000.

Yermolov, A. Yu. *Gosudarstvennoe upravlenie voennoy promyshlennostyu v 1940-e gody: Tankovaya promyshlennost.* St. Petersburg: Aleteyya, 2012.

Zaloga, Steven. *Armored Thunderbolt: The U.S. Army Sherman in World War II.* Mechanicsburg, PA: Stackpole Books, 2008.

———. *Armour of the Pacific War.* Vanguard 35. Oxford: Osprey, 1983.

———. *Japanese Tanks 1939–45.* New Vanguard 137. Oxford: Osprey, 2007.

———. *Lorraine 1944: Patton vs. Manteuffel.* Campaign Series 75. Oxford: Osprey, 2000.

———. *M4 (76mm) Sherman Medium Tank 1943–65.* New Vanguard 73. Oxford: Osprey, 2003.

———. *M4 Sherman vs. Type 97 Chi-Ha: The Pacific 1945.* Duel. Oxford: Osprey, 2012.

———. *Panzer III vs. Somua S35: France 1940.* Duel. Oxford: Osprey, 2014.

———. *Panzer IV vs. Char B1 bis: France 1940.* Duel. Oxford: Osprey, 2011.

———. *Panzer IV vs. M4A1 Sherman: Normandy 1944.* Duel. Oxford: Osprey, 2015.

———. *Spanish Civil War Tanks: The Proving Ground for Blitzkrieg.* New Vanguard. Oxford: Osprey, 2010.

———. *Tank Battles of the Pacific War 1941–45.* Hong Kong: Concord, 1995.

———. *U.S. Armored Division in the ETO 1944–45.* Battle Orders 10. Oxford: Osprey, 2005.

———. *U.S. Armored Units in the North African and Italian Campaigns 1942–45.* Battle Orders 21. Oxford: Osprey, 2006.

———. *U.S. Tank and Tank Destroyer Battalions in the ETO 1944–45.* Battle Orders 3. Oxford: Osprey, 2005.

Zamulin, Valeriy. *Demolishing the Myth: The Tank Battle at Prokhorovka, Kursk, July 1943.* Solihull, UK: Helion, 2011.

Zetterling, Niklas. *Normandy 1944: German Military Organization, Combat Power and Organizational Effectiveness.* Winnipeg: Federowicz, 2000.

———, and Anders Frankson. *Kursk 1943: A Statistical Analysis.* London: Frank Cass, 2000.

Index

Page numbers in italics indicate photographs, illustrations, and tables.

Other books by Steven Zaloga

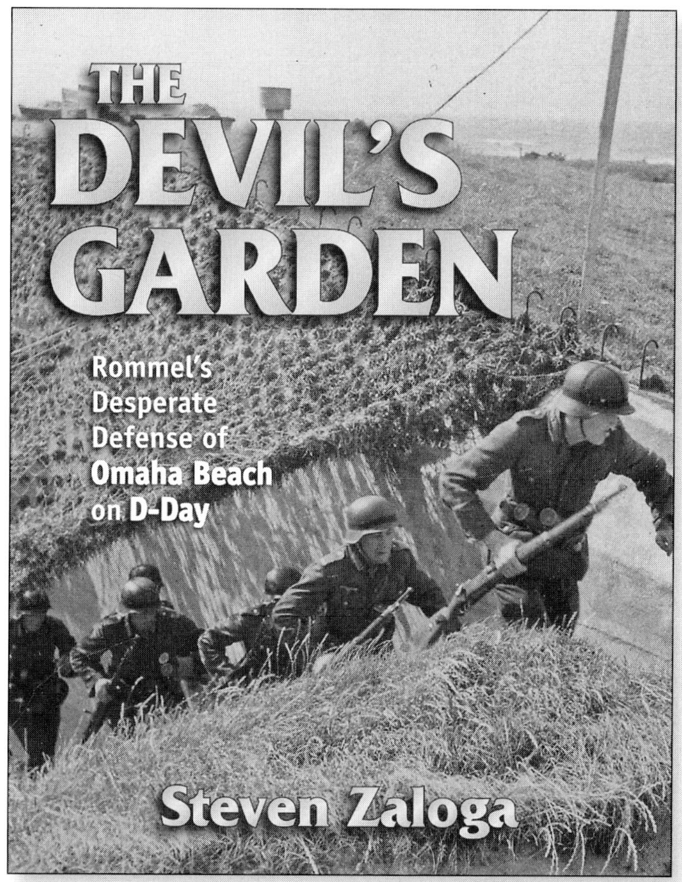

THE DEVIL'S GARDEN

Rommel's Desperate Defense of Omaha Beach on D-Day

288 pages, 240 photos, 978-0-8117-1228-6

WWW.STACKPOLEBOOKS.COM
1-800-732-3669